DSL Self-Install

You Need:
10BASE-T or
10/100 Fast Ethernet
network card

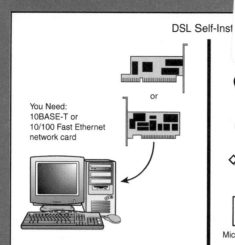

Power Supply

RJ-45 – RJ-11
Cables

Wall Mount
Plate

MicroFilter

2-Outlet
Modular
Adapter

Modem

DSL
MODEM

installation
guide

Cable Modem

You Need:
10BASE-T or
10/100 Fast Ethernet
network card

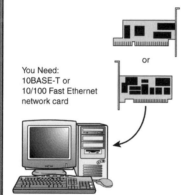

Your Cable Modem Provider Supplies:

Cable modem

- Cat 5 Ethernet cable
- Coaxial cable into home

DirecPC

What You Need:

Open PCI
slot inside
your computer

or working USB port

and an
analog
(dial-up)
modem

External   Or   Internal

What DirecPC Supplies:

PCI satellite modem

or

USB satellite modem

- DirecPC or DirecDuo satellite dish
- Mounting hardware

Hardware Quick Reference

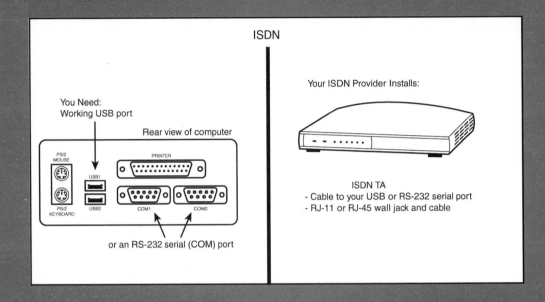

ISDN

You Need:
Working USB port

Rear view of computer

PS/2 MOUSE

USB1

PRINTER

USB2

PS/2 KEYBOARD

COM1   COM2

or an RS-232 serial (COM) port

Your ISDN Provider Installs:

ISDN TA
- Cable to your USB or RS-232 serial port
- RJ-11 or RJ-45 wall jack and cable

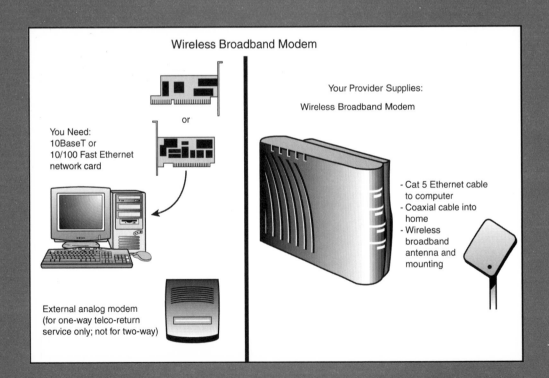

Wireless Broadband Modem

You Need:
10BaseT or
10/100 Fast Ethernet
network card

or

External analog modem
(for one-way telco-return
service only; not for two-way)

Your Provider Supplies:

Wireless Broadband Modem

- Cat 5 Ethernet cable
  to computer
- Coaxial cable into
  home
- Wireless
  broadband
  antenna and
  mounting

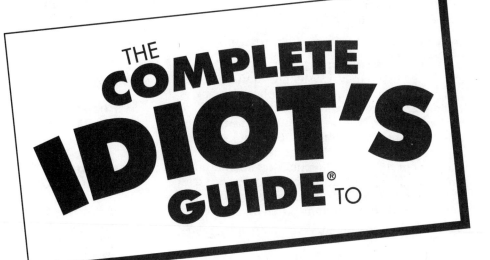

THE **COMPLETE IDIOT'S GUIDE**® TO

High-Speed Internet Connections

Mark Edward Soper

201 W. 103rd Street, Indianapolis, IN 46290

The Complete Idiot's Guide® to High-Speed
Internet Connections

Copyright © 2001 by Que® Corporation

International Standard Book Number: 0-7897-2479-0

Library of Congress Catalog Card Number: 00-106255

Printed in the United States of America

First Printing: December 2000

04   03   02   01   4   3   2   1

Trademarks

All terms mentioned in this book that are known to
be trademarks or service marks have been appropriately capitalized. Que Corporation cannot attest to the
accuracy of this information. Use of a term in this
book should not be regarded as affecting the validity
of any trademark or service mark.

Warning and Disclaimer

Associate Publisher
Greg Wiegand

**Senior Acquisitions
Editor**
Jenny L. Watson

**Senior Development
Editor**
Rick Kughen

Development Editor
Todd Brakke

Managing Editor
Thomas F. Hayes

Project Editor
Tonya Simpson

Copy Editor
Cynthia Fields

Indexer
Chris Barrick

Proofreader
Benjamin Berg

Technical Editors
Ralph Becker
Teri A. Robinson
Johannes Ullrich
Karen Weinstein

Illustrator
Judd Winick

Team Coordinator
Sharry Gregory

Interior Designer
Nathan Clements

Cover Designer
Michael Freeland

Production
Cyndi Davis-Hubler

Contents at a Glance

Contents

Foreword

Bragging rights at the office water cooler used to center on how large a hard disk your system had or how fast your over-clocked processor was. Not anymore. "How fast is your Internet connection?" is now the question that separates the serious Web surfers from the lightweight computer dweebs.

High-speed, broadband Internet connections are the future and the future is now, if it's not yesterday already. (Wait, is it yesterday already? Oh gosh, we've got to get going faster, faster, faster to make tomorrow today…). ISDN, T1, DSL, cable, or broadband in any flavor provides not only lightning-fast retrieval of current-generation Web and Internet content, its high speed affords access to next-generation content that will revolutionize the role that the Internet plays in our lives. We've come a long, long way from the early days when we could read our email as it scrolled up the screen as it was being downloaded using a 2400-baud modem. It was a major breakthrough when we hooked up our first 9600-baud screamer and for the first time the text scrolled by too fast to be read onscreen during downloading.

Indeed, the times, they are a changin'—and download times more so than anything else. The lynchpin of what might be called the Great Internet Awakening is broadband access. Streaming audio is here now, and there are services where you can store gigabytes of your favorite music on a Web server and play your favorite tunes from any computer you're sitting at. Sites such as Akoo.com have current movie trailers, the hottest music videos, radio from around the world, and full-length old-time movies, all for immediate streaming across the Internet to your computer. But to enjoy this you must have a faster Internet connection. Never has there been a greater need for speed.

But how does a person cope with trying to get a network connection to be all it can be? The computer landscape is littered with changing hardware, incomprehensible acronyms, and conflicting technologies all revolving around faster connections. The average computer user doesn't know the difference between an MTU (maximum transmission unit) and a TTL (time to live) setting. There must be a rational resource to help people who just want the benefits that a faster Internet connection can give them without having to get a degree in telecommunications engineering.

The good news is that this book gives the communications novice all the smarts they need to fine tune and/or upgrade their Internet connection to take advantage of the faster broadband technologies that are available in the world.

Stuck trying to deal with a mass-market modem that came with your computer?

Troubled by firmware follies in getting your modem upgraded to the latest standard? *The Complete Idiot's Guide to High-Speed Internet Connections* deals with each of these issues, showing you what you need to know to cope with each in turn. But that's not all, not by a long shot. Maybe a new modem is the answer; maybe adding a second modem will boost your connection speed to an acceptable level. But maybe a modem is not the way to go at all.

This book gets you up to speed with all the high-speed broadband alternatives to dial-up service that are available today. It covers all the cable conundrums you can run into trying to get your slice of the Internet pie from your local cable provider. Can the same company that provides Hollywood's celluloid marvels also provide reliable high-speed Internet service? How does it work? What do you have to watch out for? Mark Soper again comes to the rescue with everything you need to know to keep a cable modem up and running.

Digital Subscriber Lines are all the rage, and Mark sorts out the alphabet soup of different flavors that this technology comes in to keep you from suffering from DSL dyslexia. From symmetrical to consumer, asymmetrical, and lite, along with the different speed ranges you can expect from each and how much it'll probably cost, you won't feel helpless when you deal with a DSL provider. You'll know what they're offering and what you can expect to get. Plus, you'll know how to check to see that you're actually getting what you're paying for!

If you can't get cable or DSL in your location should you opt to go the wireless route and let global geosynchronous satellites beam the Internet right to your PC? How fast is satellite downloading? How do you handle upstream traffic? Again, Mark covers exactly what you need to know to make the decision about whether this is the right technology for you and if it is, how to go about getting it to actually work effectively on your system.

But the pitfalls extend beyond merely selecting the perfect broadband technology for your needs. To get the most out of whatever high-speed solution is chosen there's still the mind-boggling matter of fine-tuning your Windows installation so you can get the most out of your new Internet connection, be it ISDN, cable, DSL, or satellite. Even then you're not done, because with a broadband connection comes the very real threat of having your connection (and your computer) hacked by unsavory Internet predators. Never fear, *The Complete Idiot's Guide to High-Speed Internet Connections* shows you how to make your Windows Registry settings obey your every high-speed whim. It discusses everything you need to know about setting up firewalls and making your broadband portal onto the Internet safe from the dangers that lurk there. The truth is right here in this excellent guidebook.

— T.J. Lee and Lee Hudspeth

Authors of *Absolute Beginner's Guide to PC Upgrades*, published by Que

About the Author

Mark Edward Soper is president of Select Systems and Associates, Inc., a technical writing and training organization.

Mark has taught computer troubleshooting and other technical subjects to thousands of students from Maine to Hawaii since 1992. He is an A+ Certified hardware technician and a Microsoft Certified Professional. He's been writing technical documents since the mid-1980s and has written and contributed to several other Que books, including *Upgrading and Repairing PCs, Eleventh and 12th Editions*; *Upgrading and Repairing Networks, Second Edition*; *Special Edition Using Windows Millennium*; and *Upgrading and Repairing PCs, 12th Edition, Academic Edition*. Mark co-authored both the first and second editions of *Upgrading and Repairing PCs, Technician's Portable Reference* and is co-author of *Upgrading and Repairing PCs, A+ Certification Study Guide*. Watch for details about these and other book projects at the Que Web site at www.mcp.com.

Mark also has been writing for major computer magazines since 1990, with more than 125 articles in publications such as *SmartComputing*, *PCNovice*, *PCNovice Guides*, and the *PCNovice Learning Series*. His early work was published in *WordPerfect Magazine*, *The WordPerfectionist*, and *PCToday*. Mark welcomes comments at mesoper@selectsystems.com.

About the Technical Editors

Ralph Becker has 18 years of experience in data communications. He has served in many different capacities, including engineering, customer service, information services, and operations, and has experience with many communications technologies, such as LAN (Token Ring, Ethernet, and so on), WAN (Frame Relay, ATM, and so on), and protocols (TCP/IP, ISDN). Currently, he works at Lucent Technologies as a system administrator in the customer service operations group. Ralph lives in Massachusetts with his wife and daughter.

Johannes Ullrich has operated cablemodemhelp.com under his own company, Euclidian Consulting, since 1998. Cablemodemhelp.com is a premier hands-on resource for cable modem users. He is employed by Banta Integrated Media as lead of the Web maintenance department. In this position, he maintains and troubleshoots several high-traffic dynamic e-commerce Web sites. Johannes graduated with a Ph.D. and M.S. in physics from the University at Albany, State University of New York. Johannes was one of the early cable modem users with Time Warner's RoadRunner service in Albany, New York. His other activities include homepc.org, a dynamic domain name system, and dshield.org, a distributed intrusion detection system.

Karen Weinstein is a computer consultant living on North Potomac, Maryland. She has had more than a decade of experience in PC sales and support. Karen has helped tech edit several Que books, including *Upgrading and Repairing PCs*. She has a B.S. in business administration from the University of Maryland and can be reached at kweinst565@aol.com.

Teri Robinson is a New York-based writer and editor. When she's not grappling with her local provider over DSL service, she writes and edits for several business and technical magazines, including *InformationWeek*, *MicroTimes*, and *InternetWeek*.

Dedication

To Howard W. Bootz, my mentor and my friend.

Acknowledgements

My name is on the cover, but I've learned since I began writing books how valuable the team behind the book is to its success. Many thanks to:

Cheryl, Kate, and Jeremy, whose loyal support kept me going and who welcomed me home after many long evenings in the office.

Ed and Ian, who are at college but whose love I can sense from many miles away (although they don't always answer their email).

Jenny Watson, whose vision for helping people learn more about faster Internet connections gave me the opportunity to write this book.

Rick Kughen and Todd Brakke, whose development efforts made sure I was going in the right direction.

Greg Wiegand, who helped me understand DirecPC a lot better.

Ralph Becker, Johannes Ullrich, Teri Robinson, and Karen Weinstein, whose technical comments made sure I was on the right track.

Tonya, Thomas, and Cynthia, who kept the copy editing processes on track.

Chris, who made sure that the index helps you find what you're looking for, and Benjamin, who made sure that the text says what it's supposed to say.

The Illlustrators, who turned my (very rough) drawings into great illustrations.

Sharry, who kept everything organized and made sure I got paid.

The rest of the gang at Macmillan, who all strive to make sure you get the best computer books on the market.

Tell Us What You Think!

As the reader of this book, *you* are our most important critic and commentator. We value your opinion and want to know what we're doing right, what we could do better, what areas you'd like to see us publish in, and any other words of wisdom you're willing to pass our way.

As an associate publisher for Que, I welcome your comments. You can fax, email, or write me directly to let me know what you did or didn't like about this book—as well as what we can do to make our books stronger.

Please note that I cannot help you with technical problems related to the topic of this book, and that due to the high volume of mail I receive, I might not be able to reply to every message.

When you write, please be sure to include this book's title and author as well as your name and phone or fax number. I will carefully review your comments and share them with the author and editors who worked on the book.

Fax: 317-581-4666

Email: quefeedback@macmillanusa.com

Mail: Associate Publisher
          Que
          201 West 103rd Street
          Indianapolis, IN 46290 USA

Introduction

One-Stop Shopping for Broadband Information

Welcome to the wide, wild world of broadband Internet access! With more and more dynamic content, streaming music, and full-motion video than ever before, the Internet demands the widest "pipe" you can buy to take full advantage of the content it offers.

Up to this point, getting information about broadband Internet has been frustrating. You've had to glean some information from a hardware vendor's Web site, pluck a few pages from a computer magazine, and dig around in an ISP's online Help. And, at the end of the day, you're still not sure that you've found out what's most essential.

An Expert Between Two Covers

This book gives you a single, friendly, and authoritative source for broadband Internet. Ever been shopping for an unfamiliar product with a friend who really is an expert? You learn what's really important, how to distinguish fluff from fact, and get the best deal. I can't be with you in person to guide you through the confusion of broadband choices, but this book is the next best thing.

Broadband Internet is all about choices: which service is faster, cheaper, easier to set up and install, and easier to get in your neighborhood. You'll find that the choices you have in your neighborhood aren't the same as family or friends might have just a few miles away. This book is dedicated to helping you figure out which broadband choice is the best one for you in as painless a way as possible.

Surviving the Installation

This book is far, far more than a shopping guide to broadband choices. It also helps you decide how much of the work you might want to do yourself to run at higher speeds. Some broadband options can be like high-tech Tinker Toy sets: Put it together right, and you have a masterpiece; assemble the pieces wrong, and you have a mess. Others are "sit back and leave the (device) driving to us." This book helps you understand how the pieces of your favorite broadband solution fit together.

Some people with the same broadband solution get more benefit out of it than others. Why? You'll find out what you can do to increase speed and get more out of your favorite broadband connection.

Unlike most network books (and trust me, the Internet is the biggest network there is), this book is refreshingly free of the kind of mind-numbing detail that so richly deserves the reaction that is also its name: "My Eyes Glaze Over." If you're looking to be rocked to sleep, go get a thicker book (thicker books make better pillows!). But if you want practical, field-tested advice that isn't biased toward anyone but you—this is your book.

Fast Track to the Facts You Want

I've added some special features to help you find the most important information—fast.

Techie Stuff

If you need just a bit more detail about a topic (without the patented MEGO—My Eyes Glaze Over—sedatives!), check these out.

Bombs Away!

Let's face it—computers can "byte" you. These sections help you avoid the potential traps lurking out there. These sidebars will help you be careful.

Hang Ten!

You probably already have an Internet connection (slow though it may be), so these sections help you research the Web with the Web (neat, eh?).

You'll also find a glossary to sort out any techno-speak that has gotten past the nerd filters I've installed in my word processor.

Broadband isn't painless—yet. But if you use this book as your guide, you'll be running faster than you ever dreamed, be smarter than you ever expected to be about broadband Internet, and be very, very popular with friends who are still stuck with ordinary modems. If they come over too often to "try" your broadband, tell 'em to buy a copy of this book. Thank you for your support!

Part 1

Getting the Most Out of Your Telephone Lines

You're probably already on the Internet, but your 56Kbps modem has lost a lot of its luster. It isn't nearly as fast as you'd like it to be, and you can't wait to get a faster solution.

In this part of the book, I help you understand where your modem fits into the world of the Internet and help you fine-tune its performance.

Even if you're on the cusp of ordering broadband service, these initial chapters are important because many broadband services still use ordinary modems for uploads, and because you might be in for a long wait to get a high-speed service installed in your home or office. Whatever the case, Part 1 will help you make the most of your current modem.

Chapter 1

How the Internet Works

In This Chapter

➤ Learn how information travels around the Internet

➤ Discover how basic networking evolved to become the Internet

➤ Understand how the World Wide Web fits into the puzzle

If you are new to the Internet and high-speed connectivity, you'll find this chapter to be an excellent primer for maximizing the performance and joy you will get from your high-speed connection. I start out with some information about the Internet, including some comparisons to help you understand how data travels around the Internet and why you can use a name instead of a number to locate a particular computer on the Internet.

Next, I help you understand how networking worked before the Internet. Sometimes, you can't use the Internet to link up with another computer, so this section isn't just a history lesson, but is an easy reference to what you need to do even now to connect with some computers.

Later in the chapter, you learn that the World Wide Web is just one part of the Internet, although it's the part that most of us use most often, and you learn what happens as you click your way across cyberspace. All in all, this chapter is designed to bring you up to speed on what the Internet is and help you start to understand why some parts of the Internet are faster than others.

The World's Largest Network—And More

The Internet has been described by some as the world's largest network. It's a great nickname because it reminds us that we can go from Evansville, Indiana to Osaka, Japan with a single mouse click (instead of taking 27 hours in overstuffed airplanes routed by way of Detroit and Minneapolis). But, like most nicknames, it is less than accurate. This shouldn't surprise you. After all, you've probably seen University of Kentucky basketball coach "Tubby" Smith on TV and said to yourself, "He doesn't *look* overweight." Or maybe you've met somebody who said, "Just call me Red," and it was obvious that the last time his nickname made sense was during the Nixon Administration.

Elements of the Network of Networks

So, what's a more accurate way of looking at the Internet? A better description of the Internet is to call it the network of networks. To understand why that's accurate, let's brush up on what computer networks are.

When we call the Internet a network of networks, we're referring to the fact that the Internet can link your computer to computers all over the world that are connected to each other in small groupings called *networks* (see Figure 1.1).

Figure 1.1

A simplified view of the Internet, the network of networks. Your computer is represented by one of the small computers at the bottom of the figure. Thanks to the Internet, you can exchange information with any other computer on the Internet, regardless of where it is located.

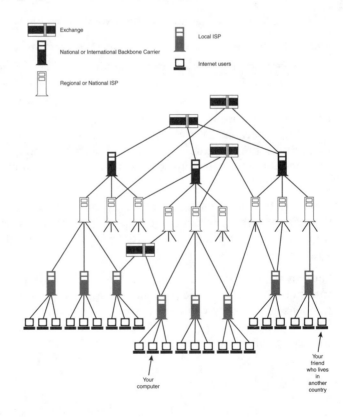

8

Computers that communicate over the Internet have several features in common:

➤ A shared software standard

➤ Connections to routable networks

➤ A shared naming system

The Software Standard Called TCP/IP

If you've ever tried to stuff a Macintosh disk into a PC and couldn't read it, or tried to explain to your crying toddler why the new Barney movie on DVD at the store won't fit into your VCR, you know how frustrating having different standards for the same kind of information can be.

Far from supporting only a single kind of computer (such as Gateway computers made on alternate Tuesdays or Lime-green iMacs with mismatched mice), the Internet performs the seemingly impossible feat of allowing Gateways, iMacs, and virtually every other computer on the market (as well as museum pieces even I can barely remember) to communicate with each other. It's amazing to think that two computers that couldn't even share a floppy disk if they were next to each other in the same office can cheerfully swap email, full-motion video, or MP3 music files over the Internet.

A suite of software (two bedrooms, bath, and laundry area not included) called TCP/IP make it possible.

What is TCP/IP? It's a collection of programming rules known as a protocol that help different kinds of computers talk to each other. A protocol is a specification; it is a common set of rules that different kinds of computers can use. This isn't easy to accomplish.

Think of the different computers connected to the Internet as being a bit like the UN's General Assembly. You've got a delegate from China lecturing the rest of the assembly, and everyone is paying (more or less) close attention, although few of the delegates even know enough Chinese to order take-out without a menu. Look closely at the other delegates, and you'll see the secret: headsets connected to hard-working translators backstage who translate the Chinese for *My government has instructed me to oppose...* into French, Zulu, English, German, Korean, and so on. Normally,

Tech Note

What the Heck Is TCP/IP?

TCP/IP—Transmission Control Protocol/Internet Protocol; TCP/IP is the standard computer language of the Internet. If you don't have TCP/IP installed and properly set up on your computer, you can't connect to the Internet, no matter how many modems or broadband connections you have running to your computer.

the UN delegates would have a hard time understanding each other, but the *network hardware* of headsets and the *network software* of simultaneous translators keeps information flowing.

Who does the translation at the UN? Nobody famous, but without them, the UN couldn't get anything done. What accomplishes the translation that allows different computer nations such as Windowsland, Macland, Linuxland, and Sunland to talk to each other over the Internet? TCP/IP.

The Many Talents of TCP/IP

What does TCP/IP help computers do? It allows you to view Web pages, send and receive email, send and receive files, and search for information. Although some of you might use your Web browser to perform all of these tasks, and some of you might use separate Web browser, email, file-transfer, and search tools, TCP/IP is the engine inside Internet software to get these jobs done.

Any computer that wants to be on the Internet needs more than to think to itself, "I really, really want to be on the Internet—really I do!" It needs TCP/IP software installed and set up correctly (more about that later) to teach it to talk to the other computers on the Internet.

Network, Take a Message

A *routable network* is a network that can send and receive messages that travel from one network to another. Before the Internet, most office and home networks were non-routable.

Routable Networks—The Information Superhighway— 1 Mile

The second factor that computers on the Internet have in common is that they are connected through routable networks.

To make this whole idea clearer, imagine that you are sending a letter to somebody living on 123 Main Street. If all you put on the letter is 123 Main Street, it will probably come back to you because you forgot to put the name, city, state, and Zip code (or province and postal code if you're in Canada) on the letter. This additional information routes the letter to the correct 123 Main Street in your state and country. (Trust me, a lot of people and businesses have addresses at 123 Main Street!)

Figure 1.2 shows how the Internet might route an email message from your computer to a friend's computer if you use different ISPs. The Internet relays email messages, Web page requests, file downloads, and other traffic in a manner similar to this millions of times a day.

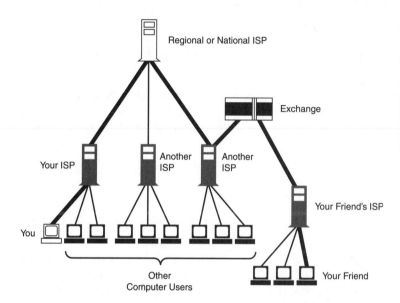

Figure 1.2

Because the Internet is a routable network, you can send an email message to your friend's computer, even though your friend uses a different ISP (Internet service provider) than you do.

In the world of the Internet, devices called, strangely enough, *routers* perform routing. These devices figure out the correct path to take a message intended for a computer called "George" in one network to another computer called "George" connected to another network. One place where our analogy breaks down is that you, the addresser of the letter, would need to add much address information to your letter, whereas on the Internet you simply click a link to send the information through all the layers it must pass to reach its destination.

This is a *very* simplified example. For more information about the details of this, see Chapter 17, "A Survivor's Guide to TCP/IP."

How Routable Networks Work—Two Comparisons

Another cool fact about routable networks is *how* they pass information from you to wherever it's going. The following examples will help you understand how routable networks work.

Hitching a Ride on the (Information) Superhighway

Imagine that you need to go to Chicago from St Louis and you face these obstacles:

➤ You have no money, so you can't buy a plane ticket.

➤ You have no money, so you can't buy a train ticket. (My favorite way to go—more scenery and more space!)

➤ You have no money, so you can't rent a car.

➤ You have no car *because* you have no money.

Okay! We've established that you're broke. But, you still need to get to Chicago. But how?

If you had money, you could go directly to Chicago. But you can't. What you can do (assuming it's a safer world than we actually live in) is hitchhike. You could hang out under the Gateway Arch or at Busch Stadium with a sign that says Chicago. Sooner or later, one of two things will happen:

➤ You'd get a ride.

➤ You'd get a ride.

(We're ignoring getting arrested for loitering, because after all, this is just an example.)

You might think the preceding text contains a misprint. It doesn't. What I meant to type was "You'd get a ride directly to Chicago" on the first line and "You'd get a ride to Springfield, Illinois, then to Peoria, then to Rockford, then to Milwaukee, then to Chicago" or something like that on the second line.

See the difference? In both cases, you get to Chicago, but in the second example you get there by various rides that take you part of the way (or sometimes a bit out of the way) en route to your final destination. Because you're hitchhiking, who are you to complain? Sit back, enjoy the scenery, and be thankful this is only an example.

It might be only an example to you, but in reality it's fairly similar to the way the Internet really works. The Internet is a network of networks that works by passing messages from one network to another until the message reaches its final destination. Seldom is the trip performed in anything approximating a straight line, but nobody's complaining.

Now, the previous example is okay as far as it goes, but like any analogy, it breaks down after awhile. This particular analogy is broken down at mile 25 on I-55 North out of St. Louis because it doesn't account for a feature of network communications called *packetized data*. As information travels on the Internet from its source to its destination, it is subdivided into data packets.

All right, what is a *data packet*? A data packet is a small portion of the total information you are sending or receiving.

To return to the example, suppose you are hitchhiking with two large suitcases and three people stop to offer you a ride: One person has a vintage sports car with leather seats but absolutely no trunk space for your luggage, the second driver is at the wheel of an ancient farm truck that hasn't had the interior cleaned since the Ford Administration, and the third driver is ferrying a carload of antique car fans in a sedan that's older than they are. Choice #1 has room for only you, and choices #2 and 3 have room for just one suitcase each. You and your luggage compare to a message that can be divided into three data packets; you represent one packet, and each suitcase represents another packet (see Figure 1.3).

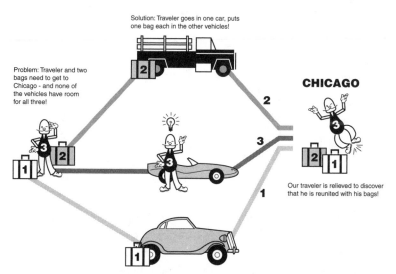

Solution: Traveler goes in one car, puts one bag each in the other vehicles!

Problem: Traveler and two bags need to get to Chicago - and none of the vehicles have room for all three!

CHICAGO

Our traveler is relieved to discover that he is reunited with his bags!

Figure 1.3

A hitchhiker with two suitcases may wind up needing to use three different cars to get to his destination. Similarly, the Internet divides up information into packets that are the right size to travel across the Internet.

If you trusted all the drivers (and for the sake of this discussion, you do), you could ask the driver of the pickup truck to take one suitcase and the driver of the sedan to take another suitcase, while you settle down in the leather interior of the sports car. You and your luggage can convoy down the highway to your destination.

In highly simplified form, that's what happens on the Internet when you send or receive information. Data is packetized to make it fit better through all types of large and small network pathways. You and your two suitcases are like a three-packet message.

Tech Note

Packet Up and Send It!

One of the many behind-the-scenes tasks that TCP/IP does for you is create data packets. When you send a file to a friend on the Internet, TCP/IP turns the file into data packets before you send it. When you get a file in return, TCP/IP reassembles its data packets into a file.

However, this analogy is also incomplete. The Internet reserves the right to send each packet any way it pleases.

Danger Danger

Don't Stop the Packets!

If you turn off your computer while you are sending or receiving email, the message you are sending or receiving will not be complete. Some of the data packets will not be sent or received, and this will cause the message to be incomplete. If you are sending or receiving a program file, the file will be damaged, and running it could cause your computer to crash.

Reunited—And It Feels So Good!

How do TCP/IP and hardware devices called *routers* work? To understand what they do, let's look at the way my family and I flew from Evansville, Indiana to Portland, Oregon a few years ago. My three sons and I flew on the Delta Connection (Comair) to Cincinnati and from there to Portland on a Delta widebody. My wife and my daughter flew to St. Louis on TransWorld Express, were delayed for several hours, and finally arrived in Portland after the men of the family on Delta. Although we went in two different directions on two different airlines, at the end of the day we were reunited in Oregon (see Figure 1.4).

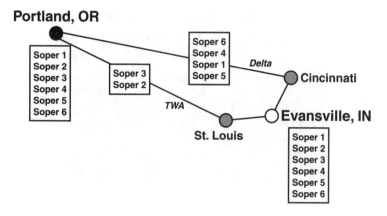

Figure 1.4

The Sopers were reunited at their destination in the same way the packets in a data file are reassembled in correct order after being routed to their destination by various routes.

Just as airlines can route different members of a family in different paths to a destination, routers (which are connected to the small networks that make up the Internet) are used to send data packets belonging to the same file on different paths to the same destination. Because TCP/IP created the data packets to begin with, it can reassemble them correctly at the destination.

Tracing the Route to Your Favorite Web Site

As you can see from the examples and comparisons, information on the Internet doesn't go directly from your computer to its destination. Instead, it can follow what appears to be a highly indirect route, and the routing can change as the traffic load on parts of the Internet backbones increases and decreases. If you're wondering about how many hops a message must take to go from your computer to another computer, you can use a command called TRACEROUTE (or the Microsoft Windows version TRACERT) to see these intermediate points on your message's journey.

To use TRACERT with Windows 95/98/Me, follow this procedure:

1. Click Start, Programs, (Accessories), MS-DOS Prompt.
2. Type TRACERT *mywebsite* (replace *mywebsite* with a real Web site name, such as my publisher's Web site: www.mcp.com), and press Enter.
3. You will see the name of each computer on the route between your computer and the Web site you specified (see Figure 1.5).
4. You can use TRACERT to look at the path to other Web sites. Type **EXIT** and press Enter to return to the Windows desktop.

Did you notice that some computers are identified only by numbers? These numbers are the IP addresses of the computers used to relay the TRACERT command. However, some computers have names and numbers. In the next section you'll discover how the Internet matches computer names to IP addresses.

15

Figure 1.5

Using TRACERT *to see the route to your favorite Web site; I chose the SIGECOM Web site because it's located in the same city (Evansville, IN) in which I live—but it still took nine hops to go there!*

The Domain Naming System—Computer Names Only a Human Could Love

The Internet has come a long way since its origins as the U.S. Department of Defense's ARPAnet in the 1960s. Along the way, many improvements have taken place in it, one of which is how computers are identified. Originally, you had to know a computer's *IP address* to locate the information stored on it. The address would look something like this:

    212.313.404.812

(This, by the way is *not* an actual IP address; it breaks about every rule out there, except for the fact that real IP addresses have up to 12 digits in groups of three as you see here. Those of you who read telephone books might recognize that these are really area codes!). As you saw in the previous section, when TRACERT is used to figure out which computers connect you to a Web site, IP addresses are used to identify the computers that link you to your destination. In fact, IP addresses are used by the Internet any time information is exchanged between two computers. From the standpoint of an ordinary human being, this is scary. Who could remember all those IP addresses, and even if you could, who'd want to? If the Internet were still strictly an IP-address based system, you wouldn't be reading this book, and I wouldn't be writing it. Fortunately, the developers of the Internet realized that something had to be done to make connecting with a computer a little bit easier.

DNS to the Rescue—How the Domain Name System Works

The secret to easy Internet access is something called the *Domain Name System (DNS)*. The Domain Name System translates the IP address of a Web site (207.46.130.49) into an easy-to-remember Web site name: www.microsoft.com (actual examples this time, by the way). The Domain Name System makes working with the Internet a whole lot easier because our brains prefer names like `www.seethenewhitmovie.com` to a long list of numbers.

Another benefit of DNS is that a single large Web site such as `www.microsoft.com` might actually use many different computers to host it. DNS enables us to go to Microsoft's Web site without worrying about which computer has the page we want to see.

Tech Note

THAT WAY ▷

The Masters of the Domain(s)

How does the DNS work? Organizations such as Network Solutions (`www.networksolutions.net`) assign domain names (the names used for Web sites and email addresses) to companies who pay fees for the rights to use a domain name for a specified period (normally one to two years). The domain name and the IP address(es) to which it points are stored in a huge database (similar in a way to a phone directory).

Each ISP has one or more DNS computers, which hold a copy of the master DNS database, which is created from the registrations performed by domain name registration companies. Whenever an individual or company purchases a new domain name, the information about that domain name and its IP address(es) are transmitted to the DNS servers all over the Internet. In a couple of days, every server will know that a particular IP address and a particular domain name go together.

Originally, the only organization in the U.S. that assigned domain names was InterNIC, which was formerly part of Network Solutions, Inc.

Today, InterNIC is a registered service mark of the U.S. Department of Commerce, and domain name registration is being handled by Network Solutions and many other competing firms. Domain name registrations can be handled through an ISP or by directly contacting any of the domain name registration services.

More About Domains

To learn more about InterNIC and domain name registrations and to see a listing of companies that can handle domain name registrations, go to the InterNIC Web site:

    http://www.internic.net

To go directly to InterNIC's WHOIS service, which shows you who has rights to a domain name, go to

    http://www.internic.net/whois.html

You also can check the WHOIS page at any of the domain name registration services for more information.

DNS in Action

When you type a Web page into your Web browser's address window and press Enter, here's what happens:

1. You type www.microsoft.com.
2. Whenever you request a Web page, your ISP's DNS server checks its database to figure out which IP address matches the name you entered.
3. When your ISP matches www.microsoft.com to its IP address (207.230.46.219), the IP address, not the name you typed, is given to the router, which relays your request to other computers.

PINGing Your Way Across the Internet

Are you wondering what IP address a particular Web site uses? You can use a program called PING to find out. PING is included with Windows, and other operating systems have similar utilities. In a later chapter you'll find out how to use PING to troubleshoot your system, but you can use PING any time to learn the IP address of a particular Web site.

Here's how to use PING if you use Windows 95/98/Me:

1. Click Start, Programs, (Accessories), MS-DOS Prompt.
2. Type PING *mywebsite* (replace *mywebsite* with a real Web site name, such as my publisher's Web site, www.mcp.com), and press Enter.

3. You will see the name of your Web site, its IP address, and statistics indicating how long it takes for a data packet to go from your computer to the Web site and back (see Figure 1.6).

Figure 1.6

Using PING to find the IP address of my publisher's Web site.

You can keep PINGing your favorite sites, or type **EXIT** and press Enter to return to Windows.

Life Before the Internet

To help you appreciate how amazing the Internet really is, here's a brief history lesson. (Don't worry, there won't be a test.)

Computer Networks

Computer networks have been around for more than 20 years. Networks were originally designed to allow computers in a single office or building to share expensive disk drives and printers. Most networks were built up from computers that ran the same *operating system* (a special program that tells the hardware and software what to do, such as MS-DOS, Microsoft Windows, MacOS, and so on).

Networks were connected to each other with coaxial cable (which looks like the wire that the cable TV people run to your set-top box) that connected to network cards inside each computer. To allow the computer in the corner office to pretend that the printer in a cubicle was connected directly to it, software known as a *Network Operating System (NOS)* was run on each computer, allowing them to share printers (my turn to print—wait your turn!) and disk drives (you'll all be able to get your files—here's yours, and yours, and yours…). Except for networks in large companies, most networks never communicated with other networks.

Calling Another Computer

The Internet has become such a big part of our lives that it's easy to forget that computers could connect to one another before the Internet was created. You'll learn how non-Internet connections work in this section. Should you care? Absolutely!

Although most people use the Internet rather than a direct connection to reach other computers, sometimes you might need to dial up another computer directly using methods just like these. If you work at home for a major corporation or do home banking, you might need to call the remote computer directly rather than use the Internet.

If your computer needed to contact a computer in a distant city, you had to purchase a modem and have somebody install it for you. But that's not all you needed. Just as a computer on a network needs special software to talk to other computers, your modem needs special software to talk to a computer that's miles away.

You'll learn more about how modems work today in the next chapter, but now I'm still trying to rid you of any nostalgia you might have for the good old days of telecommunications (a long phrase which means "it would be a lot easier without modems").

A careful search of the box the modem came in would usually locate some disks that you needed to install to allow your modem to actually work, assuming that the disks were still readable. When I first installed a modem, disks were 5.25 inches wide with thin, flexible jackets, so the term *floppy disks* still made sense. There's nothing quite so bone-chilling as seeing a disk that won't lay flat because it's been folded—and no better way to wreck your disk drive than trying to use a folded disk.

After you bought a modem (ten times slower than today's models at about five times the cost), you needed to set the modem to call the other computer. This wasn't easy. Sure, you needed to enter the phone number of the other computer, but that was just the beginning. For example, if you were calling the A&BC Corporation's computer, you might have received instructions that looked like this:

```
(812) 555-1234
    VT-100 emulation
    2400bps, 7-bit word length, even parity, one stop bit
```

What's all that mean? I'll break it down.

➤ (812) 555-1234—Well, the first line is the phone number (that was easy, right?).

➤ VT-100 emulation—The second line is the *terminal emulation*. Different brands of terminals work in different ways, so big computers were programmed to recognize one brand or model of terminal. Terminal emulation allows your computer to talk to different computer systems used in different companies by imitating the terminals used at each company.

Tech Note

And Now Arriving at the Terminal: Your Data

Terminals vaguely resemble what would happen if somebody broke into your office and swiped the computer but left the monitor and keyboard behind. On a real terminal, the keyboard has a bunch of extra keys with names like PF-17, and the CRT (which looks like a monitor but displays only green or amber text) has a bunch of connections in the back for devices such as AUX. A terminal's keyboard plugs directly into the CRT, and unless the whole rig's connected to a real computer somewhere else, nothing's happening onscreen. Terminals are sometimes called *dumb* or *smart* terminals, but because both types need to hook up to a real computer, neither type is very big in the brains department. The data you enter into a terminal is stored in a large computer, and your terminal can be connected to that computer through a telephone modem or network cable.

➤ 2400bps, 7-bit word length, even parity, one stop bit—The third line is the modem configuration. You'd take this information, plunge into your modem program's setup screens, and enter this information before you start the call to the computer at A&BC Corporation.

What happens if you set the terminal emulation or modem settings incorrectly? Your computer and the A&BC computer would have a rather one-sided conversation, something like this:

```
(Your computer). I'd like to logon, please.
(A&BC computer). %$^**^***)_# )((**(&:LKJHYO%T$R_)_)*%$$^#$^#!!!
(Your computer).  So's your old man! (hangs up)
```

Without the correct settings, your computer and the other computer are speaking different languages. In the preceding example, the A&BC computer was trying to reply with a message like "Logon Name, please," but because the settings were not correct, your computer couldn't understand the message.

File Transfer Follies

Things got even worse if you were trying to receive (*download*) or send (*upload*) a file to a computer. You'd need to choose a *file transfer protocol*. This means if you and I can't agree on how to send and receive this file, it ain't happening. The following are real-life favorites of file transfer protocols (the names have not been changed):

➤ Xmodem (Xactly what does this stand for? Does it matter?)

➤ Ymodem (Y use it? It's better and faster than Xmodem.)

➤ Zmodem (even better than X and Y put together; notice a pattern here?)

➤ Kermit (the frog prince of protocols—ugly and slow)

Tech Note

Terminal, Right This Way

In the days of MS-DOS, you needed to use the terminal program included with your modem to get the terminal emulation and file-transfer settings mentioned in this chapter.

Today if you need to make a direct computer-to-computer connection via terminal emulation with Windows, you can use the HyperTerminal program to make a connection. HyperTerminal can emulate several popular terminals and also contains file transfer protocols such as Xmodem and others. See your Windows online help or user manual for details.

The problems of convincing the remote computer to send the file you wanted would be the final factor convincing you that nostalgia for the '80s certainly can't apply to computers.

The Internet fixes all this for you—simply and easily from your standpoint—but with an immense amount of work by others around the world.

How the Internet Changed Everything

Before the Internet, you needed a vast amount of information about any computer you wanted to contact. And even though you knew what the A&BC Corporation's computer wanted to hear when you called it, a call to a different computer, such as the ZX&Y LLC's computer, would require completely different settings.

And did you notice the phone number? You made AT&T, Sprint, or MCI very happy every time you called a computer that wasn't in your local calling area. If you needed to send files or look at information for 55 minutes, that was a 55-minute long-distance call. Cha-ching!

Battle of the Networking Stars—The Internet Versus Other Networks

How did the Internet change all that? See Table 1.1 for a quick comparison.

Table 1.1 How the Internet Changes The Way You Contact Another Computer

Process/Settings	Before the Internet	The Internet
Contacting a Computer	Direct call (long distance) to each computer by modem	One call to an Internet service provider (ISP) (usually local) by modem and link to any computer or connect directly through your office or home network
Call Settings	Different for each computer	One setting to access any computer
Terminal Emulation	Different for each computer	Not needed; use a Web browser program for most content on the Internet
User Interface	Different for each computer	Same for all computers on the Internet (your browser)

As a veteran of the pre-Internet communications days, I'm stunned when I realize how much easier the Internet has made getting and sending information. In the next two sections, we'll look at exactly what makes the Internet work.

Browsers, Web Pages, and Hyperlinks

When you think of the Internet, you probably think of your Web browsing program, your favorite Web page or Web site, and clicking your way around cyberspace. Is this the totality of the Internet?

Don't Get Stuck Thinking the Web Is All the Internet

What is the Internet? If you answer the World Wide Web, you only get half credit (but don't worry, this isn't a test). The World Wide Web is what I like to call the visible or popular side of the Internet. Because this is the part of the Internet that most of you are concerned about, this book is primarily concerned with the Web.

Before the World Wide Web was developed in the early 1990s, people (primarily computer geniuses in the military and computer students drinking too much coffee in college) could use the Internet but had to use search tools with names like Archie, Veronica, and Jughead (do computer geeks read too many comics?) to locate files to download or text files to read online.

Although we still use search tools today, we have a big advantage over the comics-obsessed early Internet pioneers: We can open up a Web page in a browser and click a link to go to either a different document on the computer we're viewing or a different computer entirely. Because you can go anywhere from anywhere else (just as if you were walking on a spider web), this technology is called the *World Wide Web*, or the *Web* for short. (Some people call it the WWW, but this sounds too much like a wrestling league full of guys wearing protractors in their shirt pockets to work for me.)

Clicking Across the Web with Hyperlinks

What is the World Wide Web? The Web combines the network of features of the entire Internet with an easy way to go from computer to computer, called *hyperlinking*, which enables you to click underlined text (or a picture) to go to another Web page or Web site without typing in either a friendly DNS name or a less friendly IP address.

The idea of text links isn't new; if you've ever looked at a Help file on a computer and clicked an underlined word to see its definition, you've used an ancestor of hyperlinking called *hypertext*. Hypertext is cool, but it has its limitations. If you're looking at the Help file for program A, for example, and the answer you want is really in the Help file for program B, there's no easy way to see that information or even to know that the information you wanted is in the other location. You would

1. Need to figure out that program B was where to look for your problem's solution.
2. Start program B, open its help file, and locate the information.

Hyperlinking goes beyond hypertext because it enables you to quickly go to information on a different computer, not merely a different document. How significant is that? If you've ever seen the movie *Miracle on 34th Street*, you'll remember what a radical idea it was to have the salespeople at Macy's tell weary shoppers, "We don't have exactly what you're looking for, but Gimbal's has it!" The idea of taking you to a completely different computer for the information you need is very much like Macy's sending people to Gimbal's. That's the beauty of hyperlinking.

Surfing the Net

To access the World Wide Web, you need the following (and I bet you've already got these):

➤ A computer

➤ An Internet connection

➤ A Web browser

Although five-year-old computers with low-IQ 486 processors can be used to access the Web, a new computer does a much nicer job. New computers have faster processors and better video cards, which work together to display pages faster and play sounds and movie clips better.

The Internet connection at home usually comes from a modem (more about those in Chapter 2, "Dial-Up Modems and Internet Slowdowns,") along with a subscription to an Internet service provider (ISP). These used to cost $15–$22 per month, but several services out there from AltaVista, NetZero, and others offer you the classic all-American deal: "Trade you free services for annoying ads." A fair number of people are willing to do just that.

Danger Danger

Keep Your Guard Up

If you want to try a new ISP or install a free Internet service, find out whether your existing Internet settings will be preserved after you change services. Some new Internet services act as if they're the only ones in town: AOL version 5, for example, takes over all Internet functions on your computer and is very difficult to remove. If you want to try a new service, ask the ISP if you can create your connection manually by using the Windows Dial-Up Networking service or your operating system's normal Internet dialer.

The *Web browser* is a program that understands a language called *HTML*. The HTML language is actually ordinary text plus special tags that make text larger, smaller, **bold**, or *italic,* and indicate links to other pages on the same computer or on another computer.

Most text links are underlined, but pictures also can be used as hyperlink buttons. The easiest way to figure out whether text or graphics are links is to watch your cursor. The plain arrow cursor changes to a finger when you move it over a text or graphics link.

Tech Note

Whoa! This Sounds Complicated

HTML is an acronym for HyperText Markup Language. You can see these tags if you use the View Source or View Page Source menu option in your browser. The tags to make text italic, for example, look like this: `<I>This is italic</I>`. You can learn HTML if you want to create Web pages, but you don't need to know a speck of HTML to use the Web.

Browsing for Browsers

It's probably no surprise that the preselected home page for Microsoft's Internet Explorer is `www.msn.com` (the Microsoft Network), and for Netscape Communicator/Navigator, it's `home.netscape.com`.

Adventures in Cyberspace

When you open an Internet connection, your browser displays a home page created with a language called HTML.

More and more Web pages aren't pure HTML. If they were, or if they had just a few pictures, you might not be reading this book right now. The use of script languages such as JavaScript, motion graphics standards such as Java and Flash, and features such as sounds and movies in Web pages make the Web more interesting and slower-loading now than ever before.

The home page for most users is the home page set automatically by the Web browsing software (the program that lets you hyperlink your way around the Web).

You don't need to stay on that home page, though. You can go anywhere on the Web you like by

➤ Typing the address of a page you want to see (the URL) into the address window.

➤ Clicking a hyperlink on the page.

When you click a hyperlink, the browser fetches the page to which the hyperlink refers and displays it in the browser's window. Thanks to the network of networks design of the Internet, that page can be on a computer in California, China, or Chartres, and you can still see it—and (usually) read it. English is the dominant language of the Internet, although I once performed a vanity search for myself and found myself listed on a Russian-language Web site that was selling a translation of a computer book I helped write.

Some people have even played an Internet version of "around the world in 80 days" to see how many links it would take to go from their original page to the same page.

Sometimes your new page is displayed immediately, but more often you must wait...and wait...and wait. This might seem strange because most of the Internet is designed to

➤ Carry huge amounts of data (computer, telephone, modem, and so forth)

➤ Carry it as fast as possible

Tech Note

URL—Pronounced "Earl"

URL—Uniform Resource Locator—A standard for naming Web pages and sites. For example, the URL for Macmillan USA, the publisher of this book, is **www.mcp.com**.

The Internet uses several so-called *backbones*, which, like your own body's backbone, support the rest of the Internet. The speed of Internet backbones varies, but the current speed champ is the OC-48, which runs at 2.5Gbps (2.5 billion bits per second!), or enough capacity to handle 175,000 customers using regular modems connected at the same time. With that kind of speed, why does anybody need to wait for anything? In the next chapter, you'll find out why.

The Least You Need to Know

➤ The Internet is a network of networks, giving you access to information stored on computers around the world.

➤ You can click your way around cyberspace to find information, or just enter the name of a Web site or page (its URL).

➤ Parts of the Internet, its backbones, carry huge amounts of information at very high speeds.

Chapter 2

Dial-Up Modems and Internet Slowdowns

In This Chapter

➤ How modems work and how they connect to your computer

➤ What makes the Internet slow

➤ Why modems are the most important speed bump on the Information Superhighway

You know the Internet is slow when you connect at home; do you ever wonder why? And do you wonder why the Internet is a lot faster at the office? You're about to find out.

How Modems Work

Using a telephone line to connect computers to each other might seem natural, but in reality it's a *kludge*.

What makes connecting computers through the telephone company a kludge? The same thing that makes it easy to tell whether the call you're getting is from a relative, a friend, or a stranger misusing your first name to sell you something: the telephone's capability to transmit volume, pitch, and tone. The telephone system, you see, works with analog data, whereas a computer is strictly digital.

Tech Note

Huh?

Kludge (pronounced "kludge" or "klooge")—An inelegant workaround to a difficult situation.

Why Computers and Telephones Don't Mix

What's the difference? Analog data (like that telephone call trying to sell you a low-interest credit card) would look like a series of waves on the electronic ocean. High-pitched and loud sounds are like the crests of the waves, with the lulls between each crest representing softer and lower-pitched sounds. Digital data, on the other hand, has no graceful curves or gradual changes. It's strictly an on or off, true or false proposition (see Figure 2.1).

Figure 2.1

Digital (computer) versus analog (telephone) data transmission.

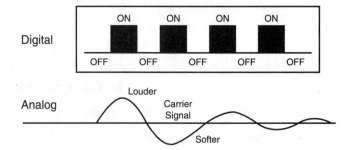

So, exactly how do digitally based computers talk to each other over a medium designed more than 100 years ago for analog-based people to talk, chat, sing, yell, and sell each other insurance policies? You need a way to convert digital signals to analog—and convert them back again. Enter the modem.

How Modems Bring Computers and Telephones Together

The easiest way to understand what modems do is to find out what *modem* is short for: **mo**dulate/**dem**odulate.

Modulation is the process of changing the digital data being sent from your computer into analog tones that the telephone companies know, love, and can transmit. Obviously, if the only computer with a modem is your computer, you'd never hear back from any other computers, so the computer you're connected to also has a modem. That modem represents the *dem* portion of modem; it demodulates the analog tones back into digital on or off, true or false signals that computers understand.

The process is illustrated in Figure 2.2.

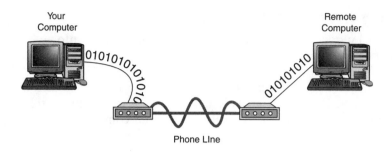

Figure 2.2

The computer on the left sends digital data (zeros and ones) to a modem, which converts the data into sounds that can be transmitted over phone lines to a remote computer's modem (on the right), which converts the sounds back into digital data.

Tech Note

The Song of the Modem

Want to hear the sounds of computers talking? Pick up an extension while your spouse or child is online and you'll hear the rasp, scratch, and screech of data in telephone-ready form. As soon as you hang up the extension, get ready for more screeching (from the computer user this time), because picking up the extension is enough to convince many modems they've lost carrier and drop the call. Want to hear really loud screeching? Pick up the extension in the middle of a huge download!

Modems, Modems, Everywhere

Modems are sometimes referred to as *telephone modems* because they are used, as we just saw, to connect two computers over telephone lines. Sometimes the term modem is used incorrectly to describe any device that connects two computers that are not on the same network, such as cable modems (which we'll discuss later). In this book, *modem* when used by itself refers to the telephone modem.

Modems come in several different physical types (or *form factors*), including

➤ Internal modems

➤ External modems

➤ PC Card modems

Although they look different, all three types of modems work the same way. Here's how to tell them apart.

The Inside Story on Internal Modems

Most people have internal modems in their computers. These modems fit into an expansion slot inside the computer and have two telephone-wire connectors on their rear brackets. Run a wire from the wall to one socket, and your modem is connected to the telephone company. Lest your telephone cry "Unfair!" at losing its connection, you can plug it into the second connector, making it easy for you to play many spirited games of Solitaire while you wait on hold for help with your computer.

Tech Note

Connector Crazy

Telephone cable uses an RJ-11 connector. Although similar in shape, this type of cable is different from the RJ-45 connectors used to connect computers and printers on a network. On some modems, you must plug the telephone line from the wall into the modem jack marked "line" or "telco" to make a connection; on others, it doesn't matter. Be sure to check the documentation that came with your modem.

Flexible Outsiders—External Modems

External modems are more popular in business circles than at home, but they have several advantages:

➤ The signal lights tell you that something is happening.

➤ You can move them around from computer to computer.

➤ You can turn them off and back on again to reset them if they get stuck.

External modems plug into either the USB (Universal Serial Bus) port or a 9-pin port on the rear of your computer called a serial or COM port. The serial port can also be identified by a symbol that resembles alternating zeros and ones: 01010. Unlike internal modems, which are found inside most new computers like Cracker Jack prizes, external modems actually cost real money.

Give Credit Where Credit Is Due—PC Card Modems

PC Card modems look like a credit card except

➤ They have more brains inside

➤ They're thicker

➤ They don't have a credit limit (but if you bid on eBay, they work just as well as any other modem to reduce your actual credit cards' credit lines!)

PC Card modems are used in notebook computers and often are too thin to accept a normal telephone cable. Instead, they can use a pop-out telephone wire (RJ-11) jack or a special cable called a *dongle* that connects to the telephone wall jack.

PC Card modems also cost real money because they are not included with most notebook computers.

Danger Danger

How to Fry Your Modem in One Easy Lesson

If you need to move your modem to another computer or pack it for a trip, make sure you follow these precautions.

The *only* type of modem you can disconnect from your computer without taking special action is an external USB modem. It's designed to be hot-swapped, which means that the computer will automatically recognize when it's connected and when it's back in your suitcase.

PC Card modems can also be removed, but you must stop the card first before you remove it. Look for a small PC Card icon on the toolbar of your Windows notebook computer. Double-click it, click your modem, and click Stop. You can remove it when you hear a low-pitched bee-doop noise.

You must turn off your computer before you install or remove internal and RS-232 serial (COM) port modems. Make sure you also turn off an external COM port modem.

Ignore this warning, and you can fry your modem (and your computer, too!).

All three types of modems share one basic characteristic with each other: They're so sloooow!

How Slow Is That Modem in Your PC?

The modem is far from the fastest device in your computer, although modems have increased in speed along with every other device in the computer. Computer speeds are usually calculated in *Megahertz (MHz)*, which measures how many million times a second current alternates (goes back and forth) inside the CPU. Modem speeds are calculated in *bits per second (bps)* transmitted (it takes eight bits to make a *byte* or character of text).

CPUs Leave Modems in the Dust

Table 2.1 compares the speeds of popular CPUs of the past and present with typical modem speeds. However, it doesn't take into account the amount of data each computer can handle during each MHz operation, so it actually understates the improvement in performance between yesterday and today.

Table 2.1   A Comparison of CPU and Modem Speeds

Year	CPU Type	Speed (MHz)	Modem Speed (bps)
1986	286	8	1,200
1989	386	16	2,400
1991	486	33	9,600
1994	Pentium	60	28,800
1995	Pentium	100	33,600
2000	Pentium III	1000	56,000

Over the 14 years in our survey, the clock speed of CPUs increased by a factor of 125, whereas the speed of modems increased by a factor of only 47. Modems didn't increase in speed nearly as much as the CPUs did; however, as Figure 2.3 indicates, maybe modems have a good reason for lagging.

The speed of your modem is just one factor that affects the speed of the Internet. In the next section, you'll find out what other factors make the Internet speedy or sluggish.

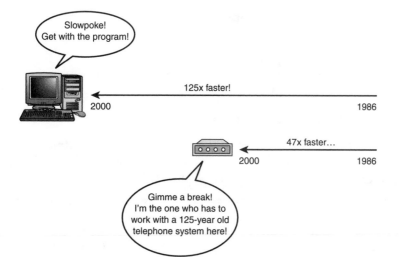

Figure 2.3

Modems work with a telephone system that was originally designed in the 1870s, so it's surprising that they run as fast as they do.

How Fast Is the Internet? It Depends

Because the Internet is a network of networks, answering the question of how fast it is seems a bit like asking how fast the American highway system is. On I-94 driving through a state like Montana, you're looking at a 75mph speed limit. But on that same I-94 running below street level through downtown Chicago, the Dan Ryan Expressway clocks at just 55mph, except at rush hour, when your real speed can be occasionally 0 mph. And, of course, just as you must drive on slower-speed streets and highways to reach the Interstate highways, some parts of the Internet are faster than others.

Information Superhighways and On Ramps

The fastest parts of the Internet are its backbones: high-speed fiber-optic cables that can carry hundreds of thousands of simultaneous connections. Depending on the provider, backbones can use any of the standards, often combined for even greater speeds, that are shown in Table 2.2.

Table 2.2   Internet Backbone Speeds

Cable Type	Speed
OC-48	2.5Gbps
OC-12	622Mbps
OC-3	155.5Mbps

Oh See How Fast This Is!

OC stands for Optical Carrier levels, referring to the fiber-optic cable construction of all Internet backbones. OC-1 is the base OC rate, 51.84Mbps. Other OC rates are multiples of OC-1. OC-48 is 48 times faster than OC-1.

Don't you wish your computer could connect directly to a backbone? Me too. Instead, your computer connects through an *Internet service provider (ISP)*, which has smaller but still impressively speedy connections.

The connections shown in Table 2.3 are used by ISPs to connect to backbones. Again, larger ISPs will often use multiple connections to support many Internet users or increase speeds.

Table 2.3   ISP Connections to Major Backbone Speeds

Connection Type	Speed
T-3/DS3	45Mbps
T-1/DS1	1.5Mbps

Definitely Speedy and Terrific!

T-1 and T-3 refer to different speeds of telephone carrier signals that transport data signals, also referred to as DS.

Discussions of ISP connections to backbones will often use either T or DS designations interchangeably. All T- and DS rates are based on multiples of DS0, which is 64Kbps (the same as ISDN one-channel basic rate).

A DS1/T-1 connection equals 24 DS0 connections. A DS3/T-3 connection equals 672 DS0 connections (or 24 DS1 connections).

All Internet backbones and ISP connections to the Internet backbones are calculated in Mbps (Megabits per second), while modem speeds are calculated in Kbps (Kilobits per second). There are 1,000 bits in a Kilobit and 1,000,000 bits in a Megabit, so even the relatively small T-1 or DS1 gateway is a lot faster than the fastest dial-up modem.

Traffic Jams on the IP

The Internet's nickname, the Information Superhighway, is an apt one because it reflects how traffic flows on the highway. As we saw in Chapter 1, devices called routers send and receive information along the most efficient routes.

Just as a driver from northwestern Indiana to Chicago can take any of several routes, data on the Internet can be diverted along many alternative routes to reach its destination. This feature was designed into the Internet from its beginnings as the Department of Defense's ARPAnet, which was designed to resist nuclear attack.

This capability to reroute data flows is useful because Internet connections can become congested with traffic for a variety of reasons:

➤ Popular Web sites

➤ Breakdowns of routing or switching devices causing data detours

➤ Inadequate capacity at an ISP's Point of Presence

Tech Note

POP Goes the Internet

The term *POP* can have two meanings. As used here, it means Point of Presence—where your computer connects to the Internet. ISPs that support dial-up connections provide you with one or more phone numbers at their POPs.

When discussing email, it means Post Office Protocol—the protocol used by email software to receive email. It sometimes is referred to as POP3, which refers to version 3 of this protocol. A reference to a POP server or a POP3 server refers to a mail server that uses the Post Office Protocol.

When a big Web event like the Victoria's Secret fashion show or a major document release from a political scandal takes place, traffic jams on the Internet can happen at the Web site's servers and at ISP connections and backbones that are connected to that Web site. In cases like this, page retrievals can take several times longer, even if the Web page you want has no connection with the event. Why? The Internet's rerouting capability is moving traffic around the delay. Instead of seeing little orange barrels appearing onscreen to tell you about rerouting, you'll just notice that the Internet is slower.

Another reason for slowdowns is that the parts of the Internet that link to the popular servers also help carry traffic bound for other servers. So, when the xGate scandal papers hit the Web, everybody's access slows a bit.

Tech Note

THAT WAY ▷

Detour Ahead

Nothing made by humanity is perfect, including the Internet. When switches or routers on major segments break down, traffic on other segments can be delayed as rerouting takes place.

If your Internet service provider doesn't have enough capacity to handle the demand, you can experience a slowdown in performance; that is, if you can get online at all. Frequent busy signals indicate that your ISP needs to add more incoming lines. However, an ISP can have plenty of lines and still provide slow performance if it doesn't have a wide enough pipe to the rest of the Internet. The best ISPs have multiple T-1 or T-3 connections to the Internet to relieve congestion and to provide a backup connection in case of problems or outages.

The Last Mile Problem

Although occasional Internet slowdowns can take place because of the reasons I discussed earlier, the real problem is the last mile between the Internet and you.

When I was a kid, a green sign a few miles from my house beckoned travelers weary of two-lane highways to the Fenton-Clio Expressway (now a part of U.S. 23 in Michigan). That highway offered 65mph speeds and no traffic lights or stop signs. The only trouble was that you had to drive across ten miles of two-lane highways with traffic lights and stop signs galore to get to the fast lane.

So it is with the Internet. Regardless of how fast the backbones are and how many T-1 or T-3 connections to the backbones your ISP installs, your computer's own connection to the Internet remains the biggest, most permanent slowdown you must contend with.

Why Your Modem Is a Permanent Traffic Jam

Table 2.4 shows how the speeds of backbones and ISP-to-backbone connections compare to a typical modem running at maximum allowed download speed.

Table 2.4   A Comparison of Internet Connection Speeds

Connection	Times Slower than Previous	Times Slower than OC-48
OC-48	N/A	N/A
OC-12	4×	4×
OC-3	4×	16×
T-3	31×	55.5×
T-1	29×	1619×
Modem (53Kbps)	29×	47170×

As you can see from Table 2.4, when your modem receives information at 53Kbps, it is more than 47,000 times slower than an OC-48 backbone!

The illustration in Figure 2.4 might make it even easier to understand.

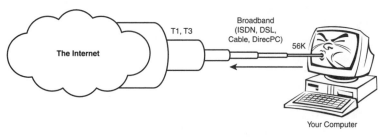

Figure 2.4

Regardless of the size of the pipe that begins your connection to the Internet's sea of information, your computer winds up drinking through a tiny straw when you use a 56Kbps v.90 modem.

In the next chapter, we'll look at how you can enhance the speed of your Internet connection without changing hardware.

The Least You Need to Know

➤ The modem in your computer converts digital computer information into sounds to transmit through telephone lines.

➤ A modem at the other end converts the sounds back into computer data.

➤ Modems have increased in speed at a much lower rate than computers in general, and are the biggest barrier to fast Internet access.

Chapter 3

Speed Up and Fix Up Your Dial-Up

In This Chapter

➤ How to keep your dial-up modem up-to-date

➤ Checking your phone line

➤ Adjusting your computer for maximum connection speed

➤ Using two modems for a single connection

➤ Taking and placing a phone call while you're online

Even if you're ready to make the leap into broadband Internet access, don't forget about your analog modem. Some forms of broadband are speedy in the download direction only, relying on your existing dial-up modem to send email and Web page requests. Even if you opt for a high-speed two-way service, you might face delays in getting the service installed. And, when you get broadband, your "ace in the hole" against inevitable system failures is your analog modem running as a backup.

So, don't discard that modem; instead, learn how to make it work better whenever you use it.

Old Modems Become New

As you learned in Chapter 2, your dial-up modem is the biggest single slowdown factor in how you experience the World Wide Web and the Internet. Because you're reading this book (and an extra thank you! if you bought it), I know you're drooling over getting a high-speed connection. So, why did I include this chapter?

As you'll discover in later chapters, some parts of the country offer you an overstuffed buffet table of high-speed choices, while others offer only promises of high-speed services to come. If you live in a part of the country where high-speed Internet is filed under science fiction—futuristic fantasy, you need this chapter.

You also need this chapter even if you're about to make the high-speed plunge. Unlike dial-up services such as AOL, Prodigy, or others which can be activated by installing the free trial CD-ROM that fell out of your cereal box this morning, all high-speed services require that new hardware (and sometimes new network cable) be installed. This can take time—sometimes a lot of time.

Finally, for those of you fortunate enough to already have high-speed service, I hope you kept your modem installed. If you did, you can always revert back to a dial-up Internet connection in case your normal service fails.

So, for all of you, here's how to keep your modem in tip-top shape until the broadband connection of your dreams arrives (or no longer is on the fritz).

Bring Me a New Brain, Igor!

Whether your modem fits inside your computer or plugs into your computer, it has a kind of a brain—not as powerful as the Pentium III, Celeron, or Athlon CPU that's inside your computer, but a type of software on a chip that tells it what to do. The pocket-protector types in the CS department call software-on-a-chip *firmware*, but whatever you call it, it can get out of date.

How can you tell if your modem's firmware is out of date? Here are a few of the likely suspects we've rounded up:

➤ Louie "Can't Connect" Nohow

➤ Jimmie "Too Slow" Pokey

➤ Al "Drop Dead" Connecshun

If your modem can't connect reliably when you try to log on to your service, doesn't connect anywhere near its rated speed, or loses connections when you're online, it's time to see if the firmware can be updated as discussed in the next section.

If you're Igor in the Frankenstein movies, you know that the order "Bring me a new brain, Igor" means it's time to go grab the shovel and dig up a recent grave. Messy, nasty work—but hey, it's the movies!

Standards, Standards, Standards

Most modems sold since 1997 are so-called 56K modems, capable of downloading information at up to 56,000 bits (56Kbps) per second (although FCC regulations prevent modems from running at speeds over 53Kbps). However, three types of 56Kbps connections exist. The old X2 and K56flex standards have been replaced by an international standard called v.90. If your 56K modem is not a v.90 model, that's another reason to see about a firmware update because most online services don't support X2 or K56flex modems at their full speeds anymore.

Confused about modem speeds? Who could blame you? Here's what the different terms mean:

➤ bps—Bits per second. Eight bits of data make a byte of data; each letter in an email message equals a byte, for example.

➤ Kbps—Thousand bits per second. Most modems are rated by Kbps: A 56Kbps modem, for example, can transfer up to 56,000 bps per second (except that the FCC says "No way!" to speeds above 53Kbps).

➤ Baud—A term that refers to signaling rate, not data rate. Early modems (such as the first 300bps models used on the IBM PC and Apple II) had identical baud and bps ratings, but baud no longer equals bps. The number of bits per baud rate vary, so referring to bps rates as baud rates is incorrect and seldom happens anymore.

What You Need to Know to Perform Brain Surgery on Your Modem

Sometimes, getting a new brain for your modem can be just as painful as shoveling at midnight. What do you need to know to get new firmware—to dig up a new brain for your modem?

➤ The brand and model number of your modem

➤ A program to unzip (uncompress) the firmware files

➤ A blank disk or two for copying the firmware files

Finding the Modem's Brand and Model Number

This is easy if it's an external modem: Just turn it over and read the label on the back or bottom of the case.

How about an internal modem? If you installed the modem yourself, see if you still have the box, the manual, or the setup CD-ROM or disks for your modem. You'll find the brand name and model number listed there.

Was your modem the Cracker Jack prize variety—built into your computer at the factory? It won't hurt to see if you can find the manual for the computer and its parts, but many of these modems are brand X models—even if you have the manual, it won't have a clue where the modem came from. Are you stuck? Nope. Look on the modem itself for the brand name and model number. If you come up empty handed, look for a sticker on the modem that lists the FCC ID#. Write it down. Either way, you can now go online and get the latest firmware brain for your modem.

Tech Note

Things You Need

If you're thinking about taking your first trip inside your computer, here's what you'll need to have handy:

➤ A Phillips-head screwdriver or hex driver—Use this to open the case and (possibly) remove cards that block your modem from view.

➤ Newspaper—A low-tech but effective non-static place to put anything you need to take out of your computer.

Don't Say I Didn't Warn You!

Precautions to take *before* you open your computer:

➤ Put some newspapers on the floor to stand on, especially if you are working on a carpeted floor. You can build up a lot of static electricity in your body, and if it decides to discharge while you have the cover of your computer open, goodbye parts or goodbye computer! Plain old newspaper is less likely to build up static electricity than the carpeting it hides.

➤ Touch a metal part on the outside of the computer case before you open it. This gives your body a chance to discharge excess static electricity safely before you open the system.

➤ Turn off the computer and unplug it. Most newer systems aren't really off when you shut them down. Instead, they go into a sleep mode, and a low level of power might still be flowing through the computer.

To open your computer:

1. Look for several screws on the back panel of your computer near the edge of the computer.

2. If your computer has a one-piece cover, remove all the screws that hold it in place.

3. If your computer has a removable side cover, remove the screws that hold the right-side (as viewed from the rear) cover.

4. Look at the back of the computer for a card with two telephone jacks; this is your modem.

5. Now, look inside your computer at your modem; can you read the brand, model number, or FCC ID? Look at both sides of the card. Write the information down here:

    Brand # _____   Model # _____

    FCC ID#_____

6. If, and only if, you can't see the information on the modem, you'll need to remove the modem from your computer.

Handle With Care

Handling your modem carelessly could destroy it. Be very careful! If your spouse, friends, or kids are more experienced with computer repair and upgrading than you are, don't be afraid to ask for help.

If you must remove the modem

1. Touch a metal part on the case again.

2. Unscrew the upside-down L-shaped metal bracket that holds the card in place.

3. *Gently* wiggle the card up and down until the card comes loose.

4. Carry it by the bracket (never by the chips on the card or the gold connectors!) and lay it on the newspaper so you can record the information.

To reinstall the modem in your system:

1. Carry the modem by the bracket and lower it into place where you removed it.

2. Line up the connector at the bottom of the modem with the motherboard slot connector.

3. Push downward to reinsert the card into the slot; it might require a fair amount of force, but if it won't go in, make sure you have it lined up correctly with the slot.

4. Fasten the card bracket to the case with the screw you removed earlier.

5. Replace the case and screw it into place.

Drivers Wanted

If you don't know the Web site for your modem maker, or all you have is the FCC ID#, my favorite Web site for drivers is WinDriver's Driver page:

```
http://www.windrivers.com/company.htm
```

You can perform an FCC ID# search, find your driver by card type or manufacturer, and even find drivers for dead boards made by companies that are no longer in business.

Make sure you look over the online instructions carefully before you download and install new firmware for your modem. If you install the wrong firmware, you'll be in bigger trouble than Igor was when he dropped the jar with the fresh brain!

If the firmware files are stored in an .EXE file, you can open the file and it will uncompress the firmware files inside. If the file is a .ZIP file, you'll need to use an unzipping utility such as WinZip.

In many cases, a firmware update, along with new driver software (see the next section) is all that you need to turn an X2 or K56flex modem into an up-to-date v.90 modem. Some vendors also offer firmware updates that turn 33.6Kbps modems into v.90 modems. See Figure 3.1 for a typical example of how modem vendors list firmware updates.

Getting Unzipped

You can download many unzipping programs. Two of the best are PKZIP for Windows, available at `http://www.pkware.com` and WinZip, available at `http://www.winzip.com`.

These Flashes are for Rockwell Chipset modems only.		
Model #	Description	File
2805C	33.6K internal modem to 56K-ready to V.90 Upgrade. The modem must be 56K enabled.	Windows fz2310db.exe
2818 2818A	K56flex ComStar Speakerphone modem K56flex to V.90 Upgrade	Windows fz2100ac.exe
2819 2819A	K56flex internal modem. K56flex to V.90 Upgrade.	Windows fz2310db.exe
2822 2901	K56flex internal modem with camera K56flex to V.90 Upgrade	Windows fz210fxvu1.exe
2836A 2837A 2838A	33.6K external modem to 56K-ready to V.90 Upgrade. The modem must be 56K enabled first.	MacOS Zoom-Uploader.bin / Windows xz2310d.exe

Figure 3.1

Some firmware updates for Zoom Telephonics modems. Note the warning at the top of the page, and note that different modem model numbers require different firmware updates.

Don't Just Call Any Number (Choosing the Correct Dial–Up Number)

Even if your modem is has the latest v.90 firmware and drivers installed, you can still have problems if you use the wrong dial-up phone number, especially if you are located in a mid-sized city or small town. In most cases, an ISP's v.90 number will work for both v.90 and standard modems that run at speeds of 33.6Kbps or lower. Because v.90 and K56flex are similar, you still might be able to use a K56flex modem with these same numbers and attain similar speeds.

Move Over and Let Me Do the Driving

You can have a v.90 modem, but like most everything in the world of Windows, a modem is just a hunk of plastic, IC chips, and solder joints without software.

If any of the usual modem problems (slow downloads, can't connect, connections drop dead) show up while you're using your modem, you should follow the steps in the previous section to download new driver software.

In most cases, if you install new modem firmware, you'll also install new driver software.

Speed Zone...Watch Out!

Despite the name, so-called 56K modems are restricted to 53Kbps downloads by FCC regulations. This restriction is due a regulation known as Part 68. Part 68 restricts the amount of power that can be run through a phone line, and running 56Kbps modems at speeds above 53Kbps would exceed the limits of Part 68. Until the FCC drops the Part 68 limitation, your 56Kbps modem won't be permitted to run as fast it was intended to.

However, if you use a dial-up number meant for 33.6Kbps or slower modems with your 56Kbps modems, you've given your modem a digital lobotomy—it can't run any faster than 33.6Kbps! Many ISPs still offer 33.6Kbps dial-up connection numbers as well as numbers for faster modems.

Refer to Table 3.1 to help your modem run as fast as possible when you connect.

Table 3.1   Matching Your Modem Type to the Best Dial-Up Number

Modem Type	Connection Number Type	Resulting Connection Maximum Speed	Acceptable?
33.6Kbps or lower	56K, v.90, X2, K56flex, 33.6	33.6Kbps	OK!
X2	X2, 56K	56Kbps	OK!
X2	56K, V.90, K56flex	33.6Kbps	No Way!
K56flex	56K, V.90, K56flex	56Kbps	OK!
K56flex	X2, 33.6	33.6Kbps	No Way!
V.90	56K, V.90	56Kbps	OK!
V.90	X2, 33.6	33.6Kbps	No Way!

In the table, any combination of modem type and connection number type with an OK! in the Acceptable column can provide the maximum speed your modem is capable of—up to 56Kbps.

On the other hand, connections labeled No Way! limit the maximum speed of your modem to 33.6Kbps—a big decrease.

If you aren't sure which dial-up number to use for your modem, contact your ISP's tech support help-desk or look at their online help to see what the best dial-up number is to use. Remember, you can connect to 33.6Kbps or slower dial-up numbers with your 56Kbps modem if you don't know what dial-up number to use.

It's Not Your Modem—It's Your Phone Line

As you learned in the previous section, using the wrong dial-up number for your modem will slow down your connection. But what if you say, "Mark, I've already got a V.90 56Kbps modem and I've already installed the latest firmware and drivers. I've called my ISP to confirm that I'm using the right 56K dial-up number. I know about the 53Kbps limitation, but I'm only getting 31.2Kbps maximum speeds! My brother-in-law lives two blocks away and he's getting 53Kbps every time he connects! What's going on?"

I don't know your brother-in-law, but I don't blame you for being upset. The problem isn't with you—or your modem—or even your brother-in-law. It's your phone line. Why?

For the Skinny on How 56K Modems Work

If you want more technical background on how 56Kbps modems work (and why they don't always work!), see the 56K Web site, located at http://www.56k.com/basics/

Basically, the whole 56Kbps modem business is based on playing a sort of technological trick on the phone system, which is, as you learned in Chapter 2, based on analog signals. Originally, the entire phone system used analog signaling, but in recent years, parts of the phone system started using digital signaling. 56Kbps modems are designed to take advantage of the partly digital nature of the telephone system today. A 56Kbps modem can break the 33.6Kbps speed limit only if it can create an unbroken digital connection between your computer and the telephone company's central office, where your call is connected to the rest of the telephone system.

Because of the explosion in demand for telephone and telephone-based services such as fax machines, credit card approval terminals, and so on, telephone systems in some places perform multiple analog-to-digital conversions, making speeds above 33.6Kbps impossible.

Testing, Testing—Is Your Phone Line Ready to Rumble?

Is My Phone Line Up to the Challenge?

3Com's Line Test page is located at http://www.3com.com/56k/need4_56k/linetest.html Follow the instructions on this page to test your phone line for 56Kbps compatibility.

If you're wondering whether your phone line is the culprit that's causing your 33.6Kbps or slower connections, use the following Web site to learn about testing your phone line for 56Kbps support.

What can you do if your telephone line isn't up to snuff? Nothing. The telephone company's attitude is "You can talk on it, and that's all that matters." You'll want to redouble your research (read the rest of this book!) to get a high-speed Internet connection as quickly as possible.

Before you blame your friendly local telephone company for giving you such a lousy phone line, make sure you aren't part of the problem yourself. Try making the following changes one at a time, and then try testing your line and connecting again:

➤ Unplug phones and other devices from the telephone jack of your modem.

➤ Unplug other phones on the phone line, even if they're in another room.

➤ Plug your modem's phone cord *directly* into the wall, instead of through a splitter or surge protector, for example.

If any of the following changes give you a faster connection, try making that change permanent, or at least change your setup when you use your modem.

Shocking!

If you find that your modem speed increases when you unplug your modem from a surge protector, don't skip surge protection completely. Every summer plenty of people wind up losing their modems, and even their computers, to power surges coming over telephone lines. Instead, install a better surge protector that also provides features such as line noise filtration and line polarity checking and correction. Some of the products with these features include

➤ Modem Saver (`http://www.modemsaver.com/`)

➤ Modem Amigo (`http://www.modemamigo.com/`)

These products can also be purchased from other online merchants.

Tweaking Your System for Faster Speed

Although the speed of your modem is largely dependent on line quality and using the correct dial-up number to support the 56Kbps flavor your modem uses, there are some subtler boosts in performance that brave souls (do I see a volunteer??) can achieve by adjusting modem and Windows Registry settings.

Gimme More!

The preceding tips are similar to some of the speed-up tips given on the Modem Troubleshooting Guide at the 56K modem site: `http://www.56k.com/trouble/connect.shtml` Surf there for additional tips and solutions.

Tech Note

Your Mileage Can Vary

Keep in mind that factors such as line condition, distance from the central switch, the quality of your modem, and the compatibility of your modem with your ISP's modems all affect the speeds of your connection. Your 56Kbps modem can make connections at speeds ranging from as high as 52Kbps to as low as 36Kbps on a 56Kbps-compliant line. The same modem can produce different connection speeds when moved from one location to another!

Danger Danger

Futzing with the Registry Is NOT for the Faint-Hearted!

Adjusting the Registry is potentially fatal to your Windows installation! Make sure that you BACK UP your Registry before you make any changes. Back up the Registry in any of the following ways:

➤ Make a copy of the USER.DAT and SYSTEM.DAT files in the \Windows folder. (These files are hidden, so you must enable the View All Files option in Windows Explorer). Use a name like USER073100.DAT and SYSTEM073100.DAT to indicate the date you made the backup.

➤ Export the Registry to a .REG file.

Adding Extra Horsepower to Your Internet Connection

What kind of changes can you make to your Internet connection by adjusting the Registry or making other Windows configuration changes? You can adjust the following:

➤ The maximum speed at which your computer talks to the serial port (also called the DTE speed)

➤ The size of the data block you can receive with your modem

➤ The ping rate (which can improve the performance of Internet games)

Changing the Computer-to-Modem (DTE) Speed

There are actually two places where speed is important in modem communications. So far, we've concentrated on the speed at which your modem can connect to another modem. This speed is sometimes referred to as the DCE rate. However, your modem must receive information from the computer before it can transmit or receive data from the Internet. The computer-to-modem speed is sometimes referred to as the *DTE rate*.

The normal speed at which computers connect to modems (DTE speed) is 115200 bps, although the modem-to-modem (DCE) speed is far less. If we can raise the DTE speed to 230400 and still connect to the other computer, we will also improve our modem's true data throughput.

Unlike other changes, this change does not require that you change the Windows Registry.

To adjust the computer-to-modem connection speed in Windows 95, Windows 98, or Windows Me:

Don't Miss This!

You'll find an excellent online reference to editing the Registry, along with additional backup tips at `http://www.halcyon.com/cerelli/regedit.htm`

Tech Note

Acronyms Anonymous

DTE—Data Terminal Equipment—The computer-to-modem connection.

DCE—Data Communications Equipment—The modem-to-modem connection.

1. Click the Start button and select Settings.
2. Select Control Panel.
3. Open the Modems icon.
4. Select your modem, and then click the Properties button.
5. Look at the value for Maximum speed. If it is already set to 230400 or higher, leave it alone. If it is set to 115200, click the down arrow and select 230400 if you can. If you cannot, the connection cannot be adjusted through the control panel.
6. Click OK, and try to connect at the higher speed.

If you can connect at the higher speed, you can keep the new setting. If you cannot connect, change the setting back to 115200 by repeating the previous steps.

Many PCI-based internal modems and modems that connect to the USB port can run successfully at DTE speeds above 115200.

The next options require changes to your Windows Registry.

Changing the Registry for Faster Gaming and Downloads

Before you decide to change the Windows Registry, you must make sure you understand what it is and what it does. Starting with Windows 95, Microsoft decided to put virtually all hardware and software settings into two files, User.dat and System.dat, which together form the Registry. Whenever you install new hardware, the Registry changes to reflect the new hardware. Add a program to Windows, and the Registry changes again.

The Registry files (User.dat and System.dat) are hidden by normal Windows Explorer settings to make it harder to delete them or change them. Microsoft prefers that nobody ever change the Registry directly, but because you can't make all the settings you'd like any other way, manual changes are sometimes the only way to get things done.

Danger Danger

Tread Carefully

Making changes to the Registry can be hazardous to your system if you don't do them correctly. A messed-up Registry can refuse to start Windows, preventing you from logging on to the Internet (or even playing a quick hand of Solitaire!).

So, be careful! I recommend that you take the following precautions before editing the Registry:

> ➤ Make a backup copy of the Registry, as discussed earlier in this chapter.

> ➤ Carefully review the proposed benefits of any Registry change.

> ➤ Remember when you use Regedit, the Windows Registry editor, that any changes (intentional or not) you make are automatically saved as soon as you exit Regedit; there is no "cancel" option.

> ➤ Whenever you can, try a utility program to make the changes because the Registry's settings are strange-looking and vary from option to option.

> ➤ Don't use a Registry setting that isn't intended to work with your version of Windows. All versions of Windows from Windows 95 up (including Windows 98, Windows Me, Windows NT 4.0, and Windows 2000) all use a Registry but in slightly different ways.

You can change the Windows Registry to

➤ Use 230400bps DTE speeds on systems that don't offer that setting—Reduces the ping rate (the delay in the round trip that signals take from your computer to an Internet server); makes Internet gaming run faster

➤ Change network values—Enhances speed for downloads

To increase the DTE speed to 230400bps on systems that don't support this feature normally, use one of the following options:

➤ Download and install Laessig Software's Powerup.Com program; it will make the correct Registry changes that will enable you to select the higher speed on most internal modems.

➤ Make changes to the modem properties in your Registry manually.

To make the Registry changes for your modem, follow this procedure:

1. Make a backup copy of the Registry!
2. Open Start, click Run, and type `Regedit` in the field provided. Press Enter or click OK to start the Regedit Registry editor.
3. Regedit displays two windows; the left window displays registry keys (which look like a folder); the right window displays values for the current key.
4. Click HKEY_LOCAL_MACHINE in the left window.
5. Click the following keys in the left window:
   ➤ System (see Figure 3.2)
   ➤ CurrentControlSet
   ➤ Services
   ➤ Class
   ➤ Modem

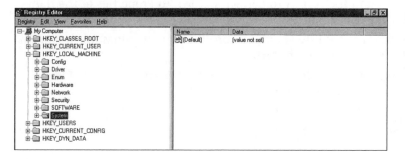

Figure 3.2

Regedit after clicking on HKEY_LOCAL_MACHINE\System\.

6. Click the plus (+) sign next to Modem in the left window. You should see a folder called 0000 beneath Modem in the left window. You might also see additional folders 0001, 0002, and so on.

7. If you have folders beyond 0000, you will need to see which folder lists your current modem (the others are for modems that have been installed previously).

8. Click the first folder (0000), and its contents are displayed in the right-hand window.

9. Look at the DriverDesc in the right-hand window to see if your modem is listed there (see Figure 3.3). If the name is correct, proceed to step 10; if not, return to step 8 and choose the next folder.

Figure 3.3

If DriverDesc lists your modem, proceed to Properties to make the changes in step 10 and beyond.

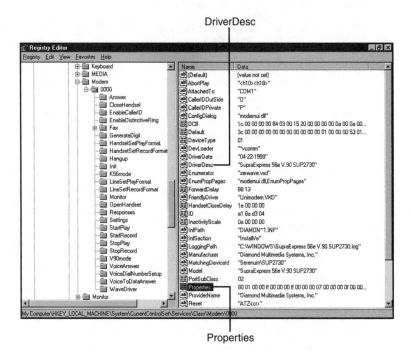

DriverDesc

Properties

10. When you have found the correct folder, scroll down to Properties in the right-hand window. Double-click Properties to display the current values listed there.

11. Before making the changes listed below, record the current values for the fourth line here (the line beginning with 0018): _____.

12. Click after the first 00 on the line starting with 0018. Your cursor should be on `0018 00 [CURSOR] C2 01` (see Figure 3.4).

13. Replace the C2 01 with the value `84 03`.

14. Delete C2 01 by pressing the Delete key twice.

15. Enter `84 03`.

16. The line should now read `0018 00 84 03` (see Figure 3.5).

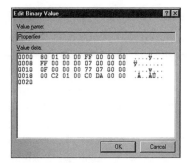

Figure 3.4

Modem Properties before replacing values on line 0018.

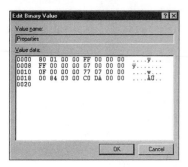

Figure 3.5

Modem Properties after replacing values on line 0018.

17. Review your changes carefully, and then click OK to exit this editing window. Close Regedit (click on Registry, Exit, or click on the X in the upper-right corner of the Registry window). Your changes are saved automatically and will take effect when you reboot your system.

Now you can set the speed as described earlier in the section called "Changing the Computer-to-Modem (DTE) Speed." If you cannot connect, you can follow the preceding steps to restore the original values for your modem. In either case, you might also need to install a modified serial.vxd (serial port driver file) if you have an external modem. Some internal modems also require this file. If you prefer to patch your system's copy of serial.vxd, you can download the Shsmod 1.7c program to make the changes for you.

You can adjust four important settings to improve the download speed of your computer: MaxMTU, RWIN, TTL, and MaxMSS.

For the Full Scoop...

You'll find links to Powerup.com, Shsmod 1.7c, and more information on making the Registry change described above at http://www. downloadit.gr/~v_laessig/ping. html

If you're mainly concerned about faster downloading of large files, use the values shown in Table 3.2.

Table 3.2   Registry Settings to Optimize for Large File Downloads

Key	Value	Registry
MaxMTU	576	System\CurrentControlSet\Services\Class\NetTrans\000x
MaxMSS	1460	System\CurrentControlSet\Services\Class\NetTrans\000x
RWIN	32120	HKEY_Local_Machine\System\CurrentControlSet\Services\VxD\MSTCP
TTL	32	HKEY_Local_Machine\System\CurrentControlSet\Services\VxD\MSTCP

There are two ways you can make these changes:

➤ Automatically, with a utility program such as MTUSpeed Pro or others

➤ Manually, through Regedit or a similar Registry-editing program

To make the changes manually with Regedit, follow this procedure:

1. Make a backup copy of the Registry!

2. Click Start, Run, and type Regedit in the field provided. Press Enter or click OK to start the Regedit Registry editor.

   Regedit displays two windows. The left window displays Registry keys (which look like folders), and the right window displays values for the current key.

3. Click HKEY_LOCAL_MACHINE in the left window.

4. Click the following keys in the left window:

   ➤ System

   ➤ CurrentControlSet

   ➤ Services

   ➤ Class

5. To make the changes for MaxMTU and MaxMSS, click NetTrans; you will see one or more folders numbered 0000 and up.

6. Open the first folder and look at the DriverDesc line in the right window. If it says TCP/IP, you need to modify or add the values for MaxMTU and MaxMSS to this folder; otherwise, try the next folder until you see the correct DriverDesc.

7. You will usually need to add entries for MaxMTU and MaxMSS to this folder. To add an entry for MaxMTU, click New, String Value, type MaxMTU (check spelling and capitalization!), and press Enter.

8. To change the value for MaxMTU, click Edit, Modify, and type 576. Press Enter.

9. To add an entry for MaxMSS, click New, String Value, type MaxMSS (check spelling and capitalization!), and press Enter.

10. To change the value for MaxMSS, click Edit, Modify, and type 1460. Press Enter.

11. When you are finished, the Registry window should appear similar to Figure 3.6.

12. Repeat steps 7–12 for any other 000x folder that has the DeviceDesc TCP/IP.

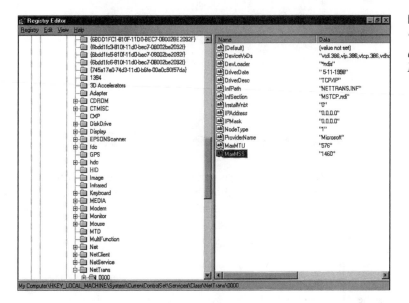

Figure 3.6

The NetTrans 000x folder after adding values for MaxMTU and MaxMSS.

13. To add the values for RWIN and TTL, click VxD in the left window, scroll down to MSTCP, and click the MSTCP folder (ignore any folders that appear beneath it).

14. You will usually need to add entries for RWIN and TTL to this folder. To add an entry for RWIN, click New, String Value, type RWIN (check spelling and capitalization!), and press Enter.

15. To change the value for RWIN, click Edit, Modify, and type 32120. Press Enter.

16. To add an entry for TTL, click New, String Value, type TTL (check spelling and capitalization!), and press Enter.

17. To change the value for TTL, click Edit, Modify, and type 32. Press Enter.

18. When you are finished, the Registry window should appear similar to Figure 3.7.

19. Close the Registry; the changes will take effect when you reboot your system.

Figure 3.7

The MSTCP folder after adding values for RWIN and TTL.

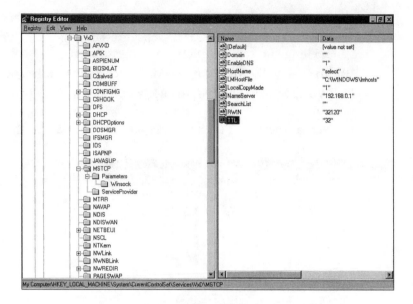

More Help

To learn how manually to make the changes listed in Table 3.2, go to `http://xtrememhz.com/reviews/how_tos/tweakinternet.html`

If you play Quake or other games over the Internet, you might find that different values will work better for you. A downloadable program called MTUSpeed Pro 4.x (see the next section) can help you optimize the correct settings.

Software That Makes Tweaking Easier

Editing the Registry by hand can be a truly scary experience, even for people like me who've been using the Regedit program for years. Fortunately, programs are available on the World Wide Web that you can use to change just the values that you need to adjust for faster modem operation. Some programs include

➤ TweakDUN 2.2—`http://www.pattersondesigns.com/tweakdun/`
➤ MTU Speed Pro 4.10—`http://www.mjs.u-net.com/home.htm`

Additional titles are available at

```
http://search.softseek.com/Internet/
Web_Browsers_and_Utilities/
Connection_Optimizers/dindex.html
```

The most famous of these, MTU Speed Pro, is available from many online sources.

Although the tips in the preceding section can produce better results, differences in systems, modems, and so on make the differences difficult to rate. If you're uncomfortable with this level of tinkering with your computer, don't do anything.

Where Can I Find It?

You can see an illustrated how-to for MTU Speed Pro and also download it from the following Web page: `http://www.exceptional.net/mtuspeed.html`

Super Glue Two Modems Together with Bonding

If true high-speed Internet access is going to take awhile to show up in your neighborhood, you might find it worthwhile to look into a feature known as *modem bonding*, especially if you already have two or more phone lines.

How Bonding Works

Modem bonding allows two or more modems to work as a single modem, providing a download speed that is the total of the download speeds of each modem. For example, if you bond two 56Kbps modems, you have a theoretical download speed of 112Kbps. Even with the 53Kbps limitation imposed by the FCC, your real maximum is still 106Kbps! Depending on the ISP, the use of two modems can be supported through MP+ (Multilink Protocol +) or Multilink PPP (MPPP). You can use any mixture of internal or external modems, and they don't even need to be the same brand, model, or speed!

Bonding can also be accomplished by purchasing a single internal card that contains two modem circuits, such as the S3/Diamond Multimedia SupraSonic II. The SupraSonic II enables you to use just one line for modem use while talking on the telephone, and then add the second line back into your modem operation when the phone call is over. Diamond calls this its Shotgun technology, and it also works when you combine one or more Diamond/Supra-brand modems with others.

Male...er, Modem Bonding

To learn more about modem bonding in general, go to

> http://www.ispcheck.com/resources/modemdbl.asp

To learn more about the SupraSonic II and Shotgun technology, go to

> www.supra.com

Follow the links to Product and Tech Support.

Will Your ISP Approve?

The bad news is that many ISPs don't support multilink connections. However, you can probably find another ISP that will support multilink connections in your area.

More on Multilink

To locate ISPs in your area that support multilink 112Kbps connections (two 56Kbps modems), go to

> http://www.ispcheck.com/access/

Enter your area code, select 112k Multilink for the access type, and click the Search button. If you are recycling an older 33.6Kbps or slower modem, ask if you can mix and match modem speeds and models; normally you will be able to.

When I searched for providers in my area code (812), I came up with 10 local and national providers supporting 112k Multilink, with prices ranging from as little as $19/month to as much as $39.95/month. So look around for a spare modem and put modem bonding to work for you. It will increase your download speed without breaking your piggy bank. You will need to have two phone lines to use this feature, but even if you need to add a second phone line, you'll enjoy the extra speed and the ability to share a phone line with your modem without losing the ability to work online.

Upgrading Windows 95 for Multilink Support

If you are using Windows 95, you might need to upgrade your Dial-Up Networking software to allow Multilink support. If the properties for your Dial-Up Networking connection do not list a Multilink tab, you must download and install Dial-Up Networking 1.3 from Microsoft's Windows 95 Web site.

Getting the Updates Online

You can obtain both of these updates from this web page:

```
http://www.microsoft.com/windows95/downloads
```

Download and install the Dial-Up Networking 1.3 Performance and Security Update, and then download and install Microsoft DUN 1.3 and Winsock Year 2000 Update.

Setting Up a Multilink Connection on Your Computer

When you decide that multilink is your best route to speed, follow this procedure to obtain and install multilink support. Remember, you need the following before you install multilink support:

➤ Another analog modem installed and working in (or connected to) your system

➤ A second telephone line to use with the additional modem

➤ A multilink account with an ISP

➤ The ISP telephone number for the second modem to dial

If your current ISP allows you to use multilink, you can modify your existing Dial-Up Networking connection properties to add support for multilink. If you need to change ISPs, you might use a proprietary dialing program, or you might also need to modify the standard connection properties. The following procedure assumes that you are modifying an existing Dial-Up Networking connection.

To install multilink support for an existing connection:

1. Open the Dial-Up Networking folder.

2. Right-click the icon for your Internet connection, and select Properties.

3. Note the modem you are currently using; you will need to choose the other modem to set up Multilink (see Figure 3.8).

Figure 3.8

This computer has the updated Dial-Up Networking version installed; note the Multilink tab.

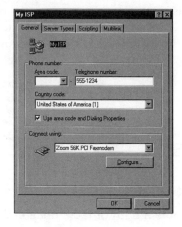

4. Click the Multilink tab.

5. Click Use Additional Devices, and then click Add.

6. Click the pull-down menu and select your new modem from the list (see Figure 3.9).

Figure 3.9

Select the modem you just installed as your additional device. You can mix and match modems with different speeds and manufacturers or use identical modems, as seen here.

7. The current dial-up number for your original modem is listed. If you need to use a different number for multilink, enter it in place of the current number.

8. Click OK to finish.

The next time you connect, both modems will be used to make the connection, so you can download and upload faster.

"We Interrupt This Online Session..." (Getting Calls While You're Online)

One of the most pressing reasons, besides download speed, for switching to a broadband service is the problem of tying up your phone line while you surf the Net. Call-waiting services by themselves don't help because most modern modems ignore the faint click that call waiting uses to signal you that another call is coming in.

Although you can adjust your modem's sensitivity to call waiting, you do so at the cost of creating a very fragile connection that will constantly hang up when any kind of line noise is encountered. A far better solution is to use one of the new, usually free, telephone answering services that intercept incoming calls and route them to a voice-mail box while playing the caller's message over your computer's speakers. More elaborate versions of these services give you additional options.

Grabbing Messages While You're Online

Services such as BuzMe (www.buzme.com), CallWave (www.callwave.com), and others take advantage of the call forwarding feature offered at minimal cost by most local telephone companies. Call Forwarding on Busy or No Answer sends the call to a special number used by the answering service, which plays a message inviting your caller to leave a voice message, which is played on your computer.

BuzMe also offers a low-cost enhanced service that enables you to select a predefined reply, type in a custom reply, or block the caller from reaching you. BuzMe uses text-to-speech technology to play your standard or custom replies for your caller. You can also take the call immediately.

Tech Note
THAT WAY ▷

Making Telephone Calls While You're Online

Combine incoming answering services such as BuzMe or CallWave with voice-over-IP outgoing call services such as PhoneFree (www.phonefree.com) or Visitalk (www.visitalk.com) and you have a good workaround to the dual problems of taking and making voice calls while you're online. Most of these services are free or cost only a few dollars per month.

If you have Windows 98 or above, you can download the new Microsoft Windows Media Player version 7, which includes telephone call software from Net2Phone. Media Player 7 enables you to make free local or long-distance phone calls to any number in the U.S. or Canada.

The Least You Need to Know

➤ You can upgrade your modem's firmware to improve its speed and reliability.

➤ You can adjust your Windows configuration to improve your modem's effective throughput, but most changes require editing the Windows Registry.

➤ You can achieve an inexpensive greater-than-100Kbps solution by using modem bonding, but you will probably need to change ISPs and you need at least two phone lines.

➤ You can use free or low-cost Internet answering services and outbound calling services to handle voice calls while you're online.

Part 2

Understanding Your High-Speed Choices

Who are the high-speed contenders, and which one is the best choice for you? You'll meet each of the major broadband Internet service types in Part 2 and learn their strengths and weaknesses in Chapters 4–8.

In Chapter 9, "Decisions, Decisions: What's the Best Choice for Me?" you'll discover a cost per MB calculator that will make it clear to you what the best online buy for you will be, and how to figure out what features are most important to you.

Chapter 4

I Smell Dollars Now with ISDN

In This Chapter

➤ Get the skinny on how ISDN works

➤ Understand why ISDN allows you to talk and connect at the same time

➤ Nail down the equipment you need to connect to an ISDN line

➤ Get down to brass tacks on the costs of ISDN

In Chapter 2, "Dial-Up Modems and Internet Slowdowns," you learned that telephones are based on analog signaling. This forces computers to use modems, which convert digital signals into analog signals and back again, to communicate with each other.

What's This ISDN Thing, Anyway? (How ISDN Works)

ISDN, the Integrated Services Digital Network, was originally developed to provide an all-digital method for connecting multiple telephone and telephony-type devices such as fax machines to a single telephone line and to provide a faster connection for teleconferencing for remote computer users.

ISDN wasn't originally intended to be used for the Internet, but because it runs at speeds of up to 128Kbps, ISDN has become a member of the broadband Internet community.

Old and Gray Technology

The network of telephone lines that connects your phone to the rest of the world is sometimes referred to as the Plain Old Telephone System, or POTS. This name reminds us that telephone lines were never designed to handle computer data. Another name for the telephone system is the Public Switched Telephone Network, or PSTN.

Is ISDN the best choice for you? Probably not if you have other choices such as DSL, satellite, or cable modems. Other forms of high-speed Internet access blow the doors off ISDN in both speed and price per Mbps of access. However, ISDN might be your only choice to exceed the 53Kbps speed limit of analog modems, so I've provided detailed coverage here.

By running multiple digital signals over the twisted-pair copper telephone wire, ISDN enables you to

➤ Use higher-speed, reliable digital communications between computers (no more modems!)

➤ Connect multiple telephone-line devices (sometimes referred to as *telephony* devices—telephones, fax machines, analog modems, answering machines, and so on) and a computer to a single phone line

➤ Use a telephony device and the Internet at the same time

So, How Is ISDN Different from a Modem?

Modems, you learned in Chapter 2, have several limitations, including slower speeds and fragile connections that easily can be broken by line noise, accidentally picking up an extension, and incoming phone calls. Modems also tie up your phone line, preventing you from being able to use your phone to talk to your Aunt Judy while downloading MP3s from the Internet.

ISDN enables your computer to run faster than modems and have more reliable digital connections, and lets you talk to Aunt Judy while you download MP3s.

The nickname "I Smell Dollars Now" for ISDN, as you'll see later in this chapter, refers to the cost and potential complexities of ISDN services.

Can Every Phone Line Be an ISDN Line?

In a word, "Nope!" Why not?

Remember Chapter 3, "Speed Up and Fix Up Your Dial-Up"? If you skipped it, that's okay—there won't be a test. In Chapter 3 you learned (or will learn) that so-called 56Kbps modems sometimes can't connect at speeds beyond 33.6Kbps because of line problems. These same problems can stop ISDN cold in its tracks.

Danger Danger

Check Your Phone Line BEFORE Subscribing to ISDN or DSL

The same problems (excess distance from the central office, too many analog/digital conversions, and quality problems) that can prevent 56Kbps modems from running at full speed and stop DSL in its tracks can also prevent ISDN service from being a viable option. In Chapter 5, "Teaching Old POTS New Tricks with DSL," which covers DSL, I go into detail about why phone lines that work perfectly well for voice traffic aren't good enough for DSL.

Most telcos (telephone companies) that offer ISDN service offer online qualification data entry screens early in the ISDN ordering process. Even if you're not serious about ISDN right now, you can use it to see whether your phone line can handle ISDN. Simply enter information such as

➤ Your area code and phone number

➤ Your apartment or suite number

➤ Your street address, city, state, and ZIP code

Click OK or Submit to transmit your location information, and in a few seconds you'll discover whether ISDN can be in your future.

How Do I Connect My Phone, Fax, and Computer?

As you'll learn in detail later in this chapter, ISDN is supplied by your local telephone company, and it was originally designed to permit telephony devices to share a single line. So, what can be attached to an ISDN line? Depending on the equipment you use to connect your home or small business with ISDN, you can connect

➤ One or more telephones—Each telephone can have its own number.

➤ One or more fax machines—As with telephones, each telephone can have its own number.

71

➤ A computer—By using the line-sharing features described in Chapter 15, "Share the Wealth: Internet Connection Sharing," additional computers can use the ISDN connection.

➤ Other telephony devices such as answering machines.

These devices attach to the ISDN line through a *Terminal Adapter*, or *TA*. TAs can be internal or external, but most telcos offer external TAs for use in small business or residential ISDN service.

Tread Carefully...

Be *as exact as possible* when you complete a qualifying questionnaire for ISDN or any other high-speed Internet service. Wiring conditions are very critical in determining whether you can use a given service. Different apartments in the same building or different homes in the same block can have different types of wiring. A slip of the finger in typing a street address or suite number could give you incorrect information about high-speed Internet availability for your home or small business.

When a Modem Isn't a Modem

ISDN TAs are also referred to as *ISDN modems*, although this isn't accurate. As you learned in Chapter 2, modems modulate digital computer data into analog sounds suitable for transmission over phone lines, and demodulate the analog tones back into computer data at the receiving end. There is no conversion with ISDN—it's digital all the way.

Calling an ISDN TA an ISDN modem reflects the popular view that a modem is any device that connects you with the Internet. It's wrong—but don't get into an argument over it.

See Figure 4.1 for a typical example of a TA and how it attaches to devices in your home or small business.

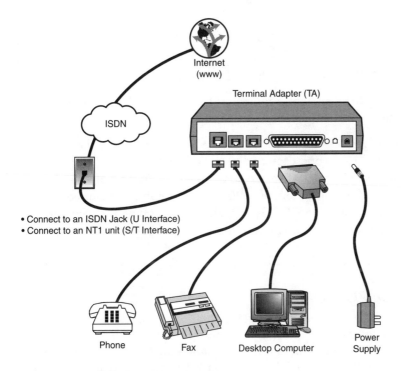

• Connect to an ISDN Jack (U Interface)
• Connect to an NT1 unit (S/T Interface)

Figure 4.1

A typical external TA, which connects to your standard telephone and fax machines through RJ-11 phone ports and to your computer through its serial port. Many external TAs now also feature a USB port for use with Windows 98, Windows Me, and Windows 2000.

BRI or PRI? What?!?

ISDN service is available in two major flavors:

➤ Basic Rate Interface (BRI)

➤ Primary Rate Interface (PRI)

Both flavors of ISDN are based on the fact that the telephone network is based on combinations of 64Kbps connections. As you learned in Chapter 3, ISPs connect to Internet backbones with a T-1 or T-3 line. A T-1 connection runs at 1.544Mbps (more than 1.5 million bits per second), which is twenty-four 64Kbps connections bundled together into a big digital *pipe*.

ISDN provides businesses and individuals their own piece of that big pipe. Both flavors of ISDN use groupings of those 64Kbps connections (called B-channels or Bearer channels) to carry information. Information isn't useful unless it knows where to go, so both kinds of ISDN also use a signaling channel (called a D-channel or Delta channel) to set up calls and carry tiny amounts of packeted data for special uses.

The differences between BRI (our primary concern) and PRI include the number of B-channels used and how they are used.

When a Kb Is Just a Thousand

One enduring mystery of the computer business is that a single abbreviation—Kb—can have so many meanings.

When measuring the speeds of modems and other telecommunications devices, each Kilobit (Kb) equals 1000 (one thousand) bits, and each Megabit (Mb) equals 1000000 (one million) bits. When measuring file sizes, instead of counting a Kilobit as 1000 bits and a Megabit as 1000000 bits, the Kilobit is measured as 1024 bits and the Megabit as 1048576 (1024×1024) bits. Rounding the values to an even number makes the math easier but seriously bothers some binary math fans.

PRI's Variable-Sized Pipe

PRI ISDN uses 23 B-channels along with a single D-channel (also 64Kbps), providing the user virtually the entire capacity of a T-1 backbone (1.536Mbps rather than 1.544Mbps because of overhead). Because most voice and data traffic doesn't require the entire 23 B-channel capacity, PRI ISDN is able to use more or fewer B-channels to handle data and voice traffic as needed. This feature is sometimes referred to as *dynamic allocation*.

PRI ISDN is far too expensive for use at home or in a small business, but the notion of dynamic allocation is still used in a simpler way with BRI ISDN, which is the type of ISDN you'd order for your home or small business.

Will That Be One B-Channel, or Two? How BRI Handles Data and Voice

In keeping with the *basic* in its name, BRI is a far simpler (and cheaper!) version of ISDN than PRI. Most BRI installations combine two 64Kbps B-channels with a single 16Kbps D-channel (producing the nickname 2B+D for this service). Figure 4.2 provides a simple illustration of a BRI connection.

Basic Rate Interface (BRI)

Two B Channels 64Kbps Each

One BRI =
2 B + D

16 Kbps D Channel

B Channels - User Voice, Data, Image, Sound
D Channels - Call Signalling, Set-up, User Packet Data

Figure 4.2

A logical view of 2B+1D BRI. Note that although three channels appear, all three run over the standard 2-wire telephone cable running into your home or office.

BRI is available in many variations, depending on your telco. Ameritech calls its service IOC-S, whereas Verizon's ex-GTE service area refers to it as Single-Line ISDN. The name can vary, but make sure your ISDN service allows your two B-channels to be bonded into a single 128Kbps connection for Internet use. It also will enable you to drop down to a single B-channel when you need to use the phone, take a call, or send a fax, and then return to full speed when the second B-channel is free.

Danger Danger

Avoiding the Killer Bs

Watch out for ISDN services packages that don't give you the kind of BRI you need. In particular, avoid

➤ Single B–channel BRI options—These limit you to a single 64Kbps channel.

➤ Two B–channels, but only one available for data—If you can't use both channels, you can't get 128Kbps service.

➤ Two B–channels plus call management and voice mail—If you use ISDN strictly for Internet access, why pay extra for telephone-oriented features?

Unlike newer types of high-speed Internet service, BRI isn't an "always on" connection. Although the connection time to get online is just a few seconds, compared to the 30 seconds to one minute timings of typical dial-up analog modem connections, you still need to dial up your ISP to get online.

BRI isn't always an "all you can eat" unlimited-connection-time service, either. Depending on which company supplies your BRI service, you can get unlimited access. However, some telcos provide you with a hefty but fixed chunk of connection time each month instead. Talk too long? Download too much? You'll pay a surcharge for every minute you exceed your allocated amount.

Can ISDN Replace Your Existing Phone Service?

In theory, the answer is "Yes, it can!"

Because ISDN supports both telephone and Internet uses, you can convert your existing line to ISDN and use the savings to offset the hefty ISDN monthly charges. Remember, you can connect a telephone and a fax machine to most ISDN terminal adapters and use them while you're connected to the Internet, as shown earlier in Figure 4.1.

With BRI ISDN charges costing around twice as much as other high-speed Internet connections, the savings you can receive by dropping your old analog service can look mighty tempting.

Should You Put All Your Eggs in a Single Digital Basket?

Consider this: ISDN, unlike your existing telephone line, isn't self-powered. Remember the last time the power went out? You could still pick up your ordinary analog phone and call the local power company to complain, or use the glowing dial for a light source, but your cordless phones that require an electrical power source didn't work at all. So, if your power fails, what would you hear with an ISDN phone? The sound of silence.

Ameritech is one of the many telcos that suggests keeping your existing telephone service as a backup in case of power failures. Are they looking out for your best interests? Yes, but don't discount the $20–$50 in line revenue they can keep receiving if you keep your analog line. So, although ISDN can replace your current phone service, in reality, the answer to our earlier question is "No."

Tech Note

THAT WAY▷

Beating Blackouts with Battery Backup Systems

If you must be able to use your ISDN line when the power goes out, check into a battery backup system. These devices contain a battery and several standard outlets for connecting a computer or other AC–powered device. Most popularly priced battery backup units are designed to run a computer and monitor for up to 10 or 15 minutes, but you might be able to keep on talking far longer if you use yours strictly for ISDN service.

You can get information on battery backup units from companies such as APC (www.apc.com) and Tripp–Lite (www.tripplite.com), among others.

How Fast Is ISDN?

As you saw earlier, if you want to order ISDN, you want the dual B-channel plus single D-channel version of BRI. Although business ISDN plans offer many confusing variations of ISDN, residential ISDN offers just a few choices. Voice only, voice and data, or voice and data and call management services usually are the only services offered to residential and small-business customers. Choose voice and data, with or without the call management services.

If you select this type of BRI-flavored ISDN as your high-speed Internet connection of choice, you'll have a 128Kbps two-way connection to the World Wide Web, news-groups, and all the MP3 files you can download when you're not using the phone or fax. You will also have a solid 64Kbps two-way connection even while you're yakking with your Aunt Mabel or your paper-clip supplier. Most terminal adapters sold for use with this type of ISDN can add or drop the second B-channel on-the-fly, so you never need to drop an Internet connection when you want to use the phone.

Unlike other types of high-speed Internet connections, ISDN runs the same speed uphill and downhill, so it's a good choice if you send many large files to other users.

Gimme an ISDN—Yes, You!

Because ISDN was originally designed to handle the increasing demands of telephony devices rather than be a pure Internet solution, your local telephone company is the place to turn to for ISDN service in many places.

ISDN Service—But Not for Your Computer?!

Be aware that many telcos often offer ISDN primarily for its business data and voice capabilities rather than for its Internet capabilities. For example, I can order ISDN today from my local telco, Ameritech, but I must use a third-party ISP because Ameritech.net (Ameritech's own ISP) isn't available in my area yet. If I want ISDN, I must locate an ISP that will

➤ Handle ISDN connections (preferably at 128Kbps!)

➤ Be available in my area (unless I *like* making long-distance calls!)

So, you might need to work with both your telco and a third-party ISP. Third-party ISP pricing can vary from the telco's offerings, and multiple ISDN-compatible ISPs might be available in your area. So, as always, shop carefully!

Ferreting Out ISDN Providers

To locate ISPs that handle ISDN calls in your area, go to

```
http://56k.com/isps/isdn/
```

This listing covers all U.S. states and territories as well as the District of Columbia. The listing also covers Australian states and Canadian provinces.

Note that both single B–channel (64Kbps) and dual B–channel (128Kbps) ISDN providers are listed. You want a 128Kbps supplier to get all the speed you're paying for.

Tech Note

THAT WAY ▷

All ISDN Is Not Created Equal

When comparing ISDN ISP pricing, watch out for these variables:

➤ Unlimited access versus blocks of time per month

➤ Surcharges, if you exceed the limits of your time per month

➤ 64Kbps versus 128Kbps—Don't buy 64Kbps Internet access if you have the typical 2B+D 128Kbps BRI ISDN service!

➤ Residential versus business access (business access costs a lot more!)

How Much Is That ISDN in the Window?

Remember how complicated it was the last time you signed up for a cellular phone? Find the ibuprofen bottle, because ISDN pricing can give you the same kind of headache.

What makes ISDN pricing such a headache? As "baby Bell" Ameritech's Web site puts it: "There are three factors which contribute to the cost of ISDN service: installation costs, monthly fee, and usage costs." Actually, they forgot a fourth factor: where you live. Unlike cable modem services, whose prices are surprisingly similar regardless of where you live, ISDN pricing is all over the map, partly because your telco is a state-regulated monopoly.

How Much Is ISDN? It Depends on Where You Live

In Michigan, for example, Ameritech's IOC-U service (data and voice) will set you back $35.12 per month, with an installation charge of $127.00 plus call plan, usage, and Enhanced 911 (E911) charges.

Move to Illinois, and you'll pay $44.11 per month and pay more for installation, too ($140.00!), plus E911 and usage charges.

Hoosiers in Indiana (and transplants to Indiana like me) get a bit of a break on installation charges compared to Illinois: $132.00, but get broken by the much higher monthly charge: $56.15 for flat rate, plus usage and E911 charges.

Internet Not Included!

And, don't forget that the charges above *don't* include ISP charges! If you want to connect to the Internet at 128Kbps, you'll need to pony up an extra $49.95 per month if you use Ameritech's own Ameritech.net ISP. Rates for third-party ISDNs can vary significantly. If you live on the West Coast, you're likely to pay a lot more for ISDN service.

Danger Danger

You Get What You Pay For

Watch out for low-ball ISDN ISP service rates. They can be for just 64Kbps rather than 128Kbps service. Unless you use your phone line continually, losing half your Internet connection potential is usually a bad idea.

All in all, you're looking at around $85–$115 per month for data/voice/Internet service, plus the one-time installation charge—and your hardware expense.

Don't Forget the Terminal Adapter!

The terminal adapter is to ISDN what the cable modem is to cable TV-delivered high-speed Internet: the missing link between ISDN and your telephones and/or computers.

Terminal adapters come in many different models, and some terminal adapters are designed primarily for telephony uses. Make sure that you order one that supports Internet connections and multiple computers if you plan to use ISDN to connect your network with the Internet. Ameritech, for example, sells a one-computer external terminal adapter (Eicon DIVA T/A) for $200, and a 4-port TA/router for use with multiple computers (Ramp Networks' WebRamp 410i) for $349.

You must buy the terminal adapter rather than lease it, but some telcos might allow you to spread the purchase price over several months.

Ameritech, my local telco, will allow me to purchase a TA from another company if I like, but it provides an enhanced warranty on the TAs that it sells. If your telco offers you the option to buy your TA from another vendor, find out how it affects service costs in case of ISDN trouble and whether the warranty provided by an outside supplier matches the warranty provided by your telco.

Adding It All Up

Although prices will vary, the cost quotation I received from my telco is typical of what ISDN services will cost you.

By the time you add the installation cost, the monthly service charges, ISP charges, and terminal adapter costs, the costs are surprising. Table 4.1 shows what it would cost you to add residential ISDN service (including voice, data, and call management services—the "V" package) for one computer to a home in the 812 area code, 464 exchange (Ameritech—Indiana pricing, August 2000). This service plan includes unlimited use; ISDN providers in your area might offer per-minute or up to X number of hours options in addition to or instead of an all-you-can-eat plan.

Table 4.1   Adding Up ISDN Start-Up Costs

Charge Type	Cost
Installation (one-time)	$152.00
Terminal adapter (one-time)	$200.00
ISDN service charges (per month)	$64.49*
ISP charges (assuming Ameritech.net—per month)	$49.95*
Total first-month cost	**$466.44**
Cost Per Month (After Initial Costs)*	**$114.44**

indicates continuing month-to-month ISDN service and ISP charges.

How good a deal is this? In many places you can get much faster cable modem or DSL service for around $50 per month, including lease of your modem, and often with no installation charge. ISDN might be the first to break the 100Kbps barrier for online service, but it's far from the cheapest service around.

The Least You Need to Know

➤ ISDN enables you to share a single phone line with two or more telephony devices, such as a phone and a fax machine and one or more computers.

➤ Basic Rate Interface (BRI) ISDN can handle up to 128Kbps Internet connections, but some ISDN ISPs can handle only 64Kbps connections.

➤ You can talk on one 64Kbps B-channel while keeping an Internet connection running through the other B-channel.

➤ An ISDN line can replace your existing telephone line, but most telcos recommend keeping your current service as a backup.

➤ ISP costs are in addition to the $35 or more per month that your telco charges for ISDN service.

➤ You can expect to pay hundreds of dollars up front for a typical ISDN Internet connection when installation and equipment are figured in, plus as much as $100 or more per month thereafter, making ISDN among the more expensive high-speed solutions on the market.

Chapter 5

Teaching Old POTS New Tricks with DSL

In This Chapter

➤ Learn how DSL works

➤ Pick the right DSL service from a bevy of choices

➤ Get a handle on confusing DSL speeds

➤ Find out whether DSL is available in your area

➤ Get to the bottom line—Can you afford it?

Digital Subscriber Line, better known as *DSL*, enables you to use the same telephone wire that comes into your home or office to carry both ordinary telephone conversations and high-speed Internet connections at the same time. If this sounds a lot like ISDN, you're right. In many ways, DSL is like a turbocharged version of ISDN that has been customized for the Internet.

Like ISDN, DSL provides you with an all-digital data connection to the Internet. But unlike ISDN, DSL is built strictly for fast Internet access. DSL is both faster and cheaper than ISDN for Internet access.

Explain This DSL Thing to Me, Okay?

How does DSL do it? A single wire for voice and data traffic—at the same time? How is this possible? Time for a little science lesson, but don't worry—there won't be a test! You know that dogs can hear frequencies that make absolutely no impact on our brains. Their ears (and brains) were made differently from ours. Dogs will go berserk because of noises we'll never hear. Similarly, DSL uses a different frequency, a much higher frequency than that used for voice telephone calls, allowing the same wire to carry both voice and data at the same time.

Connecting DSL to Your Computer

Instead of using a dial-up analog modem, DSL uses a device that is also called a modem but that connects with your computer like a network device. DSL modems can be external, connecting to your computer through a standard 10BaseT (twisted-pair) Ethernet network card, or internal, plugging into an open PCI expansion slot in your computer.

Although a few computers have shipped with a DSL modem (also capable of being used as an analog 56Kbps modem), DSL service providers, such as one of the local telephone companies, provide most DSL modems.

How does the DSL signal get to your computer? As Figure 5.1 shows, DSL typically works like this:

1. A single phone line coming to your home or office goes to a splitter, which separates the line into two; one for digital DSL signals and one for analog signals that are used with phones and telephony devices.

2. Both lines go from the splitter to a new wall plate installed as part of the DSL service. The DSL line from the splitter connects to the RJ-11 connector marked for use with the DSL modem, and the other line connects to the regular jack used for your phone.

3. A standard RJ-11 telephone cable carries DSL information from the wall plate to the DSL modem.

4. A Category 5 Ethernet cable that uses RJ-45 connectors runs from the DSL modem to a 10BaseT Ethernet network card in your computer.

DSL differs from conventional analog modems by creating a direct connection between your end of the telephone wire and the local telephone exchange. As you can see in Figure 5.2, the same telephone wire carries both digital Internet data and analog telephone calls between your home or office and the telephone company. At the telephone company, a device called a DSL access multiplexer separates the digital DSL signal from the analog phone signal. The digital DSL signal is transmitted to the Internet, while the analog phone signal goes through the ordinary phone switch and on to the telephone network.

DSL data is never run through the telephone switch normally used to route calls because switching would prevent the creation of the high-speed direct digital connection that DSL needs to work.

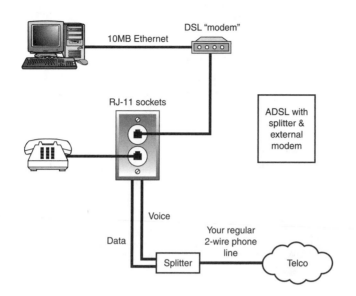

Figure 5.1

External DSL modems connect between your computer's network card and your telephone jack.

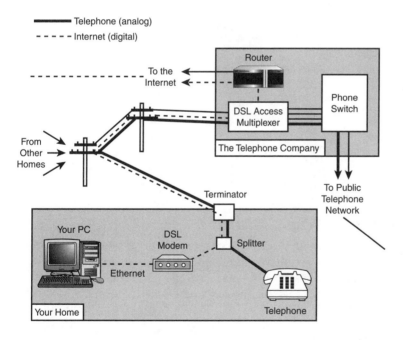

Figure 5.2

DSL data and voice travel together from your home to the telephone company (telco), which separates DSL data from voice calls. DSL data then is sent to the Internet, and voice calls (as well as faxes) are sent to the public telephone network.

Filtering Out the Voice from the Data

How does DSL keep voice calls and data transmissions on the same wire from interfering with each other? Signal-separating devices of various types are connected to the DSL modem that connects your computer to the Internet. Some versions of DSL use a device called a *splitter* (see Figure 5.1) to separate voice from data. If your DSL service uses a splitter, a technician must make a service call to your home or office to install it, making DSL very expensive to install.

Today, some versions of DSL have replaced the splitter with microfilters that are installed on your existing lines to separate phone and data traffic (see Figure 5.3). If your DSL service uses microfilters, you can perform the DSL installation yourself, saving time and money.

Figure 5.3

If your DSL service provider uses a filter instead of a splitter to separate voice and data, you might be able to install DSL yourself.

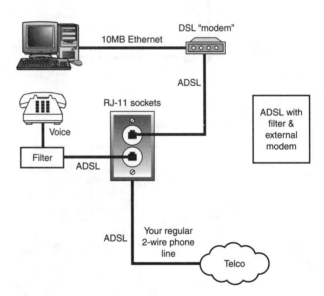

Your DSL Connection Is Yours Alone

Unlike its arch rival in speed, the cable modem, DSL service isn't shared (you'll learn more about how cable connections are shared in Chapter 6, "It's Not Just TV: It's HTTP…Cable Modems"). It doesn't matter how many people go to their computer keyboards at 6 p.m. for the Internet's take on the day's news; a DSL connection won't slow down.

The only sharing that DSL performs is with your telephone. This factor makes DSL a good choice for users who are concerned about protecting their computers from network-based break-ins. However, a DSL connection alone isn't secure enough. Because DSL is an always-on continuous connection, it can leave your computer theoretically vulnerable to attack.

See Chapter 16, "Don't Be A Bullseye: Securing Your Internet Connection," for more information on keeping your DSL connection safe from hackers.

DSL's Alphabet Soup (Types of DSL Services)

If you want to cause a fight in a bar with a lot of bandwidth-starved computer users, stand up and announce that "There's no such thing as DSL!" Before anybody decides to break a chair (or your head!), you'd be well advised to add that what you really meant is that there's no such thing as a *single* DSL standard.

DSL is the family name for many different line-sharing arrangements that run high-speed Internet connections over ordinary telephone wire.

Tech Note

THAT WAY ▶

When One Line Isn't Enough

Although all forms of DSL allow your telephone and computer to share a single phone line, regulations concerning telephone and data services in some states require telcos to run new wire just for DSL service. One example of this approach is Ameritech's SpeedPath service.

Tech Note

THAT WAY ▶

Fancy Ways to Say Same and Different

So-called *asymmetrical DSL* services enable you to download faster than you can upload. *Symmetrical DSL* services use the same speed for both download and upload. Symmetrical DSL services are more expensive and are often marketed only to business customers.

Table 5.1 shows the major members of the DSL family that are available for home and small-business users as of this writing.

Table 5.1   Major Types of DSL Service for Home and Small-Office Users

Features Service Type	Download Speed Range	Upload Speed Range	Notes
DSL Lite (*G. Lite, Universal DSL*)	1.544–6Mbps	128–384Kbps	Can be installed by customer; no splitter required
SDSL	160Kbps–2Mbps	Same	"Symmetrical" DSL
CDSL	384Kbps–1Mbps	128Kbps	No splitter required "Consumer DSL"
ADSL	1.5Mbps–8Mbps	32Kbps–1.08Mbps	"Asymmetrical" DSL

Other types of DSL are designed for use by ISPs and large businesses. The most common types of DSL that home and small-business users will encounter are G. Lite, CDSL, or ADSL.

How Fast Is DSL?

Table 5.1 indicates the theoretical limits for typical DSL speeds, but the DSL service provider will set guaranteed speeds for the types of DSL connections it provides. These guaranteed speeds will be far less than the top limits seen previously and will vary by provider and market.

Typical DSL Speeds

Table 5.2 shows DSL speeds offered by major telcos as of August 2000. Pricing data is for the service plus Internet access costs and does not include setup or equipment costs.

Table 5.2   Typical DSL Speeds from Major Telcos

Telco	Service Name	Download Speed	Upload Speed	Price Per Month
Verizon	DSL Personal	256–640 Kbps	90Kbps	$39.95
Verizon	DSL Professional	960Kbps–1.6 Mbps	90Kbps	$99.95

Telco	Service Name	Download Speed	Upload Speed	Price Per Month
Qwest	MegaBit Deluxe	256Kbps	256Kbps	$47.90
Ameritech	SpeedPath 768	Up to 768Kbps	128Kbps	$39.95
BellSouth	FastAccess	Up to 1.4 Mbps	Not listed	$49.95

Why DSL Speeds Vary

One major reason why DSL speeds vary so much is because DSL runs over the same wire as your telephone calls. The length of the wire running from your telephone connection on the side of your home or office must be no longer than 18,000 feet for most versions of DSL, and shorter wire runs are better. Some versions of DSL drop in speed as wire length increases.

Besides wire length, the quality of the wire in telephone circuits is another limiting factor. Although many newer forms of DSL are designed to compensate for less-than-perfect wiring, a newer wiring plant can support higher DSL speeds than an older plant.

But the biggest reason why DSL speeds vary is because of the choices that the real provider of DSL service, your local phone company, makes. As you saw in an earlier section, some types of DSL are faster than other types, and the telco decides which type of DSL it will support. Different flavors of DSL in different markets also means that a DSL modem in one market probably won't work with another provider's DSL type if you move or change services.

Where Can I Get DSL?

Unlike dial-up analog-modem based Internet services, which are almost always provided by an ISP separate from your phone company, DSL services can be provided by either

➤ An ISP that provides DSL services

➤ Your friendly local telephone monopoly (telco)

In major cities where a telco monopoly no longer exists, you can also get DSL from a different telco than the one your phone is using now.

You can contact an ISP that specializes in DSL or your local telephone company to ask about DSL service. However, the infrastructure that your local telephone company has in place to support DSL is the biggest deciding factor in the speeds of

DSL, the prices you'll pay for DSL, and even whether DSL is available to you. If the DSL access multiplexer equipment isn't installed in your telephone exchange, you can't get DSL.

Unlike dial-up Internet service, designed to be carried over the switched telephone network, DSL is a direct connection between your computer and the central office (CO) or telephone exchange. Although some types of DSL can be installed by the individual user, your ability to get any type of DSL is controlled by what the local telephone company has added to its exchange to support DSL. If the answer is nothing, then you can't get DSL no matter how much you want it.

What does your local telephone company (telco) need to add to its exchanges to support DSL?

➤ A splitter, with one end connected to POTS (the Plain Old Telephone System for voice) and the other end connected to…

➤ A Multiservices Digital Subscriber Line Access Multiplexer (DSLAM), which collects data from multiple splitters and sends it to…

➤ The Internet

As you can see, even if your new top-of-the-line computer comes with a DSL modem, it can't connect you to the Internet unless your telco has added the necessary equipment to handle DSL.

Unfortunately, DSL service is a long way from being universal, even for users who are within the magic 18,000 feet of the local telephone company's CO or exchange.

Tech Note

Be Careful with Those Measurements

The maximum distance listed for DSL is not map distance, it's wire distance. Because telephone wires seldom follow an "as the crow flies" path, you can't look at a map to decide whether you qualify for DSL service.

It has taken local telephone companies a long time to install the infrastructure needed for their exchanges to support DSL, although estimates indicate that more than 60% of telephone lines in the U.S. will be capable of carrying DSL signals when the necessary equipment is in place in the telcos' COs.

How can you tell when DSL service is available in your area? Many ISPs that sell DSL connections offer a lookup service; just enter your phone number, city, state, and Zip code, and the lookup service will query the telco that services your area for DSL availability. Alternatively, you can contact the local telephone company yourself.

If you don't live in a major city, take a good look at the DSL coverage maps available at the DSL Reports Web site. These maps, which provide a quick visual check for many of the major DSL network providers, indicate that most medium-size cities and small towns outside the Northeast are still on the "someday DSL" list.

Seven Reasons You Might Not Have Access to DSL— Yet

Although most high-speed Internet experts agree that the speed, security, and pricing of DSL services make DSL the best choice for high-speed Internet, many people still can't order DSL. Why not? Here are seven of the leading reasons why DSL might not be available to you—yet—even if your telco offers DSL to some customers in your area:

Can I Get DSL?

DSL Reports, one of the leading Web sites providing DSL coverage, has developed maps that indicate areas covered by major DSL service providers. See DSL Reports' coverage maps at http://www.dslreports. com/clec

➤ Your central office (CO) hasn't been updated to handle DSL yet—This process, as mentioned earlier in this chapter, is a slow one. Some multistate telcos are currently providing DSL service to only a few major cities in their market areas.

➤ You're connected to the CO by a digital loop carrier—When I first moved as a newlywed in 1977 to Evansville, Indiana (where I still live), I could easily memorize the five or so exchanges in use. I tucked them in my memory next to the area codes for major cities and metropolitan areas.

Today, with the explosion of telephony devices and increasing numbers of alternative local telephone companies in major cities, both area codes and local exchanges have grown in number. Most of us literally have no idea whether a given telephone number is a local or long-distance call away unless it uses one of the old, familiar exchanges and area codes.

How has your friendly telco responded to the huge demand for telephone numbers? Starting in the 1980s, many telcos supplemented their normal copper wiring loops with digital loop carriers (DLCs, also called SLCs). Unfortunately, these DLCs were never intended for use with a service like DSL. Some can be updated to handle DSL, but others can't and would need to be replaced. What are the odds that your telephone line is connected to the CO by a DLC? One in five!

➤ You are too far away from the CO to which your phone is connected—Most forms of DSL require that your connection to the CO be no longer than 18,000 feet (wire distance) for DSL to work. Some DSL providers won't support distances beyond 16,000 feet. Although new forms of DSL are being developed to handle longer wire runs, it's up to the telco to decide to offer these services and install the necessary equipment.

➤ Your telephone line has load coils installed—Load coils suppress the high-frequency signals that DSL uses to transmit data. Although load coils help eliminate noise on voice calls, they automatically make any phone line with load coils not DSL compliant!

➤ Your telephone line is connected to the public telephone network through a bridge tap—A bridge tap provides a convenient shortcut for the telco; rather than running your phone line all the way back to the CO, it can run your line to a phone line passing by your house or business and tap into it.

Again, as with load coils, there's no effect on voice traffic, but the high-frequency interference from bridge taps can prevent your line from handling DSL traffic.

Some telcos automatically run new wire for DSL service to bypass problems with both load coils and bridge taps.

➤ Your telephone line is picking up other forms of interference—The short length of unshielded twisted-pair telephone cable that connects your home to the network (the cable drop) can act as an unintentional antenna to pick up AM radio or other forms of interference. Some other home appliances can also cause significant forms of interference; we just bought a chair cushion that features both heat and massaging action. Turn on the massagers while the TV and computer are on and you'll see the monitor image dance gently across the CRT and the TV produce snow in August! I wonder what that massager would do to a DSL signal?!?!

➤ Rogue high-speed signals on bundled telco wires can interfere with DSL—DSL isn't the only form of high-speed data traffic on the telephone system these days. Telephone wires that run to various locations are bundled into a binder group on their way to the CO. Signals from other types of high-speed data, such as T-1 or ISDN can jump from the original wire pair over to your wire pair, interfering with your DSL connection.

Even if you qualify for DSL according to telephone records, the problems listed here could delay your DSL service, or even prevent you from getting DSL service until wiring or equipment problems are solved.

Does the D in DSL Stand for Dollars? (How Much Is DSL?)

DSL pricing varies widely, but to see representative pricing from major telcos, refer to Table 5.2 earlier in this chapter.

You can expect to pay around $50.00 a month for most telco's home-oriented DSL offerings; prices from ISPs who resell DSL service can be more. Two variables in the process that are not found in Table 5.2 include the costs of hardware and installation.

Many telcos that offer DSL provide so-called self-install kits to eliminate the cost (around $150.00) of having the telco repair person come out and set up the connection. If you've installed a hard drive or add-on card in your computer, you should be able to install one of these kits.

Some telcos provide the DSL modem that attaches to your computer at no charge, whereas others require you to buy or lease the device. A DSL modem can cost you more than $100 to buy, and leasing can run around $10/month.

Keep in mind that telcos often waive the costs of either installation or hardware, or both, to get DSL started. These promotions are the best times to order.

The Least You Need to Know

➤ DSL allows you to use your phone and your computer online at the same time.

➤ DSL service provides high-speed Internet access at a monthly rate that's about twice that of normal dial-up Internet connections.

➤ DSL service might become more common with time, but the slowness of local telephone companies to make the equipment changes needed for DSL service have prevented it from being currently available to most of the U.S.

Chapter 6

It's Not Just TV: It's HTTP...Cable Modems

> **In This Chapter**
>
> ➤ How cable modems work
>
> ➤ Differences between cable modem services
>
> ➤ Speeds of cable modems
>
> ➤ Prices and availability of cable modem service

As you've seen in previous chapters, one of the most common ways to gain faster access to the Internet is to piggyback on an existing technology. The latest example of getting more out of an existing communications medium, the cable modem, doesn't use phone lines. Instead, it rides on the same cable that brings TV entertainment into your home.

So This Wire Carries Cable TV and the Internet...

As you've seen in previous chapters, this book is dedicated to helping you find the best high-speed Internet access solution for you, your family, and your business. Although several high-speed Internet solutions are on the horizon, the first one that makes sense for most people *and* is available today in many markets is the cable modem, which uses the cable TV infrastructure to access the Internet at very high speeds. Like DSL, cable modem service is always on; as soon as you boot your computer, you have an Internet connection.

Channeling Cable Internet Data

How can the same coaxial cable that carries everything from the Cartoon Network to Speedvision into your home also carry high-speed Internet data? The same way it carries all those cable channels; the Internet data is carried over one or more channels that are not in use for cable TV programming. Thus, cable modems, unlike DSL on phone lines, fit into the native design of the cable TV medium and aren't a hack or retrofit that needs to work around limitations in cabling, at least in the downstream direction. However, depending on the type of cable infrastructure your provider has, you might need to rely on that old reliable, the analog modem, to carry your email and page requests back to the provider.

Splitting the Signals

There is no chance of accidentally receiving cable TV channels on your computer with a cable modem. Cable modems tune into cable channels that aren't used by the normal cable TV system. So why does your cable technician install a splitter when you add cable modem service to your existing cable TV service? The splitter is actually for your TV's benefit, not your computer's benefit. If you have two-way cable modem service, the cable must also carry data from your computer back to the provider. The splitter prevents upstream data from interfering with your favorite TV programs (see Figure 6.1).

Figure 6.1

The splitter prevents outbound cable Internet traffic from interfering with cable TV reception.

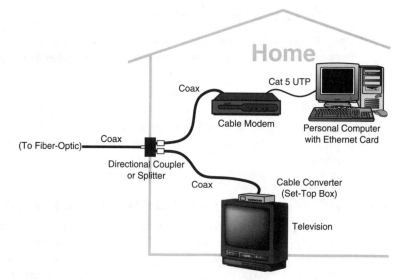

Getting Cable Internet into Your Computer

Cable modems perform a task that is somewhat similar to the ordinary analog modem they replace. Like analog modems, cable modems perform a modulate/demodulate operation on data flowing to and from the cable modem network. The information coming to your computer isn't in analog form, but it still must be converted from its cable-friendly state to a computer-ready condition.

Tech Note

THAT WAY

A Different Kind of Modem

Cable modems are necessary because the Internet data signals are brought to your computer by a carrier signal. The cable modem separates the data signal from the carrier signal. The cable modem performs a task for your computer that is somewhat similar to the job the set-top box performs for your TV: Both bring you the data that matters to the device to which they're connected. The set-top box selects the correct cable TV channel, and the cable modem selects the Internet data.

Cable modems come in two forms: internal and external. And, just as with DSL, your Internet service provider will decide which one is approved or provided. Although cable modems are already being sold in some locations, many companies bundle the cable modem with the service to make sure that compatible equipment is used with the cable modem Internet service.

External cable modems connect to your computer through an unshielded twisted-pair cable that attaches to a 10BaseT Ethernet network card inside your computer or to a USB port (usually found on the rear of your computer). Internal cable modems connect to a PCI or ISA expansion slot.

Like DSL, cable modems provide a specialized, always on, form of network connection to your computer.

You Are Not Alone in Cyberspace

After you install cable modem service and turn on your computer, your computer becomes part of a sort of neighborhood area network. This neighborhood network includes other homes or businesses near yours that also have cable modem service. Because you and your cable-modem neighbors are sharing the same channel, you're likely to notice peaks and dips in cable modem performance, especially if the neighborhood gets crowded with other users.

If you're the first one to log on to the Internet in the morning, you'll enjoy tremendous speed. However, if everyone on the neighborhood network logs on to view stock activity and the Weather Channel's online version at 6 p.m., performance can drop because you are sharing the channel.

Tech Note

Don't Panic About Slowdowns

Cable modems use variable amounts of the channel's bandwidth; just a little is used for Web surfing, page requests, and email, whereas more is used during downloading. This is why Internet traffic is sometimes described as being "bursty." Chances are that you won't see a huge slow-down unless everyone in the neighborhood network decides to download a huge file at the same time.

Danger Danger

Don't Say I Didn't Warn You!

If you decide on cable modem service, make sure you follow the steps to protect yourself outlined in Chapter 16, "Don't Be a Bullseye: Securing Your Internet Connection."

Should you be worrying about sharing your cable modem connection with other users? The concerns of many early cable modem users about being visible to their cable modem neighbors is no longer an issue if your cable modem meets the DOCSIS (Data Over Cable Systems Interface Specification) standard. More and more two-way cable systems use DOCSIS cable modems, which use encrypted data transfer to prevent simple snooping.

However, if you have a one-way cable system connection (the type that still uses a modem and your phone line), you might be at slight risk for visibility to the rest of the network because these older systems do not use encryption.

In either case, though, if you use File and Print Sharing on the computer, you risk intrusion by other Internet users, whether they are connected to your local cable modem network or not. Some cable providers help security by blocking the TCP ports used for Windows file sharing, but regardless of the cable modem type you use, you should take additional precautions.

What's Happening at the Other End of the Cable?

If you have a two-way cable modem, both downloads and uploads are carried over the cable TV media. Let's assume that you click a hyperlink.

After your page request leaves your home on the cable modem, it travels over the cable TV media to the local cable operator's network hub. The Cable Modem Termination System (CMTS) connects with the channels devoted to cable modem traffic and routes traffic from the network hub to a cable modem ISP's backbone. The cable modem ISP (companies such as @Home, Road Runner, and so on) delivers the traffic to the Internet.

When the Web page comes back to your cable modem ISP from the Internet, the cable ISP sends the page to the cable head end. The cable head end encrypts the page (for security). Then, the cable head end feeds the page to the channel assigned to your cable modem. Your cable modem monitors this channel and sends the page to your Web browser when it receives it.

Two-way cable modem service is becoming the standard, but as you'll see in the next section, it's not the only cable modem standard out there.

Types of Cable Modem Services

Only two types of cable modem service exist:

➤ Two-way

➤ One-way (also known as Telco Return, or TR)

The choice of which cable modem service you can get depends on the existing cabling in your neighborhood.

Tech Note

Fixing Up the Cable TV Plant for Two-Way Service

Most cable TV systems out there can offer their customers one-way service, but two-way service is faster and doesn't use your telephone line. What must your cable TV company do to the network to offer two-way service?

Two-way service requires the following:

➤ Hybrid fiber-optic/coaxial cabling—This type of network is fiber optic (for speed and higher capacity) from the head end to each neighborhood. Then, taps are installed to connect fiber to existing and new coaxial cables. So, the cable into your home looks the same; the difference is an outside job.

➤ Amplifiers—Two-way service means that your cable modem doesn't just receive data, it also sends out email, page requests, file uploads, and so on. Amplifiers boost the strength of the signals coming from your computer so they'll reach the head end.

What's the difference between two-way and one-way service?

Two-Way Cable Modems

Two-way cable modems use the fiber-optic cables that run from the cable TV office to your home to carry both downloaded Internet data and uploaded data (email, page requests, files) (see Figure 6.2).

Figure 6.2

Two-way cable modems use the cable TV network for data flowing both to and from the Internet.

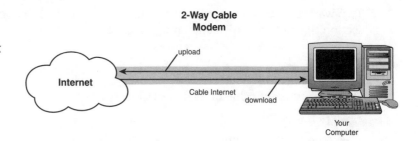

One-Way (Telco Return) Cable Modems

One-way cable modems use coaxial cable to carry download traffic only. The alternative name for one-way service, Telco Return, refers to the need to use an ordinary analog modem, such as those covered earlier in this book, to send page requests, email, and other uploaded information back to the Internet. Some TR modems have a connection to an external modem, but most can be used with the internal modems already found in most computers (see Figure 6.3).

Figure 6.3

One-way cable modems use the cable TV network only for downloads; uploads must go through a normal analog modem through the telephone system.

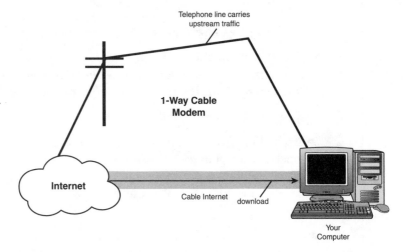

Which One Is in Your Neighborhood?

How can you tell which system your cable modem provider will offer you? Well, you can't tell by looking at your incoming cable. Both pure coaxial and fiber-optic cable TV systems still use a coaxial cable for the cabling that goes into your home or office; a converter is used to change the laser over fiber-optic data into data that can flow over coaxial cable into your home. If your cable TV provider offers digital cable TV, this requires fiber-optic service, so you'll probably have two-way service if your operator provides cable modem service.

One-Way Is Going Away

One-way cable modems represent a short-term solution for cable TV users who also want fast Internet. As more and more cable TV systems are upgraded to fiber optic, you'll see one-way cable modems become less popular in major markets, although they are expected to stay around in rural areas and in small cable systems.

How Fast Is a Cable Modem?

Some cable modem vendors claim that cable modems are as much as 100 times as fast as dial-up modems. Don't believe it; one of the problems with claims like this is that they often don't tell you what dial-up modem speed they're comparing with—14.4Kbps? 28.8Kbps? 56Kbps? You can't tell from a lot of this information.

More realistic estimates suggest that the maximum speed of a two-way cable modem system is about 1Mbps for downloads (varies with load), and less for uploads. @Home, one of the two biggest cable modem ISPs, has capped upload speeds at 128Kbps.

One-way cable modems are faster for downloads than analog modems, but not as fast as two-way systems.

How Fast Is Fast?

Although the maximum speed for a two-way cable modem is about 1Mbps for downloads, how fast can you expect to go? To find out, check with a friend who already has a cable modem in your neighborhood and try a speed test such as the ones available online from

```
http://www.cable-modem.net/features/oct99/speed.html

http://www.cablemodemhelp.com/speedtest/

http://www.2wire.com/services/bandwidth.asp
```

If you want to try any of these tests more than once, follow these tips for an accurate test:

1. Clear your browser's cache (the temporary files copied to your system). If you don't delete the files used for the speed test and you rerun it, you will get a falsely higher reading because the computer will open the files from the hard disk instead of downloading them again.

   ➤ In Microsoft IE 5.x, open the Tools menu, select Internet Options, and click Delete Files.

   ➤ With Netscape Navigator 4.x, open Edit, Preferences, Advanced, Cache, and click both Clear Memory Cache and Clear Disk Cache.

2. Try the test before 8 a.m., around Noon, around 4 p.m., around 8 p.m., and at bedtime to see when you can expect to see slowdowns.

Overcoming Potential Congestion Problems with Cable Modem Service

As mentioned earlier, because cable modems share bandwidth with other users, peak traffic can cause a drop in performance, whereas off-peak uses will be faster. The configuration, number of users per channel, and local configuration vary with each local cable modem provider.

Many cable modem providers overcome potential Internet congestion problems by setting up caching servers as part of their cable modem service. However, heavy local use can still cause slowdowns.

What is a caching server? It's a computer that stores (or caches) content that came from the Internet for reuse by other viewers.

How does it work? Imagine that you and six other football fans in your neighborhood all have cable modems from the same ISP. All of you decide to check the latest sports coverage at the ESPN home page. Normally, each request for the ESPN Web site's home page would be a separate download, as shown in Figure 6.4.

By using caching servers, a cable ISP reduces Internet traffic and still provides every football fan the ESPN home page, as shown in Figure 6.5.

Another way to look at the benefits of caching servers is to compare the situation to you and your cache—I mean cash. The Internet is a bit like your bank. There's your money—vast amounts of money, I hope—but it's inconvenient to go to the bank every time you want to buy a candy bar or a newspaper.

Your wallet or purse is like a caching server. You refresh its contents periodically by visiting your bank or ATM to get money. In the meantime, you enjoy the same content the bank provides without going to the bank.

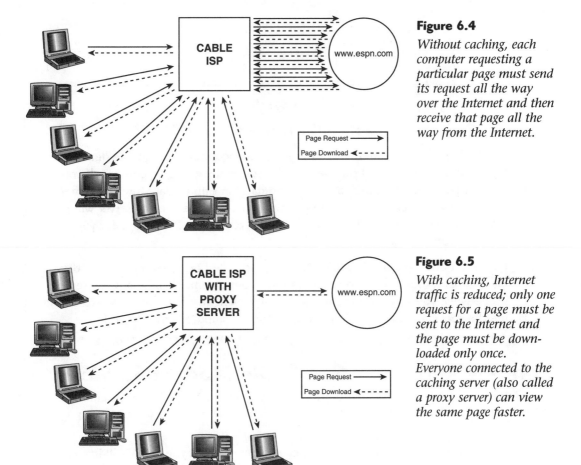

Figure 6.4

Without caching, each computer requesting a particular page must send its request all the way over the Internet and then receive that page all the way from the Internet.

Figure 6.5

With caching, Internet traffic is reduced; only one request for a page must be sent to the Internet and the page must be downloaded only once. Everyone connected to the caching server (also called a proxy server) can view the same page faster.

Just as you'd find it very slow to go to the bank or an ATM for cash every time you needed to buy a pack of gum, cable modem services would also slow down if all content were pulled directly from the Internet. By storing popular content on caching servers located between the cable modem users and the Internet, traffic to and from the Internet is reduced, making cable modem service faster.

The speeds of cable modems compare favorably with that of DSL, and cable modems are available in many more markets than DSL at present.

Getting the Freshest "Cache"

Most cable ISPs use caching servers as just described, but one possible disadvantage of caching servers is how they handle constantly changing content. If you notice that a page that provides real-time data isn't up to date, use the Refresh button on your Web browser to request a fresh copy. The caching server will generally pass this request back to the Internet, fetching the latest page for you and other viewers at your ISP.

One additional benefit of caching servers (also called proxy servers) is that they make it harder for outside intruders to hack your system. Because a proxy server sits between you and the Internet, a hacker looking for IP addresses to attack will see the caching/proxy server's address, not your computer's own IP address.

Cool—Where Can I Get Cable Modem Service?

Getting cable modem service usually is as easy as contacting your local cable TV provider to see whether the service is available in your area and then ordering the service.

It's important to realize that your local cable operator isn't the actual ISP in most cases. Instead, a small number of regional and national cable ISPs have been created to bring you the Internet through cable. Your choice of cable ISP is conditioned by the company from which you get your cable TV/cable modem service. If your city has only one cable provider, you have no choice. However, if your city has two or more cable providers, you might have a choice *if* you don't already have cable TV service.

Two of the biggest cable ISPs are @Home (founded by TCI, Cox Communications, Comcast, and others) and RoadRunner (created by Time Warner and MediaOne).

These two ISPs have exclusive agreements with cable TV companies serving 80% of U.S. households. Chances are you'll probably get your cable modem service from one or the other.

Other major cable modem providers include High-Speed Access Corporation and ISP Channel. Some cable TV providers also have their own ISPs.

Taste Before You Buy In to Cable Modem Service

You can learn a lot about the major cable modem ISPs, including how they configure your computer to work with their systems, what they require, and what level of tech support they provide, by visiting their Web sites.

@home's Web site is `www.@home.com`

RoadRunner's Web site is `www.rr.com/rdrun/`

Your Friendly Local Monopoly?

If you have only one cable TV company in town, be sure to get referrals before you jump into a cable modem deal. If a cable TV company is having a hard time keeping the Discovery Channel on the air, how good a job will they do at keeping your Internet connection working?

If your neighborhood will be getting DSL or low-cost fixed-base wireless service in the near future, look for a short-term contract or no contract at all to keep your options open.

A Fistful of Digital Dollars—How Much for Cable Modem Service?

Just as with DSL service, but unlike dial-up Internet service, the price you pay for cable modem service usually includes both the service and the bundled hardware you need to access the service. Typical residential cable modem service costs around $30–$40 per month, plus lease fees of about $5–$10 per month for the cable modem hardware.

This pricing model is similar to how cable TV is priced; you pay for the service plus lease the set-top box and other hardware. Typically, you'll also pay for initial installation, although some providers can run specials to waive or reduce the cost of installation at certain times.

Because cable modems run over the same cable as cable TV, providers often offer discounts if you subscribe to both cable modem and cable TV service. Further savings are possible if you can also get telephone service from the same vendor.

Lease or Buy Your Cable Modem?

One issue you'll confront if you decide to order cable modem service is what to do about getting a cable modem. Depending on your cable ISP, you'll have one of the following choices:

➤ Lease the cable modem for around $5 to $10 a month

➤ Buy the cable modem

At first glance, leasing a cable modem might seem like a throwback to the way that telephone service worked during the AT&T monopoly era. Then you paid month after month to lease an ancient 1937-vintage dial telephone (my grandmother actually had one of these until she died in 1998!), but you never owned it. Why not just buy the cable modem outright?

Why Cable Modem Leasing Can Make Sense

The problem with comparing cable modems to telephones is that telephones are

➤ Simple devices

➤ Standardized

Cable modems are neither. Many cable ISPs don't offer the option to buy the cable modem because their cable modems simply won't work with other cable systems' Internet options. Many different cable modem manufacturers exist, and unlike dial-up analog modems, they're often not interchangeable with each other.

DOCSIS Has the Prescription for Incompatible Cable Modems

There is a move toward standardization in cable modems. The newest cable modems are built to meet a standard called *DOCSIS* (the *Data Over Cable Service Interface Specification*), allowing cable modems from different manufacturers to be used in a DOCSIS-compatible cable system. This allows cable ISPs to switch cable modem vendors and models without needing to re-equip their systems. Because DOCSIS-certified cable modems can be used on a variety of cable systems, they are slowly becoming available for purchase.

However, even if your cable ISP gives you the option to slap your VISA card on the counter of your favorite electronics or computer superstore instead of paying bit-by-bit for your cable modem, think twice.

Sticker Shock and Scapegoats

If you've been lulled by the ultra-low prices for analog modems and dual-speed Ethernet network cards (you can buy both for less than $50 in some cases!), you're in no condition for the sticker shock that buying a DOCSIS-certified cable modem will induce—if you can find one.

After you track down a modem, expect to pay between $250–$300 for it, as shown in Figure 6.6.

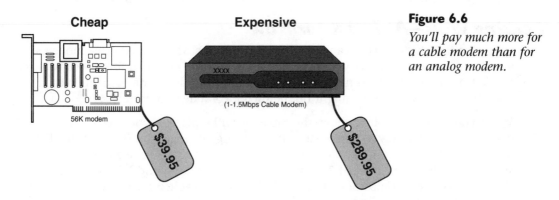

Cheap   **Expensive**

56K modem

(1-1.5Mbps Cable Modem)

$39.95

$289.95

Figure 6.6

You'll pay much more for a cable modem than for an analog modem.

Don't be surprised if, at the first sign of trouble, your cable modem operator points its finger at the alien modem you brought into the mix. Because every cable system has its own peculiarities, sometimes the cable operator might be correct to blame your cable modem.

Are Cable Modems Worth Buying?

If a new cable modem costs $300, and you can lease one for $10 a month, you'd need to keep your current service for at least 30 months (two and a half years!) or longer to make buying a cable modem pay off, compared to leasing it. And, this assumes that you have no problems with your cable modem. If the cable ISP has to send a service person to your home or office because the cable modem has a problem—and it's your cable modem, not theirs—guess who gets the bill?

Do the Math Before You Buy or Lease

Car leasing, as most car buyers learn after they lease a car, is often good only for the dealer. But with the high initial hardware cost of a cable modem versus the low lease price, leasing a cable modem is really good for you in most cases, especially if the cable modem isn't DOCSIS compliant.

Leasing Wins—At Least for Now

Given the fact that so many cable ISPs aren't using DOCSIS-certified cable modems yet, the high prices you'll pay for cable modems, and the potential for service issues, I think it still makes sense to pay a few dollars a month to lease the modem. Even if you can find a deal today, it might not be such a good deal tomorrow.

When you lease the cable modem, the cable ISP will replace it when technology changes; when you buy it, you're stuck if technology changes. If I'd buried the dial-up modems I've owned instead of just throwing them out, I'd have a row of tombstones in my backyard marked 2400bps, 14.4Kbps, 33.6Kbps, and X2 56Kbps. But, the most expensive tombstone of all would be marked cable modem. Lease it—don't buy it.

The Least You Need to Know

➤ Cable modem service is widespread.

➤ Cable modems are much faster than analog modems.

➤ Because cable modems are "always on" and transfer data so quickly, you are more vulnerable to hack attacks than with slower dial-up analog modems.

➤ Cable modems can provide you with fast service today.

➤ You're better off leasing, rather than buying, your cable modem hardware.

Chapter 7

Understanding DirecPC

In This Chapter

➤ Learn how DirecPC works.

➤ Choose the right DirecPC plan for you.

➤ Find out what kind of performance you can expect with DirecPC.

➤ Learn what you can do if you already have DirecTV or want both DirecPC and DirecTV.

➤ Find out what you'll pay for DirecTV.

If you live too far out in the country for cable TV, you're also way too far out for DSL to help you out. If you're tired of watching your analog modem sweat and strain as you download an MP3 file or a software patch, what can you do? Take a look at the southern sky. If you can see the sky, you can look up—way up—for a possible solution. DirecPC, the high-speed cousin of the popular DirecTV mini-dish satellite TV system, might fit the bill.

DirecPC isn't for everyone: As of this writing, it's a one-way system that still asks your existing modem to call up the Internet, and installing the dish can be a royal pain. However, if you're beyond the reach of wired solutions, it's worth a closer look.

From a Satellite to Your Desk

Like many other high-speed Internet services covered in this book, DirecPC is an off-shoot of a popular TV transmission medium, in this case, Hughes Network Systems' DirecTV. Like DirecTV, DirecPC receives data from a satellite orbiting the earth. DirecPC is the leading satellite-based Internet service on (and off!) earth.

Because DirecPC is satellite-based, you can get high-speed Internet service, even if you live beyond the suburban sprawl that marks the outer limits of wired high-speed services such as cable modems and DSL, or even beyond the 35-mile radius of fixed wireless Internet services.

Tech Note

Screwdriver or No Screwdriver—Your Choice!

DirecPC's satellite modems fit into either a PCI expansion slot inside your computer or connect to the USB port on most 1998 and newer computers. For more details on installation, see Chapter 13, "Getting DirecPC."

Tech Note

Big and Bigger Pipes

DirecPC's network operations center's T-3 connections to the Internet are about 30 times faster than the T-1 connections (1.5Mbps) used by some small ISPs. For more information about T-3 versus T-1 connections, see Chapter 2, "Dial-Up Modems and Internet Slowdowns."

How DirecPC Connects to Your Computer

DirecPC connects to your computer in one of two ways. It uses your choice of two types of proprietary devices called satellite modems to connect to the DirecPC satellite dish mounted outside your home.

You still need to use your existing analog modem with DirecPC. When you start a DirecPC session, your analog modem must dial the ISP you're using with DirecPC, and the analog modem is used to send page requests from your DirecPC-equipped system.

Suppose you want to see your favorite magazine's home page. You type its URL into the address window of your Web browser. When you press the Enter key, DirecPC attaches a special signal, known as the *tunneling code*, to the page request before buzzing it over the telephone system to the ISP. That tunneling code says "Hey, I really want you to send this request to the DirecPC network operations center!"

The routers at the ISP (which can also be handling ordinary 100% dial-up traffic) nod obediently and whistle for a router. "Hey, router—special deal on this one!" and send the page request to DirecPC's network operations center rather than straight to the site you entered.

The network operations center uses multiple high-speed T-3 lines (45Mbps speeds) to send your page request to the servers at your requested Web site. The same big pipes receive the page, and the network operations center (NOC) then blasts the information up to the DirecPC satellite, which sends it down to your dish and on to your computer.

Thus, DirecPC is a one-way system: While uploads (like email and page requests) must use your poky ol' analog modem, downloads "pick up speed" as they dive earthward from the DirecPC satellite to your computer. See Figure 7.1 for an overview of the entire process.

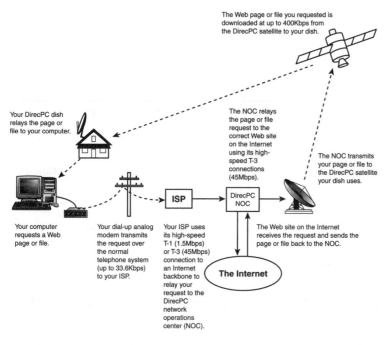

The Web page or file you requested is downloaded at up to 400Kbps from the DirecPC satellite to your dish.

Figure 7.1

How DirecPC reroutes page requests through its high-speed satellite service for downloading.

Your DirecPC dish relays the page or file to your computer.

The NOC relays the page or file request to the correct Web site on the Internet using its high-speed T-3 connections (45Mbps).

The NOC transmits your page or file to the DirecPC satellite your dish uses.

ISP

DirecPC NOC

Your computer requests a Web page or file.

Your dial-up analog modem transmits the request over the normal telephone system (up to 33.6Kbps) to your ISP.

Your ISP uses its high-speed T-1 (1.5Mbps) or T-3 (45Mbps) connection to an Internet backbone to relay your request to the DirecPC network operations center (NOC).

The Web site on the Internet receives the request and sends the page or file back to the NOC.

The Internet

Tech Note

THAT WAY ▶

How Fast Is My "56Kbps" Modem with DirecPC?

Because 56Kbps modems run at speeds above 33.6Kbps only for downloads, and DirecPC normally uses your modem only for uploading, having a 56Kbps modem doesn't matter much unless you decide to bypass the DirecPC dish (known as terrestrial mode) for special needs such as Internet gaming. Your existing 33.6Kbps modem will work just as well as a V.90 56Kbps modem.

How Much DirecPC Do You Need?

One criticism of DirecPC over the years has been the relatively high cost per hour of the service, especially when compared to the "all-you-can-eat" service available with DSL, cable modems, and some fixed wireless Internet services. The latest DirecPC service plans make DirecPC directly comparable to DSL and cable modems in cost, and cheaper than some fixed wireless Internet services.

Don't Get Bitten by Hidden Long Distance Charges!

Before you buy DirecPC, you must make sure that you can use an ISP with a local phone number. You don't need to use DirecPC's own ISP; any ISP can work, but if you must make a long-distance call to connect, you will rack up long distance charges aplenty.

You can keep your current ISP if the dial-up number is local, but if not, start looking. When DirecPC goes to a two-way system, this will no longer matter, but until then, make sure your call is local!

"All-You-Can-Eat" or "Diet" Internet with Your Choice of Plans

The Family Surfer Unlimited Plan now provides unlimited hours of Web surfing. For limited uses, you can still get an Executive Surfer plan that provides 25 hours of access per month. These residential plans are designed for one computer per hookup, but instructions for configuring Windows 98's Internet Connection sharing are available at the SelfHelp portion of the DirecPC Web site.

This Just In!

For the latest plans and other DirecPC news, be sure to check the DirecPC Web site: www.direcpc.com

Give Your Modem a Break with Turbo Newsgroups and Turbo Webcasts

Because the early versions of DirecPC were all time-limited per month and the service continues to require an analog modem for page requests, DirecPC offers two ways to receive data automatically without tying up your phone line or counting against a time-limited plan:

➤ Turbo Webcasts—DirecPC's Turbo Webcast feature lets you choose from more than two dozen popular news, entertainment, education, and technology sites that can be delivered automatically to your computer without clicking a mouse or typing a URL.

➤ Turbo Newsgroups—You can subscribe to your choice of thousands of newsgroups and have their latest postings downloaded to your computer with Turbo Newsgroups. Configuration options enable you to select how much disk space to use, how long to keep articles, and whether to use password protection for your newsgroup configuration.

Even if you select the Family Surfer Unlimited plan with its unlimited access, you might find it useful to have your favorite Web sites or newsgroups waiting for you when you turn to your computer after breakfast.

Turbo Webcasts and Turbo Newsgroups work in a manner similar to that shown in Figure 7.1. The major difference is that the pages are delivered automatically to your computer rather than by clicking on each Web site or newsgroup manually. You can set up when to receive updated information, and both Turbo Webcast and Turbo Newsgroup content is stored on your computer's hard disk in your browser's cache (its temporary on-disk storage area).

Both of these services make DirecPC much more appealing for users looking for high-speed Internet connections as a way to keep on top of news and information sources.

Email Notification Any Time with Email Alert

The latest addition to the DirecPC automation features is Email Alert. Like the Turbo Newscast and Turbo Webcast features, Email Alert takes advantage of the "always on" download channel to inform you of email you've received. This works only for email sent to `mail.direcpc.com`.

Although you'll still need to dial in to retrieve your email, the ability to receive alerts online makes it easier to keep DirecPC and your phone line coexisting happily.

How Fast Is DirecPC?

Like other one-way systems, DirecPC emphasizes its download speed, a respectable 400Kbps maximum, which is about three times as fast as ISDN and close to the performance of some of the lower-cost DSL plans on the market. You'll see every bit of this speed when you use DirecPC to download large files, such as MP3s or the latest Microsoft Office service pack. Keep in mind, though, that this speed is not guaranteed. Various factors, including Internet congestion and the controversial DirecPC Fair Access Plan, can cause slowdowns.

Web Surfing: A Mix of Speedy and Slow

Because page requests and emails go through your analog modem, you won't see any benefits at all when you send information. Web surfing is a combination of page requests (uploads) and page elements received (downloads), so you'll see overall performance increase substantially over your old analog modem connection, but not quite as much as with a high-speed, two-way connection.

Game Players See No Speedups with DirecPC

If you are among the growing ranks of Internet game players, DirecPC's download speed won't do you any good at all. Because network gaming must transmit both your moves (upload) and your opponents' responses (download), the indirect way in which DirecPC handles uploads is a major delaying factor. Game responsiveness is measured in latency, which is more popularly known as ping rates.

Tech Note

THAT WAY ▶

Latency, Bandwidth, and Why You Just Got Killed in a Death Match

Latency is the amount of time it takes for a signal to be transmitted from your computer and return to you. It is also referred to as *ping rate* because you can use a program included with Windows called Ping to see the number of milliseconds (thousandths of a second) it takes to send and receive a signal from a computer you specify.

Bandwidth refers to the speed of data transmission in bits per second (bps). DirecPC has high maximum bandwidth (up to 400Kbps), but it's not a good gaming platform because the indirect route it uses to send information (modem to DirecPC NOC to satellite to you) adds a tremendous amount of latency to your connection. Even though the speed of data transfer from the satellite to your computer is relatively high at up to 400Kbps, the time it takes to get the request to the satellite is why you'll be blown away whenever you play shoot–em-ups online with DirecPC.

DirecPC has typical ping rates between 400–600ms. This compares to ping rates as low as 30ms for gamers connected through cable modems or DSL lines. And any gamer can tell you, the lower the ping rate, the more likely you are to survive to the next round.

Can you make DirecPC faster for gaming? Only by bypassing it. You can set some programs to run in what DirecPC calls *terrestrial mode*, which sends and receives data through your modem and bypasses the dish entirely. In short, DirecPC is far from the online gamer's dream because the only way to get decent ping rates is to bypass the dish and its high-speed (but terrible ping rate) downloads!

Tech Note

THAT WAY

Distance Matters, Even for Satellites

When I was a kid in the early 1960s, Telstar, the world's first communication satellite, was launched. It wasn't very practical because it orbited around the Earth so quickly that it could send and receive TV transmissions for a relatively short time each orbit.

DirecPC and other satellite communications services are different: They use a *geosynchronous* orbit (first suggested by science-fiction writer Arthur C. Clarke in 1945, by the way!) at a distance of 22,236 miles (35,785 kilometers) above the Earth's equator. This distance makes the satellite appear stationary relative to the Earth's surface. Unfortunately, this distance also makes for a built-in latency problem because even speed-of-light transmissions between the Earth and the satellite and back again take about 240ms in each direction (for a total of 480ms).

Therefore, even a high-speed two-way version of DirecPC won't be much faster for gaming as long as the distance to the satellite is more than 22,000 miles. What could change things? Boeing and Hughes (Hughes is the parent company of DirecPC) have proposed a Low Earth Orbiting (LEO) satellite system called Teledesic that will be only 1,400 kilometers (about 854 miles) above the Earth's surface. This proposed service would offer 64Mbsec downloads and 2Mbps uploads and have a lot lower latency to boot. If Teledesic appears, it will be a far better game platform than DirecPC is now.

Having Your PC and TV Too with DirecDuo

If you're already a DirecTV user or are looking for a TV/PC solution, DirecPC's sibling, DirecDuo, is designed for you. DirecDuo uses a special dish designed to work with both services to receive both satellite TV and satellite Internet service if you order both services.

You can also order a "TV-ready" version of DirecPC which comes with the 23-inch DirecDuo dish that allows you to add DirecTV in the future.

DirecDuo can be confusing because it really refers to just the special dish designed for both TV and Satellite Internet use; it isn't a special version of DirecPC or DirecTV. If you buy a DirecDuo dish, you still need to buy the DirecPC and DirecTV hardware and services you want to use with it.

The only real difference between using a DirecDuo dish and a DirecTV and DirecPC dish together is that you just work with a single dish rather than with two separate dishes. The DirecDuo dish uses separate connections for each service.

Where Can I Get DirecPC?

DirecPC is available from a wide variety of online and retail vendors. You can use the searchable database online at DirecPC's Web site to look up both direct and retail dealers. You can specify dealers by ZIP code and by maximum distance. Because dealers have live DirecPC connections set up in their showrooms, going to a retail dealer is a good way to "try before you buy" the system.

When you enter your ZIP code and specify the number of dealers you want, you'll get their street addresses, phone numbers, and approximate distance, making it easy to go to the nearest dealer.

Coming Soon: DirecPC-Powered Broadband from Third Parties

DirecPC is becoming the partner of several broadband providers, meaning that in the future you will have a variety of service plans and prices from which to choose.

Starting in late 2000, DirecPC also will be available from Pegasus Communications Corporation under the name Pegasus Broadband powered by DirecPC. A similar service will be offered by Juno, Juno Express powered by DirecPC, in the same timeframe. Both these agreements will also include DirecPC's future two-way pure satellite version when it becomes available by early 2001. Other partnerships might also be on the horizon. Both the Juno and Pegasus versions of DirecPC are expected to use the USB satellite modem only.

You Won't Always Need Your Modem: The Coming Two-Way Service

By the time you read this, you might see an even faster DirecPC than the current version. Hughes Network Systems has announced that early in 2001 DirecPC will become a two-way system, allowing uploads at 128–256Kbps through a new antenna to their satellites, and faster downloads too: up to 40Mbps with 400Kbps for each user on a multiuser system. Hardware upgrades will be available for current one-way DirecPC users to enable them to use the new two-way system.

How Much Is DirecPC?

As with many of the high-speed Internet choices on the market, three factors are involved in figuring the price of DirecPC:

➤ Hardware

➤ Installation

➤ Monthly Service

Pricing the Hardware

You can buy the one-way DirecPC or DirecDuo system in kit form or in pieces; kits are usually less expensive.

You'll pay around $225 for the DirecPC kit in either its USB or PCI format. These kits include the DirecPC satellite dish, the USB or PCI satellite modem, and the DirecPC software. During the installation process, covered in Chapter 13, "Getting DirecPC," you can select the service you want.

Tech Note

THAT WAY

Dish or Antenna? Both!

Some people refer to the DirecPC or DirecDuo satellite dish as an antenna. Although this is technically not quite correct, I recommend that you just smile and nod when you hear this misuse. It's a dish, all right, but it picks up signals like an antenna.

Planning on TV and the Internet? Spend around $250 and get the DirecDuo kit, which replaces the DirecPC dish, which can't receive DirecTV services, with a slightly larger model that can handle any network, Internet, or broadcast. Again, as with the DirecPC kits, choose from the USB or PCI versions.

Keep in mind that you'll need Windows 98 or newer to use the USB versions of DirecPC.

Piecemeal Pricing on DirecPC/DirecDuo Components

The DirecPC dish sells for a bit under $100, and the DirecDuo version sells for a bit under $130. You'll pay a lot less for the USB version of the satellite modem ($120) than for the internal PCI version (around $200), and, as you'll see in Chapter 13, the USB version is also less painful to install.

DirecPC Installation

Can you install DirecPC yourself? Sure, if you don't mind climbing on the roof, trying to figure out which way south is, and putting a couple of holes in your inside and outside walls for the DirecPC cable between the dish and the satellite modem.

Before you reach for the toolbox (and turn to Chapter 13), take a few moments to look at the online installation guide.

Hang On...Help Is On the Way

If you find that your eyes are starting to glaze over while reviewing the online installation manual, ask your retailer about installation, or call 1-800-DIRECPC for installers in your area. You'll also find the DirecPC self-help installation guide at

```
http://www.direcpc.com/selfhelp/
```

Dish installation and cable running into your home cost around $250, but you'll want to check with your DirecPC installer for actual prices. Some retailers or installers will also install the computer hardware and configure the system for an additional fee.

Shelling Out for DirecPC

DirecPC offers several service plans, including a plan for low-volume (25 hours or less) users that costs about $30 per month (including DirecPC's own ISP) and an unlimited-hours plan that runs about $50 per month (including DirecPC's own ISP). If you prefer your own ISP, you'll save about 10 bucks a month in DirecPC charges, but you'll need to choose your own ISP and pay their charges separately.

DirecPC periodically changes their pricing and service plans, so get the latest information at their Web site: www.direcpc.com.

Hidden Costs Ahead—Hold On To Your Wallet!

Ironically, considering that rural customers beyond the reach of cable modem or DSL service are among the prime targets of DirecPC, the access numbers offered by DirecPC's own ISP are somewhat lacking in their coverage, often serving only mid-size to large cities. In my area code, 812, for example, only three local access numbers are available for approximately one-third of the state of Indiana!

Watch Your Wallet with Limited-Hours Plans

DirecPC typically charges about $2/hour (with their own ISP) or $1/hour (if you use a different ISP) for online time that exceeds the limits of their limited-hours plans. DirecPC's Executive Surfer plan, for example, limits you to 25 hours a month, or about 50 minutes per day on average online. If you spend just 10 hours over that time, you'd pay the equivalent of the extra cost needed to upgrade to an unlimited service plan.

Make sure you use the DirecPC usage check feature if you choose a limited-hours plan. You'll find it located at

```
http://utilities.direcpc.com/db2/
```

or click on the Check Your Usage link on the DirecPC Owner's Club home page:

```
http://www.direcpc.com/consumer/owners/index.html
```

What can you do if DirecPC's ISP access numbers would require you to pony up long-distance telephone fees? Stick with your current dial-up ISP or another ISP that offers you a local call for connection, and pay two bills.

Typical dial-up ISPs run around $15–$22 a month, so you'd wind up paying about $10 more a month for the combination of DirecPC plus your own ISP, compared to the DirecPC/ISP bundles listed previously.

Just How Local Is Local?

Before you decide to use DirecPC's own bundled ISP, make sure that at least one of the local access numbers for your area code is really a local call. DirecPC's local access number lookup system is available at `http://utilities.direcpc.com/pops/findpop.cfm`

119

Free ISPs

If you have a high tolerance for onscreen ads or nosy surveys, check out the many free Internet services. Some of the leaders in free Internet service include

➤ AltaVista Free Access—Download the client at

    http://www.zdnet.com/downloads/altavista/

➤ StartFree/Tritium Network—Covers about half the 50 United States. More information is available at

    http://tritium.net/

➤ Freel Network—More information is available at

    http://www.freei.com/

Getting Started—The Bottom Line

If you install the DirecPC system yourself, your first-month cost will run around $300 if you choose an unlimited access plan and use DirecPC's own ISP. Your first-month cost jumps to $550 or more if you decide to spring for professional installation.

Changes Ahead for DirecPC

As you learned earlier, Hughes has big plans for DirecPC: faster, two-way service. Also, you'll soon be able to buy DirecPC service in conjunction with Internet providers such as Juno and Pegasus.

DirecPC has already come a long way in making its service plans easier to understand and providing more bytes for the dollar. When two-way service is here, your worries about telephone number access won't matter any more.

Hot Off the Press!

Keep on top of the latest DirecPC news by checking their Web site often:

    www.direcpc.com

Love to read press releases about DirecPC and DirecTV? You'll find them at Hughes Network Services' Web site:

    www.hns.com

The Least You Need to Know

➤ DirecPC provides high-speed Internet access through satellite transmitters.

➤ You can download data at up to 400Kbps, but uploads of data and page requests must be sent through your conventional analog modem.

➤ DirecPC can optionally use the same dish as DirecTV; this combined service is called DirecDuo.

➤ You can choose your own ISP to provide local dial-up access if DirecPC's own ISP doesn't cover your area.

➤ The best value is the unlimited access plan, which provides unlimited access per month for a flat rate.

Chapter 8

Look Ma, No Wires!—Wireless Internet

In This Chapter

➤ How fixed wireless Internet access works

➤ How to find a fixed wireless Internet provider

➤ What you might expect to pay for the service

If you live beyond the reach of DSL and cable modem service, you still might be able to use a broadband Internet service. The best-known no-cable option is DirecPC, as discussed in Chapter 7, "Understanding DirecPC." However, a faster and friendlier broadband option that uses microwave transmissions might be available in your area. This chapter discusses how to select and order fixed broadband wireless Internet services.

"I'll Have Fast Internet—Hold the Wires"

If you live in a major (or not so major) city or suburb, chances are you're enjoying the delightful option of pitting the major high-speed Internet services against each other. Will you choose the pricey veteran ISDN or pass it up for its younger, faster telco rival, DSL? Will you watch techtv and download from ZDNet at the same time with a cable modem? Decisions, decisions....

However, most of you who turned to this chapter first might not be so lucky. Instead of a fast-food restaurant sign towering over the next corner, you have a silo or a grain elevator. A "short trip" into town might take you a half an hour or longer. You love country life, but many of the high-speed Internet providers could care less about you.

Fortunately, you still have choices: High-speed wireless Internet will work for some of you, and DirecPC will work for just about everyone else. One of these chapters should contain the right high-speed choice for you.

How (Fast!) Wireless Internet Works

There are two distinctly different forms of wireless Internet. We're not talking about the slow-speed wireless "mini-Internet" you can access through your Palm organizer or digital phone. Instead, we're talking about fixed broadband wireless technology, which provides Internet access to your immobile desktop system—a medium that is also used to carry TV signals. In fact, fixed wireless Internet, as you'll see in detail in this chapter, is a lot like cable modem service—but without the cable. It is often referred to as *wireless cable*.

It Uses a Dish—But, Hold the Satellite

At first glance, you might mistake a fixed wireless Internet connection on your neighbor's house for another dish-based system, DirecPC (see Chapter 9, "Decisions, Decisions: What's the Best Choice for Me?").

What are the differences?

Whereas DirecPC receives its signal from a satellite, fixed wireless Internet receives its signal from a transmission tower no more than 35 miles away. Both must be aligned in direct line of sight with the originating signal. However, fixed wireless Internet can be used in situations where line-of-sight would prevent the use of a satellite-based system because of the differences in line-of-sight between satellites and ground-based antennas.

Increasing numbers of fixed wireless Internet providers support two-way service, using the connection to both receive and send signals, while DirecPC is still strictly a one-way system for now.

Wireless Internet services typically use Multichannel Multipoint Distribution Service (MMDS) technology, which is a series of frequencies running at 2.1 and 2.5 to 2.7 GHz (Gigahertz). These frequencies are suitable for both broadband Internet and cable TV channels, so most wireless Internet providers are also wireless TV providers.

MMDS technology uses a tower to transmit MMDS signals up to 35 miles in all directions to a wireless broadband router (WBR) and head-end equipment that converts the incoming (and outgoing, in some cases) data into the appropriate formats.

When you request a page or send an email, that upload can take two very divergent paths depending on the type of fixed wireless Internet service you have. With a one-way service, you must use a dial-up connection to transmit your page requests, just as with DirecPC or one-way cable modem service. After your wireless Internet service provider receives the page, the page is downloaded through the microwave tower that transmits signals to your receiving dish.

Tech Note

What's in a Name?

The wireless broadband router resembles a cable modem and connects to your computer in a similar fashion. Some people refer to it as a wireless cable modem, although this isn't really accurate.

Tech Note

Break Out Your Wallet...

Many WBRs are designed with a built-in analog modem for use in one-way service, allowing you to remove your internal analog modem or disconnect your external analog modem. This is one of the reasons why WBRs are more expensive than cable modems.

Tech Note

Two-Way Service

Two-way services are able to transmit page requests and email from your system as well as receive pages and downloads coming to your system. Remarkably, the antenna necessary for either type of service is much smaller than a satellite dish.

Don't Count on Getting Two-Way Service

Don't assume that you can get two-way wireless service just because your friend can. Services that have only one transmission and reception point can offer two-way service for only a portion of their total service area because the antennas used at the base to receive signals might not cover as wide an area as the transmitting antennas.

The Connection in Your Home

Your computer needs a standard 10BASE-T (twisted-pair cable) Ethernet card to connect with the wireless broadband router (WBR) provided by the wireless cable Internet provider. The "cable" in "wireless cable" is a short one, running to the roof (or sometimes up a mast atop your roof) to a small square, rectangular, or oval antenna. The antenna acts as a transceiver, receiving signals from the transmitter and sending signals back to the transmitter (if you have two-way service). A typical setup for a single computer using two-way service resembles the one shown in Figure 8.1.

Figure 8.1

A wireless cable Internet connection substitutes a transceiver dish for the fiber-optic cable connection used with cable modems. But inside your house, it's just like a cable modem setup.

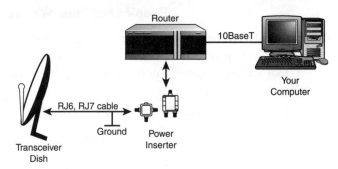

Up on the Roof

Outside your home or office, your provider might use a wide range of transceivers. Wireless cable transceivers come in a variety of sizes and shapes. Your vendor will provide this equipment as part of your installation.

The height and orientation of the transceiver (or transmitter for one-way service) are critical because the transceiver/receiver antenna must be in direct line of sight (LOS) with the provider's tower, which can be as far as 35 miles away.

Tech Note

Go on a Bender

If you can be content with one-way broadband service, you might qualify for broadband wireless service even if the provider can't establish a direct line of sight with the transmitter. Some providers will install special wireless reflectors called *benders* on a nearby object that does have line of sight with the base's transmitter. The bender will reflect wireless signals to your receiver.

Because benders cannot reflect low-power signals back to the base, you will need to use a dial-up connection for page requests, email, and uploads.

Far, Far Away at the Tower...

At the wireless cable operator's end, a tall tower with multiple antennas on all sides is used to send signals to the customer (and receive signals from your transceiver if two-way service is offered). To achieve the 35-mile maximum range provided by typical wireless cable service, these towers must be positioned on high ground, frequently a tall building or mountain, and the tower's site must be carefully chosen to provide maximum population coverage. Figure 8.2 shows the coverage area map for Ohio Valley Wireless, a wireless cable Internet/TV provider in southwestern Indiana. The star in the center indicates the location of the tower.

If you live on the edge of the coverage area, you might not be able to use the service, or a tall mast might be necessary to elevate the receiver or transceiver to receive an acceptable signal. For example, in Figure 8.2 you can see that the small cities of Mt. Vernon and Jasper are on the edge of the coverage area. Wireless access in these areas might not be available without using a tall mast to elevate the receiver.

Tech Note

Why Being on the Map Don't Guarantee Service Availability

Coverage maps like the one in Figure 8.2 can be highly misleading, especially if the provider has only a single tower installation. Do not assume you can get service until a site survey is completed because of blind spots caused by terrain or man-made obstructions such as buildings. And you might be eligible for only one-way service.

Figure 8.2

To achieve maximum coverage of the estimated 200,000+ population found in Evansville, Newburgh, Henderson, and Owensboro, the signal tower must be placed east of Evansville, the largest (125,000+) city in the coverage area.

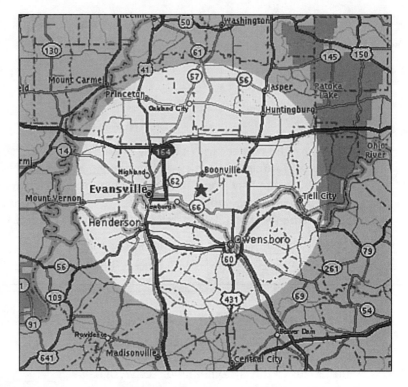

From Your Home to the Internet

The numbers in the following steps correspond to numbers in Figure 8.3.

1. After you send a page request from your computer to the wireless broadband router (wireless modem), it is relayed to your wireless transceiver.

2. When the request is received by the wireless provider's receiving antenna it is converted into computer form by the down-converter.

3. The signal is sent to an upstream router, which relays the request to the caching Web servers.

4. The caching Web servers check for an up-to-date copy of the page already stored there.

5. If an updated copy of the page exists on the caching Web server, the page is relayed to the transmitter, which sends the page back to the transceiver and onto your computer.

6. If the page is not already stored in the caching Web servers, the Web servers send the page request to the gateway router.

7. The gateway router passes the request to the ISP.

8. The request is then passed to the Internet.

After the page is retrieved from the Internet, it is relayed to the transmitter and onto your computer through the transceiver. See Figure 8.3 for a diagram of the entire process.

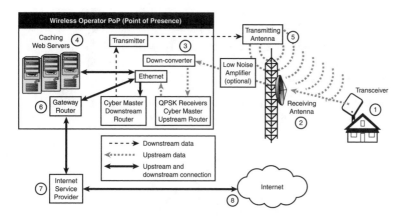

Figure 8.3

How a typical two-way wireless Internet service works. In built-up urban or hilly areas, the main tower can be supplemented by signal booster towers to cover areas that can't be in direct line of sight of the main tower.

Types of Wireless Internet Services

Originally, wireless Internet services such as cable modems were one-way; the wireless antenna provided speedy downloads, but a poky telephone modem was required for uploads, outbound email, and other transmitted traffic. This was both inconvenient and expensive because rural users sometimes needed to call a long-distance number with their modems to use the Internet.

In 1998, new regulations allowed wireless cable to be a two-way system. Increasingly, wireless cable Internet connections are now two-way, using the dish as both receiver and transmitter (hence the name *transceiver*).

Keep in mind, though, that a given wireless broadband provider can provide both one-way and two-way service in a given market. One-way service can work at greater distances from the transmitter than those distances available with two-way service.

The Nitty Gritty...

If you want to learn more of the technical background behind wireless cable, go to

    http://wcai.com/wireless_cable.htm

This page is on the Wireless Cable Association's Web site.

129

How Fast Is Fixed Wireless Internet?

Like DSL, but unlike cable modems, fixed wireless Internet is available in a variety of speeds. Offerings can vary by service provider, but I found the following speeds offered in my survey of wireless providers.

A provider in my area, Ohio Valley Wireless, offers both one-way (Telco return) and two-way fixed wireless services featuring the following speeds for both one-way and two-way services:

➤ 128Kbps

➤ 512Kbps

➤ T1 (1.5Mbps)

Maximum upload speeds for the two-way service are 200Kbps.

Who Can You Call for Fixed Wireless Internet?

Finding a fixed wireless Internet provider can be difficult at present because many of the companies in the business are just launching pilot programs to serve limited markets. If you currently use a fixed wireless hookup for cable TV service, check with your provider. These companies are leaders in pioneering fixed broadband Internet access because they already have the infrastructure in place for supplying at least one-way high-speed Internet service.

You also can find telco spinoffs such as Sprint Wireless providing this service, as a glance at the CableDataComm News Web site's list of providers will reveal.

Get the Scoop on Wireless Providers

For a list of fixed wireless Internet providers, locations, and equipment suppliers, go to

    http://www.cabledatacomnews.com/wireless/cmic12.html

Although this page lacks contact information or Web page links, you should be able to call local directory assistance for companies in your area.

To determine whether you can get fixed wireless service from Sprint Broadband, go to

    http://www.sprintbroadband.com.

Interest in and development of fixed wireless Internet access is growing. One provider, UBNetworks, claims on its Web site (www.ubnetworks.com) that "If you live in just about any major city in the USA, we will be in your area soon."

When you locate a wireless Internet provider, remember that some services have a radius as wide as 35 miles, so small towns and rural areas near the listed cities can often use the service as well.

How Much to Cut the Wire?

Prices on fixed wireless services vary with service type (one-way or two-way), service speed, and provider. Typical rates from a Midwest provider (Ohio Valley Wireless) appear in Table 8.1. Note that just as with cable modems, users who also subscribe to the TV service get a break on both monthly service fees and initial installation.

Table 8.1 Typical Wireless Network Rates

	New Customers		Current Customers	
	Monthly Charge	1-Time Install Charge	Monthly Charge	1-Time Install Charge
1-way 128K speed (telco return)	$49.95	$79.95	$39.95	$39.95
1-way 512K speed (telco return)	$59.95	$79.95	$49.95	$39.95
1-way T1 speed (telco return)	$74.95	$79.95	$64.95	$39.95
2-way 128K speed (wireless return)	$74.95	$149.95	$64.95	$109.95
2-way 512K speed (wireless return)	$84.95	$149.95	$74.95	$109.95
2-way T1 speed (wireless return)	$99.95	$149.95	$89.95	$109.95

Note that installing two-way service almost doubles the installation costs because a transceiver, rather than a less-expensive receiver, must be installed. This vendor limits its customers to 1.5GB per month of data transfers and charges five cents per MB beyond that. The odds of hitting the surcharge are astronomically low if you are primarily a Web surfer, but if you overindulge in big video downloads or guzzle MP3s, you might be in for a financial headache the morning after the bill arrives.

These rates include both antenna and cable modem rental.

Pricing from a West Coast wireless company, ISWest, is aimed exclusively toward a business clientele and offers 600Kbps download and upload speeds as shown here:

Users	Dish Monthly +	ISWest Monthly =	Total Monthly
1–5	$250	*$69.95	$319.95

(Rates for larger numbers of users also are available.)

Sprint Broadband Direct, which is being rolled out in several major U.S. cities after being tested in Phoenix, currently features up to 5Mbps download and up to 1Mbps upload service for $39.95 per month. The normal installation charge is $299.00 (waived at this writing), and equipment charges range from $299 for month-to-month service to just $99 with a two-year commitment.

The Least You Need to Know

➤ Wireless broadband service provides an alternative to cable modem or DSL service for customers who live in rural areas and other locations beyond the reach of wired high–speed Internet service.

➤ Depending on the provider, you might need to use a conventional modem for uploads and page requests; two-way service is available from many providers for an extra cost.

➤ Although pricing is often higher than for services such as DSL and cable modems, performance can be comparable.

EENY, MEENY, MINY, MO--

Chapter 9

Decisions, Decisions: What's the Best Choice for Me?

> ### In This Chapter
>
> ➤ Learn how to choose the best high-speed Internet service for you.
>
> ➤ Choose the service with the best "bang for the buck."
>
> ➤ Find out how well a service is working in your area.

When I first began to use the Internet—with a 28.8Kbps CompuServe connection a few years ago—I had no choices other than which slow-as-molasses online service I would use or which browser. Boy, are you lucky! No matter where you live, you probably have at least one (and often several) high-speed choice from which to pick. No single choice is best for everyone, so in this chapter I provide the tools you need to figure out which choice has the best combination of speed, reliability, and features for your needs.

The High-Speed Contestants

Here are the high-speed contestants in the great High-Speed Internet Road Race, all gunning their engines and looking toward the grand prize (your wallet!):

➤ ISDN

➤ DSL

➤ Cable modems

➤ DirecPC

➤ Fixed wireless

Which of these is the best choice for you? It might seem like a difficult process, but this chapter will show you how to sort through the claims and counterclaims to find that perfect solution for your unique situation.

Choosing What's Available *Today*

First of all, start by eliminating the services that just aren't available in your neck of the woods yet. This simple act can eliminate one or more technologies from many lists, especially if you live in the Midwest or in a smaller city.

Don't Waste Your Time on Services That Aren't Around Yet

Right now, for example, I'd have to cross DSL off my personal list; it won't be available in my area until early 2001. Why is this step so important? If you value your time, making a move toward high-speed service as soon as you can is one of the best things you can do for yourself and your family. If you don't separate the services you can get today from those that will be available someday, you can be doing yourself and your family or business a disservice. What about services that will be available soon? The cutting-room floor where the history of the computer industry is being continually re-edited is littered with the remains of real-soon-now technologies and services that either never made it at all or never became popular enough to make it to your neighborhood. Concentrate on what's ready now.

How can you discover which services are available to you now? Follow the suggestions in previous chapters, or see the quick-reference table on the inside back cover. Remember that most high-speed services are offshoots of cable TV or telephone services, so a call to your cable TV provider or local telco can save you a lot of time and trouble.

Tech Note

Which Broadband Services Have the Biggest Reach?

Right now, it looks like the three choices you'll have in almost any city or suburb will be cable modem, ISDN, and DirecPC. DSL still is very spotty, but third-party DSL providers are stepping in to many markets where the local telco has been slow to offer the service.

Live out beyond the glow of city lights? Look for DirecPC or other satellite-based services or, if you're not too far out of town, fixed wireless.

Is Your Computer Up To It?

Next, make sure your computer meets the minimum standards for the services you are considering (see the installation chapters for details). If you are running a Windows-based computer you bought in 1997 or later, you'll exceed the minimums comfortably. However, if you're looking at an old 486-based or early Pentium computer you've kept around primarily for Web surfing, it won't make the cut with most services. Why? Your old computer probably doesn't have enough RAM, a fast enough CPU, and might even lack a CD-ROM drive. If you've updated your old PC periodically through the years, you might be okay for now. But, if it's still in its factory configuration, forget it—it's just too slow.

Danger Danger

Why Not Upgrade This Old PC?

If you've gradually been upgrading your old computer to meet the minimum standards of your broadband provider, go ahead and use it. But what if you've been putting off upgrades for years? Should you go ahead and upgrade everything now? Nope.

Why not? Suppose you need to upgrade the CPU, RAM, hard drive, and CD-ROM drive to make your aging box fit for high-speed Internet. You could spend between $350–$450 for those components, not counting the cost of labor. Bottom line? You're not far away from an economy PC at many stores that will have a much faster CPU, a newer version of the operating system, and features such as USB ports that can make upgrading easier. If you've waited till now to upgrade this old PC, don't.

What if you're a fearless rebel, disdaining the Windows environment for a Macintosh? Maybe you've secretly replaced the Windows version in your computer with Linux (instead of Folger's Crystals). You might be out of luck; many of these services are aimed squarely at the big market leader: Microsoft. You might be able to get around this problem by installing a small network that can connect your non-MS computer with a Windows-based PC that can act as the gateway to a faster Internet (see Chapter 15, "Share the Wealth: Internet Connection Sharing," for details). With very competent computers available for around $700–$800, adding a second computer isn't nearly as painful as it once was. Use Table 9.1 to help you select the best features for you.

Table 9.1 High-Speed Internet Feature Matrix

Feature Service Type	Requires Analog Modem	Same Speed for Upload & Download	Ping Rate	Works on Notebook Computers	Can Also Support TV Channels	Self-Install Option	Replaces Existing Phone Service	Shared Bandwidth with Other Users
ISDN	No	Yes	Moderate	Yes	No	No	Yes[1]	No
Cable Modem One-Way	Yes[2]	No	Moderate	Yes	Yes[3]	Yes[4]	No	Yes
Cable Modem Two-Way	No	No	Fast	Yes	Yes[3]	No	No	Yes
DSL	No	Varies	Fast	Yes	No	Yes[5]	No	No
Fixed Wireless One-Way	Yes[2]	No	Moderate	Yes	Yes[3]	No	No	Yes
Fixed Wireless Two-Way	No	No	Fast	Yes	Yes[3]	No	No	Yes
DirecPC (current)	Yes	No	Slow	Yes	Yes[6]	Yes	No	Yes
DirecPC (future service)[7]	No	No	Moderate two-way	Yes	Yes	Yes	No	Yes

1 Most telcos recommend retaining the existing analog service as a backup

2 Can use your existing modem, or can use a modem built into the device

3 Requires separate subscription to TV service from provider

4 Option availability varies with cable modem provider; applies only to upgrades of an existing cable TV service to cable TV/cable modem service

5 Option availability varies with provider; applies only if existing telephone line is suitable for DSL and does not need to be replaced

6 Requires DirecDuo dish, DirecTV equipment, and subscription

7 Projected answers; service expected to start in 2001

Which Features Do You Care About Most?

After reviewing Table 9.1, it's time to figure out which of these features will benefit you most—or cause you the most trouble. See Table 9.2 for a feature-benefit analysis.

Table 9.2 A Closer Look at Major Features

Feature	Great Deal Terrible Deal No Big Deal	Why
Two-way service	Great Deal	Bypasses telco, so you don't tie up your telephone line and get faster uploads
One-way service	Terrible Deal	Uses your phone line for uploads, which are very slow; can't use phone while Internet connection is active.
Uses analog modem	Terrible Deal	Required to make one-way connections work, but is very slow and interferes with phone line.
Same speed for upload and download	No Big Deal or Terrible Deal	If you have two-way service, you can upload at speeds beyond 100Kbps, so it's no big deal unless you plan to host a Web server or game server. However, if you're using one-way service, you're stuck at 33.6Kbps or less for uploading, which is a terrible deal.
Ping Rate	Depends	If you live and die for the next online death match, you want an online service with a fast ping rate. But if your idea of an exciting computer game is a few hands of Solitaire, it's no big deal.
Works on Notebook	Great Deal	With more and more of us computers bringing work home, this is a great deal.
Can also support TV channels	Great Deal	If you already have cable TV, you might as well get double duty out of the cable coming into your home.

Table 9.2   CONTINUED

Feature	Great Deal Terrible Deal No Big Deal	Why
Self-Install Option	Depends	How great a deal this is depends on whether you're adept at drilling holes and whether you'd need to pay a lot for installation otherwise. If you're getting a cable modem or DSL, installation is often free, but these services are also relatively easy to self-install. DirecPC is far and away the biggest challenge to the do-it-yourself installer.
Replaces Existing Phone Service	No Big Deal	Because ISDN vendors recommend that you keep your existing phone service, you should count on keeping it around.
Shared Bandwidth with Other Users	Depends	In theory, it's always a better deal to have your own exclusive bandwidth, as with ISDN and DSL (telco-based) services. But, in reality, many shared bandwidth services are still fast enough. Get the details later in the process.

If you're like most people, the most important feature in this entire list is two-way operation. Why? Two-way operation guarantees that your telephone line stays clear while you surf to your heart's content.

How Fast Is the Service with the Features You Need?

The next step in determining the best service for you is to rank the services in terms of speed. Because many variations are available in wireless cable, cable modem, and DSL speeds, Table 9.3 uses representative examples from typical residential providers. Business versions of these services can run faster, but they'll cost you a whole lot more money.

Although download speed is far more important than upload speed for most users, Table 9.3 lists both.

Table 9.3   Broadband Internet Speeds for Upload and Download

Service Type	Typical Download Speeds (Maximum)	Typical Upload Speeds (Maximum)
ISDN	128Kbps	128Kbps
Cable Modem One-Way	512Kbps	33.6Kbps
Cable Modem Two-Way	1.5Mbps	256Kbps
DSL	128Kbps–768Kbps	128Kbps
Fixed Wireless One-Way	128Kbps 512Kbps 1.5Mbps	33.6Kbps
Fixed Wireless Two-Way	128Kbps 512Kbps 1.5Mbps	128Kbps
DirecPC (Current)	400Kbps	33.6Kbps
DirecPC (Future Two-Way Service)	40Mbps	128–256Kbps

Keep in mind that services that share bandwidth with other users can become significantly slower during peak periods.

Full Speed Ahead!

Wondering why any Internet connection seldom (if ever) runs at its maximum speed? MSN Computing Central's bandwidth speed test not only checks your current speed but also provides a concise discussion of what keeps your connection from reaching its top speed:

```
http://computingcentral.msn.com/topics/bandwidth/speedtest50.asp
```

Cable modem and DSL services are often priced similarly to each other for residential use. If you want to know which is really faster, check out this 1999 real-world test in the San Francisco Bay area:

```
http://www.keynote.com/news/announcements/pr051799.html
```

Cable Modem Help's home page lists the results of periodic speed tests of RoadRunner and @Home's cable modem services. See the latest results at

```
http://www.cablemodemhelp.com
```

Calculating the Best "Bang for the Buck"

The next factor you need to consider is which service available to you has the best "bang for the buck"—the lowest cost per Kbps of download speed.

Here's the formula you can use, along with a few sample calculations based on pricing you've seen in earlier chapters:

```
Cost per Kbps = Service Cost per month / Kbps (download speed)
```

Example 1: DSL (various telcos)

```
Service cost per month = $49.95    Speed = 768Kbps

Cost per Kbps (approximately) =  6.5 cents/Kbps
```

Example 2: ISDN service (Ameritech)

```
Service cost per month = $110.00 Speed = 128Kbps

Cost per Kbps (approximately) = 86 cents/Kbps
```

Example 3: Cable modem (various providers)

```
Service cost per month = $49.95 Speed 1.5Mbps (1500Kbps)

Cost per Kbps (approximately) = 3.3 cents/Kbps
```

As you can see from these examples, the cost per Kbps makes great deals and not-so-great deals really stand out.

Tech Note

Watch That Bottom Line!

These examples do not include equipment costs, and you should also factor these in. If you are leasing your equipment, add the rental fee to the monthly service cost. If you must buy your equipment, divide the equipment cost by the number of months you plan to keep the service and add that calculated figure to the monthly service cost.

After you add the appropriate equipment and installation charges, you can calculate the true cost per Kbps. If you learn later in your research that the service runs consistently slower (rarely faster!) than the maximums given, you can use that speed to make your calculations as "real-world" as possible.

If possible, get test results from the broadband service you are considering to use in your calculations. Because conditions vary from city to city, try to get local test figures performed on the same service you are considering. Results are likely to be lower than the maximums listed previously.

You Want Uptime and Reliability

If you live in an urban or suburban area, you're likely to have several choices that meet your requirements for speed, cost per Kbps, and other standards you select. Sometimes, you might even be able to select from more than one vendor offering a specified technology. It doesn't matter how fast a technology is supposed to be if you

➤ Can't get it installed in a reasonable timeframe

➤ Suffer frequent service outages

➤ Wind up with substandard performance

These issues aren't the kinds of factors that high-speed Internet providers are likely to boast about on their Web sites or in their brochures!

You must find out how well (or how badly) a given provider handles these issues. Here's how:

➤ Contact local providers for referrals—It's true that you'll only get the grade-A, 100% satisfied customers that way, but when you talk to them, find out *why* they're satisfied. As this book shows you, getting a reliable high-speed connection is still difficult at times, so ask about problems the vendor overcame, how good their customer service department is, and whether the customer would use that service again.

➤ Get referrals for installation—A high-speed service that can't get installed is useless. DSL in particular is difficult for some vendors to get working in many cases. When you're asking existing customers or friends about their experiences, remember to ask them about the installation process.

➤ See whether the provider or a third party runs an online forum where users can discuss problems and solutions—Newsgroups and industry-specific Web sites are good sources for this type of information. If you see a pattern of broken promises, performance below standard, and persistent problems without solutions, watch out! Keep in mind that the problems might not be with the technology, but with the vendor. Look for Web sites (like DSLReports.com) that aren't afraid to name names, listing the companies that do a great, adequate, or lousy job of providing the specified technology.

➤ Ask your friends—Chances are, you might know friends or business or church acquaintances who have already tried the high-speed technology you're interested in. Don't overlook friends and neighbors' war stories. If you overhear someone having a problem, volunteer to help, or at least listen to his or her tales of woe. The shoulder you let someone cry on could save you a few tears later.

➤ Check the local media—Local papers, TV, and radio often report bad technology news with a local flavor (after all, good news is no news, right?). If a local ISP is crashing and burning, you're likely to hear about it through one of these sources.

➤ Check the contract for specific service guarantees—Who pays if you lose your service? Can you get credit or a pro-rated bill? Is a certain level of speed guaranteed? Know what your vendor has bound itself to do before you sign on the dotted line. Remember, unlike dial-up service, which is easy to walk away from and requires just the modem you already had, you're facing a big commitment (and a big equipment bill!) from many high-speed vendors.

➤ Ask about a trial period—If you have a money-back guarantee and trial period offer, don't hesitate to tell a vendor that fails to meet reasonable expectations during the trial period to come to get their access device and their cables. After all, if they can't even take care of you during the honeymoon, what will it be like during the marriage?

Look Before You Sign

There are several Web sites you can use to help evaluate the reliability of a broadband provider before you sign the contract.

For DSL, see the DSL Reports Web site and look at the reviews of ISPs; sort them by Zip code to see how DSL is doing in your area:

```
http://www.dslreports.com/allreviews
```

For both cable modems and DSL, SpeedGuide.net's discussion forums contain a mix of topics, including spirited discussions of how broadband ISPs are doing. Start with the Cable Modems and xDSL forum, and try others:

```
http://www.speedguide.net/cgi-bin/Ultimate.cgi
```

Wondering about @Home or Road Runner cable modem service? Look at the World Wide Wait forums:

```
http://www.worldwidewait.com/homenet.html
```

```
http://www.worldwidewait.com/rr.html
```

The World Wide Wait Web site has just been redesigned to provide forums for most high-speed Internet technologies. Check out the new site at

```
http://www.worldwidewait.com/
```

For DirecPC, check out the DirecPC newsgroup:

```
alt.satellite.direcpc
```

"The Envelope Please"—You Choose the Winner

It's your money and it's your choice, but here are some reasons for picking any of the high-speed choices covered in this book.

When ISDN Makes Sense

➤ It's the only high-speed choice in your market

➤ You want symmetrical upload/download service

➤ You want the superior speed and quality of digital phone lines and fax service as well as faster Internet service

➤ You are connecting with ISDN-optimized videoconferencing or other services

DSL's the Best When...

➤ It's working—and working well—in your market

➤ You don't want to share your bandwidth with anybody

➤ You want a fast and secure Internet connection

➤ You can get free installation or can install it yourself

Cable Modems Rule When...

➤ You want the peaks of performance and don't mind the valleys

➤ It's the fastest ready-to-go technology you can get today

➤ You can lease the equipment, making your up-front expenses minimal

➤ You can get free installation

➤ You can get two-way service.

Why Fixed Wireless Is Fine

➤ You like cable modem-type service without moving back to town

➤ You hate to see the cable guys dig up your back yard

➤ You can get two-way service

DirecPC Rules If...

➤ You are too far out in the country for fixed wireless or wired broadband

➤ It's the fastest service in your part of the country

➤ The new two-way service is ready when you are

➤ You pick up the unlimited plan and have a local dial-up number for now

Your Selection Process in Review

Use the tips in this chapter to help you create a selection worksheet. Start by writing down the services available in your area. Then record the speeds and the up-front and monthly costs. Calculate the cost per Kbps for the technologies that best match your favorite features.

Finish the job by researching satisfaction, reliability, and customer service issues. A winner, or at least a couple of finalists, should emerge.

The Least You Need to Know

➤ Choosing the best high-speed service involves figuring out which technologies and providers are available in your area, as well as calculating the best prices and features.

➤ Before signing on the dotted line, it pays to find out which companies are reliable providers and avoid the rest.

➤ Different services make sense for different people.

Part 3

Getting Your High-Speed Connection Wired and Working

You've placed your order and now it's time to wait for the day your high-speed service will arrive. What do you do in the meantime? How can you prepare for installation? If you have the option to do it yourself, should you? In Part 3 you'll learn what your system needs to be ready for your favorite high-speed option, how the installation process should work, and how to do it yourself when possible.

Chapter 10

Getting ISDN

In This Chapter

➤ Choose the best ISDN provider and package for your needs.

➤ Prepare for your ISDN installation.

➤ Choose and pay for your equipment.

➤ Learn what to expect during the installation and setup process.

If you've decided that ISDN is the best broadband option for you, you're still not home free until you choose the right service plan and get ISDN installed and working. Here's how to have the smoothest ISDN setup and installation.

Choosing Your ISDN Provider

ISDN, the Integrated Services Digital Network, is an oddball in the world of high-speed Internet access. Originally designed to provide clearer telephone calls, faster faxing, and other enhanced services, it has become a popular way to get faster Internet access in areas that lack choices such as cable modem or DSL service, and where dish-based systems aren't suitable.

Because ISDN is a telephone-line–based service, you get ISDN service from your local telephone company. Want a choice? If you live in an area that has multiple local telephone companies, you might be able to compare ISDN service offerings, but for most of us, your friendly telephone monopoly is the only ISDN game in town.

What's the Best ISDN Package for You?

As you learned in Chapter 4, "I Smell Dollars Now with ISDN," ISDN comes in two forms:

A Bond That Lasts...

"Bonding" makes two separate Internet connections work as a unit. Bonding can work with both ISDN and analog modems, but ISP support for bonding isn't widespread. It's also referred to as *Multilink* (short for *Multilink Point-to-Point Protocol* or *M-PPP*).

➤ Basic Rate Interface (BRI)—Basic Rate Interface has two B-channels of 64Kbps each and a 16Kbps D-channel (used primarily for signaling). However, before you stick out your chest and say, "Ha! I'm hot stuff—128Kbps worth of two-way Internet!"—hold on. You need to make sure your Internet service provider can handle the trick needed to make those B-channels "bear" the same load.

If your ISP doesn't know how to do "bonding" (see Chapter 3, "Speed Up and Fix Up Your Dial-Up" for details), the second 64Kbps channel isn't going to do you much good. Before you sign up for ISDN with the Internet as your primary use, make sure that "bonding" is in your ISP's vocabulary.

➤ Primary Rate Interface (PRI)—The PRI form of ISDN is a 1.5Mbps connection, comprised of 23 B (bearer) channels of 64Kbps capacity each and a 64Kbps D (delta) channel for signaling. PRI-ISDN is far too expensive for use in a residential or small-business environment.

All ISPs Are Not Created Equal

If you use the telco's own ISP, you'll probably have support for bonding. However, many third-party ISPs that started out as strictly analog dial-up providers, such as CompuServe, don't support bonding, limiting your maximum speed to a single B-channel (64Kbps).

64Kbps or 128Kbps?

If you *must* use an ISP that supports only a single 64Kbps B-channel, you should plan accordingly. Typically, you can get three versions of ISDN-BRI:

➤ Data only

➤ Voice and data

➤ Voice, data, voice mail, and call management

If you are buying ISDN strictly for its Internet access features, choose the data-only service. However, if you can't use the second B-channel for data, you might want to pick up one of the other two options if your only option is the dual B-channel (128Kbps) service. Some ISDN providers offer a 64Kbps option, allowing you to tailor your ISDN speed to your ISP's limitations.

Tech Note

Beat the Clock with Data Over Voice Bearer

If your ISDN provider wants to charge a per-minute rate on your data service, see if you can get an option called Data Over Voice Bearer (DOVB). DOVB enables you to run a data connection at 56Kbps (rather than the normal 64Kbps B-channel rate) without being whacked with a per-minute connection charge. You'll need to make sure that you order Voice and Data B-channel service, buy an ISDN terminal adapter that supports DOVB, and use an ISP that supports it. Make sure that you can switch from a DOVB 56Kbps connection to a full-bore 2B (128Kbps) connection when you need the extra speed for downloading a large file.

Getting the Right ISP

As with some other high-speed Internet services, ISDN gives you a choice of ISPs. You can use either

➤ The telco's own ISP

➤ A third-party ISP

Make your choice carefully, based on these factors:

➤ Local or long-distance call

➤ Connection speed

➤ Experience with ISDN

Local Call or Long Distance?

In many parts of the country, finding an Internet point of presence (a dial-up number) that's a local call for your ordinary 56Kbps

Danger Danger

Don't Ditch That Phone Just Yet

Although one of the theoretical appeals of ISDN-BRI is that you can talk on one 64Kbps B-channel while you surf on another, keep in mind that in the event of a power failure, neither channel will work, knocking you off the air. The telcos (and most other experts) recommend you keep your existing analog phone service.

modem is no problem. However, change to ISDN and you might be looking at a long-distance call—*especially* if you plan to stay with your existing ISP. The telco's "captive" ISP for ISDN usually has local ISDN numbers available everywhere that the telco makes ISDN available. But don't assume anything; just as the cost of long-distance calls can make your dial-up Internet experience an expensive one, the same thing can happen with ISDN. If your current ISP can't connect you with a local call, find out who can *before* you place your order.

Area Code Mayhem

The explosion in new exchanges and area codes over the last few years makes it virtually impossible to tell whether an "unfamiliar" exchange or area code is actually in your local calling area. Don't guess! Call your telco and ask the customer service people whether the ISDN number is a local call for you.

Getting the Fast ISDN You Pay For

Most ISDN-BRI plans are also known as the 2B+D service: two Bearer channels running at 64Kbps each and a 16Kbps Delta channel for signaling. So, performing a brilliant mathematical calculation, you add 64 to 64 and say "all right—128Kbps here I come!"

If 128Kbps is what you want, don't forget to ask about bonding. Bonding, as you learned earlier in this chapter, turns the twin 64Kbps B-channels into a single 128Kbps logical connection to and from your ISP. Your ISDN service can do it—but can your ISP?

Again, most "captive" ISPs that are owned by telcos have no problem with bonding (also known as Multilink-PPP), but not every third-party ISP that claims to support ISDN is as capable. If your ISP can't support bonding/Multilink-PPP, you're stuck with a 64Kbps connection, even if you have full-bore 128Kbps ISDN. Get an ISP that runs ISDN as fast as your connection allows.

Experience with ISDN

The telco understands ISDN—after all, telcos invented the service—but your ISP must understand how ISDN interfaces with the Internet. I'd rather have an ISP that understands the peculiarities of ISDN than one that is primarily concerned with analog or other broadband services. Again, this might be an argument for the telco's own ISP—but don't be afraid to ask for references for any ISP you are considering before you sign up for ISDN.

Dynamic or Static IP Address?

The last option you might be able to select is what type of IP address to choose from:

➤ Static IP addressing

➤ Dynamic IP addressing

As with other high-speed Internet options, static IP addressing usually costs more (when you can get it at all) and is worth the extra money only if you need to have the same IP address all the time, as for Web hosting or teleconferencing programs such as Microsoft NetMeeting. A static IP address can also require you to change from a residential to a much more expensive business ISDN plan.

Unless you need a static IP address, take the normal dynamic IP address option and don't worry about it. You'll save money and have a far easier IP configuration to record.

Your ISDN Order, Please

The process of ordering ISDN includes

➤ Qualifying your line for ISDN

➤ Selecting your options

➤ Ordering the service

Is Your Line Good Enough for ISDN?

Because ISDN is an all-digital service, it is subject to the same type of line qualification issues as DSL. When you contact your telco about ISDN service, you will need to provide at least your area code and exchange (812-555-xxxx) to see whether you qualify for ISDN service. This information is transmitted to the telco's exchange database, which will compare the number to its records of exchanges that are ISDN-ready.

Tech Note

Wire Distance Is Not Measured as the Crow Flies

What's a "wire foot," 13 inches? No—a "wire foot" is the same as a regular foot (12 inches), but it refers to the distance the *wire* must travel from the CO to your location, rather than straight-line or road distance. That's why looking at a map to determine whether you can get ISDN won't work.

What does it take to have an ISDN-ready line? Your location must be within 18,000 wire feet of the telco's central office (CO) to permit a high-quality digital signal to be sent and received. What if you're "out in the boonies"? You might still be able to get ISDN, but only if the telco is willing to install repeaters to strengthen the signal to acceptable levels. Multiple repeaters are necessary to reach locations that are many miles from the CO.

Time to Draft Your Neighbors?

How can you convince your telco to provide ISDN service if you're beyond the normal 18,000-wire feet range? You might need help from your neighbors. For example, Scott Mueller, author of the bestseller *Upgrading and Repairing PCs*, told me that Ameritech wasn't providing ISDN service to his rural northern Illinois neighborhood when he first asked about ISDN. However, if he placed an order, Ameritech told him it would install ISDN support because another person in the area also wanted ISDN service.

After both Scott and his neighbor were signed up, Ameritech quickly set up the equipment needed to provide ISDN service to their area. So, if you can't get ISDN, see if someone else near you is interested. Between the two of you, you might get your telco to come across.

Buy or Lease Your Hardware?

Unlike many other types of high-speed Internet connections, usually you are required to buy your ISDN terminal adapter (TA), the ISDN "modem" that connects your computer to the ISDN line. Unlike the throwaway pricing common for analog modems these days, an ISDN TA costs real money: $200 or more, depending on features.

Most TAs are external, connecting through either an RS-232 serial port or a USB port (with Windows 98, Windows 2000, and Windows Me). An ISDN TA is useless for any other task, so if you're adopting ISDN as an interim solution, see if you can lease the TA rather than buy it outright.

Tech Note

Avoiding Sticker Shock

If you can't lease your ISDN TA, see if you can get "lease–like" payments. Some telcos allow you to pay for equipment over several months. Because you will also be paying for ISDN installation, you'll save yourself a kick in the wallet if you can stretch your payments over time.

Making Sure Your System Is Ready for ISDN

The basic requirements for ISDN service vary by provider, but Verizon's recommended list is typical of the hardware requirements of ISDN providers across the country, as seen in Tables 10.1 and 10.2.

Table 10.1   Typical Recommended PC System Configuration for ISDN Service

Computer hardware	Pentium MMX or Pentium II 133MHz or faster
Operating system	Windows 95/98/Me or Windows NT 4.0, Windows 2000
RAM	Windows 95—16MB Windows 98/Me—32MB Windows NT/2000—64MB
Hard disk space	2GB hard drive space (with 200MB available)
Video	Super VGA monitor (800×600 pixels) at 64K colors or more
External port	RS-232 serial port (for use with external ISDN TA)
Cabling	RS-232 cable (for use with external ISDN TA)
Drive	CD-ROM drive
Software	Microsoft TCP/IP stack

Table 10.2   Typical Recommended Macintosh System Configuration for ISDN Service

Computer hardware	PowerPC 604E 120MHz or faster
Operating system	Mac OS System 7.5 or later
RAM	32MB
Hard disk space	2GB hard drive space (with 200MB available)
Video	Thousands of colors or greater
External port	RS-232 serial port (for use with external ISDN TA)
Cabling	RS-232 cable (for use with external ISDN TA)
Drive	CD-ROM
Software	Mac TCP 2.1 or later

Minimum Configurations Equal Minimum Satisfaction!

Do yourself a favor and try to exceed the recommended minimums by a factor of at least two when you evaluate your current computer. You'll really hobble any high-speed service if you tie it to a slow computer. For example, a 300MHz or faster Pentium II, Celeron, or similar CPU (such as the AMD K6–2, Athlon, or Duron) with at least 64MB of RAM will give you a far better online experience.

If you've been looking for an excuse to buy a new computer for the family, even the cheapest new Windows PC or iMac will beat these specifications by a huge margin and give you a shiny new PC for your shiny new online service.

USB Rules!

If you have a computer with Windows 98/Me/2000 (or an iMac) and USB ports, you might be able to use the USB port instead of a serial port for your TA connection, and there are good reasons to switch.

The USB port can run at 1.5Mbps or higher, speeds far higher than the 115.2Kbps limit of the typical RS-232 serial port on current computers. If your ISDN provider is using an external TA to connect you to the ISDN line, you might be losing through-put if you attach it to a normal serial port. Why? Many external TAs can run at 230.4Kbps, twice as fast as the "speed limit" of the serial port but well within the speed range of a USB port. Most current TAs can connect to either port.

Can you speed up your serial port? Sure, by replacing it. If you are using Windows 95 or Windows NT 4.0 (which don't support USB ports) on your Web-surfin' machine, you could buy a high-speed serial port to fix the problem. But, that'll cost you $70 or more just for the card—not to mention the potential headaches of opening up your computer, finding an empty slot, avoiding hardware conflicts....

If your computer has a working USB port with the right versions of Windows, go USB! It is Plug-and-Play, easy to install, runs faster, and you don't even need to fiddle with thumbscrews!

Tech Note

THAT WAY ▷

More Alphabet Soup

Why are normal serial ports 50% slower than external TAs? It's because of their UARTs. What's a UART? UART stands for Universal Asynchronous Receive Transmit, and all true serial ports have a UART or equivalent chip connected to the port. Typical computers have UARTs called 16550AFs, which have a top speed of 115.2Kbps, half that of most external ISDN TAs.

You can buy faster serial port cards from many vendors, including

➤ SIIG, Inc. (www.siig.com)

➤ Lava Computer Mfg., Inc. (www.lavalink.com)

You can purchase any serial port card that uses a 16650 UART. This chip supports 230.4Kbps and faster speeds, allowing your TA to run as fast as possible. Although both ISA and PCI models are available from these and other manufacturers, we recommend PCI cards for more versatility, easier installation, and even better speed. See Figure 10.1 for a typical fast serial port card.

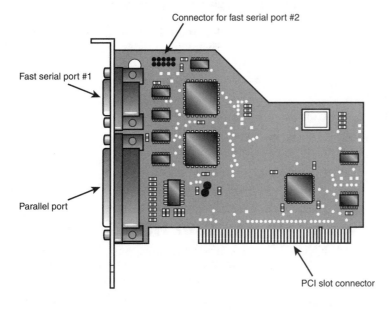

Connector for fast serial port #2

Fast serial port #1

Parallel port

PCI slot connector

Figure 10.1

Lava's 2SP-PCI card, a typical high-speed multi-port card that uses the 16650 UART for full performance with your ISDN TA.

157

Digging Up Your Operating System

Unless all your operating system files are stored on your hard drive, you need to locate your original OS CD-ROM or disks before the ISDN installer shows up. Why? You'll need to

➤ Install drivers for the ISDN TA

➤ Install networking components such as TCP/IP

Don't Get Stuck with Old Drivers

You should download the latest service packs for your operating system before you install your ISDN connection, especially if you have Windows 95. For Windows 95, I recommend installing Windows Dial–Up Networking version 1.3 and its Year 2000 update, as well as the security updates listed on the Microsoft Web site (www.microsoft.com/windows95/downloads).

If you know what brand and model of ISDN TA you will be receiving, you should also download the latest versions of its drivers. Although the technician will also have drivers, they might not be the latest version.

After you've decided what to order, made your order, and have your hardware and software ready to roll, you're ready for your ISDN installation.

Installing ISDN

The ISDN installation process involves

➤ Wiring your home or office for ISDN

➤ Activating ISDN service

➤ Installing and configuring the ISDN TA

Whose Wire Is It Anyway?—Wiring Your Home for ISDN

During the order process, you also need to determine who is responsible for wiring ISDN inside your home—your telco or you.

Some telcos take care of bringing ISDN only to your telephone service box, leaving you to perform the rest of the wiring yourself—or pay the telco's technician or an electrical contractor to carry the connection the rest of the way.

If the wiring from your service box to your wall falls to you, ask some questions before you break out the wire cutters or call an electrical contractor.

You must know what type of wiring connector you need to install for your ISDN TA. ISDN wiring can use any of the following connectors:

Getting the Inside Story

James T. Perkins has put together a very good overview of his experiences with using and installing ISDN at `http://www.inetarena.com/` `-jamester/isdn/index.html`

➤ RJ-11—This is physically identical to the standard four-wire phone jack.

➤ RJ-45—With ISDN, this isn't used to connect to Ethernet but to a TA.

➤ SJA-11—A cheaper version of the RJ-45 jack.

Which one should you install? It depends on the needs of your equipment. Originally, ISDN wiring connected to a device called an NT-1 (Network Termination Device 1), which was connected to devices that would share the ISDN line. Today, most ISDN TAs have a built-in NT-1, meaning that whatever type of cabling the TA needs to connect to the ISDN line needs to match the wall connector you install (or have installed for you). See Figure 10.2 for examples of these connectors.

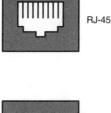
RJ-45

RJ-11

Figure 10.2

RJ-45 (top) and RJ-11 (bottom) jacks can both be used for ISDN equipment. Your ISDN TA's design determines which one you install. The SJA-11 jack (not pictured) looks and works identically to the RJ-45.

If your telco provides an "all-in-one" installation service, you won't need to worry about this.

Tech Note

The Fix Might Be in the Box!

Because many ISDN TAs can use either RJ-11 or RJ-45 wall sockets to connect to the ISDN line, they often come with an RJ-45 to RJ-11 converter cable. If your ISDN TA includes this cable, you can use a standard RJ-11 wall socket, just as you do for a normal phone connection. I recommend that you label it ISDN, though, to avoid confusion if you move your computer to a different room later.

After the ISDN wiring has been run to a wall jack and your ISDN TA is installed, you connect the RJ cable from the TA to the wall jack. Whether the cable has an RJ-11 or an RJ-45 connector at the wall socket, it snaps into place like an ordinary phone cable. Both types of cables have a plastic retaining clip that must be pressed to remove the cable after it is attached (see Figure 10.3).

Figure 10.3

Attaching the RJ cable from the ISDN TA to the ISDN wall socket.

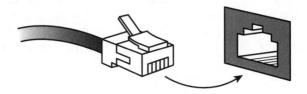

Danger Danger

Don't Forget to Coordinate "Flipping" the ISDN Switch

Find out during your ordering process when the ISDN line to your home will be provisioned (telco talk for "turned on and ready for you to use"). This date should be *before* the appointment you make for the telco installer to set up the line, so that you can get connected right away.

Attaching the ISDN TA to Your Computer

After the ISDN wiring is installed, the TA needs to be connected to your system. Most TAs used today connect to an RS-232 serial port or USB port. Whichever connector you use, the physical connection process is normally quite simple:

1. Plug the cable from the TA into your computer.
2. Fasten the screws to attach the cable to your computer.
3. If you can't find any thumbscrews—relax, it must be a USB device!

See Figure 10.4 for an illustration of how a typical external ISDN TA attaches to the ISDN line, to your computer, and to any analog devices (phone or fax machine) you plan to use it with your ISDN service.

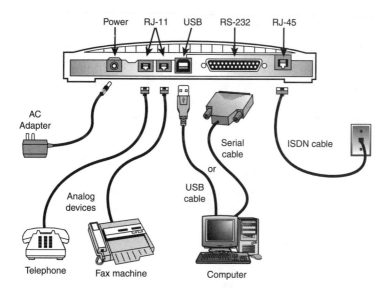

Figure 10.4

Connecting a typical external ISDN TA to your computer, telephone equipment, and the ISDN wall jack.

Tech Note

Check Those Slots!

Some TAs connect to an internal expansion slot instead of to an external port. If your telco uses this type, you must make sure you have an open expansion slot of the correct type before installation day.

Installing Drivers for the ISDN TA

If your computer supports Windows Plug and Play (PnP) technologies and you are using Windows 9x/Me/2000, your TA will be detected automatically by Windows when you start up your computer after you install or connect your TA. If you're using Windows NT 4.0 at home, you'll need to use the Have Disk feature to manually install your modem drivers. In either case, you'll need to supply the CD-ROM or disk provided with your TA to complete the installation process.

Because Windows treats your TA like a modem, you will need to complete a location screen, providing your country, area code, codes needed for outside lines, and choice of tone or old-fashioned pulse dialing. After you complete this information, it's time to connect your TA to the ISDN wall socket and configure it.

Configuring Your TA the Easy Way (?!)

ISDN configuration used to be very difficult, for the following reasons:

➤ You needed to know what kind of switch your ISDN line was connected to.

➤ You needed to know whether your equipment required a SPID (Service Profile Identifier), a number that includes your ISDN device's area code and phone number and extra digits that are used to identify the type of ISDN service you will receive.

➤ You needed to know whether you were configuring for a point-to-point (single ISDN device) or multipoint (multiple ISDN devices) connection.

➤ You needed to know the ISDN telephone number assigned to your device.

Keep That CD Handy!

Make sure you store your software CD in a safe place after you get your system running with it. You'll need it if you decide to change configurations later!

These complications led both to humorous Dilbert cartoon panels and to serious headaches for ISDN installers. Fortunately, many ISDN TAs have built-in features to minimize these problems. For example, 3Com's latest ISDN TA comes with its ISDN Line Wizard, which automatically configures the SPID and switch settings, and with the AutoSPID feature, which downloads these settings from switches that support this feature. These features are included on the 3Com Control Center CD-ROM, which is included with the ISDN TA.

After your TA has been configured with the correct telephone number, SPID, and switch configuration, you're ready to use it in most cases.

Be sure to record any information that your TA could not determine automatically.

If you need to tweak the configuration of your ISDN TA, see Chapter 18, "Tips, Tricks, and Troubleshooting for ISDN."

Getting Online with Your ISDN TA

Unlike "always on" connections that use a network interface card, your ISDN TA acts like a modem: You must dial your ISP to make a connection (although the connection time takes just a couple seconds). So, if you're a Windows user, you'll need to configure a new Dial-Up Networking connection for your TA.

If you are switching to ISDN from a previous analog dial-up Internet connection, you already have Dial-Up Networking (DUN) installed on your Windows computer.

To make a new DUN connection for your ISDN TA with Windows 9x or Me:

1. Click Start, Programs, Accessories, Communications, Dial-Up Networking.
2. Double-click the Make New Connection icon.
3. Enter the name of your ISDN ISP in the Type a Name box, such as My ISDN ISP.
4. Select your ISDN TA from the Select a Modem drop-down list.
5. Click Next.
6. Enter the telephone number (including Area Code if needed) on the next screen.
7. Click Finish to complete the connection.

After you create the connection, right-click the connection icon in the Dial-Up Networking folder and select Properties. Click Server Types, and if any of the following are checked, click the boxes to uncheck them, because they are not needed for your ISDN connection:

➤ Log on to network
➤ NetBEUI
➤ IPX/SPX Compatible

You must also set your browser to use this connection rather than your previous analog modem connection.

After you've created a Dial-Up Networking icon and set your browser to use it, you can open your browser and it will dial your ISDN TA to make your connection. Have fun!

Checking the List and Getting ISDN Right

Use the following checklist to ensure that your ISDN installation comes off without a hitch.

Before you place your order:

__ Figure out where the computer will be placed for use with the ISDN TA.

__ Check the hardware and software requirements; try to exceed the recommended standards to enjoy better performance.

__ Replace your computer if it doesn't meet the minimum standards; upgrade your computer with more RAM, and so on to meet the recommended standards if possible.

__ Decide which ISDN ISP you will use and find out what types of ISDN connection the ISP supports.

During the order process:

__ Find out who is responsible for performing your inside wiring.

__ Ask about installation specials.

__ Find out what ISDN TAs you can use and whether they can be connected to your computer with a USB port if you have Windows 98/Me/2000.

__ Purchase or lease your TA.

__ Record the expected time and cost of installation.

During installation:

__ Record the network, browser, and ISDN configuration used to get your system connected.

__ File all software and paperwork provided by the vendor.

__ Make sure you can get your system connected before the technician leaves.

The Least You Need to Know

➤ Setting up ISDN service requires coordination between your telco and your ISDN ISP. After you qualify your line for ISDN, you need to select an ISP. Your ISDN ISP should be able to support a 128Kbps connection with a local call; if not, shop around for an ISP that supports a 2B+D (basic ISDN BRI) connection.

➤ Find out in advance who wires the inside connection, and make sure that your ISDN TA comes with the correct cable.

➤ Your ISDN TA will probably connect to a serial or USB port, so make sure these ports are available before the install day. Provide the telco's technician with the operating system drivers needed to finish the job, and check the connection before the telco truck leaves your driveway.

Chapter 11

Getting DSL

In This Chapter

➤ Select the best DSL provider and plan for your needs

➤ Order and install DSL yourself

➤ Order DSL and supervise its installation by your DSL provider

➤ Track the progress of your DSL installation

Digital Subscriber Line (DSL) has the potential to be the ultimate high-speed Internet service of your dreams. Why? DSL can be faster than cable modems without the occasional slowdowns of cable modems' shared access. DSL lets you talk on your phone all day long while you surf the Net, download, and email whenever you want. And, you might even be able to install DSL yourself, helping yourself to a speedy online experience without ever having to wait for a service call.

However, DSL can also be a heartbreaker, making you wait weeks for installation and performing little better than the analog modem it replaces.

Which will it be? Choose the right DSL provider and make sure it's installed correctly, and you'll love it. If you don't supervise the process, you might hate it. This chapter helps you make sure that DSL lives up to its potential by guiding you past potential traps.

Choosing Your DSL Provider

Depending on where you live, you might not have a choice of DSL providers, or you might have two or more to choose from. Why? As you learned in Chapter 10, "Getting ISDN," regardless of where you purchase your DSL service, ultimately a telecommunications company is part of the process. This is because DSL will be provided either on your existing telephone line or, in some cases, on another line brought to your home or office by either your friendly local telco or a competing telecommunications company.

Tech Note

What's at the Other End of the DSL Cable?

Whether DSL is provided over an existing telephone wire or over new wire, when DSL data reaches the telco's central switch, it is routed to a device called a *DSL Access Multiplexer (DSLAM)*, which routes traffic to and from the Internet. Voice traffic on the DSL wire is carried by the normal public-switched telephone network (PSTN).

So, it matters more than ever who you choose for DSL service. In some markets, you can choose your telco, and if all the telcos you can choose from provide DSL service, you open up your options. Even if your locality offers only one telco, chances are there is at least one ISP specializing in DSL. Even though the telco provides the wire in both cases, you might get better service from the ISP than from the local telco's own DSL service. And, more and more telecommunications companies that are ready and willing to pull new wire to your home or business are springing up to fill in the coverage gaps caused by the incumbent telco's tardy adoption of DSL.

What does this mean for you? More choices and the possibility that your DSL can come from a third party instead of from a "baby Bell." It can also mean that you'll get a new line to your home or office as part of your DSL package.

Choosing and installing DSL sometimes involves using and learning a lot of telecommunications jargon, because DSL is a telephone line-based technology. The following are some of the most common terms:

➤ ILEC—Incumbent Local Exchange Carrier; your traditional telco, which until recently provided the only local telephone service in most cities and localities. Some ILECs still are effective monopolies, but more and more ILECs have competition from…

➤ CLEC—Competitive Local Exchange Carrier; companies other than your traditional telco that can offer local telephone (and sometimes DSL) service.

➤ DCLEC—Digital (Data) Competitive Local Exchange Carrier; companies other than your traditional telco that also offer digital/data communications services.

➤ PpoE—Point-to-Point protocol over Ethernet; an increasingly common way of handling DSL connections that requires you to log in with a username and password to make the connection.

Unfortunately, one of the reasons you're reading this chapter is likely to be the many horror stories coming from around the nation about botched DSL installations. Whether you have one, two, or three DSL providers to choose from, you need to find out who is doing the best job of DSL installation and service in your area. The ratings provided by the DSL Reports Web site are an outstanding way to get a big picture view of how well DSL providers around the country, and your local DSL providers, are living up to the promise of DSL.

In addition, other valuable sources of DSL information are your friends and associates at work, in your church or synagogue, or in clubs and civic organizations. Find out who else has DSL and how they like it, as well as how easy (or painful!) the DSL process was for them. Factor their experiences into your decision-making process.

Your DSL provider should have a proven capability to

➤ Provide reliable DSL service

➤ Live up to its DSL installation schedule

➤ Coordinate field and back-office setup to get you online

Learn the Terms

You can see the definitions for many more terms in the knowledge-base section of DSL Reports:
`http://www.dslreports.com/ information/kb`

Get the Skinny on DSL Providers

The home page of DSL Reports provides a quick "good—mixed—bad" rating on DSL ISPs and links to the details. See the home page at `http://www.dslreports.com`

Getting this kind of information before you sign on the dotted line is critical. At least one telco had to suspend DSL marketing in one state because of repeated failures to deliver DSL service in a reasonable amount of time for its customers. The constant waves of mergers in the telecommunications business and the side effects of mergers are also putting a lot of strain on many DSL users.

Later in this chapter we'll provide you with a DSL checklist that you can use to track your installation process. Use the checklist to see how well your DSL provider is living up to its commitments.

No DSL for You!?

If you're a residential customer, some of the non-telco DSL providers don't want your business. It's nothing personal, it's strictly business; that is, they want business rather than residential customers. Why? Some DSL providers are bypassing the local telco's antiquated wiring altogether and pulling their own cable. This costs major bucks, and these companies are looking for long-term commitments from businesses to pay the freight for rewiring. If you contact a DSL provider and they politely tell you, "thanks but no thanks"—that's why.

The DSL Players Behind the Scenes

If you have "competing" DSL providers asking for your business, make sure they really are competing. Many traditional telcos and data-only telecommunications companies are teaming with a small number of DSL providers to deliver DSL to you. Three of the biggest DSL providers are Covad, NorthPoint, and Rhythms. Through partnerships and co-marketing agreements, these companies sell DSL through ISPs, local telcos, and data-only telecommunications providers.

It's important to know who's behind the scenes coordinating DSL when you place your DSL order; don't hesitate to ask. You need to know so you can see whether you're really choosing between true alternatives or just the same service in a different wrapper.

Selecting the Best DSL Package

As with any other telecommunications package, you want the best service for the lowest cost. Depending on who provides your DSL service, you can have many choices or just a "take it or leave it" version of DSL to choose from.

If you have a single DSL choice, it will usually include a dynamic IP address with 384Kbps–768Kbps downstream speed and a lower upstream speed. This type of DSL service will meet the needs of most home and small-business users, although heavy users who download a lot of Web content such as MP3 files or software service packs will want to get at least 768Kbps or faster downstream speed.

Finding Out Whose DSL You're Really Getting

To find out who's partnering with the biggies in DSL to bring it to your neighborhood, check out these Web sites.

Rhythms' Service Areas map shows the states and cities where you can get service. After you select a state and city, you'll see what ISPs Rhythms uses to deliver the service.

```
http://www.rhythms.com/service_areas/service_areas.shtml
```

NorthPoint Communications doesn't offer a formalized list of ISPs at its Web site, but you can learn about its partnerships with companies such as Microsoft, Verizon, and others by scanning its press release library:

```
http://www.northpoint.net/about_press.asp
```

Covad's strategic and distributor (ISP) partners are available from links on its Partner page:

```
http://www.covad.com/partners/
```

Some typical DSL options include

➤ Fixed IP address—This is useful primarily if you plan to do Web hosting, use virtual private networking (VPN) to reach your computer remotely through the Internet, or use Microsoft NetMeeting or other collaboration software that requires or works better with a constant IP address. Availability varies widely; some DSL ISPs provide a fixed IP address at no extra charge, whereas others can charge extra for it or don't offer it at any price.

➤ Symmetrical Upstream/Downstream speed—This is also useful primarily for Web hosting or collaborations using Microsoft NetMeeting. This can require you to purchase a business-oriented form of DSL, which can be much more expensive than asymmetrical residential or small-office DSL lines.

➤ Extra Email Addresses—If several people in your family or office will share the computer, be sure to factor in the cost of enough email addresses for everyone. Residential services can offer only one or a limited number of addresses as part of the package.

Options such as personal Web hosting space can sweeten the pot, but look at availability and reliability as more important, because many Web sites offer free personal Web hosting.

Use the calculator found in Chapter 9, "Decisions, Decisions: What's the Best Choice for Me?" to figure out your best DSL buy if you have two or more plans to choose from.

Tech Note

Filling in the X in xDSL

DSL sometimes is referred to as xDSL because there are many different varieties, but for our purposes we're concerned about the two major types of DSL: Asymmetric (ADSL) and Symmetric (SDSL).

Asymmetric DSL gets its name from the faster speed of downloads than uploads. This type of DSL is far less expensive for telcos to provide because it can normally be run over existing wire to your home or office, and might even allow an easy self–install option.

Symmetric DSL provides the same speeds for uploads and downloads. This type of DSL is more expensive for telcos to provide and usually is priced for, and aimed at, a business market. Symmetrical DSL requires a technician's visit to set up and, unlike ADSL, requires new wiring to your home or office.

Ordering DSL

Remember how easy it was to sign up for a dial-up Internet connection? You just installed software from a CD-ROM that might have come in your cereal box, ponied up your credit-card number, and you had a working connection in just a few minutes. Now, forget it. DSL installation, even when nothing goes wrong (ha!), can take days or weeks or ....

Why? As you learned in Chapter 5, "Teaching Old POTS New Tricks with DSL," regardless of who you send the check to, DSL usually involves your telco, at least at the wiring level. Depending on where you buy DSL, it might also involve a separate DSL provider who manages the DSL gear at the telco's central office *and* sometimes an ISP who finishes the job of connecting your computer to the Internet using DSL.

With up to three different entities involved in the process, ordering DSL isn't simple—it certainly is a long way from booting up the "1 Zillion Free Hours!" CD-ROM that came in the cereal box!

Your First Move—Getting Qualified for DSL

Before any DSL reseller will sign you up, you will normally need to complete an online qualification form. You will need to enter information such as your street address, Zip code, and telephone number with area code. What is the DSL provider doing with this information? Mainly, they're checking a database of DSL availability to see whether your location is served by a central office (CO) that has DSL service available.

Tech Note

THAT WAY ▷

If at First You Don't Succeed, Check or Call Again

The database used to look up DSL eligibility might not include non-telco providers of DSL. If you strike out with your telco's own DSL qualification database, call or check with independent DSL providers in your area.

In my case, I first tried DSL Reports' DSL lookup service, which relies on telco information, and didn't qualify because my telco doesn't offer DSL service in my area yet. But, when I tried the lookup service provided by independent DSL provider Vectris, I did prequalify. What's the difference? The independent DSL provider (Vectris: www.vectris.com) can bypass the telco's own network to bring DSL where the telco can't (or won't). Vectris also deals exclusively in SDSL, which requires new wiring.

If you like your current dial-up ISP, you also can check with them to see if they provide DSL service in your area. Although it might be simpler to use the telco's own ISP, the experience of many users indicates that a local ISP that can work with your DSL connection is the best way to go. Why? The telco's ISP might not be a local connection, and the extra transmission time required to send information from your telco's CO to the ISP connection and back can cause high latency scores, affecting the responsiveness of online game play and the general overall speed of your connection.

Choose a Plan

After you prequalify for DSL, you will need to choose from the plans available. In some cases you might have several plans available with widely different prices. The natural tendency is to pick the cheapest one, but with a service as complex as DSL, this isn't always the best idea.

The following are some points to consider:

➤ Is quality of service guaranteed?—If your DSL connection is supposed to run at a "maximum" of xKbps, what's the minimum?

➤ Who do you call for support?—If your DSL provider refers support issues to a third-party provider (a process called *outsourcing*), do they know (or care) what the setup is in the CO? Most DSL problems aren't at the subscriber's end but are located in the infrastructure that ties the subscriber to the Internet.

➤ How good are the online support options?—Some DSL providers use the Web primarily for marketing DSL, but that's no help if you run into problems with DSL later. Take a look at the provider's DSL-specific online help before you sign on the dotted line.

➤ Can you retrieve your email from a Web-based email service if you're traveling?—The ability to get your email from a Web server is attractive for travelers and as a safeguard against a temporary outage. You can set up a free analog dial-up service from a company such as NetZero and use it on the road to access your email, or connect with it at home through your old analog modem if you have a snafu with your DSL service.

Some DSL providers charge extra for a backup dial-up connection. If you can get your email through the Web, our advice is to skip it and go with a free service.

Do You Really Need a Backup Service?

Take a detailed look at your ISP's box score at DSL Reports if you're wondering whether you need to worry about having a backup DSL-provided or third-party analog connection for getting your email. DSL Reports recalculates its DSL ISP ratings on a weekly basis, and separate ratings for tech support and reliability are factored in along with sales rating, install experience, services, and value for money. If the DSL ISPs you're considering have a C+ or lower rating for reliability, I'd consider having a backup plan.

See the DSL Reports "Good, Bad, and Ugly" ISP rating page at

```
http://www.dslreports.com/gbu
```

Is More $$ Really Better?

What's the difference among three different DSL solutions, which offer the same speed but at three different prices? More than you'd think. Often, the more you pay, the more personalized the service and the more help you'll get if you have problems. See the details in the online article "Why Pay More" at

http://www.dslreports.com/shownews/91

Place Your Order

You can place your order through

➤ Your local telco (if it provides DSL service through its own ISP)

➤ A DSL ISP

➤ A DSL news and referral site such as DSL Reports

Choose an Installation Method

In some cases, you might be able to choose between

➤ Self-installation

➤ Technician installation

You don't need to be a rocket scientist to install DSL, but if opening your computer or working with telephone wires worries you, either ask a friend to help out or opt for the technician.

Check That Line!

Because your ability to get DSL is heavily influenced by line conditions between your home or office and the CO with the DSL equipment, don't pay in advance for DSL service until you are certain that the line will work for DSL. Just looking up your address and telephone number isn't adequate. It can be tough to get a refund if something goes wrong, so don't pay until you know you're A-OK!

Be warned, though. Poor coordination between technicians who perform DSL installs and the folks who market, flip switches, and change wires at the back office and run DSL ISPs can lead to a lot of frustration over all-day waits for technicians who might not show up and or miss appointments. My opinion? Try the self-install method if it's available to you and yelp for help only if you can't get DSL working yourself.

Why Self-Installation Isn't for Everyone

Self-installing a DSL connection isn't hard if you've ever installed a network card, and on a few recent Windows PCs and most recent Macs, it's already there.

So, what's the problem? Getting some DSL providers to send you the kit. Some DSL providers use the so-called "splitterless" or G.Lite form of ADSL, which is tailor-made for self-installations. Other providers, stuck with a wide variety of telco lines that might not be suitable for DSL, or having invested in other types of DSL that require a field installation, make you get an appointment with a technician. SDSL always requires a technician's visit because new wire to your location is part of the package.

The bottom line? If you want the self-install option, ask for it up front. It doesn't always work, but it's worth a try.

Waiting for the Truck Roll

In telco-ese, the term "truck roll" is used to describe service calls, and if you aren't eligible for a self-install form of DSL, you're waiting for the truck to roll to your location before you get connected. How long will you wait?

DSL waits are legendary. In an online poll taken by DSL Reports, slightly less than half of the 1,063 respondents who took part had their service in 28 days or less. Another survey finds the average wait is 30–60 days.

Some respondents reported waiting as long as 10 weeks or more for DSL service! Self-installation can speed things up a lot, and here are other suggestions passed along by the readers of DSL Reports:

➤ Call the tech support line when the technician shows up so that the line can be activated and tested immediately.

➤ Order by calling a real human being rather than ordering online. One DSL provider's service representative estimated that ordering online adds two–three weeks to the process. Unfortunately,

In a Hurry for Speed? Try Cable Modems Instead!

DSL has many theoretical and practical advantages, but if you need to wait for a service call, you can probably get cable modem service a lot faster. I had cable modem service from @Home installed in three days after I placed the order, and that included running a new cable to my home.

information about some DSL offers can only be found on the Web. For example, when Verizon launched its DSL service in New York City in June 2000, calling the 800 number listed in the ad reached a recording that told you to go online for more information or to sign up.

➤ Watch out for DSL getting "lost in the shuffle" when your telco merges with another company. Contacts to solve DSL problems and order DSL often get moved around in the wake of mergers.

The View from Chicagoland

For a healthy dose of reality about the problems of choosing a broadband (DSL or cable modem) provider, getting service installed (45–60 days is common) and enjoying reliable service, check out this article from the June/July 2000 issue of *Digital Chicago* magazine:

```
http://www.digitalchicago.com/Mag/JJ00/Broadband/
```

Installing DSL

Unlike most other forms of high-speed Internet access, DSL offers you the possibility of performing most of the work yourself. Some telcos offer a "self-install" DSL service. Not everyone is eligible for self-install. You'll find out whether your line is eligible for self-install during the order process.

Making Sure You're Ready for DSL

Two steps are involved in preparing your system for DSL:

➤ Verify that your computer meets the hardware specifications required by your DSL vendor

➤ Locate your operating system and network card software

Hardware Requirements

Regardless of the method you choose to get DSL, your computer needs to meet (and hopefully exceed!) the requirements of your DSL provider.

With so many companies offering DSL, it's impossible to provide a comprehensive answer about system configurations here, but the following configurations are typical. Windows users need the following:

➤ Pentium CPU or equivalent (133MHz or faster)

➤ 32MB of RAM for Windows 9x or Windows Me, 64MB of RAM for Windows NT 4.0 or 2000

➤ 80–200MB of free hard drive space

➤ Microsoft Windows 95, Windows 98, Windows Me, Windows NT 4.0, or Windows 2000

➤ CD-ROM drive

➤ Ethernet 10BaseT network interface card

Prefer to get online with a Mac? If so, you'll need the following:

➤ PowerPC or faster processor

➤ Mac OS 7.6 or greater

➤ Open Transport 1.1.1 enabled

➤ 32MB RAM

➤ 25MB of available hard disk space

➤ Installed CD-ROM drive

➤ Installed 10BaseT Ethernet network interface card

➤ Operating system CD

Danger Danger

Don't Forget To Prequalify Your Hardware, Too!

The preceding lists are distilled from several DSL providers around the country. Some DSL ISPs add special requirements, such as the following:

➤ Installed dial-up modem—This can be required so that software patches can be downloaded during installation.

➤ Windows 95/95a (the original version and the retail upgrade version sold in stores) aren't supported by some ISPs; Windows Me and Windows 2000 are too new to be supported by some ISPs.

Avoid disappointments if you are trying to use an older computer; ask for the hardware requirements list before you sign up.

Almost any computer bought since about 1997 should work with DSL—*if* you add a 10BaseT Ethernet network card (iMacs, and some G3 and G4 models already have built-in Ethernet).

Why do you need a network card? Just as with cable modems, DSL uses a network card to interface the external DSL modem with your computer. Ask your DSL provider if any particular brand is recommended or required, but chances are you'll be okay if it's 10BaseT Ethernet.

See Chapter 12, "Getting a Cable Modem," for an in-depth discussion of Ethernet cards.

Operating System and Network Card Files

You also need to have your operating system CD-ROM, disks, or files on hard disk and network card drivers available in case you must install or reinstall network components.

See Chapter 12 for an in-depth discussion of this topic.

After your computer has a network card installed and you have your operating system files and network card drivers available, you're ready to self-install DSL or have the technician install DSL for you.

The DSL Dance—Explained

Wondering what goes on during the 30 days or so between ordering DSL service and installation day? If you can't self-install DSL, you can look forward to two service calls if you're not getting DSL direct from your telco:

➤ The first service call (from the telco) checks your line for DSL compatibility and installs a new line for DSL if necessary.

➤ The second service call (from the DSL provider) installs the service and makes sure it works before leaving.

Get the rest of the story from

```
http://www.covad.com/dslfacts/installationprocess.shtml
```

Do-It-Yourself DSL

If you can self-install, you should do it (or get a friend to help you). You'll have your DSL service much faster; when the line is set by the provider for DSL, you'll be online within an hour or two of the start of installation! There's no need to wait around all day (or over several days) for a service call, and you'll save the considerable money that a service call can cost.

Can You Hack It?

If you're wondering whether you can handle a self-installation, take a look at some of the self-installation guides online. Although a few details will vary, the basic process will follow one of these guides.

If your DSL ISP will configure your connection with a fixed IP address, see the following example:

http://www.dslnorthwest.net/support.html (you will need to install Adobe Acrobat Reader or use Microsoft Word to view the guides available from this page; get Acrobat Reader from http://www.adobe.com)

If your DSL ISP will configure your connection with a dynamic IP address (the most common), see the following example:

http://www.gte.com/customersupport/index.html

Follow the DSL link in the Online Help category, and then select the Verizon DSL Self-Installation Guide link on the following page.

The process of performing a do-it-yourself DSL installation includes

➤ Receiving an in-service date from the DSL vendor
➤ Receiving the self-install kit in the mail
➤ Unpacking and checking the contents of the kit
➤ Installing the kit
➤ Configuring your system
➤ Going online to test your connection

The goal for self-install DSL vendors is to provide you with your kit within about five working days. Generally, your service date will fall in the same period, allowing you to install your DSL kit and get connected as soon as you receive it—if you have already installed and tested your Ethernet network card.

Contents of the Self-Install Kit

The contents of a DSL self-install kit can vary slightly by DSL vendor, but Verizon/GTE's version is a typical example. It contains the following components:

➤ DSL modem kit—The modem comes with a power supply cord, RJ-45 Ethernet crossover cable (to connect the PC and DSL modem), RJ-11 modular telephone line cord (to connect the DSL modem and the phone jack), and modem installation manual.

➤ Five microfilters—The microfilters connect between telephones, fax machines, and other telephone devices and the wall jack to prevent interference and allow simultaneous use of telephone-based devices and the DSL Internet connection.

➤ Two-outlet modular adapter—This allows a desk phone and DSL line to share a single wall jack.

➤ DSL installation instructions.

➤ DSL troubleshooting guide.

➤ DSL software on CD-ROM.

Installing the Microfilters

The microfilters install in two different ways—between a desktop phone and the wall jack, using a two-outlet modular adapter (see Figure 11.1), or as a replacement wall jack with integrated connectors for DSL and a wall or desk phone (see Figure 11.2).

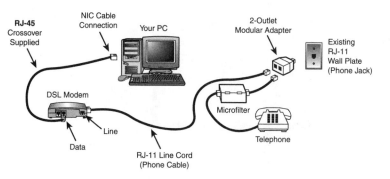

Figure 11.1

A microfilter installed between a desktop phone and the wall jack shared by the DSL connection.

Figure 11.2

A microfilter is incorpo-rated in a replacement wall jack that connects with the telephone and the DSL modem.

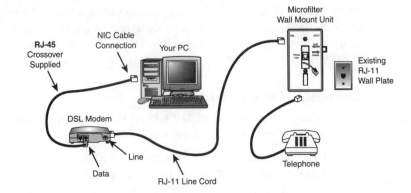

Figure 11.3 shows a close-up of the wall jack including a microfilter. You connect the DSL modem to the side of the wall jack marked DSL; your telephone to the central RJ-11 connection; and fax machines, answering machines, analog modems (for backup), or other telephone-based devices to the opposite side of the wall jack (marked ACC'Y).

Figure 11.3

A detail of the replace-ment wall jack incorporat-ing a microfilter. Attach the DSL modem to the jack marked DSL only.

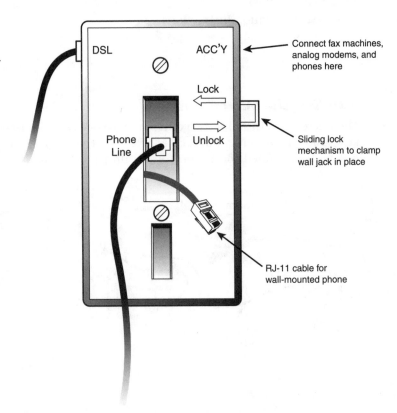

Connecting the DSL Modem to Your Computer and to the DSL Jack

The DSL "modem" (it's in quotes because it's not really a modem—we just don't know what else to call the thing that goes between a telephone line and a computer) attaches to the DSL jack on the wall mount or the two-outlet splitter by an ordinary RJ-11 telephone cord. Don't kill yourself if the dog gets hold of the one in the kit; just go out and buy another one (or find one in your junk box).

However, you'd better keep the dog away from the RJ-45 network cable that runs between your 10BaseT Ethernet network card and your DSL modem; it might not be an ordinary network cable! Some DSL modems are designed to use a "crossover" cable, which reverses some of the wires to allow a direct connection between the devices without the typical Ethernet hub or switch used in ordinary networks. Lose this cable, and you might not be able to buy one at the typical "office supplies and stereos plus a bit of computer stuff" store.

The DSL modem has only three connectors on its back side:

➤ The RJ-11 jack that connects to the telephone wall socket configured for DSL

➤ The RJ-45 jack that connects through the crossover cable to your 10BaseT Ethernet network card

➤ The power connector

See Figure 11.4 for a typical example of these connectors.

Tech Note

THAT WAY ▷

Get a Grip on Your Cables

Check your DSL modem manual to see whether it requires a crossover or standard RJ-45 network cable (also known as a Cat 5 or Category 5 cable).

RJ-11 connector and wire to phone jack with DSL microfilter

Power connector and wire to AC outlet

RJ-45 connector and wire to network card

Figure 11.4

Rear of a typical DSL modem showing the power, RJ-45 network, and RJ-11 telephone connectors.

Connecting Your Computer to the DSL Line

If you have a Windows PC, you'll find the RJ-45 connector on your network card at the rear of your computer. Run the crossover wire from the RJ-45 jack on the rear of the DSL modem to this jack. If you're an iMac lover instead, you've already got built-in Ethernet. Remove the access cover on the left side of your iMac unit and attach your crossover cable to the jack. See Figure 11.5 for details.

Figure 11.5

Remove the access cover on your iMac to find the RJ-45 port for the iMac's built-in Ethernet network connection. It's between the USB ports (left) and the RJ-11 modem connector (right).

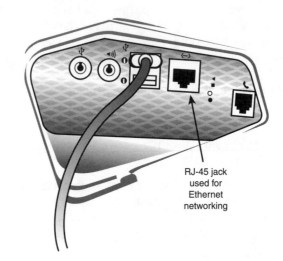

Figures 11.6 and 11.7 show the results after two common forms of DSL self-install kits are set up.

Figure 11.6

A DSL self-installation that uses a microfilter between the telephone and a splitter, allowing the DSL line and telephone line to use a standard wall jack.

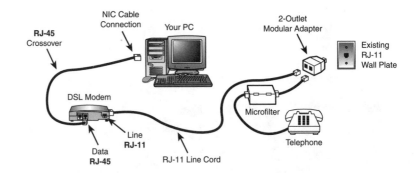

Installing the Setup Software and Configuring Your System

After you've connected your DSL modem to a telephone jack equipped with a micro-filter and connected the modem to your network card, you're ready to install the DSL software supplied with the self-installation kit. Follow the CD-ROM's prompts to set up your connection. You might need to install a new version of your favorite Web browser.

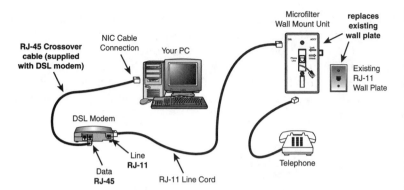

Figure 11.7

A DSL self-installation that places the microfilter inside a replacement wall plate. The DSL line is connected to a socket marked DSL on the wall plate, and the telephone is connected to a socket containing a microfilter marked ACC'Y or telephone.

If you need to perform a manual software configuration for some reason, you will need to set up the following:

➤ Your network card's TCP/IP configuration

➤ Your Web browser's connection type

If you have a dynamic IP address, you won't need to make any changes to the default Windows TCP/IP configuration, which assumes a server-assigned IP address. If you have a static IP address, check with your ISP to get the correct IP configuration settings, including IP address and others.

If you need help with TCP/IP configuration, see Chapter 17, "A Survivor's Guide to TCP/IP."

Your Web browser should be set to use either "direct connection to the Internet" or "local area network." No proxy settings are needed with a typical DSL connection.

Testing Your DSL Connection

If you have completed the self-installation process on or after your service-start date, turn on your DSL modem, check its status lights, and open your Web browser. You should be connected to the Internet!

If you're having problems getting your DSL connection working, see Chapter 19, "DSL Tips, Tricks, and Troubleshooting," for common problems and solutions.

Have the DSL Provider Do It For You

If your line isn't suitable for "do-it-yourself" DSL, or if your DSL provider doesn't offer this option, you will need to schedule at least one service visit to get DSL service.

When you schedule the DSL installation appointment, you might need to wait all day for the technician. If you get a choice between a morning and afternoon appointment, take the morning slot (but don't plan to do anything in the afternoon). Because adding DSL to an existing phone line can be tricky, a technician can get "hung up" on previous appointments to yours and might arrive late—or not at all. Of course, you know how that goes if you've ever needed telephone, appliance, or electronics service or delivery.

Make Sure Your Line Is Ready

If you are getting your DSL through an ISP, find out who is responsible for coordinating the physical installation and the provisioning of your DSL line. If your line isn't ready for DSL when the technician arrives, you can't get online.

Misery Loves Company

For a vivid example of the problems that can take place in coordination between a telco and an ISP providing DSL service, see the three-part Upside op-ed piece by Adam Feuerstein starting at

```
http://www.upside.com/texis/mvm/opinion/story?id=39776d950
```

Scroll down to the bottom of the page to see the start of the story and link to part two.

Part two is located at

```
http://www.upside.com/texis/mvm/opinion/story?id=397771300
```

Part three is located at

```
http://www.upside.com/Opinion/3980bc440.html
```

Providing the Physical DSL Connection

The technician will either locate an unused wire pair for use with DSL or pull a new phone wire for DSL. To avoid interference between your existing telephones and your new DSL wiring, the technician also installs a splitter to isolate DSL and telephone traffic.

The technician will connect the DSL side of the splitter to a wall jack that will be used to connect to the DSL modem. After the splitter and wall-jack wiring are finished, make sure the technician stays around to test the connection!

Tech Note

THAT WAY ▷

Wondering What the Tech Does with the Wires?

Rewiring an existing telephone connection for DSL is a complex process meant to be performed by a trained technician, although some brave amateurs (like the folks at smellyeyeball.com) have also performed it. If you're wondering what's so hard about a tech–installed DSL line, you can find out at the "Don't Do It Yourself PacBell DSL Page" at

```
http://www.smellyeyeball.com/dsl/
```

Testing the DSL Connection

If possible, install any DSL software provided and configure your TCP/IP connection while the wiring is taking place, especially if the technician doesn't carry a notebook computer that can be used to test the DSL connection.

After the wiring is done and your software is installed, plug the DSL modem into the wall socket and your computer and try to connect. If you have problems and the technician is still present, you should be able to determine whether the problem is with the modem, your computer, or with the telco. If the DSL service isn't "turned on" at the telco end, you won't get connected until it is.

Sharing Your DSL Connection

Unlike most cable modem providers, most DSL providers have no problem with simple Internet-connection sharing arrangements such as those discussed in Chapter 15. However, you should wait until your DSL connection is installed and working before you worry about how to share it.

Keep Your Connection to Yourself for Now

Don't try to share your DSL connection until you've used the "stock" installation for a few days. Whether you use Microsoft's Internet Connection Sharing (ICS) or a third-party gateway or proxy server program, you will need to change your system's configuration to share your Internet connection. If you try to set up sharing at the same time you set up your high-speed connection, you might not know whether your high-speed connection or sharing software isn't working if you are having problems.

Your DSL Check List

Use the following checklist to track the progress of your DSL installation.

Before you place your order:

__ Figure out where the computer will be placed for use with the DSL connection.

__ Check the hardware and software requirements for your DSL service; try to exceed the recommended standards to enjoy better performance.

__ Replace your computer if it doesn't meet the minimum standards; upgrade your computer with more RAM, and so on to meet the recommended standards if possible.

__ Find your operating system CD-ROM and network card drivers; keep them safe until installation day.

During the order process:

__ Ask for a self-installation kit if available.

__ If you can't use the self-install option, ask about installation specials; you might be able to get reduced-price or even free installation if you ask about it.

__ Find out about network cards; does your DSL provider supply one or do you need to get your own? What models are recommended or required?

__ Record the expected time and cost of installation.

__ Determine when DSL service will be turned on; the telco should activate it before your service visit or self-installation kit arrives.

__ If you are ordering DSL from an ISP (not the telco itself), get contact information so you can avoid problems with missed appointments, DSL lines that aren't ready, and so forth.

During installation:

__ Read the self-installation kit instructions carefully before you get started.

__ Record the network and browser configuration used to get you connected.

__ File all software and paperwork provided by the vendor.

__ Make sure you can get connected before the technician leaves.

__ If you can't get connected, contact both the telco and the ISP to find out who is at fault.

__ Be polite but firm if you run into problems until you get a satisfactory resolution.

Dear Diary...

Both for your own benefit and for the benefit of other DSL users, take a few minutes to register for the free DSL Reports DSL Diary service before asking a lot of questions. You can review other users' experiences before and during your installation and use it to track your own installation online. Go to

    www.dslreports.com/

Open the Tools menu and select the DSL Diary to read other entries or to create your own (free login required).

The Least You Need to Know

➤ DSL service provides a highly secure way to get broadband access to the Internet.

➤ Technician-provided installations can get bogged down in coordination problems between telco and the DSL ISP (even if the telco is acting as the ISP).

➤ Use the self-installation method if you can to save time and aggravation in getting online.

Chapter 12

Getting a Cable Modem

In This Chapter

➤ Choose the best cable modem provider and package

➤ Start the order process

➤ Learn what happens during the installation process

➤ Create a checklist to track your cable modem installation progress

Cable modems aren't the perfect high-speed Internet technology, but for more and more people (including me), they'll do just fine until something better comes along. Although cable modems aren't available yet to everyone within the reach of cable TV, cable companies across the U.S. are scrambling to upgrade and refit their systems to allow Internet traffic to flow to your home over the same cable that carries TV channels. This makes cable modems one of the most widespread high-speed Internet solutions available.

This chapter shows you how to make sure you choose the best cable modem service for your needs and have it installed correctly.

Choosing Your Cable Modem Provider

In the not-too-distant future, you might be able to call your cable TV provider and add cable modem service as easily as you add football or movie channels to your cable TV service today.

It isn't quite as simple as that yet. Some cable TV providers haven't discovered the Internet yet, and those that have offer spotty coverage. If you already have cable TV service, call your existing cable TV provider and ask about availability, or use online qualification databases such as those mentioned here to check your address for service.

Can I Get Internet With My Cable TV?

Use CableModemHelp's search engine to see whether cable modem service is available in your area. Enter your ZIP code and you'll find out who your cable operator is and whether they provide cable modem service in your area.

```
http://www.cablemodemhelp.com/cable.htm
```

You can also look up your cable company on Cable-Modem.net's Service Availability page:

```
http://www.cable-modem.net/gc/service_availability.html
```

If you're a satellite subscriber or antenna TV viewer not subscribing to cable, or if your current provider isn't providing Internet access, see whether you have an alternative choice. More and more areas of the country have replaced the traditional cable TV monopoly with a "duopoly" approach; check with cable company "B" if company "A" can't help you.

Abandon Choice, All Ye Who Enter Here

Live in an apartment? Your cable modem choice (if any) is determined by the cable service available to your building. If the cable service at your apartment building doesn't have cable modem service available, you'll need to look at alternatives such as DSL.

Why Cable Modems Aren't Available Everywhere

Can't get cable modem service from your existing cable TV provider? You're not alone. Two-way cable modem service (the best kind to get) requires major investments by the cable provider. Some cable network investments, such as fiber optic to the curb, bring benefits for both cable TV and cable modem users by allowing more (digital) channels for cable TV and providing the bandwidth necessary for two-way service. However, both one-way and two-way cable modem services also require the cable operator to install expensive equipment at the head end to connect cable modem traffic to the Internet. Two-way service also requires the cable operator to install repeaters to boost the signals coming back from individual cable modems to the head end.

Selecting the Best Cable Modem Package

As you learned in Chapter 6, "It's Not Just TV: It's HTTP...Cable Modems," cable modem service comes in two major forms:

➤ One-way (also called *telco return*)

➤ Two-way

Tech Note

Your Telephone Line's Still Busy with Telco Return

One-way (Telco Return) cable modems use your telephone line for all traffic from your computer to the Internet. So, if you are trying to free up your telephone line by switching to cable modem service, one-way won't do.

If you can't get two-way cable modem service, see whether you can get DSL service (which never ties up your phone line) to your home or office.

Which type of cable modem service you get depends on how your neighborhood is wired for cable. If your provider hasn't converted your neighborhood over to fiber-optic, you'll be stuck with one-way cable and still need your existing analog modem for sending out Web page requests and email. Cable systems are rapidly converting to "fiber to the curb" all fiber-optic systems, though, and this means the odds of having two-way cable are increasing and are especially good for you if your cable TV provider is using a newly installed infrastructure.

Most cable modem services are provided in conjunction with one of the two major national cable modem providers:

➤ @Home

➤ RoadRunner

Typically, because of how cable modems work, you don't have a lot of options to choose from when you order cable modem service.

IP Addresses and You

The IP address identifies your computer to the Internet. There are two varieties: fixed and dynamic.

A fixed IP address means that your computer will always have the same identity when you're online. Having a fixed IP address is necessary if your computer will be used as a game server (to host interactive games) or a Web server (to provide Web pages to other users), but usually isn't available for home cable modem users.

A dynamic IP address changes whenever you connect to the Internet, but it also slightly minimizes the chances of having your computer attacked by intruders.

If you really, really need a fixed IP address, you might need to look at other types of broadband service, but for Web surfing, email, downloading, and other typical Internet uses, dynamic IP addresses are fine.

Cable modem services for home use aren't designed to host servers, for example, so fixed IP addresses usually are not available. Cable modem speed varies, but it isn't broken down into various performance levels as with typical fixed wireless or DSL services.

Ordering Cable Modem Service

Unlike services such as DSL or ISDN, which often require pre-qualification and line testing to see whether your location qualifies for high-speed service, and which can bury you in a blizzard of service plans to sort through before you can say, "do it," the process of ordering cable modem service is extremely simple:

1. Contact your local cable TV/Internet provider to see whether service is available in your area.

2. Set up an appointment to have the service installed.

Most of the installation is performed by a cable operator service technician, so your primary tasks are to

➤ Be at home or at the office when the technician is scheduled to arrive.

➤ Make sure your system is ready for the installation.

Danger Danger

Wallet Check! Save Money on Your Cable Modem Installation

Getting cable modem service can cost up to $150.00(!) or as little as $0. What can you do to make sure your installation cost is as low as possible (or even nothing)?

Get in on the ground floor—if you take advantage of "grand opening"-type specials when new cable modem service rolls out in your area, you might be able to get free installation, and sometimes even a month of free service.

Don't be shy—ask! If you have a choice between two cable modem services, or if DSL is showing up in your area, you might be able to pit provider against provider. Ask about a deal, and drop a hint that you can—and will—go elsewhere. If the provider wants to gain market share, you might get a better deal on installation.

Add cable modem service to your existing cable TV service. The actual cost to the provider of adding cable modem service to an existing cable TV installation is far less than installing a brand-new service. You deserve a break—and you should ask for it.

Install your own network card. Thanks to Windows Plug-and-Play technology, network cards are easy to install. Pay the cable modem installer to put your network card in, though, and you've spent $30 or more for the privilege.

Getting Your System Ready for Cable Modem Service

Before the technician arrives to bring you the wonderful world of broadband, you need to be ready for it. How can you get ready for broadband? By having the software and hardware on hand that the technician needs to complete installation—a lucky rabbit's foot never hurts, either.

First, your system must meet or exceed the minimum standards for cable modem service (exceeds is better!). @Home requires or recommends the equipment listed in Table 12.1.

Table 12.1   @Home Minimum and Recommended Hardware

Component	Windows Minimum	Windows Recommended	Macintosh Minimum	Macintosh Recommended
Operating System	Windows 95/98/ NT 4.0/2000 Professional	Windows 95/98/ NT 4.0/2000 Professional	OS 7.6.1 or higher	OS 7.6.1 or higher
CPU	Pentium equivalent	Pentium 166 equivalent or higher	PowerPC 601	PowerPC 603
RAM	16MB	32MB or more	24MB	50MB or more
Free disk space	125MB	125MB or more	50MB	50MB or more
Network Card*	10BASE-T Ethernet	10/100 Fast Ethernet	10BASE-T Ethernet	10/100 Fast Ethernet

*The network card may be provided by the cable modem provider at extra cost.

Surf

Your computer also must have a CD-ROM drive to install the software.

Don't let the network card requirement scare you. Any computer, office supply, or appliance superstore that also sells computer network hardware will have lots of 10BASE-T Ethernet or Fast Ethernet cards to choose from at low prices. The requirements for RoadRunner cable modem service are similar but more detailed.

Are You Ready to Run with RoadRunner?

You can read the "official" requirements for RoadRunner's cable modem service at `http://www.rr.com/rdrun/` Click on the Residential Service button, and then on the Requirements button.

Tech Note

THAT WAY ▷

The Newer, the Better

If you don't know much about your computer, use this rule of thumb. If your computer is less than three years old, it should be okay for cable modem service, but watch out for computers that are older; they often aren't fast enough.

Any computers you can buy at a store today, including the lowest-cost Windows PCs or iMacs, are more than good enough to run cable modem service.

Before you run out and buy a brand-new Windows computer running Windows Me, though, make sure that Windows Me will work with your cable modem service.

I've created a more user-friendly version of what RoadRunner requires in Table 12.2.

Table 12.2   RoadRunner's Required and Recommended Hardware

| | Running Windows? | | Have a Mac or iMac? | |
	Minimums	Better	Minimums	Better
How fast and what kind of processor (CPU)?	Pentium or equivalent 75MHz	Pentium or equivalent 166MHz	Power PC 75MHz	Power PC 166MHz or faster
How much RAM (memory)?	At least 32MB	64MB or more	At least 24MB	32MB or more
How much free hard disk space?	At least 110MB	At least 150MB	At least 30MB	At least 50MB
What kind of a video card?	Super VGA (all computers since about 1991 have had SVGA)	Super VGA with 16-bit (65535 colors) colors	16-bit (65535 colors) colors	24-bit color (16.8 million colors)

Table 12.2   RoadRunner's Required and Recommended Hardware Continued

| | Running Windows? | | Have a Mac or iMac? | |
	Minimums	Better	Minimums	Better
Do you need a sound card?	No, but it's useful (think MP3s!)	Get one!	No, but it's useful (think MP3s!)	Get one!
Do you need a network card?	Yes; 10BASE-T or 10/100 Ethernet unless you have Windows 98 or Windows 2000 (These can connect via a USB port)	Yes; 10BASE-T or 10/100 Ethernet unless you have Windows 98 or Windows 2000 (These can connect via a USB port)	Yes; 10BASE-T or 10/100 Ethernet (iMacs and some other models have one built in)	Yes; 10BASE-T or 10/100 Ethernet (iMacs and some other models have one built in)
What operating system?	Windows 95/98, NT Workstation 4.0 with SP3, Windows 2000 (Windows 2000 requires Pentium 133MHz or faster CPU and 650MB of free disk space on a 2GB or bigger drive)	Windows 95/98, NT Workstation 4.0 with SP3, Windows 2000 (Windows 2000 requires Pentium 133MHz or faster CPU and 650MB of free disk space on a 2GB or bigger drive)	Mac OS 7.6 or higher	Mac OS 7.6 or higher

198

Most computers purchased from 1997 to the present should meet or exceed these minimums. However, if you've been using an old 486-based, early Pentium or "classic" Macintosh for Web surfing, it's time to retire it for one of the inexpensive and surprisingly powerful low-end Windows or iMac systems available at stores everywhere.

Fixing Common Shortcomings of Your System

As you can see from Tables 12.1 and 12.2, both Windows PCs and Macs are okay for cable modem service. Here are the most common shortcomings that typical systems at home might have:

➤ "Wrong" operating system

➤ No network card

➤ No operating system CD-ROM or files

➤ No network card drivers

➤ No backups of your system

In this section, we'll help you make sure your system is ready to go online with a cable modem.

The "Wrong" Operating System

Windows Me, the newest version of Windows for home users, might take a while to gain official support from the major cable modem providers. As this book went to press neither RoadRunner nor @Home listed Windows Me on their lists of supported operating systems. Does this mean you can't use Windows Me with a cable modem?

Not necessarily. A search of the Computing.Net Web site (a popular Web site for getting tips from other users) found that a lot of the problems some users have had with Windows Me and cable modems appeared to be caused by

➤ Trying to use a pre-release (beta) version of Windows Me. Buy the final release.

➤ Upgrading from Windows 98. The upgrade was very smooth for some users and a big problem for others.

➤ Problems with the cable modem hardware and Windows Me or Windows 2000. Whereas external cable modems are connected through your network card or USB port, internal cable modems used by some one-way systems must have drivers installed for your operating system. For example, some 3Com internal cable modems lack drivers for Windows Me or Windows 2000, and 3Com has no plans to create new drivers.

My advice? If you're using Windows 95 or Windows 98, stay with these versions for now because the cable modem provider can help you.

If you already have Windows Me, find out which cable modem models your cable modem provider uses for installations, and check with the cable modem vendor to see whether the cable modems will work okay with Windows Me. If some cable models used by your provider work and others don't, request a cable modem model that works with Me. Even though Windows Me might not be on the "official" list of supported operating systems, checking on compatibility before installation day can help you have a trouble-free installation.

Getting Advice from Other Users

The Computing.net's Windows Me discussion board features a wide range of user messages and help on Windows Me, including cable modem and Internet issues. You can browse or search it at

```
http://computing.net/windowsme/wwwboard/wwwboard.html
```

Think I'm worrying too much? I know how similar Windows Me is to Windows 98 in its networking features (I contributed several chapters to Que's *Special Edition Using Windows Me*, after all!), but try to explain the similarities to a technician. Keep in mind that if you are trying to use an "unapproved" operating system it will be the first item on the blame list if your cable modem installation doesn't work.

To see which version of Windows you have (if you are running Windows 95 or later), follow these steps:

1. Right-click the My Computer icon on your Windows desktop and select Properties, or open the Windows Control Panel and open the System icon.

2. You will see the version of Windows installed on your system, as well as the amount of RAM you have installed and your computer processor type (see Figure 12.1).

Operating system version

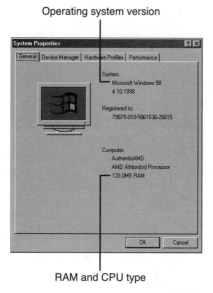

RAM and CPU type

Figure 12.1

The author's computer exceeds the minimum requirements by a wide margin in both operating system and RAM. The CPU type is displayed, but not its speed.

Tech Note

How Fast Is My Computer?

If you're not sure how fast your CPU is, watch your computer at startup. Most computers display a brief information screen that tells you the CPU type and its speed.

If your computer doesn't display the CPU speed at startup, compare the processors on the following list to what Windows reports. Any of the following CPUs are more than fast enough for use with a cable modem Internet connection:

AMD K6, K6-2, K6-III, Athlon, Duron

Intel Pentium Pro, Pentium II, Pentium III, Celeron

Cyrix M2, Cyrix III

Late-model Pentiums that are 166MHz or faster are also okay.

No Network Card

Unless your cable modem operator is going to fix you up with a one-way cable modem, you're going to wish you could change your modem into a network card instead. You can use two types of network cards with an external cable modem—10BASE-T Ethernet and 10/100 Fast Ethernet.

Both of these cards use a type of cabling called *unshielded twisted-pair (UTP)*, which resembles a telephone wire but is thicker. Similarly, the RJ-45 jack used by the Ethernet network cable resembles the RJ-11 telephone jack but is also larger. Most external cable modems use a short section of UTP cable to connect with your computer. Unlike the analog modem, which comes in almost all computers, an Ethernet card (or built-in Ethernet) is a feature provided with very few computers.

Tech Note

THAT WAY ▷

Check Your Computer—You Might Get Lucky!

Some recent computers, notably the iMac series and some G3 and G4 PowerMacs from Apple as well as a few Windows PCs made for office computing, have a network card or network port already included. Look at the back of your computer and compare the connections you see there with Figure 12.2 to see whether you have a network jack. If you have an iMac, see Figure 11.5 in Chapter 11, "Getting DSL," to find its network port.

Network cards aren't very expensive any more, though, and you might even be able to score a free one. Many companies currently are dumping their Ethernet hardware for a newer technology, not-so-creatively named *Fast Ethernet*. You might be able to save a few bucks by checking with the techs at your office and having them fish a 10BASE-T Ethernet card out of the scrap pile. Before you pick up a 10BASE-T or 10/100 dual-speed Ethernet card at the store or take one from the office junk pile, though, you'd better find out which ones are supported by your cable operator and whether a network card is supplied as part of your cable modem service.

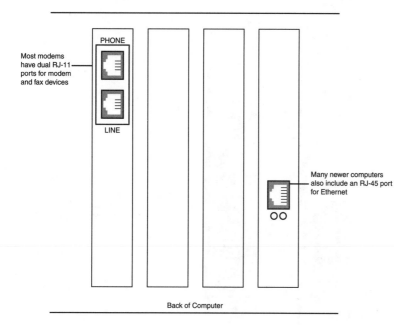

Most modems have dual RJ-11 ports for modem and fax devices

PHONE

LINE

Many newer computers also include an RJ-45 port for Ethernet

Back of Computer

Figure 12.2

The back of a computer with both an analog modem card (left) and Ethernet card (right). On some computers, these ports might be located near other built-in ports such as parallel or USB.

Tech Note

Connector Conundrum

Ethernet cards that use 10BASE-T cable have a connector on the card bracket that resembles the one used for telephone wiring (called RJ-11), but it's wider and has connections for eight wires. This connector is cryptically known as an *RJ-45 connector*.

Some older Ethernet cards don't have this connector but have either a connector with 15 pins or a round barrel-shaped connector. These were used for Thick or Thin Ethernet coaxial cable and can't be used with 10BASE-T cable. Some networking cards have both, and it's a-okay to use one because your cable modem will just ignore the other connector (see Figure 12.3).

Figure 12.3

Three types of Ethernet cable connections.

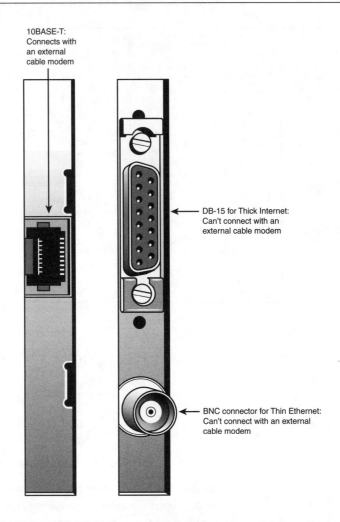

10BASE-T: Connects with an external cable modem

DB-15 for Thick Internet: Can't connect with an external cable modem

BNC connector for Thin Ethernet: Can't connect with an external cable modem

@Home supports any 10BASE-T or 10/100 Ethernet card that you want to use, but RoadRunner supports only the models listed in Table 12.3.

If you can't locate a supported card at your favorite store or don't want to install it yourself, ask your provider for the cost of the card plus installation.

If you're squeamish about opening your computer to install a network card, and if you have Windows 98, you might be able to substitute an external Ethernet connection that plugs into your computer's USB port. Some @Home and other cable providers support this configuration. However, check with your cable operator first for support and which brands and models are acceptable.

Table 12.3   Network Cards Approved for Use with RoadRunner Cable Modem Service

Manufacturer	Card Model	Attach to Computer Through
3Com	EtherLink XL 3C900-TPO	PCI bus slot (internal)
3Com	EtherLink III PC Card 3C589C-TP	PC card (PCMCIA card); For notebook computers
3Com	EtherLink III Card 3C562-TP (Win 95)	PC card (PCMCIA card); For notebook computers
3Com	Parallel Tasking Ethernet Adapters 3C509B-TP	ISA bus slot (internal)
3Com	Parallel Tasking Ethernet Adapters 3C590-TPO	PCI bus slot (internal)
SMC	EtherEZ PC Card SMC8020T 10BASE-T Adapter Type II	PC card (PCMCIA card) For notebook computers
SMC	EtherEZ SMC8416T Ethernet Network 10BASE-T Adapter	ISA bus slot (internal)
SMC	EtherPower SMC8432T 10BASE-T Adapter	PCI bus slot (internal)
Intel	EtherExpress Pro/10 with Flash (RJ45) PCLA8225B	ISA bus slot (internal)
Intel	EtherExpress Pro/10 (RJ45) PILA8420	PCI bus slot (internal)

Wondering which kinds of slots your computer has? After you (or a technically minded friend) open the case, take a close look inside. You're likely to see slots that resemble those shown in Figure 12.4.

Because ISA slots are older than dirt, in computer years, most computers built since 1998 have only one or two of them. Very often now, the only ISA slot is a combination ISA/PCI slot, as you can see in Figure 12.4.

The good news is that it's physically impossible to put the wrong kind of card in the wrong slot. As you can see in Figure 12.5, typical ISA and PCI network cards look similar at first, but note the differences in the connector types at the bottom of the cards.

Tech Note

THAT WAY ▶

PCI Is Perfect for Most Systems

As you saw in the previous table, you can use one of two slot types for your desktop computer:

➤ ISA (also called Industry Standard Architecture)

➤ PCI (also called Peripheral Component Interconnect)

Although the ISA slot is physically bigger (see Figure 12.4), it is much slower than the PCI slot and has been completely replaced by the PCI slot on most of today's computers.

If you have an open PCI slot, you should use it for your network card because PCI is faster and is the current standard. Use an ISA slot only if no PCI slots are available on your computer.

No Open Slot

Unless your cable modem can connect to an USB port, you will need an open expansion slot inside your computer. In most cases, the slot will be used (as you saw in the previous section) for a 10BASE-T or 10/100 Ethernet card. If you are getting one-way cable modem service, the cable modem will plug directly into the slot.

What can you do if you are out of open slots? If you have no open slots inside your computer and you can't use a USB connection for your external cable modem, you will need to remove an existing card to free up a slot.

If you don't even like looking at your computer's case, let alone what's inside it, this presents a problem. Which card can you sacrifice? If you're installing a two-way cable modem system, the best candidate for being "voted off the island" with Survivor-esque cruelty is your analog modem. But, if you're stuck for now with a one-way system, scrapping your modem is not even an option because you'll need it to send data out from your computer.

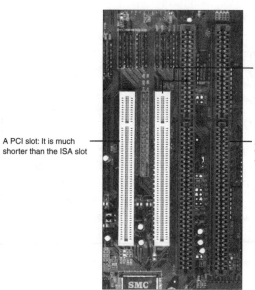

Figure 12.4

PCI, ISA, and combo slots in a typical computer.

A "combo" slot: You can insert either a PCI card (left) or ISA card (right) into the slot, but you cannot use both

A PCI slot: It is much shorter than the ISA slot

An ISA slot: It is much longer than the PCI slot and is usually made from a different-colored material

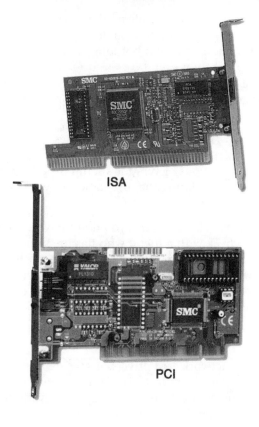

ISA

PCI

Figure 12.5

An ISA network card (top) and a PCI network card (bottom). Photos courtesy SMC.

207

Throw Me Lifeline!

A serial port or USB port can be a lifesaver. If you need to use an analog modem and your system requires that you free up an expansion slot to fit in a one-way cable modem, try using a serial or USB port to connect an external modem. Although it's an expensive option, an external analog modem that connects to one of these ports can let you detour around internal slot congestion.

(To learn more about serial ports, see Chapter 10, "Getting ISDN.")

No Operating System CD-ROM or Files

During the installation of your network card and cable modem, you need your operating system CD-ROM, disks, or files on hard disk to complete the process. Frequently, the CD-ROM becomes missing in action not long after a computer is brought home from the store, or it might not even be present for so-called *OEM* versions of Windows preinstalled on a computer. (OEM stands for *Original Equipment Manufacturer* and refers to versions of Windows supplied with a computer, not bought at retail as upgrades.)

If you can't find a CD-ROM of Windows files, click Start, Find, Files or Folders and search for a folder called Cabs. If present, this folder should contain several files that end in .CAB and contain compressed versions of Windows setup files. Note the location of your .CAB files, and use these files during the installation of your cable modem.

What can you do if you've lost your Windows CD and you don't have a Cabs folder with the Windows files? You could check with a friend who has the same version of Windows to borrow the CD in case you need to install new files during the installation of your cable modem. Otherwise, you could try to find the same version of Windows for sale at a store. If all else fails, upgrade to the latest version of Windows supported by your cable modem provider.

No Network Card Drivers

Your network card is useless without network card drivers. If you are responsible for supplying the network card, visit the card manufacturer's Web site with your current dial-up connection and download the latest drivers and diagnostic testing software for your card and operating system. Install the card and use the diagnostic testing software (this software should come with some form of instructions) to ensure your network card is working before installation day, or you very well might have problems getting online.

Look Out!

Believe it or not, there's a big difference between an operating system CD and the so-called "recovery" or "system recovery" CD supplied with many new computers. The latter is designed to reset your computer to its original factory settings; it usually deletes all your data files if you run its setup program. If your computer was supplied with a system recovery CD instead of just a generic Windows disc, you will normally have .CAB files on the hard drive for hardware or feature installation as listed previously.

No Backups of Your System

You should take time to back up your entire system's contents before the installer arrives. During the cable modem installation process, your computer gets moved around and opened, and new software is installed. If anything goes wrong, you might blame the installer, but that won't get your data back.

If you are concerned mostly about backing up the information you created, be sure to put the contents of the My Documents, My Pictures, My Files, and other folders you use to store documents, pictures, accounting, and so forth on a disk or high-capacity storage drive (CD-RW, LS-120 SuperDisk, or Zip drive). Chances are nothing will go wrong, but you'll feel better if you protect yourself.

The Best Backups

One of the best ways to back up important information on your computer is with the new breed of high-performance, low-cost (under $200) rewritable CD drives. Many models include backup software you can use, or you can buy backup software separately.

Installing the Cable Modem Service

For most users, the installation process is generally the easiest step in having a cable modem installed. All you have to do is be home when the cable guy (who hopefully does not look like Jim Carrey) shows up. However, depending on the reliability of your cable provider, that can be easier said than done! Generally, the process works as follows.

If you already have cable TV service, the technician arrives at your home or office and installs a device called a *splitter* where the existing coaxial cable enters your home or office. A new coaxial cable then is run from the external splitter to the room containing your computer.

If you are getting a two-way cable modem, the cable modem is connected to the coaxial cable in the room containing your computer. From there, a network cable, of the unshielded twisted-pair (UTP) variety, is run from the cable modem to your computer's network card. If the card isn't already present, the cable technician is usually the one to install it in your computer. Setup software, provided by the cable company, is then installed. Typically, this includes a version of Internet Explorer specifically customized for use with your cable modem. For example, @Home's version of Internet Explorer features a customized local content index and other quick-access options.

A one-way cable modem configuration is a little different. Just as with a two-way cable mode, the one-way cable modem is connected to the coaxial cable, but one-way cable modems fit inside your computer. Most one-way cable modems fit into an ISA slot.

The network configuration in your computer must be completed according to the technician's work order, and the cable modem must be turned on and allowed to synchronize with the cable network for as long as 30 minutes after being connected to the coaxial cable. After these processes are complete, you should be able to connect to the Internet.

The technician should give you an instruction manual, software, and any additional tips you need. If he doesn't, make sure you specifically ask for them! You also should make careful notes and, if possible, read along in the manual while you get briefed on your new setup. If the technician says something that the manual contradicts, find out who's right.

Self-Install Your Cable Modem? Maybe You Can!

Some cable modem providers offer a self-installation option for existing cable TV customers. Typically, a self-install kit provides you with everything you'd need to add cable modem service to an existing cable TV installation. For example, 3Com's self-installation kit for its cable modems includes the following:

➤ Short coaxial cable (6 feet)

➤ Long coaxial cable (25 feet)

➤ Cable line splitter

➤ Cable line clips (10 black, 10 white)

➤ Wrench

➤ Installation CD

➤ Installation guide

➤ User's guide and reference source

Check with your cable modem supplier to see whether self-installation is available to you. If it is, you can save time and money, however, many suppliers don't offer self-install yet.

Self-installation works best for upgrading relatively recent cable TV installations. If your installation dates back several years, you can have deteriorated external coaxial cable, the wrong standard of coax for use with a cable modem, or other problems that should be dealt with by the provider's own installer.

Avoiding Installation Problems

Problem #1: Your computer is in the "wrong" room.

Make sure you tell your cable provider where your computer will be located and whether you have a crawlspace and an external wall available for the cable drop when you place your order. Providers often need to budget extra time (and charge you more for installation) if your computer is on an upper floor or away from external walls, because a "wallfish" (not a rare type of trout!) is needed to run the coaxial cable to the correct location.

If you need to move your computer to a different room after the cable modem service is installed, call your provider to see whether you can just connect additional coaxial cable to the original installation or if additional hardware is needed.

Problem #2: Your computer isn't working properly.

If you can't load CDs with your computer or are having other technical difficulties, you'd better postpone your appointment until you get your computer fixed. A technician can't—or, very likely won't—fix your computer and install the cable modem hardware at the same time.

Problem #3: You have marginal cable hardware.

Coaxial cable standards have changed over time. If your technician needs to change your old RG-59 coaxial (obsolete) to RG-6 (current), let the installer take the time to do the job right.

Problem #4: You are going to replace your computer soon.

When you replace your computer, you must reinstall your cable modem software and network card. Here are some tips to help you get an installation you can move to another computer.

➤ Get a PCI network card—If the cable modem provider also supplies you with your network card, insist on a PCI-based network card if you have at least one PCI slot. Why? The once-common ISA slot is fading from use; I just bought a new HP Pavilion as a second computer for my small office and found it had no ISA slots. Your new desktop computer might, if you're lucky, have one ISA slot, but it's sure to have at least two or more PCI slots.

➤ Keep your software safe—Don't forget to keep the CD-ROM with the cable modem installation software in a safe place; you'll need to reinstall from the CD (and also from the new computer's operating system) when you set up the new computer.

➤ Write down the TCP/IP and browser settings—Also, you'll need the TCP/IP and browser configuration settings used by your cable modem provider. Sometimes this information is found on the work order. Grab a copy of it if possible.

Remember that a one-way cable modem has special settings for both the cable modem and your analog modem.

Tech Note

Finding the TCP/IP Settings

Sometimes the correct TCP/IP settings for your computer can be found on a sticker attached to the cable modem. You can also use the tips in Chapter 17, "A Survivor's Guide to TCP/IP," to look up your settings and record them.

If you change network cards, you might need to contact the cable modem provider. Why? Each and every network card has a unique number called the MAC number. Some ISPs use the MAC number to identify the computer that has the authorization to use your cable modem connection. You should ask your installer or the cable modem provider's help desk to see if this is necessary for you.

Your Cable Modem Checklist

Before you place your order, do the following:

___ Figure out where the computer will be placed for use with the cable modem.

___ Check the hardware and software requirements; try to exceed the recommended standards to ensure better performance.

___ Replace your computer if it doesn't meet the minimum standards; upgrade your computer with more RAM and so on to meet the recommended standards if possible.

During the order process, do the following:

___ Describe the location of the room carefully; determine whether a wallfish is necessary.

___ Ask about installation specials; you might be able to get reduced-price or even free installation if you ask about it.

___ Find out about the network card; does your cable modem provider supply it, or do you need to get your own? Which models are recommended or required?

___ Record the expected time and cost of the installation.

Before installation, do the following:

___ Run ScanDisk to test your drives for errors; fix any errors reported. Many technicians run ScanDisk as part of the installation process. If disk errors are reported, some techs won't finish the job or might make you sign a waiver.

___ Check the Windows Device Manager to see whether all your hardware is working correctly. Right-click on My Computer, select Properties, and click on the Device Manager tab. If you see hardware marked with a yellow exclamation point (!), the hardware is not working correctly. Some technicians will also make you sign a waiver or might not be able to finish the installation if these problems aren't corrected.

During installation, do the following:

___ Record the network and browser configuration used to get you connected.

___ File all software and paperwork provided by the vendor.

After installation (but before the tech leaves), do the following:

___ Make sure you can get connected to the Internet.

___ Make sure your computer is still working correctly, especially if the tech installs the network card for you or installs an internal cable modem. Some techs will disable sound cards or other hardware if there are conflicts between the network card or internal cable modem and your existing devices.

Thank the technician for setting up your system, but don't let the tech drive away until you know everything is okay.

The Least You Need to Know

➤ The order process for cable modem service is easier than for many other broadband services, but you will still need to make sure your computer is ready for broadband.

➤ The most common change you must make to your system is to add a network card.

➤ A few cable modem providers allow self-installation, but you will need a technician's visit for most installations.

➤ You must make sure that your system and your Internet connection are both working correctly before the technician leaves your home or office.

➤ It pays to make notes and ask questions to be sure you can change computers or network cards after your cable modem service is installed.

Chapter 13

Getting DirecPC

In This Chapter

➤ Select the best DirecPC plan and hardware for your needs

➤ Choose between DirecPC and DirecDuo

➤ Order and install DirecPC yourself

➤ Order DirecPC and supervise its installation by others

➤ Consider alternatives to DirecPC

DirecPC is the most widely known satellite solution to high-speed Internet access. If you're beyond the range of wired solutions, such as DSL and cable modem, or fixed wireless microwave-based broadband solutions, DirecPC gives you a way to get much faster downloads than are possible with your 56Kbps analog modem (uploads will use your analog modem until the two-way service debuts in 2001).

This chapter helps you go the distance from choosing the best DirecPC service package all the way through watching the first Web pages delivered by satellite show up on your computer screen. I also tell you how to get more information about some of the up-and-coming satellite rivals to DirecPC.

Time for the Usual Disclaimers

DirecPC is not available in Alaska and Hawaii. What about elsewhere? Although systems based on DirecPC are available in many different countries around the globe, differences in the satellites used mean that different dish types are used in different countries, the DirecPC software is different, and the services might even have different names.

Selecting the Best DirecPC Package

As you learned in Chapter 7, "Understanding DirecPC," DirecPC currently offers two different plans for home users:

➤ Family Surfer Unlimited—This plan offers unlimited online hours every month.

➤ Executive Surfer—This plan has a limit of 25 online hours per month; hours above 25 per month are charged at $2 per hour if you use DirecPC's own ISP, or $1 per hour if you use your own ISP.

Unless you live alone *and* have an iron-clad grip on your Web-use habits, you'd better get the Family Surfer Unlimited plan. Take it from somebody whose family ran up a $70.00 CompuServe bill after one month in the days of metered service—you don't want to play "watch the clock" when you're online!

And Now, for the Latest Deal from DirecPC

DirecPC has offered several plans over its history, and because you'll need to sign up for a plan during the DirecPC installation process, take a moment to go to the DirecPC Web site for the latest plan and pricing information: http://www.direcpc.com

AOL and DirecPC? It's Here

If you're an AOL fan and are also considering DirecPC, you can now combine the two into a single service. AOL Plus Powered by DirecPC uses DirecPC hardware to bring you AOL content (including the Internet). This version of DirecPC is exclusively for Windows 98 users and features a new version of the USB satellite modem and new software.

You can upgrade your current DirecPC to AOL Plus Powered by DirecPC by purchasing a new USB satellite modem with software. You can reuse your existing DirecPC satellite dish and cabling, but you will need to reposition your dish because AOL Plus uses different satellites than the normal DirecPC service does.

You can get more information about AOL Plus by calling 1-888-849-3200, or from the Web.

The term AOL Plus is also used for AOL's high-speed DSL service available in some markets.

You'll buy and install the same hardware regardless of which service you select, but if you're wanting to improve your satellite TV as well as Internet choices where you live, you have another choice to make before you buy your system and get it installed.

AOL Plus: Hot Off the Web

For the latest information about AOL Plus Powered by DirecPC, go to the AOL Plus section of the DirecPC Web site: http://www.direcpc.com/aolplus/

DirecPC or DirecDuo?

DirecPC is the "Internet-only" cousin of DirecTV. But, if you want both TV and Internet on the same dish (and who wants two mini-dishes to worry about?), go with DirecDuo. DirecDuo supports just TV service, just Internet service, or both at the same time.

Any way you slice it, if you are even thinking about adding DirecTV service, go with the DirecDuo dish instead of the normal DirecTV dish. It's slightly larger and a bit more expensive than the DirecTV dish, but having only one dish to mount and aim makes it worth buying. When used for DirecTV service, you can view any DirecTV program and service package with your DirecDuo dish.

Get the Latest Dish on DirecDuo

Need more information on the DirecDuo hardware packages? Go to the DirecDuo Web site at http://www.direcduo.com/

Ordering DirecPC

All right! You've looked over the DirecPC information and made your choice: It's time to get some satellite Internet action. How do you get your DirecPC connection started?

The DirecPC ordering process works like this:

1. Buy the equipment.
2. Install the equipment yourself or have it installed for you.
3. Run the DirecPC software on CD-ROM to sign up for the service package that you prefer.

When deciding to purchase DirecPC equipment you still have choices to make:

➤ What equipment you should buy

➤ Who should get your money

You can buy DirecPC equipment from any of the sources described in Chapter 7:

➤ Local retailers

➤ National appliance and electronics chains

➤ Online retailers

Because DirecPC offers you the choice of self-installation or professional installation, you should probably make your choice of dealer based on more than just the lowest price. Here are a few questions worth learning the answers to before you lay down your money:

➤ If you are looking at a package deal that includes both hardware and installation, how experienced is the dealer with DirecPC installation?—Although DirecPC is similar to DirecTV in some ways, aiming the antenna is a lot trickier.

➤ Can you return your dish for a refund within a few days, or are you forced to return a defective dish to Hughes Network Systems?—A no-hassle return policy is probably worth paying a few dollars extra up front.

➤ Are you getting fresh product, or have the dish and satellite modem been sitting around for quite a while waiting for a buyer?—Older products come with older software that will need to be updated as soon as possible.

➤ Is the product in stock, or must it be special ordered?—If the dealer doesn't stock the product, the odds of getting good answers to your questions might not be very high.

Regardless of where you purchase your equipment, be sure you get everything you need. After all, the guy in a trench coat in that back alley with the unmarked van might offer a good deal, but if you're not getting the following equipment, you're getting short-changed:

➤ DirecPC or DirecDuo dish

➤ PCI or USB satellite modem (comes with software)

➤ Universal mounting kit

➤ Self-installation kit (if you plan to install the dish and cabling yourself)

Some vendors sell all the pieces as a kit; others make you buy it piecemeal. After you have your equipment, though, you're ready to install it—or pay somebody else to install it. Before you make that decision, review the rest of this chapter.

Pliers? Phone Call? You Decide

Before you decide whether to put the dish up yourself or pay a pro to install it yourself, do two things:

➤ Call DirecPC at 1–800–DIRECPC to locate a professional installer in your area.

➤ Take a look at the DirecPC installation documents online at

```
http://www.direcpc.com/selfhelp/
```

By reviewing the steps needed to install the hardware before you decide how to install DirecPC, you'll be better able to judge whether you want to do it yourself or not.

If you decide to opt for professional installation, you can expect to pay between $170–$200 for "partial installation" and between $230–$270 for "full installation"; prices vary, so contact your installer for your best price. What's the difference?

➤ Partial installation (dish-only installation) puts you in charge of installing the satellite modem and the software while the installer worries about falling off the roof while placing the antenna, grounding the system, and running the coax.

➤ Full installation (dish and modem installation) makes you a bystander while the installer does everything.

Especially if you opt for the USB satellite modem with Windows 98, you should choose the partial installation option; by setting up the computer yourself, you'll save money and headaches and have your system online faster. If your system isn't compatible with the USB satellite modem and you're a rookie at installing cards like the PCI satellite modem inside the computer, go for the full installation option.

If you've already had experience with coaxial cable, you might prefer to perform the entire job yourself.

Making Sure Your System Meets the DirecPC Requirements

DirecPC requires a bit more "oomph" in the CPU department than DSL or cable modem service, but on the upside, it requires less disk space. The following are the requirements:

Tech Note

USB, PCI, and Other Alphabet Soup

What's PCI? What's USB? Why should you care? These acronyms refer to the two ways you can connect a DirecPC satellite modem to your computer. The good news is that if you're running Windows 98, installing a DirecPC satellite modem can be as easy as running a wire from the back of the external satellite modem to a universal serial bus (USB) port on the back of your computer. If you hate crawling around on the floor, make one of the kids do it!

What if you're running Windows NT 4.0 or Windows 95? You'll need to pop open your computer and insert an internal satellite modem into a peripheral component interconnect (PCI) slot inside your computer. You can also use the PCI satellite modem with Windows 98, but if you can use the USB version, you might not want to use PCI.

Are you wondering how to tell what the USB port and PCI slot look like? See Figures 13.1 and 13.2.

Figure 13.1

You can use any USB port on your system for the USB version of the DirecPC satellite modem shown in Figure 13.3. The USB ports might be marked by the fork-shaped USB logo or by name as seen here.

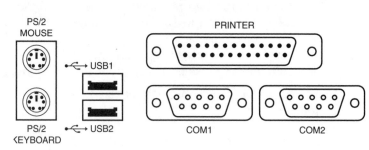

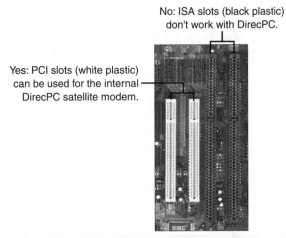

No: ISA slots (black plastic) don't work with DirecPC.

Yes: PCI slots (white plastic) can be used for the internal DirecPC satellite modem.

Figure 13.2

If you don't have a USB port handy on your Windows 98 system, or if you're running Windows 95 or Windows NT 4.0, look inside your system for an open PCI slot for the internal version of the DirecPC satellite modem shown in Figure 13.3.

DirecPC works the same way regardless of which modem type you choose. To see what the external (USB) and internal (PCI) satellite modems look like, see Figure 13.3. Table 13.1 breaks down the DirecPC hardware requirements.

External satellite modem (requires USB port and Windows 98)

Internal satellite modem (requires PCI slot and Windows 95/98 or NT 4.0)

Figure 13.3

The DirecPC external USB satellite modem (left) and PCI card internal satellite modem (right).

Table 13.1 Hardware Requirements for DirecPC— USB and PCI Versions

Hardware	Requirement
USB Satellite Modem	
Dish placement (outside)	An unobstructed line of sight to the south*
Processor	200MHz Pentium-type CPU with available USB port
Memory	32MB RAM (minimum) and 20MB of hard disk space
Modem	28.8Kbps or faster
Operating system	Microsoft Windows 98
Other requirements	Internet service provider (normal dial-up account or ISDN), which DirecPC can provide

Table 13.1 Hardware Requirements for DirecPC— USB and PCI Versions Continued

Hardware	Requirement
	PCI Satellite Modem
Dish placement (outside)	An unobstructed line of sight to the south*
Processor	200MHz Pentium-type class with available PCI port
Memory	32MB RAM (minimum) and 20MB of hard disk space
Modem	28.8Kbps or better
Operating system	Microsoft Windows 95/98 or Windows NT 4.0
Other requirements	Internet service provider (normal dial-up account or ISDN), which DirecPC can provide

For installations in the Northern hemisphere. DirecPC satellites are geosynchronous, orbiting the equator at a distance of about 22,000 miles. For installations in the Southern hemisphere, an unob-structed line of sight to the north is needed.

Note that you don't need a network card with DirecPC, but you do need to have either an open PCI card slot or to be running Windows 98 with an open USB port. If you're out of PCI card slots on a Windows 95 or Windows NT 4.0 computer, you'll need to juggle some cards around to free up a slot, because DirecPC no longer uses the ISA slots shown in Figure 13.2 for its satellite modem.

Installing DirecPC Yourself

Should you install DirecPC yourself? Good question! Unlike the self-installation version of DSL, which never exposes you to the outside air, a DirecPC installation will require you to briefly don the caps of a

➤ Satellite dish technician

➤ Coaxial cable wiring specialist

➤ PC hardware technician

Outside of some carnies I saw as a youth, most of us don't have that many heads to put these caps on. Don't underestimate this challenge, because you might need to jump through such hoops as climbing on your roof, poking holes in your walls and ceiling, and, even more daring, popping open your PC.

The DirecPC Web site's Self-Help section is a useful resource if you plan to install the system yourself. And, later in this chapter I'll bring you help for some of the details that aren't covered as adequately online as you might like.

If you've installed other satellite dishes for TV, you'll find that the DirecPC installa-tion is similar, although the antenna pointing routine is more involved. If you're new to this, don't panic; by the time you finish this part of the chapter, you'll be ready to decide which way to go to get connected with DirecPC.

Tech Note

Hey, What About Me? (and 2000?)

If you have the latest versions of Windows (Windows Me and Windows 2000), you might be feeling a little miffed right now because neither of these versions is listed in the compatibility guidelines shown earlier. What's the inside scoop?

Although neither version is officially supported by DirecPC, the news is much better for Windows Me users than for Windows 2000 users. Windows Me, which is an update to Windows 98, typically works quite well with DirecPC. Comments on the DirecPC newsgroup available at http://www.deja.com discussion site indicate that you'll have the best luck if you use Windows Me + DirecPC on a computer with factory-installed Windows Me or a Windows 98 system upgraded to Windows Me; installing Windows Me to an empty hard disk doesn't work as well. You can use either the USB or PCI versions of the satellite modem.

The news isn't so good for Windows 2000. Although Windows 2000 is a replacement for Windows NT 4.0, its hardware support is completely different than NT's. You'll need to wait for Windows 2000 drivers or set up a network and use your Windows 2000 computer as a client. See Chapter 21 for details.

Nine Steps to Going Online with DirecPC

When you receive your DirecPC or DirecDuo system, what's the first thing you'll do? Unpack it! Just like the birthday kid who can't wait to open the presents, you'll be eager to unwrap your system and get started. But take a deep breath, slow down a little bit, and do the following:

1. *Carefully* unpack your DirecPC or DirecDuo system—There are a lot of small parts in the box; make sure none of them get lost.

2. Inspect components for damage—If you're buying DirecPC off the shelf at a retailer, I hope you skipped the box that looked like Godzilla stepped on it. If you get a damaged unit despite your best efforts, return it pronto!

   If you bought DirecPC from an online or mail-order retailer, take a careful look at the shipping carton before you sign for it. If the carton looks like Godzilla found it anyway, contact the delivery company. If the carton appears okay but the dish or other components are damaged, contact DirecPC for replacement instructions.

3. Install the DirecPC satellite modem—You'll need to use it to receive signals from your antenna when it's time to point the dish at the satellite.

4. Install the DirecPC software—The modem will just sit there looking useless until the software's in the system. You need all three: DirecPC antenna, DirecPC satellite modem, and DirecPC software to tell the antenna where to go.

5. Install your antenna and mount—When the antenna is installed and pointed in (approximately) the right direction, you're ready to run the software.

6. Run the DirecPC auto-setup program—The program contains a satellite pointing program; use it to aim the antenna toward the DirecPC satellite.

7. Register your DirecPC system—Enter the ISP you want to use and select the DirecPC service plan you want.

8. Configure your computer to use DirecPC Turbo Webcast and Newscast services if you want.

9. Start using the Internet with DirecPC.

Installing the DirecPC Hardware and Software in Your Computer

It might seem backward to you, but you need to install the DirecPC USB or PCI modem and install the DirecPC software before you can aim the satellite dish. Why? The DirecPC CD has a satellite dish locator feature that, when installed first, will help you align your dish correctly.

Before you have the luxury of installing the DirecPC software, however, you must install the DirecPC hardware. Slip on your computer installer hat and prepare to crawl under the table or pop open your computer.

The DirecPC satellite modem can be either a PCI card (for Windows 9x and Windows NT 4.0) or a USB external device (for Windows 98 only). What exactly is a "satellite modem?" Either type of device is a proprietary device that works especially with DirecPC; the link between the DirecPC or DirecDuo dish outside your home and your Web browser runs straight through the satellite modem.

Don't confuse the internal DirecPC card with a 10BASE-T or 10/100 Ethernet network card (see Chapter 12). The only reason to have a network card in a computer that uses DirecPC is to share the DirecPC connection with other computers over a network.

You will need to shut down your computer to install the PCI satellite modem card, but the USB satellite modem can be plugged into your computer while it's running.

For details on how to install the PCI satellite modem card inside your computer, see the discussion of removing and installing an internal modem in Chapter 3. Use Figure 13.2, earlier in this chapter, as a visual aid to help you locate your PCI slots inside your computer.

What happens the first time you turn on the computer after connecting either type of satellite modem? If you are using Windows 95 or Windows 98 (or Windows Me), you can normally perform a Plug and Play installation:

1. The computer detects the new satellite modem during Windows startup—The Update Device Driver Wizard starts and prompts you for the DirecPC CD-ROM, which contains the drivers for both types of satellite modems.

2. Pop the DirecPC CD-ROM into your computer and browse to the CD-ROM's drive letter—It might take about five to ten seconds for the drive to spin up, so don't panic if your system doesn't display the .INF driver files needed to install hardware right away.

3. Both the oemset95.inf driver file used by the PCI satellite modem and the dpcusb.inf driver file used by the USB satellite modem are on the CD-ROM; after the appropriate file is displayed and loaded, Windows will detect your modem. Click Finish to continue.

4. Swap your DirecPC CD-ROM for the Windows CD-ROM if prompted; although the satellite modems aren't network cards, network files (such as TCP/IP protocol files and others) will need to be installed.

5. After installing the network files, Windows will look on the Windows CD-ROM for the bicndis.sys (PCI modem) or dpcusb.sys (USB modem) drivers and not be able to find them (duh! they're on the DirecPC CD-ROM). Switch back to the DirecPC CD-ROM to finish installing your modem.

6. Restart your computer if you are installing the PCI internal satellite modem; the USB modem doesn't require a restart.

To learn more about the Update Device Driver Wizard, see Chapter 19, "DSL Tips, Tricks, and Troubleshooting." If you have problems with any part of the DirecPC installation process, see Chapter 21, "DirecPC Tips, Tricks, and Troubleshooting."

Tech Note

NT Ain't So Easy

Are you installing the DirecPC PCI satellite modem into a computer running Windows NT 4.0? NT 4.0, unlike Windows 95, Windows 98, and Windows Me, isn't Plug and Play; you must install the satellite modem drivers manually. If you need help installing the modem, go to the DirecPC Self-Help site and look up Satellite Receiver Adapter – Driver Installation:

```
http://www.direcpc.com/selfhelp
```

After you've restarted the computer, it's time to take off the computer hardware tech hat and put on the dish and cable installer hat (if you've decided to install the DirecPC or DirecDuo dish yourself). You'll go back to the computer later to aim the antenna, but first you must assemble the antenna, mount it, and run the coaxial cable from the dish to your satellite modem.

Dish and Cable Assembly and Installation Tips and Hints

After the DirecPC satellite modem is installed, it's time to assemble and install the DirecPC or DirecDuo satellite dish. DirecPC provides two forms of guidance to help you get your dish installed right:

➤ A series of manuals in Adobe Acrobat PDF format on the DirecPC installation CD-ROM—Acrobat Reader software (which you need to read the manuals) is also supplied on the CD-ROM

➤ The DirecPC Self-Help Web site

These provide a detailed description of the installation process, so what I'll do for you in this section is give you some tips and pointers that aren't available there.

Tech Note

THAT WAY ➤

Get the Most Out of Self-Help

If you decide to use the DirecPC Self Help Web site, I suggest that you

➤ Visit the site before you start the installation process and print out the pages

➤ Click the figures to display a larger, more detailed view and print out those pages

➤ Number the pages for easy reference

You'll find the Self Help web site at

```
http://www.direcpc.com/selfhelp/
```

Choosing the Best Location for Your Satellite Dish

You need an unobstructed southern view if you're installing DirecPC in the northern hemisphere (an unobstructed northern view is needed if you are installing DirecPC in the southern hemisphere). You must make two adjustments with your dish to aim it correctly:

➤ Azimuth—The angle in degrees between true north and the point on the horizon directly beneath the satellite; always a positive number, measured clockwise. For example, a 45-degree azimuth would be the same as northeast, a 90-degree azimuth would be east, and a 270-degree azimuth would be west (see Figure 13.4).

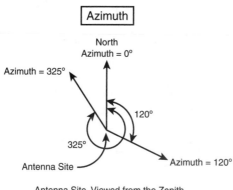

Figure 13.4

The azimuth will vary according to two factors: the satellite your DirecPC installation will use and your location on the ground relative to that satellite

➤ Elevation—The angle in degrees between the horizon and the satellite; always measured in positive numbers. For example, a 45-degree elevation would be halfway between the horizon and vertical (see Figure 13.5).

During the DirecPC dish aiming procedure, you will need to move your dish from side to side to adjust the azimuth, and pivot it up and down to set the elevation. If you have obstructions blocking your view, your dish might not be able to "see" the satellite.

After you've settled on a location, it's time to install your dish. The online Self-Help Guide provides step-by-step instructions for typical installations.

Regardless of where you install the dish, be sure you

➤ Mount the antenna so that you start out with a plumb mount (perfectly straight up and down)—A crooked mount will make it much harder to locate the satellite.

➤ Mount the antenna securely—If the antenna wobbles, you will lose your signal and go off the air.

➤ Make sure you can reach the adjustments at the rear of the dish—These must be used to correctly point the antenna during software installation.

227

Figure 13.5

The elevation will vary according to two factors: the satellite your DirecPC installation will use and your distance from the equator. The farther from the equator you are, the lower you'll set the elevation of the satellite dish.

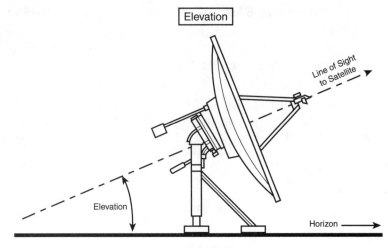

Satellite Antenna Side View

Tech Note

Put Away the Drill—There's Another Way to Use Your Chimney

The increased elevation that a chimney can provide makes it a logical place to put your DirecPC dish mount. However, you don't need to drill holes in the brick as suggested in the online Self-Help guide. Instead, you can attach the dish mount to one corner of your chimney and strap it into place with a satellite chimney mount kit (about $20–30).

After you've attached the dish to its mount, it's time to install your coaxial cables.

What's in the DirecPC Self-Install Kit?

Before you order your DirecPC system, I encourage you to decide where you want to put your dish, especially if you are planning to install the dish yourself. Why? You want to know how much coaxial cable you'll need to connect your dish to your satellite modem and whether the typical self-install kit has enough.

The official DirecPC self-installation kit contains the components listed in Table 13.2. Other "self-install" kits might omit some components.

Table 13.2   Components in the DirecPC Self-Installation Kit

Quantity	Component
1	RG-6 weatherproof F-to-F coaxial cable, 25-foot length
1	RG-6 weatherproof F-to-F coaxial cable, 100-foot length
1	#8 aluminum grounding wire, 50-foot length
1	Angle finder
4	11 1/2-inch cable ties
8	Cable clips
1	F-type grounding block with mounting hardware
1	Wall plate with mounting hardware
1	Water pipe ground clamp
1	Pole-mount grounding lug with mounting hardware
1	Silicone sealant, 1-ounce container
1	Compass
10	Cable clips for RG-6 coaxial cable
5	Hex-head machine bolts, 2 1/4-inch×3/8-inch
2	Lag bolts, 3-inch×3/8-inch
8	Lag bolts, 2 1/2-inch×3/8-inch
12	Cement-coated nails, 16d

This kit is designed to include everything you need to connect the DirecPC dish to your DirecPC satellite modem. However, a grounding rod is not included (the kit assumes you'll use a water pipe), and you might need additional coaxial cable, especially if you are using both the TV and Internet features of the DirecDuo dish. See the next section for a list of additional components you can add to the standard kit or substitute for the components in the standard kit.

Planning Your Cable and Grounding Block Installation

Before you can aim your dish and start receiving Internet data with your DirecPC dish, you must connect the cables to your dish and to your satellite modem.

At the dish, the coaxial cable attaches to a device called a low-noise block (LNB). It's the gizmo at the end of the arm that projects from the dish. What does it do? The LNB amplifies the microwave signal received from the DirecPC satellite and converts in into a signal that can be sent through the coaxial cable you attach to the LNB. And on to your satellite modem?

Get Me More Coax—I've Got DirecDuo

You will need to run three coaxial cables (one for DirecPC and two for DirecTV) between a DirecDuo satellite dish and your home if you use both DirecPC and DirecTV. You will also need to purchase additional grounding equipment for the two coaxial connections used by the DirecTV portion of the DirecDuo dish.

Are you not sure whether you want DirecTV service yet? Most folks advise running the additional coax anyway so you're ready to add TV to your service in the future.

Skip on By If George Will Do It

If you've called a professional installer, you can rest easy until it's time to install the DirecPC software. However, if you're Mr. (or Ms.) Self-Install, pay close attention to all this stuff.

Almost. Sure, the signal gets there, but you actually need two lengths of coaxial cable:

➤ One runs from the LNB to the grounding block

➤ The other runs from your grounding block to satellite modem

If you are installing the DirecDuo dish instead of the normal DirecPC dish, you need three lengths of each cable because the LNB for the DirecTV part of the dish uses two coaxial connectors (if you have two receivers), and the DirecPC portion uses one.

So, before you buy or build your cable (let alone install it!), you also must decide where to install the grounding block. If you are planning to use a cold-water pipe as a ground, you can put the grounding block in a location near a cold-water pipe, such as the basement. If you plan to use a grounding rod, the grounding block should be installed outside.

Figure 13.6 shows a typical attic location for the grounding blocks on a DirecDuo installation.

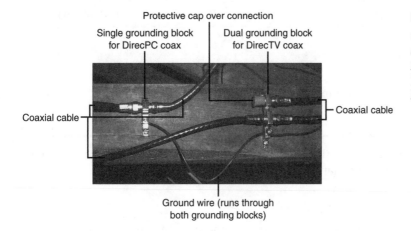

Protective cap over connection

Single grounding block
for DirecPC coax

Dual grounding block
for DirecTV coax

Coaxial cable

Coaxial cable

Ground wire (runs through
both grounding blocks)

Figure 13.6

Grounding blocks with coaxial cable used in a DirecDuo installation. This user has only one DirecTV receiver.

After you decide where to place your grounding blocks, you'll know how much coaxial cable to buy or build. You can use Table 13.3 as a planning chart to help you determine how long each cable section should be. Table 13.4 is an example of a completed planner.

Table 13.3   Blank Cable Planner for DirecPC/DirecDuo Installation

LNB Type	LNB to Ground Block	Ground Block to Device (Satellite Receiver or Modem)
DirecPC		
DirecTV #1		
DirecTV #2		
	(Record distance in feet or meters above)	

When you record the estimated lengths you need, allow sufficient slack for adjusting the cable at both ends. If you are installing a DirecDuo dish, complete DirecTV lines 1 and 2 as well as the line for DirecPC.

Table 13.4   Completed Sample Cable Planner

LNB Type	LNB to Ground Block	Ground Block to Device (Satellite Receiver or Modem)
DirecPC	10 feet	30 feet
DirecTV #1	10 feet	50 feet
DirecTV #2	10 feet	50 feet
(DirecTV lines for DirecDuo dish)	(Record distance in feet or meters above)	

Note that the cable distances for the DirecTV coaxial cables could be different if your receiver is in a different room than the computer with the DirecPC satellite modem.

Building Your Own Self-Install Kit

The standard self-installation lacks some of the components you need, can include components you don't need, and has fixed lengths of coaxial cable that aren't suitable for every installation. You can use the following lists of components to help you "roll your own" kit, or supplement a standard self-install kit. Stores such as Radio Shack or others that stock cable TV and antenna wiring components are good sources for these components and tools.

The screws and nails found in the self-install kit can be purchased at a local hardware store. You can buy a magnetic compass at a local sporting goods store. The remainder of the items in the self-install kit can be replaced by components available at electronics stores such as Radio Shack.

➤ RG-6 coaxial cable—If you find that the coaxial cable lengths in the self-install kits aren't adequate, you can buy prebuilt cables in lengths ranging from 25 to 100 feet. If you must run the cable past sources of interference, such as heaters or electric motors, consider quad-shielded RG-6 cable.

➤ Bulk RG-6 cable and connectors—If you must install your dish on a tower away from your house, you might need more than 100 feet of cable, and if you are installing a DirecDuo dish for TV and Internet service, you'll need multiple lengths of cable. In these cases, buy bulk cable and connectors you can cut to the lengths you need. See the following section for details.

➤ Grounding equipment—Electrical storms can damage your dish, and if the current is carried into your home, your satellite modem and even your computer could be damaged or destroyed. The DirecPC self-install kit contains the grounding block and ground wire but assumes that you have a water pipe nearby for grounding the dish assembly. My advice? Buy a grounding rod long enough to reach moist earth (an 8-footer should do it in most places), pound it into the ground, and run your ground wire to it. It's safer than trying to figure out where the nearest cold-water pipe is.

➤ Wall and cable sealant—There's no getting around it: DirecPC requires you to put a hole through your wall to get the coaxial cable from your dish into your home. The standard self-install kit provides a small tube of silicone rubber sealant; you might need to buy more. And, to prevent damage to your cable, consider adding a set of feed-through bushings, which snap into both the outside and inside holes to provide a smoother hole for insertion of your cable. You should also buy weatherproof tape to wrap around your outside connections.

➤ Rubber boots—Not for your feet, for your cable connectors. While you're safe, warm, dry, and online inside, your dish will be taking a beating from rain, snow, sleet, hail, drizzle, or whatever your local climate's bad weather feature happens to be. By covering the coaxial cable connectors with protective boots, you minimize the risk of corrosion damaging your cables and taking your Internet downloads off the air. You can substitute weatherproof tape, but the boots are a more elegant solution that still don't cost very much.

Building Coaxial Cable, Piece by Piece

Do you have a cable run too long for the prebuilt cable in the usual self-install kit? Want smaller holes in the side of your house? Hate the usual black color of prebuilt coax? Putting in a DirecDuo dish and TV tuner along with your DirecPC service? These are all good reasons to buy what you need to build your own coaxial cable.

What do you need to build coaxial cable yourself?

➤ Bulk RG-6 coaxial cable—Cable can be purchased by the foot from some stores or in boxes that contain a 500-foot spool of cable. Make sure you buy cable that is rated for both outdoor and indoor use. You can sometimes get white coax as an alternative to basic black. You'll spend about 20 to 24 cents per foot on quad-shielded outdoor/indoor cable at typical stores; standard cable will be less expensive but not as resistant to interference.

➤ RG-6 F-type connectors—Each end of the cable needs a connector. By threading the raw cable through the wall, you can have smaller holes and a less conspicuous installation. If you use quad-shielded cable, you must use a crimp-on connector; standard cable can use a twist-on connector. Either type will run you about $1 each.

See Figure 13.7 for details of the cable and connectors.

Figure 13.7

F-type connectors and RG-6 coaxial cable before stripping and assembly.

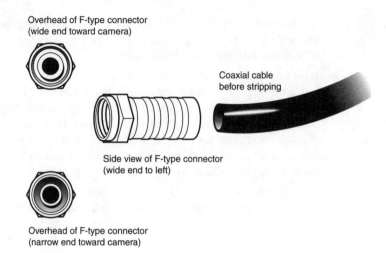

Overhead of F-type connector
(wide end toward camera)

Coaxial cable
before stripping

Side view of F-type connector
(wide end to left)

Overhead of F-type connector
(narrow end toward camera)

To prepare your cable for assembly, you also need

➤ Coax cable cutter—It's tempting to just grab your pocket knife to cut the cable, but don't do it. The coaxial cable cutter has curved blades that won't flatten the cable while it's cut, making it easier to install the connectors. It's around $7.

➤ Coax wire stripper—After the cable has been cut, you must strip the outer coating off to allow the connector to be twisted onto the cable. It's about $12.

➤ Crimping tool—If you install quad-shielded cabling, you will need to crimp the F-type connector to each end of the cable after you slide it onto the end of the cable; standard cable can use twist-on connectors. A good crimping tool runs around $16.

See Figure 13.8 for details of these tools.

After the cable is stripped (see Figure 13.9), the narrow end of the F-type connector is twisted over the stripped end of the cable. The crimping tool is used to fasten the connector to the cable. The result also appears in Figure 13.9. Both ends of the cable are assembled in the same way.

After you have bought or made the cables you need, attach them to your mounted antenna, grounding blocks, and satellite modem. Figure 13.10 shows how the coaxial cable is mounted on a DirecPC dish.

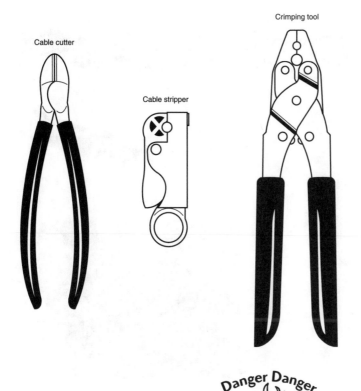

Cable cutter

Cable stripper

Crimping tool

Figure 13.8

Cable cutter, cable stripper, and crimping tools; you'll use each of these tools to finish each end of your cable.

Danger Danger

Build the Cable or Break It? Your Tools Will Decide

If you've decided that building your own coaxial cables is the way to go, don't cut corners by trying to use pliers to crimp the cable connector or a knife to cut or strip the cable. The tools just mentioned are designed to do the job right. If you use pliers instead of a crimping tool, for example, you'll damage the cable and connector. You'll damage the cable if you try to strip the cable with a knife. It pays to buy good tools if you plan to do it yourself.

Figure 13.9

The F-type connector and stripped cable before assembly (top) and after assembly and crimping (bottom).

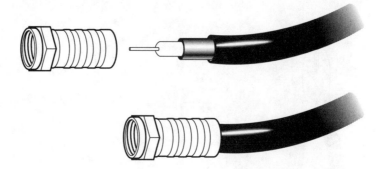

Figure 13.10

A typical installation of coaxial cable to the LNB of the DirecPC antenna.

If you have a DirecDuo dish, you will also have a dual LNB for use with up to two DirecTV receivers. See Figure 13.11 for details of its coaxial cable.

Figure 13.11

Two different views of the LNBs on the DirecDuo antenna.

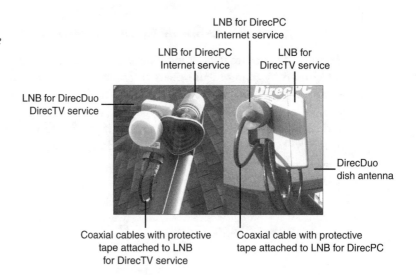

After you have connected the coaxial cable to both your dish antenna and to the satellite modem, you can install your DirecPC software to align the antenna and get connected to the service. Figures 13.12 and 13.13 show you where to connect the coaxial cable to both types of satellite modems.

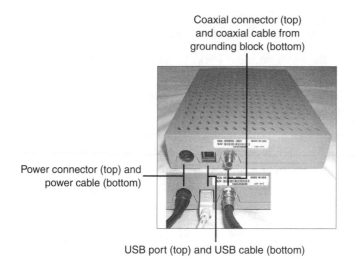

Coaxial connector (top)
and coaxial cable from
grounding block (bottom)

Power connector (top) and
power cable (bottom)

USB port (top) and USB cable (bottom)

Figure 13.12

Connectors on the DirecPC USB satellite modem.

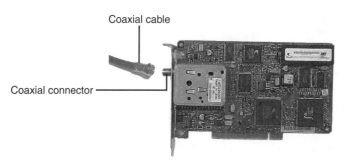

Coaxial cable

Coaxial connector

Figure 13.13

Connectors on the DirecPC PCI satellite modem.

It's Software Time!

It won't be time to relax just yet, but you should take a moment and smile after you've installed the satellite modem, assembled and installed the antenna, and strung the coaxial cabling. You're halfway home.

What's left? You still need to install the software and aim the antenna.

Check and Double-Check

Before you start the DirecPC software installation process, make sure your regular analog dial-up modem is still plugged in and working properly. You will need to use it during installation to help set up your antenna, register your system and set up a service plan, and go online.

If you needed to unplug the telephone wire from the analog modem while you were installing the satellite modem or coaxial cable, make sure you plug it back into the correct jack on the rear of the analog modem. Look for "Line" or "Telco" markings to make sure (some modems don't care which jack you use).

The same CD-ROM used to install the satellite modem software also contains the DirecPC software. Getting started is easy:

➤ Slide the CD-ROM into your CD-ROM drive

➤ Open Windows Explorer

➤ Browse to the CD-ROM's drive letter

➤ Double-click Setup to start the process

During software installation, part of the time you can sit back, but you'll need to supply some information as the software does the following:

➤ Sets up your modem

➤ Sets up your dial-up connection

➤ Registers you for the DirecPC service plan you prefer

➤ Configures your network settings

➤ Points your antenna

Next, DirecPC configures your dial-up modem and uses it to call the Registration server. You can use the Properties buttons to make any adjustments you like, but if your modem has worked well for you with your previous online service, it should be okay (see Figure 13.14).

During the registration process, a status bar appears on your screen. After your system is registered and you have selected a service plan, you must select an Internet service provider (ISP). You can keep your current ISP or use a DirecPC dial-up number.

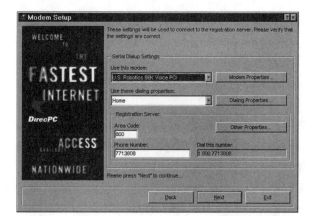

Figure 13.14

Verify that your modem has been identified and that the correct registration number is being used before you continue.

Make Sure the Call Is Local

As you learned in Chapter 7, you must use an ISP that's a local call for you. If you're happy with your current ISP (except for the speed), select Other from the list and continue to use it with DirecPC.

If you select Other (meaning that you're going to stick with your current ISP, thank you!), provide the area code and phone number, username and password, and connection type (usually PPP, the Point-to-Point protocol seen in Figure 13.15) to set up your connection. If you use DirecPC's own ISP, you choose by city and state.

When you finish the ISP selection, it's about time to drag yourself out of your chair and prepare to go on the roof. Next stop—Antennaland!

Aligning the Dish Antenna

The antenna alignment process uses the DirecPC installation program to provide the basic information you need to align your antenna, but it won't go back up on the roof for you. Unlike the antenna rotors still common in rural areas for TV, there's no motor on the DirecPC dish—pointing it is up to you!

This is *not*, repeat, *not* a one-man (or one-woman) operation. No way! Why not? After all, after you select the city and state where you live, you get aiming coordinates, right (see Figure 13.16)? That's a start, but the coordinates you see onscreen are approximations. You still need to fine-tune your antenna to make sure the signals that have come 22,000-odd miles to your neighborhood come in strong enough to be detected.

239

Figure 13.15

If you are sticking with a non-DirecPC ISP, supply all the information requested here to set up your connection.

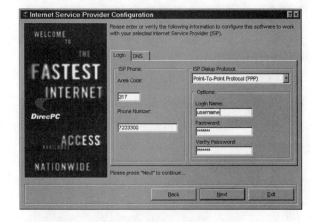

Figure 13.16

Record the values for your location and prepare to adjust the antenna. You're not finished until you hit a signal strength of at least 100.

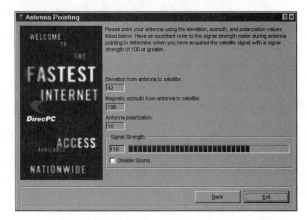

After you write down the settings displayed for your location, it's time to take your tools and go to the roof because the process of adjusting the antenna for adequate signal strength requires adjusting three factors:

➤ Azimuth

➤ Elevation

➤ Polarization

You adjust azimuth and elevation by moving the dish from side to side and up and down, whereas you adjust polarization by moving the antenna reflector. All the nuts on the rear of the antenna will need to be loosened (see Figure 13.17).

Tech Note

Two Out of Three Ain't Bad

If you've already installed some sort of satellite dish before, a lot of this will seem familiar. The major difference between a DirecTV, Dish Network, or USSB dish installation and DirecPC is the polarization setting.

If you are installing DirecDuo for use with both DirecPC and DirecTV services, be sure to set up the dish for the DirecPC service first! Aiming is far less critical with the DirecTV service than with DirecPC because there are more DirecTV satellites.

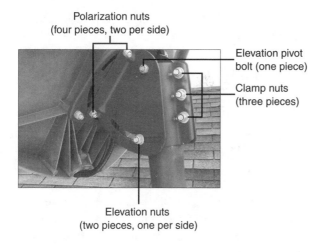

Polarization nuts
(four pieces, two per side)

Elevation pivot
bolt (one piece)

Clamp nuts
(three pieces)

Elevation nuts
(two pieces, one per side)

Figure 13.17

To allow adjustment of the azimuth, elevation, and polarization of your dish, loosen all the screws indicated.

Adjust the polarization first to the value provided by the DirecPC setup program. Note that a positive polarization value uses the scale below the zero value, and a negative polarization value uses the scale above the zero value (see Figure 13.18).

Figure 13.18

This antenna has been set to the 10 degrees polarization setting called for by the setup program.

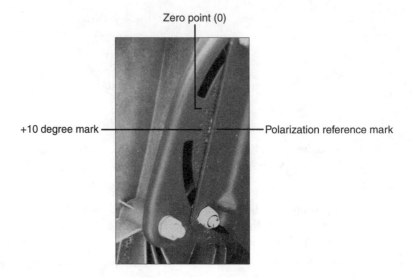

Zero point (0)

+10 degree mark ——————

———— Polarization reference mark

Next, set the elevation to the figure provided by the DirecPC setup program. Tighten the elevation bolts but not the pivot bolt.

Tech Note

THAT WAY ▷

Lining Up a Crooked Dish Can Be Plumb Hard

The elevation and azimuth values provided by the DirecPC setup program should be very close to the final values if you have a properly mounted dish. If your dish is mounted on a pole that is not plumb (completely vertical), you'll have a harder time making the final adjustments using the signal strength indicator.

Finally, set the azimuth. Pull out your magnetic compass and hold it away from you and from the dish (to avoid being attracted to the dish, your belt buckle, or your wallet chain), and find magnetic north. Check the value given for the magnetic azimuth by the DirecPC setup program, and turn the dish mounting until the value lines up with the azimuth figure.

Use a pencil and place a pencil mark at the actual setting, then one at 3/4-inch on either side of the actual setting. Turn the dish to the right-most pencil mark for starters to help adjust for the difference between magnetic and true north.

Are we there yet? The same setup screen that provided you with these values will tell you. Return now to those thrilling days of yesteryear—or at least back a couple of pages to Figure 13.16. Notice the moving bar that indicates the strength of the satellite signal. When that bar reaches a strength of 100 or better, stop and tighten down the nuts on the dish and get ready to rock and roll! Not there yet? Here's where it can get a bit tricky.

If you've been a lone wolf so far on this installation job, it's about time you made a friend. Grab your spouse, teenager, or a bored passerby to help you make the final adjustments. You need somebody to monitor the computer and let you know when the signal strength hits the happy 100, and the last thing you need is to be running up and down ladders to make fine adjustments.

If the antenna location is far enough away from the computer that you can't reasonably shout, "More, more, now stop!", you need some way to communicate. If you have a couple of cordless phones, a pair of walkie-talkies (even Power Rangers or Pokemon will do), or a couple of those very, very handy FRS (Family Radio Service) handhelds, you're in business. In fact, if you're stuck without a friend (but have a couple of cordless phones), you can leave one phone on next to the computer and take the other phone with you to act as a monitor, because the computer will beep (its way of saying "Stop already!") when you hit the signal jackpot.

Why all the communications hardware? Simple. You must make tiny adjustments in the antenna position to get a decent signal, and the computer will take at least 10 seconds to make up its mind if you're warmer or colder every time you move the dish.

You have three adjustments to make. Which one should you do first? Adjust the magnetic azimuth in one-eighth of an inch increments toward the center pencil mark. Make a movement, wait 10 seconds or so, and listen for a change of tone. When the tone indicates that you have sufficient signal strength, presto! Congratulations!

Follow the instructions in the DirecPC Self Help guide to make final adjustments, and tighten up the antenna to keep those settings. Then, grab a cold one and sit down (but first, get off the ladder!).

No Signal? Double-Check Everything

If you keep moving the azimuth until you've gone past both the center and left-hand pencil marks, you have a problem. Check the following:

➤ Cabling back to the ground blocks and to the computer

➤ Modem is turned on and connected to coax

➤ Obstructions

➤ Recheck magnetic azimuth readings (move 15 feet in front or behind the antenna—don't fall!—and avoid metal objects such as cars and belt buckles)

Box or Call Your Way Out of Trouble

If you have problems picking up the satellite, see the following document on the DirecPC Helpfile site, which describes the "box" method for locating the satellite:

> http://www2.direcpc.com/helpfiles/troubleshoot/troubleshoot_
> antpointing.htm

If you are unable to locate the satellite, you might be able to call an installer to handle this part of the task for you at a lower price than would be charged for typical installation.

Click Exit to complete the antenna pointing process.

Getting Online with DirecPC

When your computer has "seen" the signal from the DirecPC satellite, your hardware configuration is over, and you're ready to get going with DirecPC. The DirecPC software has five components, but all you need to use to get started is

➤ DirecPC Navigator service—This is the front end of the DirecPC software, making the connection to DirecPC and providing menu-driven access to any of the major features of DirecPC

➤ Turbo Internet—This provides the connection features of DirecPC

The fastest way to get online with DirecPC is to click the DirecPC Navigator icon in the Windows system tray. You also can right-click the Navigator icon in the system tray and select Connect. Either way, Navigator dials your ISP as shown in Figure 13.19.

The DirecPC software automatically opens your installed browser when you're connected, so you'll start enjoying fast downloads right away. When you're finished, click the Disconnect button to get back your phone line.

If you're perfectly happy with the DirecPC defaults, just relax and enjoy the system, but if you want more control over the DirecPC software and hardware, turn to Chapter 21 to learn configuration, setup, and speedup tips and tricks.

If you're having problems, Chapter 21 also can help you troubleshoot your installation.

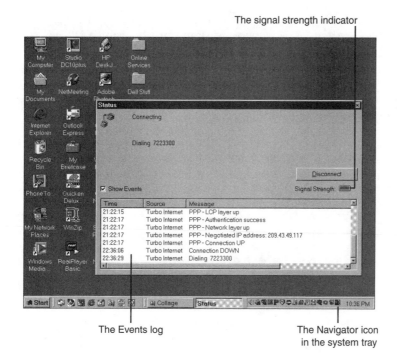

The signal strength indicator

The Events log

The Navigator icon
in the system tray

Figure 13.19

The DirecPC Navigator dials your ISP. The signal strength is indicated below the Disconnect button, and if you enable Show Events as seen here, you can see a log of all activity.

Two-Way Rivals to DirecPC

DirecPC has always offered fast download speeds but has been frustrating for many users because, like all one-way broadband systems, it requires you to give up your telephone line while you use it. For a long time there was no widespread alternative to DirecPC, but new services are now becoming available to give you a two-way satellite solution.

First is DirecPC's own two-way solution, due to kick off sometime in 2001. Details were still sketchy as this book went to press, but download speeds are expected to match or exceed the current 400Kbps download speed per user, and uploads are expected to run at 128Kbps to 256Kbps. Current DirecPC users will be offered upgrade kits to retrofit their current equipment for the new service.

Another two-way service that has been tested for a while has just undergone a name change: Israel's Gilat-to-Home's two-way service, beta-tested in the United States in mid-2000, has changed its name to Starband. Starband service is being sold by MSN retailers including Radio Shack stores in the United States, DISH Network retailers, and direct from Microsoft. Starband offers

➤ Two-way service through internal or external Starband satellite modems—Two PCI slots are required for the internal version (one for receive and one for send), but the external version connects to the USB port.

➤ 24-inch by 36-inch satellite dish can also receive Dish 500 programming (EchoStar, parent company of Dish Network, is a major partner in the Starband service).

245

➤ A DISH Network system can be upgraded to Starband by replacing the dish with a Starband dish—The current DISH Network system must be using a DISH Network satellite located at 110 degrees or 119 degrees azimuth.

➤ Typical download speeds range from 150Kbps to 400Kbps.

The design of the Starband dish is similar to the one-way DirecPC dish, but it's a little larger and it has a transmitter as well as a receiver.

Getting the Latest on Starband

The Starband Web site (formerly Gilat-to-Home) has the latest information about Starband service and package deals. See it at

```
http://www.starband.com
```

Your DirecPC/DirecDuo Checklist

Before you place your order:

___ Decide whether you want to keep your current ISP or change to DirecPC's own ISP. Use the Find a DirecPC POP search page online at `http://utilities.direcpc.com/pops/findpop.cfm` to see whether a DirecPC POP is a local call for you. Remember, you don't want to pay for a long-distance phone call whenever you connect to DirecPC!

___ Check the hardware and software requirements; try to exceed the recommended standards to enjoy better performance.

___ Upgrade your computer with more RAM to meet the recommended standards if possible.

___ Decide whether you want the DirecPC or DirecDuo dish; get the DirecDuo dish if you plan to add DirecTV later or if you already have DirecTV and want to use just one dish for both services.

___ Decide whether you want to install the dish yourself or pay an installer to do it for you.

___ Decide whether you want the internal PCI card satellite modem or the external USB satellite modem; you must be running Windows 98 to use the USB satellite modem.

__ Make sure you have an open PCI slot (for internal satellite modem) or working USB ports (for external satellite modem).

__ Make sure you have a working analog modem. You can use the same analog modem you used with your previous dial-up Internet connection.

During the hardware order process:

__ Order the components you need (choose one from each of the following groups):

Satellite dish

➤ DirecPC dish

➤ DirecDuo dish

DirecPC satellite modem

➤ PCI external

➤ USB internal

Universal mount

Satellite access software

Are you planning to add DirecTV now (requires DirecDuo dish)?

__ Yes—Choose a receiver:

➤ Silver—Basic unit

➤ Gold—adds one-touch VCR record and S-video outputs

➤ Platinum—Adds Dolby Digital A/V output

Select one of the following:

__ Self-install kit—Choose from the following:

➤ DirecPC only

➤ DirecTV (use with a DirecPC kit for DirecDuo including DirecTV)

__ Full or partial (dish-only) installation (no kit needed)

Does DirecPC vendor provide installation?

__ No—Call 1-800-DIRECPC for an installer.

__ Yes—Arrange for installation and ask about installation specials.

__ Record the expected time and cost of installation.

During installation:

___ Record the antenna settings used to locate your satellite

___ File all software and paperwork provided by the vendor in a safe place. My publisher's dog found the DirecPC CD-ROM a tasty snack!

___ Make sure you can get connected before the technician leaves.

The Least You Need to Know

➤ You need an unobstructed view toward the equator to receive DirecPC service.

➤ You must attach an external dish to your home or apartment to use DirecPC.

➤ You must connect a satellite modem to your computer to receive DirecPC.

➤ You can build your own cables or buy the same cables and hardware used for satellite TV installations.

➤ Aiming the dish is similar to aiming a USSB or DirecTV dish, but it requires more precision.

➤ The software installation process is also used to aim the dish.

➤ Starband is a new two-way satellite Internet system with download speeds similar to those of DirecPC.

Chapter 14

Getting Wireless

In This Chapter

➤ Choose the best wireless provider and package

➤ Learn how the ordering and installation process works

➤ Make sure you get the service you're paying for

Fixed-base wireless Internet, which broadcasts Internet traffic from tall microwave towers, has had a modest market reach when compared with its wired competition. Although fixed-base wireless providers have always offered performance comparable to cable modem or DSL service, some are now going head to head with the wired broadband competition in more and more metropolitan areas. If fixed-base wireless meets your broadband needs, this chapter's for you.

Choosing Your Wireless Provider

Fixed-base wireless Internet service providers are often the same people who offer "cable TV without the cable." Just as cable TV's infrastructure can carry both TV and Internet traffic, the tall microwave towers that transmit cable TV to areas beyond the reach of wired cable operators can also carry the Internet to your computer.

Tech Note

Wireless Doesn't Mean Satellite

Although both fixed-base wireless and DirecPC services use antennas rather than cables to bring you the Internet, that's where the similarities end. Fixed-base wireless broadband uses microwave towers, whereas DirecPC and similar services from other vendors use a satellite. It's far easier to provide two-way service with a microwave tower than with satellites, which is why most fixed-base wireless providers already offer two-way service to at least some subscribers, and why DirecPC's two-way service is being introduced in 2001.

If you already use fixed wireless TV service, check with your existing provider. Utilities, cable TV providers, and even telcos are beginning to provide wireless service in some locations.

Finding Wireless Service

You'll find a list of wireless broadband Internet providers at `http://cabledatacomnews.com/wireless/cmic12.html`

After you locate a provider, find out the following:

➤ Which kind(s) of service are offered?—Two-way fixed wireless is preferred, especially if you do a lot of uploading or need an "always on" connection, because it doesn't tie up your telephone line. However, it might not be available to you, depending on where you live.

➤ Which speeds are offered?—Depending on the provider, you might have a wide range of speeds to choose from, or just one or two options. If you can choose from a range of speeds, be sure to look at pricing. The cost per month will increase as speeds increase on multi-speed services.

➤ How long has the company been providing Internet access?—As with anything else in the computer business, experience pays. If your provider is new in your area, find out if they have experience in other markets. Competition is scarce in many markets, but you don't want to pay for indifferent service; remember, you can use satellite-based services in a pinch.

Don't forget to ask for references, and if you're concerned about looks, see what type of antenna and installation are required to get you online. Antennas vary, but some wireless services use antennas that are quite small.

Getting Qualified for Wireless Service

Just because you live or work within the service radius of a fixed wireless service provider doesn't mean you're ready to order the service. Most providers must do a *site survey*, in which the provider sends a technician to your home or office to determine whether you can receive the *microwave signal* (see Figure 14.1). During the visit, the technician will do the following:

➤ Check the line of sight from your location to the transmitter

➤ See whether you qualify for two-way service

➤ Determine where and how to position the antenna

Call the provider or fill out an online form to request the site survey.

Tech Note

You Might Already Be Qualified

Qualifying for fixed-base wireless broadband service means that your location can receive and (for two-way service) send the microwave signals used by the service.

Site surveys are more common with single-antenna services that serve both rural and city areas. If you are looking at an urban/suburban fixed-base wireless service that uses repeaters, coverage is far more widespread, and advance site surveys might not be necessary.

A typical site-survey truck can carry a retractable antenna boom as much as 80 feet long. After the surveyor arrives at your home or office, up goes the antenna. After the antenna boom is elevated and pointed at the *head end* (wireless talk for the big microwave tower that sends and receives data), signal strength is measured for both received data (one-way service) and sent data (two-way service).

Depending on the results obtained, you might need to

➤ Install a taller tower than the one covered by the standard installation—Be sure you find out how much the antenna costs.

➤ Settle for one-way broadband—Some wireless Internet providers aren't equipped to cover the entire service area with a receiving antenna.

Tech Note

THAT WAY ▷

> ## Why You Might Only Qualify for One-Way Service
>
> Wireless Internet services with only a single head-end facility might sometimes choose to receive data from only a portion of their service areas. The receiving antennas they use, unlike transmitting antennas, are directional in nature. They must have multiple receiving antennas to widen the service area for two-way service. Also, because of the low-power transceivers used to send data back to the head end, service areas might be limited to a shorter distance (about 15 miles) than the 30- to 35-mile distance available for receiving data.

After the site survey has been completed and your home or office has been qualified to receive wireless service, you're ready for the next step: deciding on the best service package for your needs.

Selecting the Best Wireless Package

Although fixed-base wireless Internet service closely resembles cable modem service in its hookup, they couldn't be further apart in their choices. Whereas cable modems offer you a "one-size-fits-all" service package with a single speed and single type of connection, some wireless providers offer you a wide range of choices. Choices can include

➤ One-way (telco return) or two-way service

➤ Varying speeds

➤ Symmetric (same speed both directions) or asymmetric (faster for downloads than uploads) service

➤ Fixed or dynamic IP addressing

What should you choose? First, choose two-way service if it's available to you. Remember that with one-way service, you'll still be tied into a phone wire to send information and data to the Internet. Two-way wireless service, like two-way cable modem service, eliminates the need to tie up your phone line for Web page uploads and email sending. You'll send and receive data through the wireless dish.

Next, take a good look at the service speeds offered for two-way service. You'll want the fastest download speeds you can afford. Try to get at least a 256Kbps download service (faster is obviously better!); many providers offer services ranging from 64Kbps through 128Kbps, 256Kbps, 512Kbps, up to 1.5Mbps.

The Best Isn't Always the Cheapest

If your broadband wireless provider has a range of service plans, watch out for the cheap ones! Some providers charge a lot less for one-way than for two-way service, but one-way service uses your phone line for page requests and other uploads. You'll probably be happier with a lower-speed two-way service that keeps your phone line open than with a speedier one-way service that subjects callers to busy signals.

If the provider offers a committed information rate (CIR), think carefully; you might be able to get by with a less-expensive service and still enjoy all the speed you want most of the time. What makes CIR special? Well, services sometimes tell you they can give you speeds that'll toss a tank around like a tumbleweed in the wind. In reality, your average speed might not be much better than a speedy modem (yet still a lot more expensive). Usually, this is because you must share your Internet bandwidth with other subscribers. When you're all logged in downloading files and Web pages simultaneously, there's much less room for your data to get through, resulting in a slower connection. *CIR* is the actual speed that is guaranteed to be available to your connection, regardless of how many other people might be using the service. Your service should never be slower than the CIR.

Maximum or Minimum Speed—Better Find Out First!

Some wireless Internet providers do not indicate whether the service speeds provided are CIR; if the term "CIR" is not used, *do not* sign up for their service until you find out, in writing, if the speed listed for the service is the maximum speed (which could drop) or the CIR speed.

It's important to remember that CIR speeds can represent a floor, not a ceiling, on your connection speed. Some vendors who offer CIR-based pricing offer a low-cost *bursting* option that lets your connection run at up to the maximum bandwidth available on the service. How does bursting work?

Assume that you have a 64Kbps CIR connection. If you don't have a bursting option, you will have a 64Kbps connection all the time, regardless of how busy the service is. Now, assume that you have the same CIR connection but with the bursting option. If the service has a maximum bandwidth of 11Mbps, for example, but 1.2Mbps of bandwidth isn't in use at a given time, your speed bursts to 1.2Mbps. If 640Kbps of bandwidth isn't in use, your speed bursts to 640Kbps, and so forth. When a lot of users are on the system, your speed drops toward the CIR, but when the system has few users, your speed can become astronomically faster as your system bursts to use the (temporarily) excess bandwidth.

How much does the burstable option cost? Not much in some cases. For example, Acc-Net, a wireless provider in Marion, Ohio, offers burstable speeds up to 11Mbps or available bandwidth for just $5.00 a month more than the guaranteed CIR speed of any of its connections, which start at 64Kbps CIR. Because Internet traffic is *bursty*, with peaks and valleys, adding the burstable option to your order, when available, is a no-brainer. Try a low CIR with bursting option to save money, and if you don't like the overall speed, you can usually upgrade immediately to a faster CIR.

Remember, a CIR rate by itself limits you to that speed, but CIR plus bursting gives you all the excess bandwidth there is at any given moment.

Save Money and Skip Symmetrical

Many providers might offer you symmetrical service at an added price. *Symmetrical service* means you get the same guaranteed speeds regardless of whether you're sending or receiving data from the Internet. You'll pay a lot more for symmetrical service than for asymmetrical service, which provides a download speed that's faster than the upload speed. Unless you're planning to host a Web server of some sort or use teleconferencing software, such as Microsoft NetMeeting, your upload speed is usually less important than your download speed. Symmetrical service offerings are usually aimed at (and priced for) business users. Look for asymmetrical offerings to save you money without sacrificing usefulness.

Dynamic IP Is Okay by Me

Finally, what about the IP address? Again, as with the question of whether you should spend the money on symmetrical service, we'd vote no, unless you're hosting a Web site or need to have a fixed IP address for other specialized reasons. You'll save money and be a bit safer online if you have a dynamic IP address.

Tech Note

Minding Your I's and P's

Dynamic IP addresses provide your computer with a different Internet identity whenever you connect; a fixed IP address means that your computer is identified the same way whenever you connect. Most fixed-base broadband wireless providers use dynamic IP addressing, which helps minimize the chances of your computer's being targeted specifically for intrusion. A fixed IP address, if available, will cost more but is of little use except for Web servers, which are normally not allowed on a wireless connection.

Ordering Wireless

How does the typical wireless ordering process work?

As discussed previously, the first thing you must request is a site survey from most providers to determine whether you can receive the microwave signal that carries wireless traffic. You can place your order after you qualify for wireless service. During the order process, there are some potential budget-busting issues you must watch out for, including the following (see Figure 14.1):

➤ The installation cost if you don't qualify for a standard installation

➤ The cost of the wireless broadband modem and whether you'd be able to reuse it at another location

➤ The cost of installing the network card if you don't want to buy it and do it yourself

Why You Might Not Qualify for a Standard Installation

Wireless providers typically charge for antenna installation, which generally includes an antenna, a tower or mount up to a certain height, and up to a certain amount of coaxial cable to carry the signal to the wireless broadband modem that connects your computer to the service. Will you qualify for the standard installation? It depends on the result of the site survey.

Figure 14.1

Before you sign on the dot-ted line for wireless ser-vice, find out about your installation costs, decide whether you should buy your wireless broadband modem, decide who should supply and install the network card, and make sure your computer's ready for the service.

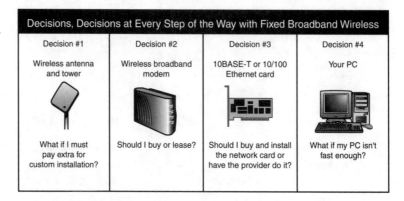

Decisions, Decisions at Every Step of the Way with Fixed Broadband Wireless

Decision #1	Decision #2	Decision #3	Decision #4
Wireless antenna and tower	Wireless broadband modem	10BASE-T or 10/100 Ethernet card	Your PC
What if I must pay extra for custom installation?	Should I buy or lease?	Should I buy and install the network card or have the provider do it?	What if my PC isn't fast enough?

The details of the equipment included in the standard installation vary with the provider, but the provider's goal is to make sure you get an unobstructed line of sight to the transmitter or transceiver at the operator's head end. In some cases, the site survey can reveal that you'll need a higher tower on your home, need to use a tower placed away from your home (and thus might also need to use more than the allo-cated amount of coaxial cable), or might need a larger or more powerful antenna than usual. The results of the site survey, in short, determine not only whether you can receive fixed-base broadband wireless service but how much it will cost you to have it installed.

Danger Danger

Have a Backup Plan

If you find that your proposed wireless installation will be far more expensive than you anticipated, be prepared with alternatives:

➤ Could you use a nearby neighbor's building for your antenna to avoid the expense of a tower?

➤ Is it time to trim a few branches from a tree that's blocking the signal?

➤ Can you negotiate a deal to spread the extra installation cost over the life of the contract?

➤ Should you consider satellite-based services such as DirecPC instead?

Having a backup plan can help you deal with unforeseen obstacles in the way of getting online with a broadband wireless connection.

If you need a special tower, antenna, or other "special" installation features, get the total cost up front. If you experience sticker shock, find out whether you can stretch out the payments over the first year of your contract, or whether a lower-cost service (such as one-way) would also help you get a cheaper installation.

Buy It or Lease It? What to Do About Your Wireless Broadband Modem

The wireless broadband modem provides the link between your antenna and your computer. Like the cable modem it resembles, the wireless broadband modem isn't a throwaway item; typical models can cost between $200 and $500!

Find out at ordering time whether you have to pay an equipment deposit and whether you must buy or can lease your modem; in most cases, you'll be using a one-way or two-way modem somewhat similar to those used on cable Internet systems.

Does it pay to buy your wireless broadband modem? Probably not. Unlike cable modem service, which is rapidly converting to the *DOCSIS* standard (which allows the same DOCSIS-compatible cable modem to work on any DOCSIS-compliant service), wireless broadband modems lack a single uniform standard. For example, Hybrid, one of the leading broadband wireless vendors, makes wireless modems that work with only its head-end equipment. On the other hand, Vyyo's broadband wireless modems are DOCSIS-compliant, enabling them to work with normal cable TV–delivered Internet services, as well as with wireless Internet. The bottom line? If you buy a wireless broadband modem today and move in a couple of years, it's likely that your modem won't work on another wireless (or cable modem) system.

Tech Note

Why Wireless Broadband Modems Are So Expen$ive

At first glance, a wireless broadband modem is very similar to a cable modem, but many wireless broadband modems cost twice as much as cable modems. Why? There's more inside a wireless broadband modem, including a complete analog modem on many models (used for one-way service). Wireless broadband modems are also designed to connect to a transceiver or a receiver, depending on the service the client receives.

Before you can make a definitive choice about leasing or buying the modem, you'll need to find out exactly how much money you'll need to spend. Use the calculations in Chapter 9 to determine the true cost of broadband wireless service: Run the numbers for both a lease and for outright purchase of the unit. In most cases, you'll find that buying the modem won't pay off unless you plan to keep the service at least three years or longer. Don't forget to ask who's responsible if the modem fails. Generally, if you are leasing it, the provider takes care of it, probably with an immediate equipment swap. If you own it, you're looking at a warranty that might expire in a year or two, and the problem of losing your service while you wait for an exchange of or repair to your unit.

Don't clobber your pocketbook with a bad decision about whether to buy or lease your wireless-cable modem. Although leasing looks better than buying a modem that might not work in some locations, consider how long you'll be using wireless and the benefits of leasing rather than buying your modem. One wireless company, for example, charges $500 for the cable modem but will lease it to you for $35/month. If you're planning to keep wireless service for 15 months or longer, you'll save money by buying the modem. But, if the modem fails after you buy it, who pays? You might be better off keeping up the monthly payments for the peace of mind that comes from service and replacement costs being borne by the wireless operator. Still prefer to buy? Find out whether you can get an extended warranty.

Making Sure Your System Meets the Requirements

Equipment requirements for wireless systems vary a great deal. Some services can handle Windows PCs, Macs, and UNIX/Linux systems with ease, whereas others are strictly limited to the Microsoft world or the Apple dimension.

Tech Note

THAT WAY ▶

How Old Is Your PC?

Typically, computers that are no more than three years old are fine for use with any high-speed Internet service, including fixed wireless broadband. Older computers might not have fast enough CPUs, enough RAM memory, use the correct version of Windows or Mac OS, or have enough free disk space. Check the provider's recommended hardware to make sure your system is up to snuff, especially if your computer was bought in 1997 or before.

In most cases, whether you go with one-way or two-way systems, you will need a 10BASE-T Ethernet network interface card. Some providers supply one for you, but if they charge more than $20 for the card, go out and get one yourself. Decent cards can be had for $10–$20. One-way cable modems can include an analog modem or might work in conjunction with your existing modem. For more information about network cards, see Chapter 12.

Don't forget to find your operating system CD or disks because you likely will need them to install TCP/IP and other network components during the installation. For more information about TCP/IP configuration, see Chapter 17.

Installing Your Wireless Service

When the technician comes to install your broadband wireless service (not to be confused with the initial site survey you must go through), the first stop is outside. The technician looks for the following:

➤ The location selected by the site surveyor to place the antenna

➤ A grounding block left over from a previous cable TV installation

The antenna must be mounted at the elevation and direction previously noted by the site surveyor. A tower might need to be installed to hold the antenna, depending on terrain and other factors.

Don't be surprised if the installer aims the antenna away from the head-end if you can get only one-way service. Some wireless providers use *benders*—reflectors mounted on other microwave towers or tall structures (including a farmer's silo!)—to "bend" or reflect the signal to the antenna if the line of sight doesn't enable a direct pathway. And you thought those years of playing pool were wasted!

Tech Note

THAT WAY ▶

When It Comes to Coax, RG-6 Rules!

Coaxial cable standards have changed over time; the former RG-59 standard once used for cable TV and antenna installations has been replaced by RG-6, which is also used by DirecPC and cable modem installations as well as by most fixed wireless broadband services.

If you previously had cable or satellite TV using the correct coaxial type and the cable is still in place, the installer's job is a lot easier. He or she can run coaxial cable from the antenna to the grounding block used previously, and the existing coaxial cable coming from the grounding block into your home or office can be reused. Otherwise, after the antenna goes up, the hole (in the wall) goes in to route your coax to your wireless-cable modem.

After the wireless-cable modem is attached to your computer and turned on, you're ready to go. Setup is easy because the modem already has the correct Internet settings, including

➤ An IP address (to identify the modem to the head end)

➤ A gateway address and DNS server address (so your computer can access the Internet via the modem)

➤ A DHCP server (which assigns your computer its own IP address)

➤ The broadcast frequency to monitor to pick up data headed for your computer

Don't Have an IP Headache

Because the modem knows the settings when it's delivered, the only IP setting your computer needs is Server Assigned IP Address (and your technician will do that for you). If you want to know what it all means, see Chapter 17. Otherwise, relax and surf!

Your Wireless Checklist

Before you place your order, do the following:

__ Get a site survey done; you can't get broadband wireless service without it!

__ Look over the proposal carefully to determine your up-front costs.

__ Decide whether you want to buy or lease the wireless modem.

__ Find out about network card requirements.

__ Figure out where the computer will be placed for use with the wireless modem.

__ Check the hardware and software requirements; try to exceed the recommended standards to enjoy better performance.

__ Replace your computer if it doesn't meet the minimum standards; upgrade your computer with more RAM and so on to meet the recommended standards, if possible.

__ Buy and install the network card and locate all your operating system and network-card software.

During the order process, do the following:

__ Ask about installation specials.

__ Record the expected time and cost of the installation.

During installation, do the following:

__ Record the network and browser configuration used to get you connected.

__ File all software and paperwork provided by the vendor.

__ Make sure you can get connected before the technician leaves.

The Least You Need to Know

➤ Broadband wireless service requires a site visit to make sure you can receive the signal.

➤ Your installation costs can vary according to the equipment needed to provide line-of-site to the transmitter.

➤ You can select from a variety of speeds with many services.

➤ A low CIR (committed information rate) guaranteed connection speed combined with a bursting option gives you the benefit of a faster connection during off-peak periods and can save you money.

➤ Wireless broadband modems are often much more expensive than cable modems, and leasing can make sense in many cases.

➤ You must add a 10BASE-T Ethernet card to most systems to prepare them to connect to a wireless broadband modem.

➤ Your wireless broadband modem is preprogrammed with the TCP/IP configuration you need to connect to the Internet.

Part 4
Connection Sharing and Security

You have a high-speed connection, but can it be safer? Can you share it with others in your home or small office? Read Part 4 to discover how to keep snoopers out of your broadband system and how to share it with family or co-workers.

It doesn't cost much to secure or share your high-speed connection, but it costs plenty if you don't.

Chapter 15

Share the Wealth: Internet Connection Strategies

In This Chapter

➤ Clearing Internet connection sharing with your Internet provider

➤ How to do it with built-in Microsoft tools

➤ The benefits of proxy servers and external sharing devices

➤ What you need to add to your systems

➤ Tips for getting sharing to work for you

Now that you're enjoying your broadband Internet connection, have you noticed how everyone else at home or at the office is giving you funny looks? Have you noticed new bookmarks or favorites showing up in your Web browser after you've been out to lunch? What's going on?

Envy! They want what you've got: a faster way to the Internet. You can ignore them, but if you do, you'll have to deal with your co-workers, your spouse, or your kids constantly sneaking onto your computer for the rush of faster connections and blink-and-you'll-miss-it downloads. You could fight them off, but why not make everybody happy by learning how easy it is to share your connection?

Making Sure Sharing Is Okay with Your ISP

As you'll learn in this chapter, sharing a single high-speed Internet connection is relatively simple. However, you'll also find that high-speed ISPs are all over the map about whether to encourage, discourage, or prohibit connection sharing.

In a review of major high-speed providers, typical cable modem providers either want an extra fee for shared access, even for home use, or don't support shared access at all. Major DSL providers typically are less hostile, even allowing their ad copy to push shared access using a local area network of a single DSL connection as a benefit of your high-speed connection. However, regardless of your high-speed connection provider, you're pretty much on your own when it comes to *how* to share that fast pipe into your home or office.

That's where this book, and specifically this chapter, come to the rescue.

Need to Log In? One to a Customer, Please!

If you use an ISP such as AOL that requires you to log in to the service, you probably can't share that service over your network unless you are willing to ask everyone to get a separate account with that provider. However, ISPs that don't use a login procedure often allow sharing.

What You Need to Share an Internet Connection

So, you're tired of fighting off the other folks who want a piece of your fast Internet action. What do you need to share it?

The chief requirement is that you have an existing network between two or more computers. Then, depending on which solution you choose, you might need to add one or more of the following:

➤ Connection-sharing software, either built in to your operating system or purchased from another vendor

➤ A second network interface card (to connect the sharing computer with the others on the network)

➤ A router attached to (or including) a hub or switch (to connect all the computers together and allow Internet access)

In the following sections, you'll get the help you need to make Internet connection sharing work for you.

Types of Internet Sharing Solutions

There are three major types of Internet sharing solutions you can use:

➤ Gateways
➤ Proxy servers
➤ Routers

What's the difference between them? Glad you asked.

You Can Share Your Modem, Too—But Should You?

This chapter discusses Internet connection sharing when you use a network card to connect to your broadband device, although you can also share an ordinary analog modem. I'm not too keen on sharing an analog modem Internet connection because slow connections get even slower.

If you think that your 56Kbps modem is struggling to handle a single connection, just ask yourself how well it will work when two or more users are trying to surf. You'll think that the molasses clogging up the works just got thicker. And if you use the network for more than Internet sharing, you'll watch the whole network slow to a crawl when one user downloads a big file.

Another problem comes from preferences for different dial-up networks. For example, if one of you likes NetZero and somebody else wants Earthlink, you'll need to decide whose dial-up connection will be used on the network. Yes, you can share a dial-up Internet connection, but I don't think you'll like the results.

Gateways

A gateway, which is an access point that allows one network to enter another network, can be the least expensive and least complicated way to share an Internet connection. One computer that connects to the Internet can become the gateway to other computers. Simplified gateway features are included in Windows 98 Second Edition, Windows 2000, and the newest member of the Windows family, Windows Me.

When you use a gateway to create a shared connection, the computer with the gateway acts like a doorway to allow Internet connections from other computers.

Gateways and ICS

A gateway can be either a computer or another network device that has the intelligence to connect one network with another, such as a router. As you'll see, Windows ICS is a low-cost gateway for your home or small-office network because you can use the computer with the shared access as if it's just another computer on the network.

Proxy Servers

Proxy servers resemble gateways in many ways, because both allow a single computer's Internet connection to be shared by one or more additional computers over a network. Proxy servers, unlike gateways, can enhance the security of a network. Proxy servers can

➤ Filter page requests and reject requests for pages from unapproved sites or pages containing unapproved content—This feature is also used by many family-friendly dial-up ISPs such as Lightdog and Mayberry USA. By using a proxy server with content filters to your network, you get the same protection for your family, even if your ISP has no family-filtering options.

➤ Cache (store) Web content requested by one user so that other users can view the same page without sending another page request to the Internet—This technique is frequently used by cable and wireless operators to relieve Internet congestion and speed up access.

➤ Block unauthorized access from the Internet to the computers on a network—Using your proxy server as a firewall to protect yourself from hackers is something that any broadband Internet user, even home users—like you—should be concerned about. (You'll learn more about Internet security in Chapter 16.)

Tech Note

Mileage Can Vary

This list of proxy server features is a general list; be sure to see the list of specific features supported by a particular proxy server program before you buy and install it.

Routers

Routers are hardware devices that connect between computers and connections to the Internet. Internet service providers use routers to route Internet traffic to and from your computer. Routers are also used on large non-Internet networks to route traffic. Historically, most routers have been too expensive and too complicated for the home or small office user. But recent developments in low-cost routers make routers useful for Internet connection sharing.

Several routers made for use with broadband networks feature a built-in switch or hub, so that multiple computers can be plugged directly into the router.

In the following sections, you'll learn more about all these solutions for Internet connection sharing.

Figure 15.1 shows a typical small workgroup hub, and Figure 15.2 shows a typical router/switch combination.

Tech Note

Switch, Hub, and Router—Which Is Which?

It isn't always easy to tell the difference between a switch, a hub, and a router, but you can do it.

A hub is the simplest network device used to connect computers. A hub has four or more connections for RJ-45 network cables and signal lights on front. A hub sends the signal it receives from one computer to all the other computers connected to the hub and divides the bandwidth between all the computers connected to the hub. Hubs aren't very smart.

Switches resemble hubs but with two important differences. A switch creates a direct connection between the computer sending data and the computer receiving data, and a switch provides a full-speed connection for each computer connected to it. Switches are like hubs with a brain transplant.

Routers send data from one network to another; these are often combined with switches.

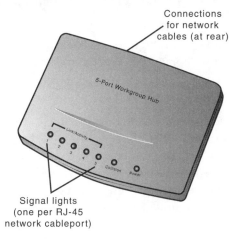

Connections for network cables (at rear)

5-Port Workgroup Hub

Link/Activity

Collision   Power

Signal lights
(one per RJ-45
network cableport)

Figure 15.1

The green lights on the hub are lit when data is passing from one computer to another. This hub uses an AC adapter for power (photo courtesy of Linksys).

Figure 15.2

This router/hub is designed to allow multiple computers to share a single DSL or cable modem connection (courtesy of Linksys).

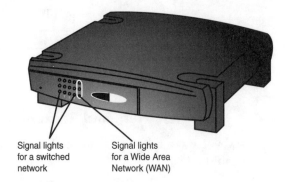

Signal lights for a switched network

Signal lights for a Wide Area Network (WAN)

Switch lights indicate traffic, full-duplex connection (doubles speed), and 10Mbps or 100Mbps connection speed. The WAN lights indicate a connection with Internet, activity, and diagnostics.

Danger Danger

When Sharing Means Sharing Trouble

If you use either ICS or a proxy server, you should always be concerned about the possible drawbacks of using a computer to share an Internet connection. The following are some of the gotchas:

➤ You must leave the computer with the Internet connection on all the time to allow access for other computers. If the computer is located near a bedroom, I hope it isn't a noisy beast or you can keep the family awake.

➤ You'd better hope that nobody's in the middle of a big download if your gateway or proxy server crashes. When the gateway goes down, so does everyone's Internet connection. You can encourage more careful computing by showing everyone how to use bookmarks and Favorites to set their favorite Web pages and encourage people to use download managers like Go!Zilla, which can resume an interrupted download to help minimize the angst when problems occur.

If you try ICS or a proxy server and find these kinds of problems are really annoying, look at using a router instead to share your Internet connection.

Microsoft's Solutions

Starting with its venerable Windows for Workgroups 3.1 and 3.11 versions, Microsoft has long provided built-in support for Local Area Networks (LANs) as part of its Windows operating systems. This tradition continued with Windows 95, 98, and the new Windows Me, as well as with the office-oriented Windows NT and Windows 2000 operating systems.

Windows 95 and 98 were introduced before the high-speed Internet craze had really taken hold. Although both support LAN connections and dial-up modems, you were on your own if you were trying to share an Internet connection on computer A with computer B. That changed when Microsoft released its Second Edition of Windows 98.

The Microsoft Gateways to the Internet

Starting with Win98SE, Microsoft supports Internet Connection Sharing (ICS) with all current versions of Windows, including the home-oriented Windows Me and the office-oriented Windows 2000 Professional. All three versions of Windows use a sharing method called a *gateway*. When the computer that has the Internet connection is set up as a gateway, other computers can use its access as an open door to the Internet.

To use ICS with a high-speed Internet connection such as a cable modem or DSL, you need to have two network interface cards in your computer. One is to connect with the cable modem or DSL modem, and the other is to connect with the other computers in your home or small-office network.

Tech Note

More Bang for Your Buck

ICS also can be used to share a single dial-up connection with additional networked computers; you don't need to wait for a broadband connection to share the Internet.

Setting Up ICS with Windows 98 Second Edition

ICS requires changes to both the gateway computer (which shares its Internet connection with others) and the computers that will share that connection.

To set up Internet connection sharing with Windows 98SE, perform the following tasks on the computer that is already connected to the Internet (the gateway computer):

1. Make sure that your high-speed Internet connection is working.

2. Click Start, Settings, Control Panel, Network to see the brand name and model number of the network card that is connected to your broadband connection. You will need to specify this information during step 5.

3. Install a second network interface card (NIC) in your computer; note the brand name and model number because you will need to specify this information later in the installation process.

Warning: Sharp Curves Ahead

If you've already set up your own home network, setting up ICS should be fairly easy. However, if you are new to setting up a network, you could easily get in over your head in no time. Be sure to work slowly and carefully as you follow each step, and review the Web sites listed for extra help before you get started.

If you need a painless way to learn about networking your home or small office, pick up a copy of *The Complete Idiot's Guide to Networking, Third Edition,* by Bill Wagner and Chris Negus, Alpha Books/Que, 2001.

4. Make sure that your gateway computer can "see" the other computers. This means that other computers on your network are visible when you open Network Neighborhood.

5. Install the ICS software on the gateway computer; install it with the Add/Remove Programs icon in Control Panel. Select the Windows setup tab; you'll find it under Internet Tools.

6. As soon as you install ICS, it starts. Click Next on the introductory screen (see Figure 15.3).

Figure 15.3

The Internet Connection Sharing Wizard's opening screen.

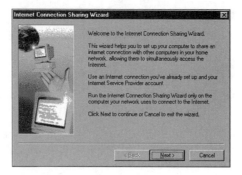

7. Select the network card you are using for the Internet connection. If you have two network cards that are the same brand and model, it will be the #1 NIC because you installed it first. Click Next (see Figure 15.4).

8. The next screen tells you that ICS will be creating a client configuration disk (CCD) that will be used to set up the other browsers on the network. Click Next (see Figure 15.5).

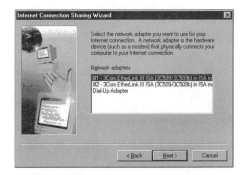

Figure 15.4

Network card #1 is the adapter with the Internet connection.

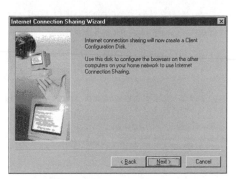

Figure 15.5

The client configuration disk isn't really necessary, but click Next to continue past this screen.

9. When you are asked to insert the disk to create the CCD, skip this step. You can set up the clients manually, which I'll get to later in "Setting Up the ICS Clients."

10. Click Finish to complete the Internet connection sharing process; reboot the computer.

This completes the installation of the Internet Connection Sharing software.

After you reboot the computer, you must complete the setup of ICS:

1. Click Start, Settings, Control Panel, Internet.

2. Click the Connections tab and make sure your system is set to Never Dial a Connection.

3. Click the Sharing button to see the ICS Control Panel; select both Enable Internet Connection Sharing and Show Icon in Taskbar.

4. Make sure that the network card that is attached to your cable modem, DSL modem, or other high-speed Internet connection is selected in the Connect to the Internet Using menu.

5. Make sure that the network card that will be connected to the other computer(s) is selected in the Connect to My Home Network Using menu (see Figure 15.6).

6. Click OK twice when you are finished; reboot the computer if prompted.

There's No Trick to Installing a NIC

Installing a second network interface card (NIC) isn't hard if you pay attention to the following:

➤ Buy the same speed (10BASE-T or 10/100 Fast Ethernet) that you use on the rest of the network.

➤ Make sure you have an open expansion slot in your computer (see Chapter 12 for details).

➤ Ground yourself by touching the inside of the case after you open your computer.

➤ Don't touch the card's chips or its gold-plated connector; hold it by the card bracket.

➤ Remove the empty card bracket blocking the slot from the rear of the computer.

➤ Carefully and firmly plug the card into the slot.

➤ Follow the card's instructions for installing the card's driver software.

See Chapter 3 for more details on opening your computer and working with internal cards.

Figure 15.6

Use the Internet—Connections dialog box to complete the setup of the Internet connection sharing gateway computer.

Figure 15.7 shows you how your ICS computer connects to a DSL or cable modem and to other computers in the network.

Setting Up the ICS Clients

After you set up ICS on the gateway computer, you need to perform the following tasks on the computers that will share the Internet connection (clients). These instructions assume that each client computer already has a network card installed.

For a Helping Hand...

For a useful visual tutorial and troubleshooter for ICS for both Windows 98SE and Windows 2000, go to
`http://www.timhiggins.com/sharing/icsinstall.htm`

1. Open the Internet icon in the Control Panel.

2. Click the Connection tab; make sure that Connect to the Internet Via a Local Area Network is selected.

3. Install the TCP/IP protocol on each client computer if it is not already installed. For Windows 95/98/2000, use the Network icon in the Control Panel to see if TCP/IP is already installed. If not, choose Add, Protocol, Microsoft, TCP/IP to install it.

4. Select TCP/IP→(your network card) in the list of network components, and click Properties to see the TCP/IP properties.

5. Make sure that Obtain an IP Address Automatically is checked.

6. Click OK and restart the computer as prompted.

After you restart both the ICS server (which has the Internet connection to share) and the ICS client(s) (which will share the connection), you should be able to access the Internet on the client computer(s) as well as on the host computer.

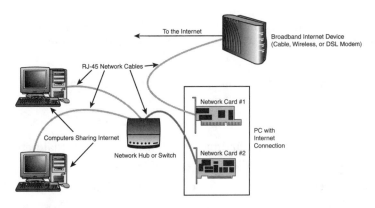

Figure 15.7

When Windows 98SE ICS or Windows Me Home Networking is used to share a broadband Internet connection, two network cards are used; one connects to the broadband device, and the other connects to the network as seen here.

Got DirecPC? Get ICS Right!

Because DirecPC uses a dedicated satellite modem for downloads but an ordinary analog modem for uploads, you need special instructions to get DirecPC to work correctly with Microsoft ICS. You'll find a well-illustrated step-by-step procedure on the DirecPC Web site at

`http://www.direcpc.com/consumer/owners/notes/icsinstall.html`

Please read all the way through this Web page before you proceed because you'll need to use Regedit, the Windows Registry editor, near the end of the process (you'll find help for using Regedit in Chapter 3).

How ICS Changes the Gateway Computer's Network Configuration

After ICS is installed, you will see that the network card that connects your computer to the Internet is labeled (Shared) when you view Network properties, and the network card that connects the computer to the other computers (for Internet sharing) is labeled (Home).

The original settings for the Shared network card (including any options such as a fixed IP address, gateways, and so on) are assigned by ICS to TCP/IP→Internet Connection Sharing.

Before ICS is installed, a direct connection is made between the Internet and your network card:

The Internet→Your Network Card

After ICS is installed, Internet Connection Sharing→TCP/IP becomes a "virtual network card," funneling Internet data to your physical network cards:

The Internet→Internet Connection sharing→Your Network Card (Shared)

For more information on TCP/IP, see Chapter 17, "A Survivor's Guide to TCP/IP."

Setting Up a Gateway with Windows Me

Windows Me, introduced in the fall of 2000, is similar in many ways to Windows 98SE. However, it uses a different setup procedure for its Internet connection sharing, which is included as part of the new Home Networking Wizard. You need to run the Home Networking Wizard on the computer with the Internet connection you want to share, and use it to create Home Networking setup disks you can use with other computers on the network.

Protect Yourself!

Before you run the Home Networking Wizard, you'll want to set a restore point for use with the new System Restore feature. Click Start, Help. Select Use System Restore from the Fix My Computer section. Select Create a Restore Point and enter a description such as My Computer Before Running Home Networking Wizard. Windows Me will store the current state of your computer, allowing you to use System Restore to roll back the clock in case of problems. Click OK when prompted to finish.

You should also record the current TCP/IP configuration for the network card that connects your computer to the Internet. See Chapter 17.

Setting Up the Gateway with the Home Networking Wizard

You must also install Internet Connection Sharing (ICS). To install ICS on a Windows Me computer, follow these steps:

1. Open the Add/Remove Programs icon in Control Panel.
2. Select the Windows Setup tab.
3. Select the Communications category.
4. Click the Details button.
5. Scroll down to Internet Connection Sharing and click on the box to put a checkmark in it.
6. Click OK twice to install ICS.

After ICS is installed, the Home Networking Wizard starts automatically.

To set up the Home Networking Wizard to share a high-speed Internet connection, follow these steps:

1. Click Next on the introductory screen; follow the link to Using Home Networking if you need help setting up your hardware (see Figure 15.8).

Figure 15.8

The Home Networking Wizard for Windows Me.

2. The next screen asks if you use the Internet on this computer. The default is Yes, A direct connection to the ISP using your network interface card (NIC). Verify that the correct NIC is selected, and click Next (see Figure 15.9).

Figure 15.9

The Home Networking Wizard is used to set up the ICS gateway (as in this example), the ICS client, or networking without ICS sharing by selecting different options on this screen.

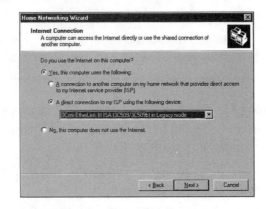

3. Select Yes to share your Internet connection with other computers on the network. Verify that the correct NIC is selected, and click Next (see Figure 15.10).

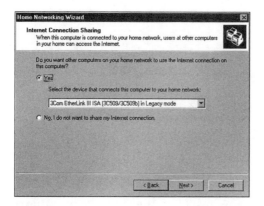

Figure 15.10

If two different models of network cards are installed, make sure that the model listed is being used for the Internet connection.

4. Select Yes on the next screen to create a Home Networking Setup (HNS) disk (for use on computers running Windows 95/98).

5. Insert a formatted floppy disk and click Next to create the HNS disk; any data on the disk is deleted (see Figure 15.11).

Figure 15.11

Unlike the disk that Windows 98SE creates for its version of ICS, the Windows Me HNS disk is useful and should be created.

6. Click Finish to complete the changes to your configuration made by the HN Wizard. Remove the HN setup disk you made in step 5, and reboot the computer if directed to do so.

7. After the computer reboots, a message appears onscreen that the HN setup is successful. The message also reminds you to use the HN Setup disk to share this connection with Windows 95/98 computers or to run the HN Wizard on another Windows Me computer to share this connection. Click OK to close the reminder (see Figure 15.12).

Figure 15.12

This message is displayed after you reboot to let you know that the HN Wizard is completed, and to tell you how to proceed to set up the rest of the computers on your network.

What the Home Networking Wizard Does to Your Computer

To see the changes in your system after installing the Home Networking Wizard, right-click My Network Places and select Properties, or open the Network icon in Control Panel.

You will see a new protocol, the Internet Connection Sharing Protocol, listed next to each of your network cards. You will also see TCP/IP (Home) listed next to the network card that connects to the rest of the network, and TCP/IP (Shared) listed next to the network card that connects to the Internet. These additional settings allow the other computers on the network to use this computer as a gateway after the Home Networking setup disks or HN Wizard are run to allow them access. Just as with the Windows 98SE version of ICS, Windows Me's version creates a TCP/IP→Internet Connection Sharing binding that takes over the original TCP/IP configuration of the network card connected to the Internet.

You should also click the Identification tab while viewing Network components and note the computer name and workgroup name. The same workgroup name must be used on other computers that will share the Internet connection with this one.

Using the HN Setup Disks on Windows 95/98 Computers

After you run the Home Networking Wizard on the computer with the Internet connection, you're halfway to your goal.

However, you're not finished until you use the Home Networking (HN) setup disks on computers running Windows 95/98 to set up their connections. You might also need your Windows setup disks or CD-ROM to complete the installation.

To install Home Networking/ICS with the HNS disk:

1. Insert the disk into a floppy drive on the Windows 95/98 computer.
2. Click Start, Run.
3. Type **A:\Setup** to start the installation process.
4. Click Next on the introductory screen.

Microsoft Doesn't Always Know Best

Microsoft recommends using the workgroup name MSHOME with the Home Networking Wizard. If you are trying to share a cable modem or other shared-medium connection, do not use this name. If any other family or office on the same connection also uses MSHOME for its workgroup, Windows will put their computers in the same workgroup as yours. This will make it very easy for them to access your computer! Make up your own workgroup name instead.

Note that some cable modem operators such as @Home require you to use their default workgroup name for the cable modem installation. In that case you will need to use their workgroup name for your network.

Does Your Internet Connection Still Work?

After you set up the ICS or Home Networking Wizard on the host computer (the one with the Internet connection), take a minute to make sure you can still access the Internet before you set up the other computers on the network.

If you can't, don't panic. See the Troubleshooting section at the end of this chapter.

5. After the files are copied, on the next screen select Yes, This Computer Uses a Connection to Another Computer to Access the Internet. Click Next (see Figure 15.13).

6. Enter the name of the computer and the workgroup name (see Figure 15.14). The name of the computer should be unique; the workgroup name should be the same as that used on other computers in your network. Click Next.

Figure 15.13

As with the Home Networking Wizard, the HN Setup disk can be used to set up both Internet sharing and networking without sharing.

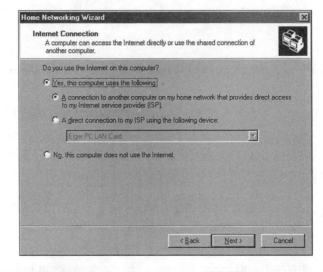

Figure 15.14

Give each computer on your network a unique name, but use the same workgroup name for all computers in your network.

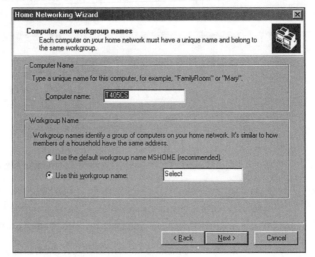

7. If you want to share the My Documents folder and its subfolder, click the box to checkmark it. Don't forget to specify a password! You can also share printers connected to this computer. Click Next after you specify a password (step 8).

8. If you specify a password, a password entry box appears. Enter the password into the first field, and then re-enter it in the second field to confirm it. Click OK to continue.

9. Click Finish to save the changes. Insert the Windows setup disk or CD-ROM if prompted to install networking files. Remove the HNS disk, and reboot the computer when prompted.

10. The same reminder message you saw after installing the HN Wizard appears. Click OK (because you've read it already).

When you run the HN Setup disk on the computers connected to the gateway, the following TCP/IP configuration is created on each computer:

➤ IP Address—Obtained automatically (each computer is assigned a different address)

➤ WINS Configuration—Disabled

➤ Gateway—192.168.0.1 (the IP address of the TCP/IP [Home] NIC installed in the computer with the shared Internet connection)

➤ Enable DNS

➤ Host: enter the workgroup name

➤ DNS Server—192.168.0.1 (the IP address of the TCP/IP [Home] NIC installed in the computer with the shared Internet connection)

To view this information, open the Network icon in Control Panel, scroll down to the entry for TCP/IP→(your network card), and click Properties.

For more information about TCP/IP configuration, see Chapter 17.

Your Internet settings (for Internet Explorer and other Microsoft programs) are also changed by the HN Setup disk to Connect to the Internet via a Local Area Network. To see this change, open the Internet icon in the Control Panel and click the Connection tab.

Setting Up ICS with Windows 2000 Professional

Windows 2000 Professional, the replacement for Windows NT Workstation, also features built-in Internet connection sharing, but you don't need to install special software to enable it. Instead, follow this procedure to set up your shared Internet connection:

Take Time to Do It Right!

Don't forget to use the worksheets in Chapter 17 to record the settings for both your ICS/Home Networking host and the other computers on the network. If somebody at home or in the office decides to play around with the settings, having a hard-copy record can help you get things fixed in no time.

1. Make sure the high-speed Internet connection is working correctly.

2. Open the My Network Places icon on the Desktop and right-click the icon for your high-speed Internet connection. It will be called Local Area Connection #.... Rename it Internet.

3. Install a second network card in the computer with the Internet connection.

4. Connect the second network card to other computers in the network; open My Network Places to see whether the other computers are visible before continuing. Rename this connection LAN as shown in Figure 15.15.

Figure 15.15

Windows 2000's network connections as shown after you rename your original connection to the Internet "Internet" and your connection to the other computers "LAN."

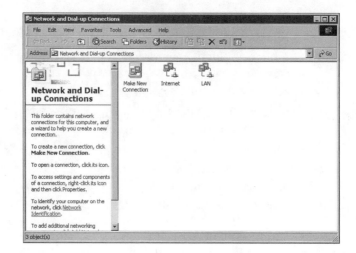

5. To set up sharing, right-click the My Network Places icon on your desktop, select Properties from the menu, right-click Internet (see step 2), and select Properties again.

6. Click the Sharing tab. Put a check mark next to Enable Internet Connection Sharing for This Connection. This allows the other computers connected to this computer to share the Internet connection (see Figure 15.16).

Figure 15.16

Enabling Internet connection sharing in Windows 2000 after you install the second network card.

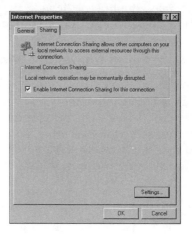

7. Click OK. A warning is displayed onscreen to remind you that the LAN adapter (network card) on this computer will be set to the IP address 192.168.0.1. Other computers that want to connect to this computer for Internet sharing must set their TCP/IP configuration to obtain an address automatically. Click Yes to finish.

To set up the clients who will connect with the Windows 2000 Professional computer that is sharing its Internet connection, use the same TCP/IP configuration listed for the Home Networking setup disk given previously.

Remember that the computer acting as the gateway (the one with the Internet connection) must be running for other computers to share its connection. If the other computers can't see the computer with the Internet connection through Network Neighborhood, My Network Places, Local Network Connections, or the Windows Explorer, they can't share the connection either. If you have problems with any version of Windows ICS, see the "Troubleshooting Your Shared Connection" section at the end of this chapter.

Proxy Servers

As you learned early in this chapter, proxy servers are "gateways with brains," providing a similar "Internet this way!" feature with extra benefits for security and connection speed. Although proxy servers were once always expensive and hard to install, newer proxy server programs oriented to small offices and home networks are easier and cost-effective. Many can even be downloaded in fully functioning trial versions that give you up to 30 days to work with the program.

Don't Forget...

Don't install a proxy server program until you remove Internet Connection Sharing from Windows Me and Windows 98SE. Use the Add/Remove Programs icon in Control Panel and select the Windows Setup tab to remove ICS before you install proxy servers, because proxy servers require different settings than does ICS. For Windows 2000, reverse the setup process listed above.

You don't need to remove the Home Networking setup program installed from disk for Windows 95/98 computers.

The following are some of the leading proxy servers for home and small-office use:

➤ Ositis WinProxy (http://www.winproxy.com/)
➤ Sybergen SyGate for Home Office
   (http://www.sygate.com/products/gate_ov.htm)
➤ Deerfield.com WinGate (http://wingate.deerfield.com/)

Try Before You Buy

You can find links to the trial versions of most of these programs and many others at the Proxy Servers section of WinFiles: `http://www.winfiles.com/apps/98/servers-proxy.html`

If you are starting from scratch to build a home or small-office network, look for boxed network kits that contain two network cards, a hub or faster switch, and some cable. These kits often contain a proxy server program, saving you the expense and time of downloading one. You will need to add an additional network card to your purchase, though, because proxy servers, like ICS gateways, use two network cards.

Differences in Proxy Server Programs

When you look at a proxy server for your home or small office, consider the following factors:

➤ How many users will you connect to the Internet?—Unlike Windows ICS or Home Networking, proxy server programs count off the number of users connected and won't work with any additional users beyond the limits built into the program. So, if you have a three-user proxy server and you want to share the Internet with four other users, you need to buy an extra license to allow #4 to join the Internet-sharing party. Sometimes you can't buy individual licenses but must buy a version for six, ten, or more users, even if you only need five or eight licenses total. Carefully count, and leave room for expansion.

➤ How easy (or hard) is the configuration?—As you'll learn in Chapter 17, this standard language of the Internet can be very difficult to set up if you must specify the settings yourself. One difference between home and small-business versions of proxy servers is the level of setup automation; if just thinking about IP addresses gives you an Excedrin headache, look for no-brainer installation features. Many proxy servers have easy installation somewhat similar to the Home Networking feature of Windows Me, but others assume that you'll love playing with arcane network setups. Read the online help for the programs you're interested in to see which proxy server programs most tax your brain.

➤ What about extra features?—Although all proxy servers enable Internet connection sharing and caching of pages, some programs provide extra features. Some of the additional features you might want include

   ➤ A built-in firewall to protect your systems from being hacked and attacked by intruders.

   ➤ TCP/IP port mapping to allow game playing, chatting, and other two-way traffic to flow directly from each computer to the Internet—Keep those death matches coming!

➤ Content filtering to block offensive or time-wasting Web sites and searches—This is great for keeping the kids out of the Web's red-light districts.

➤ Integrated antivirus scanning to stop viruses before they can mess up your computers.

To get the features you want in a proxy server, you might need to add optional features at additional cost or upgrade to a better version of the proxy server.

Tech Note

THAT WAY

Let Proxy Do It!

Using a proxy server to provide features such as Web content filtering, firewalls, and antivirus makes your life easier by

➤ Protecting all the computers on the network from a single location.

➤ Allowing easier configuration of protection features. You change the proxy server settings, and all the computers on the network are protected the way you want.

Routers

Routers have been used for years to enable multiple computers on a network to access the Internet. Because a router displays only a single IP address to the Internet but allows multiple computers on your network Internet access, it can save money over buying direct access for additional computers and also provide limited firewall capabilities.

Most routers for Internet use cost $500 or more, but several models introduced recently are priced for the home and home-office or small-office markets.

Leading models include

➤ Linksys EtherFast Cable/DSL Router (model BEFSR41 features a four-port 10/100 Ethernet switch)

➤ Nexlan ISB2LAN

➤ D-Link DI-701 DSL/Cable Residential Gateway (router)

➤ Umax U-Gate 3000 Cable/ADSL Modem Sharing Gateway (router with 4-port 10/100 Ethernet hub)—also allows Web hosting with a dynamic IP address!

Get the Dish on Internet Sharing Options

Visit www.SpeedGuide.net for a wide range of tips for broadband users, including detailed reviews of these and other Internet sharing solutions.

Some cable modems can act as routers for multiple IP addresses instead of allowing a single IP address to be shared among several users. If you don't mind paying $5 or so a month for an additional IP address, you might prefer to use this method for sharing your cable modem connection with an additional user.

Troubleshooting Your Shared Connection

1. If you are using a computer as a proxy server or gateway (Internet connection sharing, and so forth), make sure it can connect to the Internet before you try to connect anybody else. If your gateway is broken, nobody can get on.

2. Make sure you specify the correct network card to configure when you are setting up the gateway computer, which has two network cards. Mix up the network card connected to the Internet and the one connected to the rest of the computers, and both the Internet and local connections will stop working.

3. If your Internet connection was working until you installed a second identical network card for use with ICS, try switching the network cables between cards. Windows 98SE's version of ICS can get confused about which card is used for the local network and which one is used for the Internet.

4. Use the worksheets in Chapter 17 to record TCP/IP settings for the Internet-connected network card and the local network-connected network card in the gateway computer, as well as for each computer that will share the connection.

5. If you are planning to use a sharing program with a one-way broadband connection, make sure that the program you want to use will support it, and follow the special instructions for setting up both your network cards and your modem.

6. If you're having problems, check the simple stuff first. It's easy to forget to plug in network cables, plug in the power supply for the hub, switch, or router, and so forth. Eliminate dumb mistakes before you start digging into the guts of TCP/IP.

7. If you need to change TCP/IP settings, read Chapter 17 first if you're unfamiliar with such things as IP addresses.

8. If you are using Microsoft ICS, check Microsoft's Web site for technical notes and clarifications on ICS and home networking.

9. Check third-party vendors' Web sites for technical notes and clarifications on their sharing programs.

10. Make sure you have your Windows and network card CDs or disks handy for installing new features.

11. If the gateway computer is connected to a telephone jack using a phone line splitter, the network might not work.

Tech Note

Different Is Good

Even though you'll need to keep another set of driver software around, it might be better to use a different brand of network card for the local connection to the other computers just so the name is different from for the network card going to the Internet connection.

The Least You Need to Know

➤ You can share an Internet connection by having one computer act as a gateway for others or one computer act as a proxy server for others, or by using a hardware device called a router.

➤ Windows 98SE, Windows Me, and Windows 2000 all feature a simple built-in gateway: Internet connection sharing (ICS).

➤ You can share either a dial-up connection or most two-way broadband connections (including DSL, cable modem, ISDN, and DirecPC) with ICS.

➤ ICS provides easy setup for the other computers in the network through standard settings or, in Windows Me, the use of a Home Network Setup disk.

➤ You can choose from many different proxy server programs, many of which can provide extra security and content filtering options not available with ICS.

➤ A router can also be used to share an Internet connection, and using one avoids the need to keep one computer running all the time.

Chapter 16

Don't Be a Bullseye—Securing Your Internet Connection

In This Chapter

➤ How to keep snoopers out of your computer

➤ Why shared hard disks and an IP address that never changes invite trouble

➤ What firewalls are and what they do

➤ Routers can do more than share a connection

Theoretically, any computer that's connected to the Internet at any time can be the target of online vandals. Your risk of attack was small when you were connected through a dial-up connection because you were online for only short periods of time. But most broadband connections are always on, and many don't require any special login procedure. The result? Your computer is vulnerable hour after hour unless you take the precautions discussed in this chapter.

The Dangers of "Always-On" Internet Access

So, you're finally done with slow Internet service. No matter when you show up at your keyboard, day or night, you're just moments away from a fresh MP3 tune, a video, or the latest news, weather, and sports. Congratulations! By the way, who else is looking at information on your computer?

It's no joke, and no paranoid fantasy. Internet access, especially the "always on" variety, can open you up to

➤ Strangers rummaging around in your hard disk files

➤ Strangers taking over your computer as a way station to attack another PC

➤ Your passwords, credit card numbers, and other confidential data being silently lifted away and sent into cyberspace

Think it's just a theory? Ask Catherine Palmer or Jim Jarrard.

Palmer watched her computer displaying her financial files onscreen while she was away from the keyboard, and later discovered that her credit cards had been maxed out by intruders who had accessed her computer through its Internet connection.

Jim Jarrard left his computer on overnight to complete a big download. Big mistake. An intruder installed a remote-control program on Jarrard's machine, but Jarrard got lucky; his computer locked up before the remote-control program could start stealing his information.

Get the Chilling Details

You can learn more about Catherine Palmer's story at

> `http://www.usnews.com/usnews/issue/991004/nycu/hackers.htm`

Learn more about Jim Jarrard's story at

> `http://www1.pcworld.com/heres_how/article/0,1400,17759,00.html`

What happened to Ms. Palmer and Mr. Jarrard could happen to you. But, you can take the "kick me" sign off your computer; you don't need to be a bullseye any longer. Low-cost and free tools available online and at local stores, as well as common-sense approaches to system setup, can keep *your* computer and *your* data *your* property.

Sharing More Than Just the Experience with Cable Modems

As you learned in Chapter 6, cable modems are a special sort of fast connection. Unlike their telco rivals ISDN and DSL, which give you a one-to-one connection to high bandwidth, cable modems divide up a big pipe among several users. In fact, if your computer is connected to a cable modem, it's connected to a local area network along with other cable modem users nearby. This is illustrated in Figure 16.1. And, like the family in the mobile phone commercial who finds a strange woman hacking away at their birthday cake, you might also be surprised to find out how easy it would be for your cable modem neighbors to "hack" away at your information.

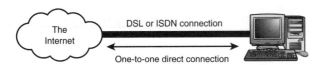

Figure 16.1

A shared media broadband connection such as a cable modem sets the stage for security problems because you're essentially on a local area network with other users.

Tech Note

"Doc Sis" Solves the Shared-Access Problem

If your cable modem uses the DOCSIS standard, you don't need to worry about shared access issues because each cable modem has an encrypted connection to the network. However, one-way cable modems and non-encrypted two-way cable modems can pose a security risk.

Are You Inviting Your Neighbors Over for Free Hard Disk Viewing?

It's very easy with most recent versions of Windows to set up your system for hard disk and printer sharing. Just click the File and Print Sharing button in your Network properties sheet, checkmark the I Want to Give Others Access to My Files and I Want to Let Others Use My Printer boxes, and restart your computer, and you have the beginnings of a big security hole.

With the rise of home networks using telephone lines, radio waves, or power lines to connect computers, and with the addition by Microsoft of Internet connection-sharing features into Windows 98SE, Windows 2000, and Windows Me, the odds are good that many of you have done exactly this—and now you need to be concerned.

Here's how you can find out whether your cable modem is putting you at risk of uninvited guests:

➤ Open Network Neighborhood or My Network Places (name varies with the version of Windows)

➤ Open the Entire Network icon

➤ Do you see several computers listed? If you do, you're sharing your broadband connection with the computers you see listed.

And, if you can see them, they can see you.

Some versions of Windows, such as Windows Me, show you shared folders, as shown in Figure 16.2.

Figure 16.2

A shared-media broadband connection displaying folders on many different computers in different homes or offices.

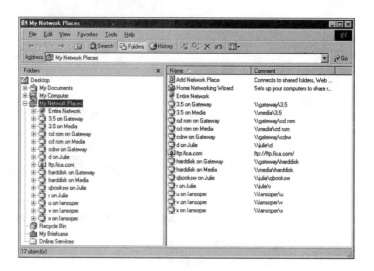

Some of the computers listed might have passwords, but it's likely that many of them do not. If a shared folder doesn't have a password, anyone who can see it can

➤ Click it

➤ Open it

➤ Read its contents

➤ Alter its contents

➤ Delete its contents

It's like leaving your car doors unlocked or forgetting to lock up your house when you leave for work. Somebody who is nosy, bored, or downright malicious is likely to "break in" and mess with your stuff.

Don't Believe Me? See For Yourself

You shouldn't open other people's folders that you can see in Network Neighborhood or My Network Places (see Figure 16.2). However, follow this link to learn how vulnerable unprotected shares on a cable modem network can be:

http://pcmike.com/Special%20Reports/cable%20modem%20flaw.html

After following the preceding link, I hope you're concerned about what people might be able to see and do on your system. In the next section, you'll learn how to block this security hole.

Why You Need to Lock Down Your System

If:

Your computer is connected to a shared broadband medium such as cable modems

And:

Your computer has one or more shared drives or folders

And:

Your computer uses Windows 95/98/Me

And especially if:

> You don't use passwords on shared resources

you are asking for trouble!

Making sure that only the people you want to use your computer can get on your computer isn't easy with the popular Windows 95/98/Me family of operating systems. Why? These versions of Windows are designed to let users in rather than keep strangers out.

Protect Others by Protecting Yourself

There are lots of good reasons to protect yourself online, but you might not realize that you also protect others when you secure your system against intruders. Here's why.

Intruders would rather take over an innocent bystander's computer and use it as a launching pad for their attacks on other computers than start attacks from their own computers. That way, the bystander's computer (and the bystander) wind up getting blamed for the damage actually caused by outside intruders. Secure your system, and you take away the ability to use it as a Trojan Horse against other computers.

Therefore, securing your system actually does your online neighbors a good turn as well as yourself. The Golden Rule works—even in cyberspace.

Sharing Too Much with Share-Level Access

Although all these versions of Windows are designed to let you access shared drives and folders *and* share drives and folders with other users, these features were designed before the popularity of the Internet. Remember the pre-Internet networking world you learned about in Chapter 1? It was a world in which small networks were like isolated islands, cut off from each other. In small-office or family networks, if you trusted your co-workers or family, you didn't need passwords.

Today, even small networks can become part of the world's largest network, the Internet, whenever computers on those networks connect. And, with many broadband Internet connections, you're automatically a part of the network whenever your computer is running.

Windows 95/98/Me—A Little Too Friendly for Network Neighbors?

The big problem with the sharing methods used by Windows 95/98/Me is that there's no provision for a user list. With Windows NT and Windows 2000, if you're not on the list of users, you're locked out of shared resources. You can't even log on to the Windows desktop! But Windows 95/98/Me are wide open. If you don't enable passwords for each shared resource, anyone who can see those resources can open them, read their contents, and perhaps even delete them.

Your nosy neighbors aren't the only ones who are trying to find out way too much about your computers. Hackers who think you're just an IP address are also interested in you—very interested.

Beyond the Network Neighborhood—Threats from the Internet

Think your home or small-office computer isn't interesting enough to be hacked? Think again. Worms like 1999's Pretty Park have been used to transmit confidential information back to the distributor of the worm and allow remote control and access programs to be run on your computer. Back Orifice is another remote-control program that is beloved by hackers who want to know what's on your PC.

Closing the Front Door to Internet Threats

Until this year, the primary way in which dangerous programs like Pretty Park could enter your computer was by disguising themselves as innocuous screensavers, animations, or other types of email attachments.

After the ILOVEYOU disaster of May 2000, which brought many corporate email systems to their knees, you were probably one of the many people who finally took the threat seriously. Maybe for the first time in your life you bought antivirus software and installed it. And you might even keep the signature files up-to-date to catch email-borne invaders in the act. Good work! You've locked the front door.

However, your computer also has a back door. The same full-time Internet access you're paying big bucks to enjoy and use can also be used against you.

How easy is it for a hacker to find your system on the Internet—and then go after it? It depends, in part, on the type of IP address you have.

The Bad, the Ugly, and the Terrible

What's the difference between Trojan Horses, worms, and viruses? All three represent harmful computer programs that must be kept off your computer to keep your information safe, but there are some differences between them.

➤ Trojan Horse—A harmful program that pretends to be a harmless program or data file.

➤ Worm—Spreads itself from system to system through email or network connections. Some worms are basically harmless, but others, like Pretty Park, can be used to send information from one computer back to the worm's originator. Worms are often launched as Visual Basic scripts attached to email messages.

➤ Virus—A program that can attach itself to the boot sectors of hard or floppy drives or to programs and can spread itself from system to system; it usually includes a payload (action that harms or destroys data) that is triggered when a particular date, file access, or other event defined in the virus takes place.

Static Versus Dynamic IP Addresses

Depending on which high-speed Internet service provider and plan you choose, you might have a choice between a *static* and a *dynamic* IP address. As you'll learn in Chapter 17, "A Survivor's to TCP/IP," the IP address is used to identify your computer to other computers on the Internet. Unfortunately, if you have the same IP address every time you connect to the Internet (a static IP address), your computer is easier to hack than if your computer has a different IP name each time you venture online (a dynamic IP address).

A fixed IP address isn't the only way that your computer can be vulnerable. As you saw earlier in this chapter, shared-medium broadband adds another layer of danger to your online experience. And, even if your IP address changes whenever you connect, automated tools used by hackers on the prowl for open systems can find your computer.

Haven't Locked the Front Door Yet?

Get antivirus information, scanning services, and software from the following sites.

The Symantec Antivirus Research Center has a comprehensive listing of viruses, Trojans, and worms, as well as a list of major hoaxes. Check it out at

    http://www.sarc.com/

You can get more information about Norton Antivirus, Norton Utilities, and Norton System Works (which also contain Norton Antivirus) from Symantec's Web site:

    http://www.symantec.com

Trend Micro, makers of PC-cillin 2000 antivirus software, also offers free online virus scanning at

    http://housecall.antivirus.com/

McAfee offers both installable antivirus software and online virus scanning by subscription along with free trial offers at

    http://www.mcafee.com

TCP/IP Ports = Unlocked Doors to Internet Intruders

How can a hacker access your computer when he or she can't see it in their Network Neighborhood?

Such access can be through ports designed into the TCP/IP protocol; these so-called software ports are used to all the TCP/IP protocols to allow multiple operations to take place at the same time.

For example, your Web browser (such as Internet Explorer or Netscape Communicator) uses TCP port 80, whereas the file transfer protocol (FTP) process (also referred to as a daemon) uses TCP port 21. This allows you to download a file from an FTP or Web site while you surf for new Web pages. Ports 0–1023 are referred to as *well-known* ports because they have specified uses. Ports 1024–49151 are called *registered* ports because they can be used by several programs. Ports from 49152–65535 are referred to as *dynamic* or *private* ports because they can be used by any program.

More About TCP Ports

The best thorough, yet non-techy explanation I've ever seen for what TCP ports do and how they can be used by intruders to attack your computer can be found at the Gibson Research Corporation Shields-Up Web site:

```
http://grc.com/su-ports.htm
```

Whenever a TCP process involving two computers is started, a port must be opened on both computers to make the connection. What makes a TCP port dangerous to your computer? Whenever your computer connects to the Internet, several TCP services such as email, FTP, and others start listening for a request to open a port.

Any TCP connection, including one started by an intruder, can ask for one of these ports to be opened, and the TCP process will obediently flip open the door and say "come on in!" After that port is opened, if you don't have a firewall, you have no way to stop whatever that TCP connection was set up to do.

You can compare the use of TCP ports to an old-fashioned telephone switchboard. To complete a call, the operator connected a wire to link the incoming call to the telephone in a particular office. Similarly, well-known TCP/IP ports are "connected" to a particular task that TCP/IP performs. Port 80, for example, is used by your Web browser to receive and display pages. You might need to specify a port number with some Web-based email systems to retrieve your email, such as

```
http://mail.someserver.com:9999
```

Ports that are left open for use by legitimate processes can also be exploited by intruders. Many port-scanning programs are used both by the curious and by the malicious to discover the following information about computers on the Internet:

➤ Their IP addresses (fixed or dynamic)

➤ Their shared folders

➤ The contents of those folders (if they are not password-protected or if the passwords are cracked by the intruder)

How much intelligence does a would-be intruder need to have to run a port-scanning program? Not much: He or she simply needs to enter a range of IP addresses to scan, sit back, and watch unsuspecting computers cough up their deepest secrets.

Figure 16.3 shows how TCP's willingness to open ports to any computer that asks puts your data at risk.

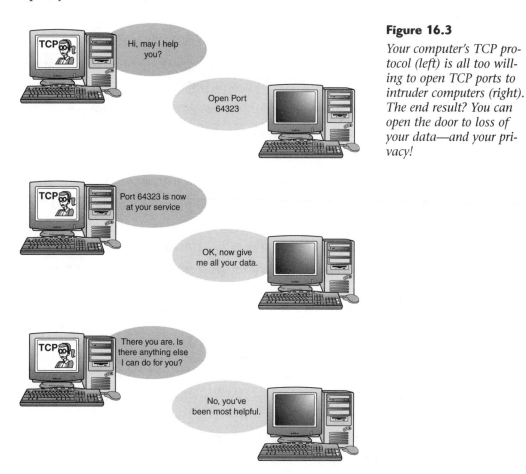

Figure 16.3

Your computer's TCP protocol (left) is all too willing to open TCP ports to intruder computers (right). The end result? You can open the door to loss of your data—and your privacy!

Keep in mind that passwords can be broken, sometimes very easily, by intruders who use password dictionaries and other tools. Therefore, you need to keep intruders out of your computer to begin with.

While You're Out, Pick Up Some Security— Hardware and Software Solutions

To stop the merely curious (like your next-door cyberneighbors on a cable modem system), a password might be enough. But to stop serious intruders who scour the Internet looking for weak spots, you need to erect a barrier against getting burned. In fact, what you need is called a *firewall*.

Shields Up, Captain!

For a horrifying look at how easy it is for port scanners to find computers on the Internet with shared folders, take a look at the following site:

    http://grc.com/su-danger.htm

This is part of Gibson Research Corporation's Shields Up! security site.

Which ports are attacked by popular Trojan Horse programs such as Back Orifice? Find out at

    http://www.sans.org/newlook/resources/IDFAQ/oddports.htm

What Firewalls Are and How They Work

Computer firewalls are designed to prevent access to a computer or network from outside that computer or network. Originally, firewalls were expensive and complicated and were used to protect corporate networks, because large networks have long been connected to other networks.

However, with the rise of the Internet, firewalls have become an important need for any computer user with an Internet connection. Firewalls work in two ways:

➤ Examining incoming traffic to see whether it should be allowed to enter

➤ Examining outgoing traffic to see whether it should be allowed to exit

Unauthorized incoming or outgoing traffic is blocked by the firewall. In corporate networks, a separate computer is used as a firewall to prevent unwanted outsiders from party-crashing the company's private network. You can now install firewall software on your own PC to provide protection for its contents.

Firewall Software for Home and Small-Business Users

Several personal firewall programs are now available for your download and purchase, including

➤ ZoneAlarm

➤ Norton Personal Firewall 2000 (also part of Norton Internet Security 2000)

➤ McAfee Firewall

➤ BlackICE Defender

Of these, one of the most effective is also the least expensive: Zone Labs' ZoneAlarm.

Tech Note

Hard Facts About Firewalls

Software firewalls are good, but hardware firewalls are even better at protecting your computer or network from unwanted intruders. For home use, the software firewalls discussed in the following text are more than adequate protection, but a business network or a home business will want the extra protection of a hardware firewall.

To learn more about all types of firewalls, I recommend Terry Ogletree's *Practical Firewalls* (Que, 2000).

ZoneAlarm—Powerful and Free for the Home

The least expensive (free for home users and just $19.95 for business users) is ZoneAlarm. It has the following major features:

➤ Can block all Internet access while allowing file sharing across your home or office network

➤ Disallows Internet traffic unless you specifically allow it on a per-application basis

➤ Blocks unused TCP ports

➤ Can hide all TCP ports, making your system "disappear" to port scanners

➤ Emergency Stop feature to immediately stop outgoing traffic

➤ Automatic Lock feature to block Internet access while you're away from your desk

Don't Just Take My Word for It

I'm not alone in raving about ZoneAlarm. Major computer magazines and Web sites such as PCWorld.com, ZDTV, *PC Magazine*, and many others love it. Find excerpts from these and many other reviews, and links to the full stories, at http://www.zonelabs.com/news.htm

➤ MailSafe, which places Visual Basic scripts (like the notorious ILOVEYOU/Love Bug virus) in isolation until you can see whether they're harmless

➤ Automatic updating over the Web

ZoneAlarm is easy to use, and abundant help is available online (see Figure 16.4).

Figure 16.4

ZoneAlarm's main menu.

Free for the Download

Download ZoneAlarm from www.zonelabs.com, which also has links to many great reviews of the product. A complete annotated list of ZoneAlarm's features is at

    http://www.zonealarm.com/zonealarm/za_features.htm

An enhanced commercial version called ZoneAlarm Plus is designed for network use. Learn more about it at

    http://www.zonelabs.com/zap.htm

Routers and Switches

If you are also planning to share your fast Internet connection with others in your home or small office, there's a hidden benefit to using a small router/switch device such as Linksys' 4-port Instant Broadband EtherFast Cable/DSL Router. This device provides both router capabilities and four switched 10/100 Ethernet ports, allowing fast network traffic and fast access to the Ethernet. Because it uses a feature called NAT (Network Address Translation) to connect the computers plugged into it to access the Internet, it acts as a firewall.

You can use it along with a program like ZoneAlarm to provide a two-layer hardware/software protection scheme for your home or small-office network.

Putting It All Together

To keep your high-speed Internet connection safe and secure, you need to do the following:

➤ Use passwords on every shared resource

➤ Use and maintain antivirus software

➤ Avoid drive and folder sharing on your Internet-connected computer if possible

➤ Install and maintain personal firewall software

Get the Scoop...

Linksys also offers many other types of low-cost, nicely featured home and small-office network hardware. Learn more about the Linksys router and the rest of the Linksys family at http://www.linksys.com

Stopping Your Network Neighbors from Getting Too Neighborly

If you have shared resources on your computer, password-protect them—no ifs, ands, or buts. If your spouse, your kids, or your co-workers are worried about forgetting them, remind them that Windows will remember the passwords for them with its password cache feature.

Don't use obvious passwords like C for the C drive. Use 8-character or longer alphanumeric (a combination of letters and numbers) passwords. Make a printed list of passwords and store it safely away *where you can find it.*

Change passwords periodically to stay on the safe side.

How to Keep File Sharing off the Internet

Ideally, the computer with the Internet connection would be set to share *nothing* with any other computer. In practice, small-office and home networks seldom follow this rule. Why is this a problem if you use passwords?

When you install Windows 95 and 98 and add a network card or a modem, these versions of Windows add file and print sharing to all network components, including the TCP/IP protocol that gets your computer to the Internet.

As you've seen previously in this chapter, TCP/IP's use of ports makes your computer "port bait" for scanners, especially if you have shared folders.

NetBEUI to the Rescue—With Some Help from Steve Gibson

Another network protocol, NetBEUI (NetBIOS Extended User Interface), is as dumb as a brick when it comes to the Internet but is perfect for sharing a drive or printer with other people in your office.

Throw Me a NetBEUI

Steve Gibson's "Network Discipline for Windows 9x" page, describing the process in detail, is available at http://grc.com/surebinding9x.htm

The perfect situation is to have NetBEUI running your home or small-office network and use TCP/IP only for the computer that accesses the Internet. Unfortunately, Microsoft binds (connects) all protocols and services together. Follow the link in the next note to see a detailed procedure that will help you use TCP/IP only for the Internet and NetBEUI for everything else.

Time to Fight Viruses

If you're not already using antivirus software, it's time to buy the latest version from a major vendor (such as Symantec's Norton Antivirus 2000) and install it. Use the quick scan feature to check important system files whenever you start your computer, and use the automatic protection features to scan downloads and incoming email. Then, keep it up-to-date by downloading and installing the latest virus signatures and patches.

Do You Need to Buy a New Version Next Year?

Even though antivirus vendors supply virus signatures for older versions of their software, buying a new version shortly after its released is best. Why? A new version adds new features, including new detection methods, as well as updated virus signatures. If you just update an old version, these new features and detection methods aren't available to you.

Building a Firewall Between the World and You

Test Fire It First

After you install your firewall, you can test that it is working properly by reading this ZDNet article and following the links it contains: http://www.zdnet.com/zdhelp/ stories/main/ 0,5594,2422273-1,00.html

Put down the trowel; as you learned earlier in this chapter, the kind of firewall you need isn't made with bricks and mortar, but with bits and bytes.

Buy or download your preferred firewall, install it, and learn how to adjust its settings. The firewall is the last brick in the barrier between you and unwanted intruders, whether they live next door or ten thousand miles away.

Check with Your ISP

Your Internet service provider can also have useful suggestions for preventing attacks on your system. Many ISPs are now providing detailed anti-hacking tips on their home pages, but others are still ignoring the very real security risk that the "always on" nature of broadband Internet brings to their customers.

Sometimes the reasons why cable and DSL providers don't provide more firewall information is that, ironically enough, firewalls and similar security measures can make it more difficult to diagnose a system problem. If you are using a firewall such as ZoneAlarm or Symantec, inform the tech people of this when you call in for help.

Don't Forget About Your Firewall!

Right after my son, Jeremy, installed ZoneAlarm for our home computer, we couldn't get connected. I thought that we'd had some kind of a hardware failure or TCP/IP addressing problem, but a quick look at the Windows 95 toolbar revealed the real problem. I'd forgotten that Zone Alarm was installed and was set to lock the Internet connection. It took only a moment to unlock the Internet and get going.

The Least You Need to Know

➤ Internet connections, especially shared-media and "always on" connections, are not secure from attack.

➤ Both shared folders and TCP ports leave your computer open to intruders.

➤ Antivirus software can stop viruses, Trojan Horses, and worms from attacking your system, but does not fix TCP port vulnerabilities.

➤ You can test your computer's vulnerability to attack at Web sites such as Steve Gibson's Shields Up!

➤ Personal firewalls such as Zone Alarm are recommended for home use, and hardware firewalls are recommended for office or home-business use.

➤ Use personal firewalls and antivirus software to help protect your system against all types of intruders and attacks.

Part 5

Squeezing More Out of Your High-Speed Connection

Any computer system will have problems sooner or later. Part 5 shows you the most common problems you can experience with your high-speed connection and what you can do about them.

First, you'll start off by learning how to understand and document TCP/IP, the language of the Internet. A mixed-up TCP/IP configuration means trouble with any high-speed connection, so this chapter comes first.

Next, you'll learn how to solve the unique problems of each form of high-speed access. From avoiding big slowdowns with DirecPC to fixing a broken cable modem or DSL connection, Part 5 keeps your high-speed connection running the way you like: fast, friendly, and almost invisible.

Chapter 17

A Survivor's Guide to TCP/IP

In This Chapter

➤ What an IP address is and why it can sometimes change.

➤ How to read and change your network configuration.

➤ How addresses are generated as needed.

➤ How to record system information to protect yourself in case your system loses its settings.

TCP/IP is the language of the Internet. If your computer doesn't speak TCP/IP, your efforts to surf the Web will wipe out in your home office or den. How much do you need to understand about it?

You don't need to be a TCP/IP expert (that could take years!), but if you want to keep your computer running, understanding the basics of how TCP/IP is configured is essential.

What's an IP Address?

Back in Chapter 1, "How the Internet Works," you learned that TCP/IP, the Transmission Control Protocol/Internet Protocol, is the network protocol suite that all computers connected to the Internet must use to communicate with each other.

One of the essential parts of any network protocol is a means of identifying each computer or processing device with a unique identifier. TCP/IP calls this identifier the IP (Internet Protocol) address. Think of an IP address as being similar to a mailing address. You can't send a letter to Jim Smith unless you also know the street address, city, state, and ZIP code where Jim Smith lives. Why do you need to supply all that information? Because there are many Jim Smiths in the world (and another one was probably just born while you were reading this paragraph). You want the right Jim Smith to get your letter.

In the same way, each computer connected to the Internet at any one time has a unique IP address, so that only messages for that computer are sent to that computer or received by that computer.

How important are IP addresses? If your computer doesn't have a valid IP address, you can't connect to the Internet or contact another computer.

Tech Note

Shhh—Keep It To Yourself!

Two types of IP addresses are used on the Internet:

➤ Private—Private IP addresses are also referred to as non-routable. Computers connected to most corporate networks, as well as most computers connected using analog modem or broadband Internet connections such as cable modem or DSL, might also use private IP addresses. Different networks can use the same private IP address ranges because these IP addresses will never be seen by the public Internet. Private IP addresses must be converted into a unique public IP address when a computer with a private IP address connects to the Internet.

➤ Public—Also referred to as global, public IP addresses can be accessed by any computer on the Internet and are unique to each computer. Web and game servers, search engines, online magazines, e-commerce sites, and other Web sites you can visit online have public IP addresses.

A Simple Example of How IP Addresses Work

I discuss where IP addresses come from (no, they're not brought by the IP Fairy!) a little later in this chapter, but right now I want to show you how IP addresses are used.

But first, a disclaimer:

"No actual IP addresses or Web sites were harmed (or used) in the creation of this example."

Tech Note

Rules for TCP/IP Addresses

What does a TCP/IP address look like? Any TCP/IP address is comprised of four groups of numbers:

Private, non-routable IP address ranges are as follows:

A-class 10.0.0.0–10.255.255.255

B-class 172.16.0.0–172.31.255.255

C-class 192.168.0.0–192.168.255.255

Addresses with higher numbers are used by public sites. For example, the IP address for www.microsoft.com is 207.46.130.45. You'll find www.yahoo.com at 216.32.74.50.

The highest value you'll see in any part of an IP address is 255.

Suppose your computer has an IP address of 10.20.30.40, and you click a link that takes you to a site called www.erewhon.tv.

What happens when you click on the link? Basically, your mouse click sends a message that (in English) would translate something like this:

```
Computer 10.20.30.40 wants to see the home page at www.erewhon.tv.
```

Your ISP's Point of Presence (POP) receives the request through its gateway computer. It's called a gateway (even if it came from a company that doesn't put cow spots on the box) because the gateway computer acts as your computer's doorway to the Internet. The gateway transfers messages to and from your computer to the rest of the Internet.

What happens next? Your request to see a page on the www.erewhon.tv server next must go to a computer called a DNS Name Server. Each ISP (and all other domains on the Web) has at least two name servers, a primary and one or more secondary name servers. They *resolve* (techno talk for match up) the name www.erewhon.tv to the IP address of the computer that hosts the www.erewhon.tv Web site (let's assume it's 23.46.22.44). As you learned in Chapter 1, these name servers act something like enormous telephone directories. Just as the telephone system would convert your request for Jim Smith's telephone number to something like (812) 555-4567, similarly, the DNS name servers use the computer's IP address rather than the Web site name to request the page.

Tech Note

Deciphering Domains

An Internet *domain* is a series of network addresses that are related in some way. For example, all Web sites that end in .com are part of a domain. Similarly, all sites that end in .cc, .net, and .org belong to different domains.

The Domain Name System matches so-called "second-level" domain names like whatis.com with the Web sites www.whatis.com, www1.whatis.com, and so on. In other words, all sites that have whatis.com at the end of the name are part of the whatis.com domain. Each ISP is also a domain.

By the way, if you're looking for concise definitions of computer terms, try

```
http://www.whatis.com
```

After the name server finds a match:

```
Send requests for pages on www.erewhon.tv to computer 23.46.22.44
```

The name server uses that information to send the request to the correct computer:

```
Router, tell computer 23.46.22.44 to send its home page to computer
10.20.30.40
```

The message is duly relayed on through layers of layers of ISP routers, gateways, and exchanges on its journey to IP address 23.46.22.44. In English, it would read something like this:

```
IP address 10.20.30.40 wants to see the home page of IP
address 23.46.22.44. Pass it on
```

You can imagine what a mess you'd have if people were doing this exchange of messages. If you've ever played the party game Telephone, where you start a message at one end of a row of players and checked the result at the other end, you know what I mean.

But, if you don't, here's an example:

During World War I, when runners, rather than radios, were used to send messages from the front lines back to headquarters, the urgent plea was given (so the story goes):

"Send up reinforcements, we are going to advance."

But after being relayed from runner to runner, headquarters was mystified to receive the following message:

"Send up two and fourpence, we are going to a dance."

It's a good thing that computers don't change the message the way people do.

Finally, after many, many, many message relays, IP address 23.46.22.44 (which is the www.erewhon.tv Web server) gets the message. It sends out its Web page (including any pictures, Java content, and so on) back to 10.20.30.40. Eventually, IP address 10.20.30.40 (your computer) sees the page onscreen.

This amazing process takes only a few seconds in many cases. Figure 17.1 helps you visualize the process.

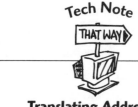

Translating Addresses

For the sake of simplicity, and to prevent inadvertent use of actual public IP addresses, I'm using private IP addresses in this example. In real life, if your computer has a private IP address, the address will be translated into a public IP address before your page request is sent to the Internet.

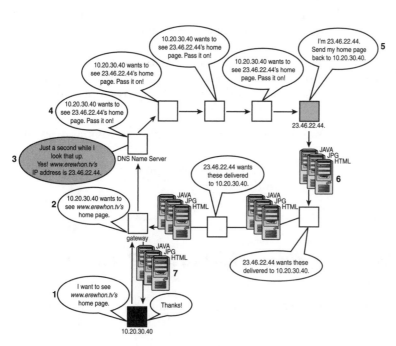

Figure 17.1

When you click on a link to a Web server's home page, you begin a process that involves looking up the Web server's IP address and relaying the request to that computer.

Use the numbers in Figure 17.1 to step through the following process:

1. Your computer requests another computer's home page.
2. Your ISP's gateway relays the request to the ISP's DNS Name Server.
3. The name server matches the Web site name to its IP address.
4. The name server sends the page request through a router to the IP address needed.
5. After being relayed by other computers, the request arrives at the Web server specified in step 1.
6. The Web server sends the contents of the home page back to your computer.
7. Your computer receives the contents of the home page and displays the page in your browser.

Where Do IP Addresses Come From?

Whenever you set up a computer to use TCP/IP, it must be assigned an IP address. IP addresses are assigned to computers in two different ways:

➤ Static IP addresses—A static IP address is assigned to a particular computer for full-time use. It never changes.

➤ Dynamic IP addresses—A dynamic IP address is assigned to a computer on an as-needed basis. It can (and does) change from time to time.

As you'll learn in the following sections, the TCP/IP settings for your computer will vary depending on which type of IP address your ISP wants you to use. But regardless of the details, make sure you use the IP address type your ISP is expecting. What happens if you fiddle around with your IP address settings?

➤ If you use a static IP address and delete it from your TCP/IP configuration, you can't get online.

➤ If you use a dynamic IP address and your TCP/IP configuration doesn't use the correct method to receive it, you can't get online.

The bottom line is, don't play with IP!

At the Dawn of Internet Time, the Static IP Address Ruled

Originally, the Internet used only static IP addresses; every time a particular computer connected to the Internet, it would use its own unique address; for example, 012.345.678.910.

This worked well as long as the Internet was strictly the haunt of scientists, researchers, military men, and nerdy college students with pocket protectors. When the World Wide Web opened the Internet to everyone in the early 1990s, the idea of giving every computer on the Internet a full-time ID that never changed wasn't going to work. There weren't nearly enough IP addresses in the world for everyone online at eBay, chatting with AOL Instant Messenger, and so on. And, to make matters worse, some networking devices and network computers need more than one IP address.

Tech Note

Deep Diving Into IP Addressing

If you really want to learn way more than you need to about IP addressing, including the rules for which addresses can be used on the "real" Internet and which addresses are for private networks, here's a very technical document from network vendor 3Com. It's not bad in the early going, but don't dive too deep:

```
http://www.3com.com/nsc/501302.html
```

For a somewhat easier take on this topic, but still more than you really need to know, go to the Whatis.com Web site and search for IP Address:

```
http://www.whatis.com/
```

In fact, the current IP address scheme for the Internet allows for only a bit over 4 billion unique addresses. If everyone on the planet (six billion and counting) goes online at the same time, we'd have to tell two billion of them to log off! Even though that's not going to happen any time soon, the pressure on the current numbering system is building. Why? Because even if everyone in the world isn't logging in at once, many systems and users are using more than one address at the same time!

Beating the Number Crunch

How does the Internet handle the huge number of new users? The following are two answers to the increasing numbers of new users:

➤ Routers—As you learned in Chapter 1, routers make the connections between different networks and route data from one network to another. Without routers, the Internet in its current form couldn't exist. Routers also have the capability to allow multiple computers connected to a single router to share a single IP address.

➤ Dynamic IP addressing—This feature takes advantage of the fact that everyone with access to the Internet doesn't use it at the same time. This allows us to share a relatively small number of IP addresses among a larger number of users.

Dynamic IP Addressing to the Rescue

Help, we're running out of numbers! Cousin Bob can't get on eBay and Aunt Petunia can't look up her New York Times crossword online!

We might already be experiencing headaches like this if those crafty computer experts hadn't come up with *dynamic IP addressing*. For the vast majority of users, whenever your computer connects to the Internet, it doesn't do so with its own IP address. Instead, it is assigned a temporary one from a pool of available IP addresses when you log in. When you disconnect or get disconnected (I hear a sigh from AOL users), the IP address of your computer dives back into the pool for someone else to claim when they go surfing. Most dial-up modems work this way. Just like a pair of bowling shoes that have helped countless amateurs throw endless gutterballs, strikes, and spares, dynamic IP addresses are recycled over and over again as computers connect to the Internet and disconnect again.

Here's how it works:

1. You start an Internet connection.

2. A computer at the ISP uses a feature, cryptically called Dynamic Host Configuration Protocol (DHCP), to dip into a fishbowl of IP addresses and pulls one out for your computer.

3. This is where your computer and the one you're logging in to for Internet access start talking. "Here, this time you're number 10.8.72.98. Be sure to return this number when you're done." "Thanks, I will," your computer replies, and you and your PC go surfing on your merry way.

4. Each Web page request you send out comes from your computer at address 10.8.72.98. The Web page then is returned to your computer at that number. When you disconnect, the IP address returns to the fishbowl for use by another computer. Figure 17.2 helps you understand how the process works.

Figure 17.2

A simple look at how dynamic IP addresses are assigned by DHCP.

Using the numbered steps below, follow along with Figure 17.2:

1. Your computer starts an Internet connection, but you don't have an IP address yet.

2. You use DHCP as a sort of digital fishing pole to retrieve an IP address from the pool of available IP addresses your ISP has for its clients.

3. After you catch an IP address, you use it to make your Internet connection.

4. When you stop working on the Internet, you throw back the IP address so another computer can use it.

Fortunately, you will almost always catch an IP address on the first cast!

Even though the vast majority of surfers get assigned an IP address dynamically these days, some still have one address all to themselves. These are called *static* IP addresses. Which kind of address do you have? Chances are if you were never told your IP address when signing up for your Internet service, you have a dynamic one. Just like the bowling shoes that have been around since approximately the era of Fred Flintstone, dynamic IP addresses don't cost much of anything; the Internet service provider is assigned a group of them to use over and over again.

Tech Note

Always-On Connections and Dynamic IP Addresses

How can an always-on connection still have a dynamic IP address? Many broad-band devices, such as cable modems and wireless broadband modems, act as DHCP servers. When your computer connects to these devices, the broadband modem will provide a private IP address for your computer. When you connect to the Internet, your private IP address is changed into a public address to enable your computer to retrieve pages.

Because you can get on and off the Internet (or just stay on for hours and hours with a fast two-way connection) with either type of address, you might wonder "who needs a static IP address?", especially because some providers who offer these charge more per month.

Do You Need a Static IP Address?

Because a dynamic IP address makes configuring your computer a lot easier, and it works just fine for most purposes, why worry about a static IP address? Some types of broadband Internet access don't even offer static IP addresses, while others can cost you more money every month. Is a static address a big deal? Is it worth changing broadband access types, providers, or service plans for?

You need a static IP address if

➤ You are running a Web server

Normally, Web servers are identified by a domain name (URL) such as www.erewhon.tv. However, sometimes when you do a search on the Web, you might find that a server that has content you want to view is identified by its IP address instead of by its URL. You can go to the Web site by entering the IP address into your browser window.

Whether or not you register a domain name for your server, it must have a fixed IP address so it can be located on the Web at all times.

➤ You are using other software or services that need to identify you by your IP address.

A couple programs that might be easier to use with a static IP address include some online games and online collaboration with Microsoft NetMeeting.

What can you do if you don't know your IP address and need to find out what it is? If you need to know your actual IP address to troubleshoot a connection problem, the easiest way to discover this information is to use WINIPCFC (covered later in this chapter).

What if you discover that your IP address is a private address? (addresses that start with 10., 172., or 192.)? If you are playing an online game or trying to use another service where you need to know your IP address, the private address isn't the answer you need. As you learned earlier, these addresses must be converted into public IP addresses when you access Internet sites.

Presto-Chango, Alikazam, a Public Address Is What I Am!

To learn what your public IP address is, go to Lawrence Goetz's IP Info Site:

```
http://www.lawrencegoetz.com/programs/ipinfo/
```

Remember, it can vary from what your network settings or WINIPCFG lists for your IP address because of the conversion from private to public IP addresses. You should check this information each time you need it because it can vary.

In addition to the issue of having too many users for too few addresses, there is another important reason why a dynamic IP address is usually better than a static one. A static IP address makes it easier for your computer to be targeted by intruders who are looking to wreak havoc. A dynamic IP address is not a great deal of security, but it can certainly make a hacker's job more difficult if your computer has, for some reason, become a target.

How to See (and Set) Your IP Address, and a Whole Lot More

Depending on exactly the kind of broadband connection you have, and whether or not you still need your trusty analog modem to do part

Port Scanners Can Still Find You

Having a dynamic IP address isn't sufficient to keep you safe online. Be sure to review Chapter 16 for the full story on Internet security.

of the job, you may need to view (or change) your TCP/IP properties for your network card and for your dial-up network connection.

Some of the settings are the same, but the network card can use more settings, depending on what your ISP requires.

Tech Note

Don't Forget Your ISP Setup CD or Disk

As essential as correct TCP/IP configuration is to getting online, you also need to run your ISP's setup program when you first configure your system. In addition to setting up your TCP/IP properties, the setup program can also be used to add other configuration information to your system that must be present to make a connection.

If you can't connect, check your TCP/IP properties and follow the hardware troubleshooting guidelines given in the following chapters. If the TCP/IP properties and hardware configuration both appear to be correct, you should rerun your ISP's setup program to restore any special drivers, Registry keys, or other setup information needed to get online.

Accessing the TCP/IP Properties for Your Network Card

Many broadband solutions use a 10BaseT or 10/100 Ethernet card as the connection. To view the TCP/IP properties for your network card, do the following with Windows 95/98/Me (Me instructions, when different, will be in parentheses like this):

1. Right-click the Network Neighborhood icon on the desktop (Me: My Network Places) and select Properties from the menu, or open the Network icon in the Control Panel.

2. As shown in Figure 17.3, scroll down the list of components and highlight a listing that looks like this:

   ```
   TCP/IP->(your network card name)
   ```

   You'll also see TCP/IP→Dial-Up Adapter and TCP/IP→Dial-Up Adapter #2 (VPN Support). Ignore these.

Tech Note

THAT WAY ▷

Where's My Network Neighborhood?

If you don't see Network Neighborhood or My Network Places on your Windows desktop, there are two possible reasons.

First, your network might not be configured correctly—you can still see your network properties from the Network icon in Control Panel, allowing you to see whether your network card and TCP/IP protocol are properly installed.

Another likely culprit is that someone has installed Microsoft Power Toys and used the TweakUI program to hide the Network Neighborhood icon. You can rerun TweakUI to unhide Network Neighborhood; see Microsoft's Web site for details.

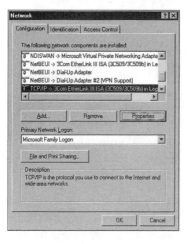

Figure 17.3

You must select the TCP/IP→network card combination before you can view its properties.

3. Click the Properties button to view the TCP/IP properties for your network card. The IP address tab is displayed first, as shown in Figure 17.4.

The TCP/IP properties for your network card, regardless of brand, are divided into categories that use some fairly arcane lingo. It can all sound and look very complicated, but there's nothing here you can't handle, so hold back any thoughts of, "I'll never understand this." Each of these categories has a tab on the Properties sheet:

➤ IP Address

➤ WINS Configuration

➤ Gateway

➤ DNS Configuration

➤ NetBIOS

➤ Bindings

➤ Advanced

Why You Need to Take a Look at TCP/IP Properties

Most ISPs provide some sort of setup program to configure these options for you. So, why learn about them? It's all too easy to change or delete settings (Windows 95/98/Me aren't designed for high security), and you might need to make manual changes if your ISP requires you to reconfigure your settings because of changes at their end of the connection.

Danger Danger

Look, But Don't Touch

Don't click OK when you finish looking at your TCP/IP properties. If you accidentally made any changes, they're saved to your Windows configuration and you might not be able to get back on the Internet. Instead, use Cancel to discard any changes you made by mistake and exit the Network menu. A worksheet is at the end of this section that you can use to record your current settings. If any of the settings are changed from your current values, this can make the job of setting things right again easier.

You can also use WINIPCFG (covered later in this chapter) to view some of the same information. Unlike the Network properties sheet, WINIPCFG displays information without giving you the chance to make a mess by editing settings.

TCP/IP Configuration Varies by Connection Type

How much of this information do you need to know? The answer to that question varies with the type of connection you have. If you have a connection that uses a static IP address (it never changes), you have a whole lot of looking to do. A static IP address changes the default settings of these IP properties sheets:

➤ IP Address

➤ Gateway

➤ DNS Configuration

A dynamic IP address is much simpler. Generally, the only tab that might vary from its default settings is the WINS Configuration tab.

If you are looking at the configuration for a computer that is sharing an Internet connection, the settings you are concerned about might vary from what is listed here. For Windows Internet Connection Sharing, see Chapter 16. For third-party sharing programs, see the documentation included with each program for details.

What about the Bindings, Advanced, and NetBIOS tabs? The Advanced tab seldom, if ever, needs adjustment. Your ISP can tell you whether you need to make any changes on this tab. The Bindings and NetBIOS tabs can be used to see if you are vulnerable to Internet cracking; they're discussed later in this chapter.

Let's start with the IP address because most changes to your properties start here.

Got Apple? Open Transport Help Is a Click Away

If you're using an iMac, iBook, or PowerMac, you use the Apple Open Transport TCP/IP Control Panel to configure and view your TCP/IP settings. Most of the settings and terminology are similar to those used by Microsoft Windows, but the layout of the Open Transport Control Panel is different than Windows's TCP/IP properties. For an online guide to Open Transport's TCP/IP Control Panel, go to

```
http://til.info.apple.com/techinfo.nsf/artnum/n75085
```

IP Address Settings

As you have probably already deduced, being the discriminating reader that you are, the IP address setting is crucial to getting online. Get this wrong and you can't get on the Internet.

You have two choices here:

➤ Use Obtain an IP Address Automatically (the default) if you use a dynamic IP address (the IP address changes whenever you log on to the Internet).

➤ If you have been given a specific IP address, you need to select the other radio button, Specify an IP Address (see Figure 17.4).

Sharing Makes for Special Settings

If you use an Internet-sharing program like Windows ICS or a switch and router for sharing, the settings for computers that share the Internet connection are different than for the computer with the connection. See Chapter 15 for more information. If you don't have a clue what this means, then pretend you didn't see this!

Figure 17.4

If your ISP uses dynamic IP addressing, the IP address and subnet mask are blanked out, as shown here.

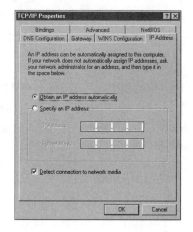

If, like most broadband users, you have a dynamic address, you can leave this tab at its default settings and go about your business. For a static address you must fill in two fields: IP Address and Subnet Mask. You need to get these numbers from your Internet service provider (see Figure 17.5).

WINS Configuration

What does this property tab do? It is used along with the IP address tab (see above) to select where your IP address comes from (see Figure 17.6).

Figure 17.5

A typical static IP address and subnet mask; if you have a static IP address, both fields must be completed with the values supplied by your ISP.

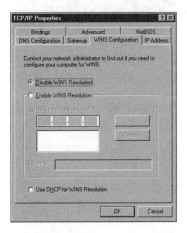

Figure 17.6

This computer has both WINS Resolution and DHCP disabled because it has a static IP address.

Think of IP Address and WINS Configuration as conjoined twins; you must set both with the correct values to get your IP address to work.

➤ If you entered an IP address and subnet mask on the IP address screen, leave this tab set to Disable WINS Resolution (the default).

➤ If you selected Obtain an IP Address Automatically on the IP address screen, you will normally select Use DHCP for WINS Resolution unless you are setting up a computer that shares another computer's Internet connection.

➤ If you are using Internet Connection Sharing or a third-party connection sharing feature, these settings can vary; see Chapter 16 or your program's documentation for details.

Tech Note

THAT WAY ▷

When You WINS, Your Home Connection Loses

You'll never need to enable WINS Resolution for a home Internet connection. WINS is used for IP address configuration on corporate networks that have Windows NT or Windows 2000 servers.

Gateway

One of the benefits of a dynamic IP address is that you don't need to worry about setting the IP address for your computer. You don't even need to set the gateway's IP address; you can leave it blank (the default).

However, if you have a static IP address or if you're connected to another computer or device that provides you with Internet access (Windows ICS or a router) you'll need to enter the IP address of the device that's acting as a gateway (see Figure 17.7).

DNS Configuration

DNS is short for *Domain Name System*. As you learned earlier in this chapter, DNS servers are used to match URLs to the host computer's IP addresses. Each ISP and domain normally have at least two DNS name servers. Figure 17.8 shows a view of the DNS Configuration page.

Figure 17.7

This computer uses a static IP address, so it requires a gateway entry. If it uses a dynamic IP address, no gateway would be used.

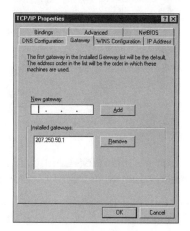

If your computer is configured to obtain a dynamic IP address using DHCP, DHCP also provides the IP addresses of the DNS servers to your computer. You must enable DNS only if you have a static IP address or if you are using some types of Internet sharing on your network.

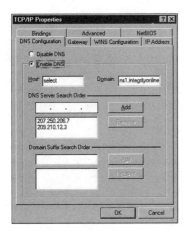

Figure 17.8
This computer can check two name servers for DNS information.

When you enable DNS, you will also need to fill in the following fields:

➤ Host

➤ Domain

➤ One or more DNS servers' IP addresses—Typically, an ISP will have at least two DNS servers

➤ A domain suffix server (by name)

NetBIOS

NetBIOS is a relatively unintelligent network protocol that, unlike TCP/IP, can't be routed. Some small networks use both NetBIOS and TCP/IP, but as you'll see, this isn't a great idea.

If you are concerned about Internet security, Microsoft's default of using TCP/IP to carry NetBIOS network traffic (as in Figure 17.9) is potentially dangerous. Why? The combination of NetBIOS networking, file sharing, and Internet access makes your computer a magnet for Internet vandals, crackers, and intruders because NetBIOS "security" isn't very secure at all.

To unbind NetBIOS from TCP/IP to help improve the security of shared folders on your network, see Chapter 16.

Figure 17.9

*Microsoft enables
NetBIOS network traffic
to travel over the TCP/IP
protocol, but this default
setting allows shared
folders to be visible over
the Internet if File and
Print sharing is also
enabled.*

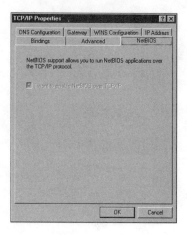

Bindings

If you want to keep a multipage document or other related papers together, you stick
them in a binder, which holds them together. Similarly, networks use *bindings* to refer
to which network components work together by using a particular protocol. Thus,
the Bindings properties tab lists the network components that use the TCP/IP protocol.

If File and Print Sharing is listed here, you might be exposing your shared folders to
everyone on the Internet! See Chapter 16 to learn how to disable this dangerous
feature. Figure 17.10 shows a view of the Bindings page.

Figure 17.10

*On this computer, TCP/IP
is bound to File and Print
Sharing, which is a
common security problem.
Everyone on the Internet
could access your shared
folders if you don't use
passwords!*

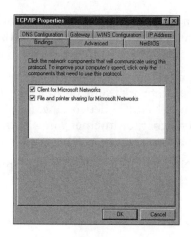

If you need to make any changes to your network configuration, you might need to
insert your Windows CD-ROM to install new network files, and the system will need
to reboot.

Sharing Is Nice, But Not With the Internet

Shared folders enable other computers on your network to use a different computer's hard disk or CD-ROM drive. But when you combine shared folders and the Internet, you set the stage for a huge security risk. Even if you use passwords to control access to a shared folder on your network, you must take the additional precautions covered in Chapter 16.

Use Table 17.1 to record your TCP/IP settings.

Table 17.1   TCP/IP Settings for Your Network Card

Tab/Field	Values	Notes/Instructions
General		
IP Address assigned Subnet Mask	___.___.___.___ ___.___.___.___	If automatically is Yes, leave these fields blank
Automatically Assigned	(_) Yes	
WINS Configuration		
Enable/Disable WINS Resolution	(_) Enable (_) Disable	If Enable, add one or more WINS Servers
WINS Server	___.___.___.___ ___.___.___.___ ___.___.___.___	Complete IP address field, then click Add button for each server
Scope ID		Enter the same value to restrict NetBIOS traffic to only those computers with same ID
Use DHCP for WINS Resolution	(_) Yes	Can be selected only if DHCP server has been detected.

Table 17.1   TCP/IP Settings for Your Network Card
Continued

Tab/Field	Values	Notes/Instructions
Gateway		
Insert Gateways	___.___.___.___ ___.___.___.___ ___.___.___.___	Complete IP address field, then click Add button for each server
DNS Configuration		
Enable/Disable DNS	(_) Enable (_) Disable	If Enable, complete remainder of fields
Host		Enter name as specified by ISP
Domain		Enter name as specified by ISP.
DNS Server Search Order	___.___.___.___ ___.___.___.___ ___.___.___.___	Complete IP address field, then click Add button for each server
Domain Suffix Search Order		Complete name field, then click Add button for each server
NetBIOS		
Enable NetBIOS	(_) Enable	Can't be selected without over TCP/IP special configuration; see Chapter 16
Advanced		Varies, can be skipped
Bindings		Specifies bindings (network components) that will use this protocol

Accessing the TCP/IP Properties for Your Modem

Some forms of broadband Internet access still use a modem rather than a network card. If you have either of the following broadband connections, you need to read this section:

➤ DirecPC—The one-way service uses an analog modem.

➤ ISDN—The ISDN terminal adapter (TA) acts like an analog modem.

332

As with broadband connections that use a network card, incorrect TCP/IP properties for your modem will prevent you from connecting to the Internet.

Follow these steps to view your connection's TCP/IP Properties with Windows 95/98/Me:

1. Open the Dial-Up Networking folder—Click the Start button, Programs, Accessories. On some versions of Windows, you must then click Communications. After you see the shortcut for Dial-Up Networking, click it to open it.

2. You probably will have only one dial-up connection displayed, along with a Make New Connection icon. If you have more than one dial-up connection icon, look for the one that lists the name of your ISP.

3. The icon for your dial-up connection to your ISP will usually list the name of your ISP (see Figure 17.11).

Figure 17.11

A typical Dial-Up Networking folder with an Internet connection icon.

4. Right-click the icon and select Properties from the menu.

5. When the Properties dialog box appears, click the Networking tab.

6. Click the TCP/IP Settings button to bring up the dialog box shown in Figure 17.12.

As with the network card's TCP/IP properties sheet, any errors in the TCP/IP setup will prevent you from accessing the Internet.

What properties do you need to set to help your modem connect with the Internet?

➤ IP address—Most dial-up connections use a server-assigned IP address (dynamic IP), but if your provider has assigned your computer its own full-time (static) IP address, enter it instead. Remember, wrong IP means no Internet for you!

➤ Name server addresses—You might need to enter the IP addresses of DNS servers and/or WINS servers even if you have a server-assigned IP address. Remember, incorrect name server entries mean that you can't connect to a Web site by its URL, but only its IP address (yuck!).

➤ IP Header compression—Some ISPs use this option to speed up data transfer; others don't. Set it according to what your ISP wants.

➤ Use Default gateway on Remote Network—Enabling this option connects you directly to the Internet gateway. As with IP Header compression, set this according to what your ISP wants.

333

Figure 17.12

An example of TCP/IP settings for a dial-up connection. Note that the server provides the IP address but the name server values are specified. Some ISPs don't require a name server.

But I Don't Know What My ISP Wants!

Many ISPs have online help for checking the configuration of your dial-up connection. If you want to stay ahead of the game, visit your ISP's help page before you have a problem and save the pages that list the correct configuration for your modem.

If you use Internet Explorer 5.5 or above, use the Save As Web Page – Complete or Web Archive – Single File to save the page with all the graphics on your own hard disk. Then, you'll have a file you can use with your Web browser or print out even if you can't get connected.

Your Dial-Up TCP/IP Configuration Worksheet

You can use the following worksheet to record the correct values for your dial-up connection:

Field	Values	Notes/Instructions
IP Address	___.___.___.___	
Subnet Mask	___.___.___.___	

Field	Values	Notes/Instructions
Server Assigned IP Address	(_) Yes	If Yes, leave IP address and subnet mask fields blank
Name Server Addresses	(_) Server Assigned (_) Specify	If Specify, enter values in fields below
Primary DNS	___.___.___.___	Enter IP addresses at left; enter 0.0.0.0 if no value is given
Secondary DNS	___.___.___.___	
Primary WINS	___.___.___.___	
Secondary WINS	___.___.___.___	
IP Header compression	(_) Enable (_) Disable	Place check in box to enable; clear check box to disable
Use Default gateway on Remote Network	(_) Enable (_) Disable	

If you make a printout of your ISP's help pages as suggested earlier, this will help you complete this printout.

Using WINIPCFG

If your system uses a dynamic IP address (which can change every time you go online), you can find out your current IP address and much more with a Windows program called WINIPCFG.

Run it from Start, Run, and it will display the IP address and other information about your system. Because you might have more than one Internet-capable connection on your system, use the pull-down menu to select your modem (referred to here as a PPP adapter) or your network card to see its IP address and default gateway (see Figure 17.13).

If you need additional information about your Internet connection, such as the default host or the IP address of your DHCP server or DNS server, click the More Info button. See Figure 17.14 to see an example of this information. Click OK to close WINIPCFG.

Figure 17.13

Run WINIPCFG and select your network card to see its current IP address and default gateway.

Tech Note

WINIPCFG to the Rescue

If you have a problem with your TCP/IP configuration, your ISP might ask you to use WINIPCFG to troubleshoot your configuration. Because WINIPCFC lists much of the same information you can see by viewing your TCP/IP configuration through the Network icon, it's a safe way to learn about your system's TCP/IP settings.

Figure 17.14

WINIPCFG displays your host, your DNS servers, and many more facts about your TCP/IP configuration when you click the More Info button shown in Figure 17.13.

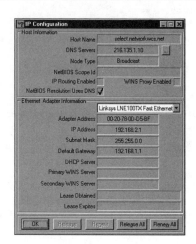

Special Notes for Sharing a Connection

In Chapter 15, you learned about various ways to share an Internet connection. Keep in mind these important differences between the TCP/IP configurations we've reviewed in this chapter and the special configurations discussed in Chapter 15:

➤ If you use two network cards in a computer acting as a gateway, they will have different TCP/IP configurations because one connects to the Internet broadband device and the other connects to the other computers on your network.

➤ If you use Microsoft Windows's Internet Connection Sharing (ICS), the original TCP/IP configuration for your network card (before sharing the connection) is transferred to the Internet Connection Sharing network device.

➤ The configuration for workstations sharing another computer's Internet connection is different than the configuration for the computer with the connection. The settings vary according to what Internet sharing software is used.

See Chapter 15 for details.

Tech Note

THAT WAY ▷

Keeping the Details Straight

If you want to use the worksheets in this chapter to record information about your connection–sharing computers, make photocopies of the worksheets and clearly mark which sheet is for the computer with the Internet connection and which records information for the computers that share the connection.

The Least You Need to Know

➤ The single most important TCP/IP configuration setting is the computer's IP address.

➤ Private IP addresses are converted into a public address when transmitted across the Internet.

➤ Some computers use a static IP address that doesn't change, while others use a dynamic IP address that is assigned by the ISP's server or by the broadband Internet device.

➤ You should record the TCP/IP configuration of your network card or modem to allow easier recovery from tampering or configuration errors.

➤ You can use WINIPCFG with Windows 95, Windows 98, or Windows Me to see your current IP address and many other details about your system.

➤ The TCP/IP configuration of a system that uses Internet sharing (either as a host or a client) will be different than that of a system that doesn't share its Internet connection.

➤ You might be able to rerun your ISP's connection software to reset your TCP/IP configuration if it has been altered.

Chapter 18

ISDN Tips, Tricks, and Troubleshooting

In This Chapter

➤ Get the most out of your ISDN connection

➤ Solve problems with your ISDN connection, both by yourself and with the help of ISDN technicians

---

When compared to other broadband solutions such as cable modems, DSL, fixed wireless, and DirecPC, ISDN is far and away the slowest broadband solution. However, you can make ISDN work faster and better for you with the tips in the first section of this chapter.

You'll find that your fast-dialing ISDN line will keep you online longer and more often than your old analog modem, and you're sure to be madder than ever if anything goes wrong with it. Use the second part of this chapter to troubleshoot your connection and keep yourself online.

ISDN Tips and Tricks

As you learned in previous chapters, ISDN is the slowest broadband connection covered in this book, even when you combine both 64Kbps B-channels (bearer channels, carrying data) into a single 128Kbps Internet connection. Several ways exist to help you get the most out of your connection, including the following:

➤ Optimizing Windows Registry settings for faster downloads and ping rate

➤ Switching to a faster connection for your external TA

➤ Using a download manager to improve download throughput

➤ Using browser synchronization to preload popular Web sites to your computer

Optimizing Windows Registry Settings

In Chapter 3, "Speed Up and Fix Up Your Dial-Up," you learned that your analog modem could gain better throughput by adjusting settings in the Windows Registry, the master database of all Windows hardware and software settings. This is also true for ISDN, although the specific values to use might be different. Table 18.1 shows the Registry settings that are most often added or changed to optimize ISDN for faster downloading of large files and better ping rates for gaming.

Tech Note

THAT WAY ▷

Faster Pinging Makes Better Gaming

The ping rate is the time it takes for a data packet to go from your computer to the target computer and return. It's sometimes referred to as latency, and ISDN offers good ping rates (which you can improve) because of its symmetric 128Kbps upload and download speeds.

For more about pinging and gaming online, see Chapter 7.

To learn how to use the Registry to make the changes listed in Table 18.1, review the section on making Registry changes in Chapter 3.

Table 18.1   Registry Settings to Optimize ISDN

Key	Value	Registry
MaxMTU	1500	System\CurrentControlSet\Services\Class\NetTrans\000x
MaxMSS	1460	System\CurrentControlSet\Services\Class\NetTrans\000x
RWIN	32120	HKEY_Local_Machine\System\CurrentControlSet\Services\VxD\MSTCP
TTL	32	HKEY_Local_Machine\System\CurrentControlSet\Services\VxD\MSTCP

To make these changes, you can

➤ Install Registry-tweaking software, such as TweakDUN, to make these changes for you; TweakDUN and other software listed in Chapter 3 will also work with ISDN connections.

➤ Follow the procedures given in Chapter 3 for making changes to your Registry with Regedit, substituting the values in Table 18.1 for those given in Chapter 3.

Tech Note

Tweaked It Once? Tweak It Again!

The values used for MaxMTU, MaxMSS, RWIN, and TTL for analog modems to speed up downloading and ping rates are different than the values needed for ISDN.

If you have previously made Registry tweaks (either with software or manually) to speed up your analog modem, it's essential that you redo the settings for ISDN. If you don't, ISDN will run more slowly than on an untweaked system. See Table 18.1 for the Registry keys you need to adjust and the values you need to use.

Switching to a Faster Connection for Your External TA

Your computer uses an ISDN terminal adapter (TA; also incorrectly called an ISDN modem) to connect with the Internet when you have ISDN broadband service. Most ISDN terminal adapters can now be connected to either an RS-232 serial (COM) port or a USB port. Unless you replaced your built-in serial ports with a high-speed port as discussed in Chapter 10, "Getting ISDN," you might not be getting the fastest performance from your TA.

If the following are all true about your ISDN connection you should forget using the serial port and use the USB port instead for the connection:

➤ You are using a TA with a maximum connection speed of 230.4Kbps and a USB port

➤ Your computer has USB ports

➤ You are using Windows 98/98SE, Windows Me, Windows 2000, or a Mac

Why Your TA Needs a Faster Connection

Many TAs have a maximum DTE (computer to modem) connection speed of 230400bps (230.4Kbps), but most onboard serial ports support only 115200bps (115.2Kbps). If your TA can receive data from your computer at a faster rate than your computer can send it, your computer represents a bottleneck, and you're not going to have as fast a connection as you deserve.

The USB port can handle connection speeds of up to 12Mbps, far faster than any ISDN TA.

Use the cable supplied with your TA to connect it to the USB port, and read the documentation to see whether any configuration changes to your dial-up connection are necessary to make the switch. In most cases, no changes will be needed. For a Windows computer, you should verify that your TA is still visible in the Windows Device Manager. Changing to a USB connector will give you faster performance for both downloading and Internet gaming.

Can you add a USB port to a computer that doesn't have one? Yes, you can, but remember that you must use Windows 98/98SE, Windows Me, or Windows 2000 to make a USB port work for you. A machine that doesn't have USB ports probably has Windows 95 installed, and you'd need to buy both a Windows upgrade ($90 or more) and a USB card (about $30) to make this work.

Because these cards plug into a PCI slot inside your computer, you must open up your case to install it or recruit that tech-head friend we all have to do it for you.

After you install a USB card, Windows detects the newly enabled USB port and loads the software drivers necessary to enable you to use it. You might need to insert your Windows CD-ROM to finish the installation.

USB Devices—Any Number Can Play!

If you already have at least one USB device (such as a Web camera, a mouse, keyboard, printer scanner, or anything else) working on your computer, you can connect your ISDN TA to any open USB port on your computer.

Most computers have two or more USB ports. If you need to locate the USB port on your computer, look for a dime-sized rectangular port. The port might be marked USB or use the fork-shaped USB logo seen in Figure 18.1. Most computers have USB ports on the rear panel, but they are sometimes located on the front or side panels.

Some of your USB devices might also act as USB hubs, providing a connection for additional USB devices. For best results, plug your ISDN TA directly into the computer's own USB ports. To free up a USB port on your computer, move another USB device to the USB connection on a USB hub.

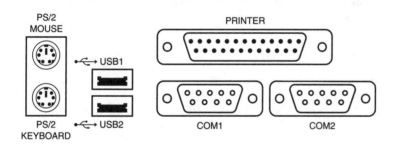

Figure 18.1
Typical location of USB ports and the USB logo in relation to other ports on a desktop computer.

Using a Download Manager

A download manager enables you to download files much more quickly than your browser can by itself. How do download managers work? They use many technological tricks to speed up downloads, including

➤ Establishing multiple connections to the same file at various Web sites—The download manager creates a single download file from multiple connections.

➤ Finding the fastest server that has the file you want—Popular utilities and software updates are often stored on multiple sites that mirror the contents of the original site. By testing each download site, a download manager can download your file from the fastest site.

➤ Scheduling downloads for off-peak hours—The Internet gets busy in the morning and in the early evening. For example, if you download after midnight, you'll get faster downloads and not be juggling downloads while you're doing other work on the computer.

Basically, a download manager's job is to get you the files you want—fast!

After you install a download manager, it is integrated with your browser. This means that when you click on a file you want to download, the download manager's own high-speed download features take over.

Turbo Charge Your Downloads

Some of the most popular download managers include Go!Zilla, available from

> http://www.gozilla.com

Download Accelerator Pro, available from

> http://www.downloadaccelerator.com/

Most download managers, including these titles, are free (advertising–sponsored) programs.

Late versions of Netscape Communicator feature Netscape Smart Download, which provides faster downloading without the need for third-party software. If you like Netscape but are not using version 4.7 or above, download the latest version of Communicator from

> http://home.netscape.com/computing/download/

Using Browser Synchronization to Preload Your Favorite Web Sites

Let's face it; there must be more than 300 million Web pages, but you couldn't care less about most of them. There are a few sites you visit every day, though, and odds are you'd like to view them more quickly. Synchronization is the process of automatically bringing you the latest version of your favorite Web sites. Because you can set up synchronization to take place at off-peak hours, you save time in browsing your favorite sites because the pages will already be stored on your computer's hard disk.

If you use Microsoft Internet Explorer version 5.0 or above, you can use the View Offline and Synchronize features to bring your favorite "hot off the Web" sites to your computer while you have breakfast or fix dinner. You must follow two procedures to make this possible:

➤ Select the sites you want to use for offline viewing—The contents of the site are copied to your computer's hard disk for instant viewing.

➤ Select how and when to synchronize the sites you select—Synchronizing loads updated content to your system.

To select your favorite Web sites for offline viewing with IE 5.0 or above, follow this procedure:

1. Go to the Web site you want to use offline.
2. Go to the page you want to start with.
3. Select Favorites, Add to Favorites, Make Available Offline (see Figure 18.2).

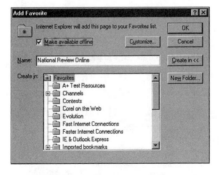

Figure 18.2

A Web page marked for offline viewing is copied to your hard disk.

4. IE starts copying the current page (text and graphics) to your computer so you can read it whether or not you're connected to the Internet.
5. Repeat this for each site you want to view offline.

After you've selected the sites you want to view offline, you must select when to synchronize them; *synchronizing* downloads the latest content for that page. To set the synchronization schedule, follow this procedure:

1. Click Tools, Synchronize.

2. From the list of offline favorites, select one and click Properties.

3. Click the Schedule tab to set up when you want to synchronize the page. Normally, synchronizing takes place only when you select Synchronize, but to have the browser download pages automatically for you, you need to select a time and frequency.

4. Click Add to select a time and frequency (see Figure 18.3). Choose the check box to have the computer automatically connect to the Internet if you don't leave your ISDN connection running at all times.

Figure 18.3

Select the frequency of updates and the time of day to update the pages. You can also provide your own name for the update. For a news-oriented site that posts new pages around midnight, updating every day around 3 a.m. is appropriate, as selected here.

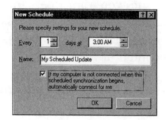

Repeat these steps for each site you want to synchronize automatically.

Figure 18.4

This site will download one layer of pages below the current page, but it will use no more than 500KB of disk space.

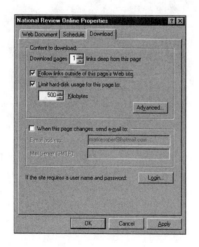

Setting Synchronization

For sites you want to review in the morning, set synchronization to take place between midnight and 6 a.m. For sites you want to review after work, set synchronization to take place about an hour before you get home. You can adjust the synchronization schedules as necessary.

If you often find yourself clicking on page links from the main page you synchronize, you can also download pages at one or more levels beneath the main page to allow them to be viewed offline. Use the Download button to select how many levels to download and how much disk space to use.

Be very careful about the number of levels you select with Download. I recommend one link deep for most pages to avoid running out of disk space. You also should limit the hard disk use for a favorite site to the default of 500KB (see Figure 18.4).

Troubleshooting Your ISDN Connection

Now that you have a fast Internet connection, you're probably more of a cyborg (part person, part computer) than ever before. If you can't get online, you feel like part of you is missing. But, if you fire up your computer, click your browser, and nothing happens, follow some excellent advice from the book *The Hitchhiker's Guide to the Galaxy*—don't panic!

When things go wrong with your computer, you're probably tempted, like most folks, to look at the most serious, weirdest possibility. I call this kind of thinking "X-Files troubleshooting," and I don't recommend it. Normally, a far better way to find problems is to start with the simple, obvious stuff and work your way up to the serious, weird, and tricky. William of Occam, born hundreds of years before computers, didn't need a computer when he created "Occam's Razor," a troubleshooting credo I live by:

> "One should not increase, beyond what is necessary, the number of entities required to explain anything."

In plain English, Occam was saying, "The simplest solution is usually correct." In computers, as in life, he's usually right. And that's especially good news with ISDN, where troubleshooting a problem can get very tricky indeed.

Please use the following notes *along with help from your ISP!* Because ISDN configurations vary so much, using the wrong troubleshooting method could make matters worse, not better!

To use the following methods correctly, you must know the following:

➤ Which type of ISDN service you have

➤ Which telephone number(s) you dial

➤ Which brand and model number of ISDN TA you have

Call your ISDN ISP with this information, keep the book open to this chapter, and you should be able to get your connection running correctly with less pain and stress.

ISDN problems can be sorted into two major categories:

➤ Can't connect at all

➤ Can't connect at the full speed you're paying for

Rest assured, I can help you with both kinds of problems. We'll start by following my own advice, beginning our troubleshooting with the easy solutions and working up to the more complicated ones.

Can't Connect at All

An ISDN connection should normally take just a few seconds to start after you open your browser. If you can't connect at all, you should check the following items:

➤ No power to your ISDN TA

➤ Bad or dead ISDN line

➤ Port or cabling problems

➤ Hardware conflicts

➤ Terminal adapter (TA) problems

Checking Your ISDN TA for Power

If you can't connect, you should first check the power light on your external ISDN TA. If it's not glowing, check the following:

➤ Is the power switch turned off?

➤ Is the AC adapter plugged tightly into the TA?

➤ Is the AC adapter plugged tightly into the wall outlet?

If you plug your TA into a surge protector, also check the following:

➤ Is the surge protector turned off?

➤ Is the surge protector plugged tightly into a wall outlet?

Check the wall outlet with a lamp if you aren't sure it's working. If the outlet itself isn't working, check your circuit breaker box or fuse box.

Finding Out Whether Your ISDN Line Is Dead

The easiest way to see whether you have a dead ISDN line is to plug an ordinary telephone into your ISDN line:

1. Disconnect your ISDN TA from the wall jack.

2. Plug your telephone into the wall jack using the cable that normally runs from the wall jack to the ISDN TA if possible.

3. Pick up the receiver; if you don't hear anything, your ISDN line is dead. If you hear hissing and clicking, the ISDN line is working.

The toughest part of that test is probably crawling around on the floor to get to the ISDN jack!

If your ISDN line is dead, plug your telephone back into the regular phone jack, reattach your ISDN TA to the ISDN jack, and call your telco to get your ISDN line fixed.

Don't Damage Your Wall Jack, Jack!

Ordinary telephones use RJ-11 cables, whereas ISDN can use either RJ-11 or the larger RJ-45 cable connector. If you plug an RJ-11 cable into an RJ-45 wall jack, you might damage some of the pins. Some ISDN TAs use a special cable that has an RJ-45 connector on one end and an RJ-11 on the other end. If the ISDN TA uses the RJ-11 connector and the wall socket uses the RJ-45 connector, you can unplug the cable from the ISDN TA, plug the cable into the phone, and check the phone line without damaging the socket.

If you have to use an RJ-11 cord to plug into an RJ-45 wall socket, the pins damaged aren't pins 4 and 5 (used for ISDN), so you'll still be able to use the jack for ISDN without any problems. However, that jack should be replaced if you plan to use it for Ethernet in the future.

Serial Port or USB Port Problems

Most ISDN TAs connect through your computer's serial port or USB port.

Start with the obvious problem:

➤ Loose or disconnected serial or USB cable

If your TA is connected through the serial port, turn off your TA and your computer before you reattach the serial port. You can fry one or the other if you attach the cable while they're running. Use the thumbscrews on the cable to tighten it to both the computer and TA's serial port.

If your TA is connected through a USB port, you can reconnect it while the computer and TA are turned on because USB is made for hot-swapping. Firmly insert the USB cable into the USB port on both devices.

➤ Bad RJ-11/RJ-45 Cables

With both external and internal TAs, an RJ-11, RJ-45, or combo RJ-11/RJ-45 cable runs between the digital port on the TA and the ISDN jack. If either end of the cable is loose, or if the cable itself is damaged or cracked, you won't be able to connect.

Hardware Conflict with Another Device

If you recently added another interface card to your Windows computer, you could be having a hardware conflict that prevents your TA from working. This is most likely to happen if you are using a TA that connects to your serial (COM) port, but it could also happen if you use an internal TA that attaches to an ISA slot.

To find out whether you have a hardware conflict with a Windows 9x/Me/2000 computer, follow these steps:

1. Right-click the My Computer icon on your desktop and select Properties, or click Start, Settings, Control Panel. When the Control Panel window opens, look for the System icon and double-click it.

2. When the System Properties dialog box pops up, click the Device Manager tab to see a list of device categories.

3. If the serial port or internal ISDN TA is marked with a yellow exclamation point (!), you have a conflict with another device. If it is marked with a red X, as shown on the Communications Port in Figure 18.5, Windows has disabled the device.

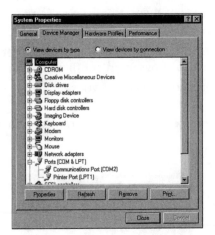

Figure 18.5

The red X indicates the serial port has been disabled.

To enable a disabled (red X) port or internal TA, follow this procedure:

1. Click the port or internal TA and select Properties.
2. Click the General tab and look at the Device Usage options; if a check mark is in the Disable in This Hardware Profile box, click it to clear it. You will need to shut down and restart your computer to re-enable the port.

Follow these steps to resolve a device conflict (yellow !):

1. Click the port and select Properties.
2. Click the Resources tab and look at the Conflicting Device list; the devices that conflict with the serial port or internal ISDN TA are listed.
3. You should try to change the settings on the conflicting device to resolve the conflict with your serial port or internal TA.
4. To change the settings used by a conflicting device, click on the device in Device Manager and select Properties.
5. Click the Resources tab, and you will see the resources (IRQ, DMA, I/O port, memory address) used by the conflicting device. The most frequent cause of conflicts include the IRQ and I/O port address settings.
6. If the Use Automatic Settings box is checked, clear it to allow settings to be made manually.
7. After you clear Use Automatic Settings, you might be able to select a different basic configuration for the device. Use the Conflicting Device list to see when you have chosen a basic configuration that no longer conflicts with your serial port or TA.
8. You also might be able to directly choose a setting by clicking on the setting and choosing another setting. If you get a message that says This Resource Setting Cannot Be Changed, you cannot change the option.

351

9. After you change the card's setting, click OK. You might need to shut down and restart your computer to finish the process.

10. If you are unable to change the conflicting device's settings, repeat steps 4–9 with the serial port or internal TA to choose non-conflicting settings.

11. After you solve a conflict, the properties sheet for your serial port will resemble the one in Figure 18.6.

12. If you are still unable to resolve the conflict, contact your computer maker for help.

Figure 18.6

This serial port no longer has a conflict.

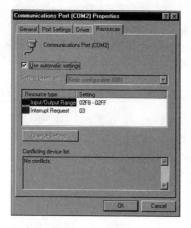

Terminal Adapter Problems

Your ISDN TA must be working correctly to enable you to access the Internet via your ISDN line. The first way to tell whether your TA is working is to watch its front panel signal lights. The number and description of the lights can vary from one TA model to another, but these are typical:

➤ Alert—If this light is on, you have a connection problem. The color of the light might indicate the nature of the problem.

➤ Power—This light should be on whenever the TA is in use; use the check list earlier in the chapter to diagnose power problems.

➤ B1 and B2—These lights indicate when these 64Kbps B-channels (bearer channels, used for data) are connected to the Internet. When you make a 128Kbps connection, both of these lights should be on. If you see only one light when you are connected to the Internet, you are getting only 64Kbps connection speed.

➤ SD and SR—When you send a page request or email message from your computer, SD (Send Data) should light up. When you receive a page or file from the Internet, RD (Receive Data) should light up.

➤ DTR—When your Web browser or other program is communicating with your ISDN TA, this light comes on.

➤ CD—When you have made a data connection with a remote site, this light comes on.

➤ Alert—This light should be off under normal conditions. On the 3Com/US Robotics TA, a blinking amber light indicates an ISDN connection problem. Contact your ISDN provider for help. A blinking green light indicates that there is voice mail waiting for a phone connected to one of the analog jacks.

If no lights appear on your TA and you've checked the wall outlet, the AC adapter, and the on/off switch, it's probably dead. Contact your vendor and get repair or replacement help.

Can't Connect at the Correct Speed

When you make an ISDN connection, you usually see a message appear onscreen indicating the ISP you've called and the connection speed. On a Windows 9x or Me computer, a small icon also appears in the taskbar next to the clock. Move your mouse over it to see the current connection speed, or click it to bring it to the middle of your screen.

On a 128Kbps connection, you should see 128000bps or 128Kbps appear when you check the speed. Also, if you have an external TA, both the B-channel lights (often referred to as B1 and B2) should be lit to indicate that you have a 128Kbps connection.

If you are not seeing the status message or signal lights listed previously, you are not getting a 128Kbps connection. Several causes are possible for an incorrect connection speed, which we'll cover in the following sections. You might be having the following problems:

➤ There is a problem with the quality of your line.

➤ Your software is not dialing the correct telephone numbers.

➤ Your Windows Dial-Up Networking software is not configured correctly.

➤ Your ISDN TA is not using the correct initialization string.

➤ Your ISDN TA is not configured correctly.

➤ Your ISDN TA needs an internal software update.

Finding Line Quality Problems

If it takes a lot longer to download anything than normal from any Web site, your ISDN line might be having problems.

How Fast Is Fast Enough?

Not sure whether you're getting the ISDN speed you paid for? Try one of these sites for a fast and easy-to-view connection speed test:

    http://mac56ktest.com/

    http://www.info-techs.com/speedtest50.html

    http://dsljump.net/speedtest1.html

A variety of factors can prevent these sites from giving you perfect information, but if you check and record your speed at several sites when you first get ISDN and compare the results later, major differences could indicate a line quality problem. Be sure to check other factors before you complain to your ISP provider about speed issues.

With a 64Kbps (one B-channel) ISDN connection, you should have results around 55Kbps–64Kbps. With a 128Kbps (two B-channel) ISDN connection, you should have results around 110Kbps–128Kbps with these tests. If your results are slower, your ISDN line might have quality problems.

Line problems can take place in one of two locations:

➤ Inside your home or office

➤ Outside your home or office

To avoid problems inside your home or office, make sure you use the cables supplied with your ISDN TA. If these are too short or become damaged, use only approved replacements. Inferior cables can cause your signal quality to go down, as can using cables that are way too long. Avoid running your cables near interference sources such as fluorescent lights or electric motors because they can really do a number on your connection speed.

To find problems outside your office, ask your telco to perform a bit error rate test (BERT) on your ISDN line. Bit errors force the Web site to resend information to your computer or force your computer to resend information to the receiver. If the line has too many errors, it causes your true speed to be considerably lower than the speed you're paying for. The telco will need to service your line to fix problems found by a BERT, and these repairs are the telco's responsibility, not yours.

Incorrect Telephone Numbers

Unlike typical analog modems, ISDN TAs on a 128Kbps connection must usually dial two numbers to make the connection, because the 128Kbps connection is really two 64Kbps connections acting as one. Sometimes you dial two separate numbers, but more often your TA must dial the same number twice. If you are getting only a 64Kbps connection, your TA might not be dialing the second number for you.

To find out which numbers the TA is dialing to make your connection, open the software you use to make your connection. Sometimes this is a proprietary program shipped with the TA, but it's more likely that you use the standard dial-up software provided by your operating system. For example, if you are using Windows 9x or Me, you probably are using the Dial-Up Networking software to set up your connection. To see which phone number you are using to make your connection, perform these steps:

1. Click Start, Programs, Accessories, Communications, Dial-Up Networking to open the Dial-Up Networking folder.
2. Right-click the icon for your connection.
3. Select Properties.
4. Next, you see the area code and phone number listed for your call on the General tab. If you see the number listed like this: 555-1212, this is the most likely cause of your problems; you must dial two separate numbers or the same number twice to make a 128Kbps connection.

Normally, you must set the number on the General tab to dial all the numbers needed to make your connection. For example, suppose you need to dial local numbers 555-1234 and 555-3456 to make your 128Kbps connection. You must enter both numbers into your communications software to make this connection.

To do so, be sure you select the General tab in the Properties dialog box and then enter both numbers, separating them with an ampersand (&). For this example, you would enter 5551234&5553456, as shown in Figure 18.7.

If your ISP wants you to dial the same number twice, you would enter the number this way: 5551234&2.

Above all, though, ask your ISP for the correct number to use and where to enter it.

Incorrect Dial-Up Networking Configuration

If you cannot enter the second dial-up number as seen in the previous section, Windows Dial-Up Networking is not set correctly to enable you to enter a nonstandard number format. Fortunately, the solution is very simple: Uncheck the box next to Use Area Code and Dialing Properties on the General tab of the Dial-Up Networking properties for your connection (refer to Figure 18.7). Unchecking this box (just click it to uncheck it) enables you to enter the number(s) needed with the ampersand or any other special characters you need to insert, as shown previously in Figure 18.7.

355

Figure 18.7

To enter two numbers in the Dial-Up Networking properties sheet for your connection, use an ampersand between the numbers.

If you must enter area code information, just do so when entering the rest of the number. Using 1 for long distance and a fictional 999 area code, the previous example would then be 19995551234&19995553456.

Incorrect Initialization String

If you can't connect at the correct speed, you might need to adjust the initialization string used by your ISDN internal TA. Your ISDN TA is treated as if it's an analog modem, and when you dial a connection with either a "real" analog modem or an ISDN TA, a series of commands called the *initialization string* is sent to your TA before the number is dialed. Some of these commands are used to set it to connect at the proper speed for your ISDN service type.

The initialization strings for your TA are available from either your ISP's online help or telephone help desk or your TA vendor's online help or telephone help desk.

Tech Note

Initialize to Change Your Modem's Defaults

Initialization strings are commands sent to your modem or TA that override its normal operation. Most modems and TAs come with a manual detailing the commands that can become part of an initialization string. *Don't* change initialization strings unless your ISP or TA vendor concludes this is the best solution.

If you and your ISP decide that changing initialization strings is a good idea, here's how you do it with Windows Dial-Up Networking:

1. Click Start, Programs, Accessories, Communications and Dial-Up Networking to open the Dial-Up Networking folder.

2. Right-click the icon for your connection, and click Properties.

3. If it's not already selected, select the General tab.

4. The modem information is listed below the Connect Using label; make sure your TA is listed there.

5. Click the Configure button.

6. Click the Connection tab.

7. Click the Advanced button.

8. Enter the correct initialization string, supplied by your ISP, in the Extra Settings field, as shown in Figure 18.8.

9. Click OK until you return to the Dial-Up Networking folder.

Figure 18.8

Using the Extra Settings window for a modem initialization string.

Don't Risk It—Copy It

Typing in an initialization string manually is very difficult to do correctly, thanks to the use of characters such as @, %, and =. If you can copy the correct information from a Web page to your system and paste it into the setup for your modem, you'll avoid the risks of messing up your modem with incorrect instructions. To do so, simply highlight the initialization string with your mouse, right-click it, and choose Copy. Now, go to the Extra Settings field, right-click there, and select Paste. Voilà!

Reconfiguring Your TA

Sometimes, as with any other piece of computer equipment, your TA can become confused and require a bit of a rest. If you are suffering from low connection speeds or an inability to dial a number but the modem's status lights and your own tests don't indicate any problems, try clearing the TA's temporary memory. Turn off an external TA for about 30 seconds and turn it back on to clear its temporary memory. Then, restart your connection.

If turning it off and restarting it doesn't work, you might need to reconfigure it for your type of ISDN service. Before you do this, however, find out whether it has a reset switch. The reset switch returns the TA to its factory-shipped configuration. Then, you can reconfigure the TA as needed for your ISDN service. To do that, you must run setup software provided with your TA and get the correct settings for the following:

➤ Your type of ISDN service (2B+D, Always On/Dynamic ISDN, or others; your ISP can provide this information)

➤ Your telephone number(s)

➤ Your SPIDs (Service Profile IDs, which are used by some ISDN ISPs to identify your service type and phone numbers)

Keep the ISP's help desk guys on the line when you must reconfigure your TA or perform the other troubleshooting tasks covered in this chapter. You'll want to ask them what to do next if the first thing you try doesn't work.

Installing New Software Into Your TA

Most ISDN TAs have *flash* memory, a special type of memory chip used for the "software on a chip" called *firmware*. As you first learned in Chapter 3, firmware fixes can improve the performance and stability of all types of Internet connections.

To learn more about firmware, see Chapter 3, "Speed Up and Fix Up Your Dial-Up."

Just as analog modems can benefit from new firmware, so can ISDN TAs. Because problems with a flash software upgrade have the potential to turn your TA into a useless hunk of plastic and circuit boards, you should perform this step as a last resort. The specifics of the procedure vary from TA model to model, but generally you must

➤ Download new firmware.

➤ Run an installation program to copy the firmware to your TA.

Your TA vendor can tell you how to use a terminal program such as Windows HyperTerminal to check the current firmware revision of your TA.

The Least You Need to Know

➤ You can improve the speed of your ISDN connection by using Registry fixes, and if you've already tweaked the Registry, you must put in the appropriate ISDN settings.

➤ Switching to a USB connection for your external TA will boost the performance of your connection.

➤ You can download files and Web pages off-peak by using download managers and browser synchronization to avoid peak-period traffic jams.

➤ Power, cable, and device conflicts all have the potential to prevent you from connecting.

➤ You can use signal lights on the front of your external TA to find line and connection problems.

➤ You must dial the correct numbers to get a 128Kbps connection with your TA.

➤ You can reconfigure your TA or install new firmware to solve persistent connection problems that originate inside your TA.

Chapter 19

DSL Tips, Tricks, and Troubleshooting

In This Chapter

➤ Get the most out of your DSL connection

➤ Solve problems with your DSL connection, both by yourself and with the help of DSL technicians

---

DSL can provide the most satisfying Internet experience you've ever had because of its high speed, but it can also be frustrating when trouble strikes. The first part of this chapter provides you with a variety of ways to coax even more speed out of DSL, and the second part helps you put DSL back upright and on the information superhighway again if it tips over.

DSL Tips and Tricks

DSL (Digital Subscriber Line) is among the fastest broadband solutions discussed in this book. But, as with almost anything else, you can make it run even faster. Some of the leading tips and tricks for your DSL connection include

➤ Windows Registry tweaks

➤ Changing Web browsers

➤ Replacing network card drivers

➤ Modifying the Hosts file to point directly to your favorite sites

Increasing Speed Through Registry Tweaking

The Windows Registry contains many settings that control how every aspect of Windows 95 and above performs. In many cases, the standard Registry settings limit the speed of DSL for downloading or game playing. Changing Registry settings allows your computer to give you faster downloads of large files and better ping rates for Internet gaming.

The speed of DSL, like other broadband connections, can be improved through Windows Registry tweaking. The settings needed for DSL can be made by

➤ Installing and using Registry-tweaking software

➤ Making manual changes to the Windows Registry

The same software and methods covered in Chapter 3, "Speed Up and Fix Up Your Dial-Up" also work for DSL connections. However, you must use different values than those recommended for analog modems. The Registry changes recommended for ISDN connections in Chapter 18, "ISDN Tips, Tricks, and Troubleshooting," are also recommended for use with DSL connections. See those chapters for details.

New Network Card Drivers

The connection between your DSL modem and your computer is made by a 10BASE-T Ethernet network card. Just like any other hardware connected to your computer, special software called device drivers (*drivers*, for short) make network cards work. Out-of-date driver software can cause problems with reliable connections and download speed.

Fast Track to New Drivers

Go to the Windrivers Web site to find links to your network card manufacturer for drivers, help line, and other questions: http://www.windrivers.com/company.htm

If you haven't upgraded to the latest drivers for your network card, take a few moments next time you're online and download them. You can determine the model number of your network card by using the Windows Device Manager; iMac users should go straight to Apple's Web site for updates because your Ethernet connection is built in.

Upgrading your network card drivers is especially important if you installed your network card with the drivers found on the Windows 95 or Windows 98 CD-ROMs; these drivers are old! Newer drivers are normally more stable, use less memory, and provide an all-around better network experience.

Tech Note

Checking Your Driver Version and Date with Windows

If you use Windows 95/98/Me/2000, right-click My Computer and select Properties. Click the Device Manager tab, and click the plus (+) sign next to network adapters. Click your network card and select Properties. To see the Driver date and version, click the Driver tab (see Figure 19.1).

If the driver for your network card is more than a year old, check with the network card manufacturer to see if a newer driver is available. You will need to know the brand and model number of the network card to get a new driver.

After you've downloaded the network card drivers, here's how you install the new drivers with Windows 9x or Me:

1. Expand the driver files to their own folder; use an unzipping program such as WinZip or PKZIP if the files are downloaded in the .ZIP format.

2. Open the Windows Device Manager (Start, Settings, Control Panel, System, Device Manager tab).

3. Open the Network Adapters section (click the plus sign).

4. Select the network card, which will have Ethernet or Fast Ethernet in its description, and click Properties.

5. Click the Driver tab.

6. Click the Update Driver button (see Figure 19.1).

7. The first screen of the Update Device Driver wizard appears. Click Next to start the search for new drivers.

8. You can select either Search for a Better Driver or Display a List of All the Drivers in a Particular Location. Select Search for a Better Driver.

9. Specify the location (folder) where the new driver is located using the Browse button, select the driver file, and click Next.

10. Follow the prompts to complete the installation of the driver; you might need your Windows CD-ROM.

Figure 19.1

The Driver tab can help you find out the date of your current network card driver and update you to the latest driver.

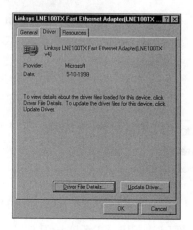

Replacing Your ISA Network Card with a PCI Network Card

If you installed an ISA network card when you installed DSL, consider replacing it with a PCI version. PCI cards are faster, are easier to configure, and will fit into most future computer models. You can pick up a decent PCI-based NIC for under $20, a small price to pay for better performance now and better compatibility later.

For more information about ISA versus PCI network cards, see Chapter 12, "Getting a Cable Modem."

Browser Tweaks for IE

You can also adjust the Microsoft Internet Explorer Web browser by means of a Registry tweak if you're feeling brave—and if you want to download Web pages faster. The more connections that Internet Explorer makes to a Web page's elements (the text and graphics included on the page), the faster you'll see it appear onscreen. You can double the number of connections IE will make to a Web page you are download-ing to speed up the page-fetch process. You can download the patch (see sidebar) from the SpeedGuide Web site.

Alternatives to IE

Internet Explorer isn't the only browser game in town. If you're looking for faster Web browsing and downloading, try Opera 4.x, the browser from Opera Software. Opera has always been much faster than IE, and current versions also work well with multimedia-rich Web sites and high-encryption e-commerce sites. Opera costs $39, but you can try it free for up to 30 days. The non-Java version is only a 1.9MB down-load, but you'll probably prefer to get the Java version, which is still only 9.3MB in size.

Get Those Pages Faster, Thanks to SpeedGuide

Want the benefits of Registry changes but don't want to fiddle with the Registry by hand or take time to experiment (and then recover from any faux pas)? The SpeedGuide Web site has the Registry fixes you need already created for insertion into your Registry, including

➤ Windows 95 and 98 DSL patches

➤ Windows 2000 DSL patches

➤ Windows 95 and 98 DSL patches for PPPoE connections (DSL connections that require you to log in)

➤ Windows 9x and 2000 back to default patches

➤ Internet Explorer patches

Download them from the Cable Modem patches section of

```
http://www.speedguide.com
```

Make Your Downloads Sing with Opera

To learn more about Opera or to download an evaluation copy, go to

```
http://www.operasoftware.com
```

If you prefer to stick with a browser based on Internet Explorer, take a look at the Voyager 5000 browser from Smartalec Corporation. It's faster than IE, maximizes screen area, and has a total download size that's much smaller than for IE.

Finding Voyager

To download Voyager 5000, go to

    http://www.tweakfiles.com/misc/voyager5000.html

For more information about other system-optimization products from Smartalec Corporation, visit its Web site at

    http://www.smartalec2000.com/

Adding Your Favorite Sites to Hosts

As you've worked with DSL or other broadband services, have you ever noticed how it takes a few seconds to locate your favorite Web site after you enter its URL or click a bookmark/favorite in your browser?

The Blame the Name (Server) Game

The IP address of the DNS server used by your computer might be listed in the TCP/IP properties for your Internet connection or might be stored in the memory of your DSL modem or other broadband device.

For more information about DNS, see Chapter 1. For more information about where you specify the DNS server, see Chapter 17, "A Survivor's Guide to TCP/IP."

The reason for the slowdown is that the Internet's DNS name servers must translate the URL into the IP address for your site before retrieving the site. For example, the IP address for www.myfavoritemovie.org rather than the URL is used to fetch pages from that site. No matter how many times a day you go to the same site, your computer can't remember which URLs and which IP addresses go together.

As with all shortcomings found when working on computers, there's a way around this inconvenience. Windows has a file, called Hosts, that—with a little bit of effort on your part—can memorize the URL and IP address match-ups you use most often.

If you add the sites you use most often to a Hosts file on your system, the performance difference is amazing; sites literally pop onto your screen because you're bypassing the normal DNS to IP address translation step. If you want to learn more, get the full details from the Tweak3D.net Web site.

DSL Troubleshooting

Your DSL connection is going to feel more and more like a part of your brain the longer you have it. Of course, the down side to that is if your DSL starts having problems, you're going to feel as if you've been through a digital lobotomy. To avoid such exercises in frustration, use this section to restore your DSL connection to health as quickly as possible.

> **For the Most from Hosts and Much More**
>
> You can learn how to create a Hosts file and many terrific speedup tips from Dustin "TimmyC" Jones's article on tweaking your DSL connection. Read the entire article at http://www.tweak3d.net/tweak/cable/print.shtml

Dial-Up Configuration

Although DSL is a network rather than modem-based technology, some DSL installations require the user to connect to the network manually. This type of DSL is often referred to as *Point-to-Point Protocol over Ethernet (PPPoE)*. If the DSL modem is internal, the installation might place an icon in the Windows Dial-Up Networking folder and use a setup that is virtually identical to an analog modem dial-up configuration.

The major difference in the configuration of a DSL modem versus an analog modem is in the telephone number entry. A cryptic hexadecimal code is used in place of the normal, easy-to-recognize telephone number on the General tab of Dial-Up Networking. For example, instead of 555-1212, you'd see a number that looks something like this example from the Hiwaay.net Web site:

```
NI 1023FFFFFFFF000CDFB6B194
```

If your DSL is configured this way, be sure that the hexadecimal entry used in the phone number field is correct. Also, make sure that the TCP/IP configuration (which uses the Server Types tab) is also correct.

Don't Put the Hex on Your PPPoE Connection

You should record the PPPoE hexadecimal connection number in a safe place, because it is much longer and harder to remember than a normal dial-up number.

You can see an example of this type of DSL configuration online at the following site:

```
http://www.hiwaay.net/support/dsl/3060-4060adsl.html
```

Releasing and Renewing Your IP Address

Most DSL connections use a dynamic IP address, which is assigned by the DSL modem or by the Internet service provider every time you connect with your DSL modem. Occasionally, your address can become corrupted, which can cause you to lose your connection. Fortunately, the fix is simple for Windows 9x/Me users:

1. Click Start, Run, and type WINIPCFG.
2. Press Enter.
3. Select your Ethernet card from the pull-down menu.
4. Click Release, and then Renew (see Figure 19.2).
5. Click OK to close the program.

Figure 19.2

Releasing and renewing your IP address can fix minor connection problems.

Windows NT 4.0 and Windows 2000 users should follow these steps:

1. Open a command-prompt session.
2. Type the command ipconfig/release to release the IP address back to the server. This allows you to get a new IP address.
3. Type the command ipconfig/renew to receive a new IP address from the server to replace the one discarded in step 2.

Network Card Problems

Your network card is the connection between your computer and your DSL modem. If your network card stops working, you'll lose your DSL connection. You can have problems with your network card during initial installation or after it's been installed. What can go wrong with your network card? Network card problems can include the following:

➤ IRQ and other hardware resource conflicts

➤ Damaged installation

➤ Hardware problems

Tech Note

THAT WAY ▷

Easier IP with Apple

Sticking to their reputation for easier use than Windows, Macs, iBooks, and iMacs release and renew their dynamic IP addresses periodically by default.

Avoiding Hardware Resource Conflicts

Network cards typically use two hardware resources:

➤ An interrupt request line—Used to signal the CPU for attention, as in "Hey, CPU, I got some data right here!" (IRQ)

➤ A range of I/O port addresses—Every device you stuff into your computer needs a unique range to avoid problems

You need a network card that works correctly, and the best way to avoid problems with IRQ or I/O port address conflicts is to buy a new network card. Why? Trying to wedge one of those dumb-as-a-brick ISA network cards you rescued from the office junk pile into one of today's overcrowded computers is just about impossible, even for a 16-year veteran of the PC wars like me.

The solution to IRQ conflicts and installation headaches is to forget about reusing the ISA card you dragged home from the office junk bin. Instead, go directly to the store and buy a PCI 10/100 dual-speed Ethernet card that supports Plug and Play. You can pop it into your computer in about five minutes and Windows will take care of the configuration for you. PCI cards support Plug and Play and can share IRQ settings on most recent computers. As a result, you'll have a working network card in no time.

If you installed an ISA network card and it's working for you, great! Just keep in mind that you might have a problem with it when you install another card. If it ain't broke, don't fix it, but remember that PCI plus Plug and Play means that you don't need to break a sweat about your network card.

If you install a new add-on card inside your computer and cannot connect to the Internet, it's a good bet that you have a conflict between the new card and your existing network card.

369

Tech Note

THAT WAY ▷

Why ISA Network Cards Are for the Birds

I've installed a lot of ISA cards over the years since they were introduced in 1984, but I hope I never have to install one again. Why not? ISA cards have two fatal strikes against them (and one is more than enough):

➤ Most don't support Windows Plug and Play—You must use the Windows Device Manager, locate unused settings, and hope the card uses the settings that are left. Then, you need to flip switches, move jumpers, or run a DOS-based (yuck!) configuration program to set the card to the available settings. This can take a long time, even for an experienced installer.

➤ ISA cards are IRQ hogs—Even if you have a late-model ISA card that supports Plug and Play, any ISA card demands its own IRQ or it can't work. A lot of computers out there today, including the one you might have, don't have a lot of open IRQs (numbered 0–15) left.

To see whether you have a hardware conflict with a Windows 9x/Me/2000 computer, follow these steps:

1. Right-click the My Computer icon on your desktop and select Properties.
2. Click the Device Manager tab to see a list of device categories.
3. If your network card is marked with a yellow exclamation point (!), you have a conflict with another device.

If you discover that you have a device conflict between your network card and a card you just installed, you can

➤ Remove the new card and install it in a different expansion slot if possible— Some systems use different hardware settings for each expansion slot.

➤ Follow the procedure given in Chapter 18 to resolve the device conflict by changing the settings on the new card.

➤ If the card you just installed is an ISA card, try a PCI version of the card—PCI cards are normally Plug and Play and can share IRQ settings on most systems, eliminating much of the risk of a hardware conflict.

➤ If the card you just installed is a PCI card but the network card is an ISA card, replace the network card with a PCI card if you have enough PCI slots.

For more information about ISA and PCI slots and cards, see Chapter 12.

Solving a Damaged Network Card Installation

If your network card is Plug and Play and it has stopped working, chances are there's a problem with the installation record in the Windows Registry rather than the card itself. You can use the Plug and Play feature to "heal" the network card by removing and reinstalling the card. Here's how it works:

1. Follow the instructions given in Chapter 17, "A Survivor's Guide to TCP/IP," to record your current IP settings for your card; you might need to reinstall the card and replace the configuration when you finish.

2. Open the Device Manager and select your network card; click Remove.

3. The card is removed from the listing, and you are prompted to restart your system.

4. Leave the card in the computer and restart your system. When Windows boots up, it recognizes the card like it's seeing it for the first time and starts the Add New Hardware Wizard to reinstall the network card on your computer. Keep your Windows CD-ROM and your network card driver diskette or CD handy because you might be prompted to insert it.

5. If you are unable to connect to the Internet after your network card is reinstalled by Windows, check the card's TCP/IP configuration. Change any settings needed to match the settings you recorded in step 1.

If the TCP/IP settings have been corrupted, this fix will repair the problem.

Does My Network Card Work?

The Windows Device Manager is notoriously unreliable at detecting whether hardware actually works. As long as the card doesn't become a black hole for electrons, the Device Manager thinks it's working okay, even if you can't Web surf across the room, let alone across the world.

If you can connect to the Internet, your network card must be working, but if you have checked your modem, cables, and other options and you can't connect, it's possible your network card has failed.

The best way to determine whether your network card is working is to use the diagnostic software that ships with most cards. Insert the disk or CD-ROM in your computer and look for a Setup program or Diagnostics folder, or check the manual to figure out which program to run.

Testing Your Network Card? DOS Awaits!

I seldom use MS–DOS commands anymore (it's just sooo easy to click my way around the computer), but if you decide that you need to test your network card, there's no getting around it—you'll need to start a DOS prompt session as discussed later.

Why? The diagnostics and testing software supplied by network card makers can't work when Windows is hanging around in the background. In other words, you can't just click on the MS–DOS prompt option from the Windows Start button and run the testing program within an MS–DOS window. You need the real thing, but fortunately, as you'll see later, a version of MS–DOS that's real enough for even a network card diagnostics program comes with Windows 95, Windows 98, and Windows Me.

The details of the tests vary from card to card, but a card that fails the tests will not work properly when you try to use it to connect to your DSL line (see Figure 19.3).

Figure 19.3

This network card is passing all the tests so far; a FAIL *message indicates it should be replaced.*

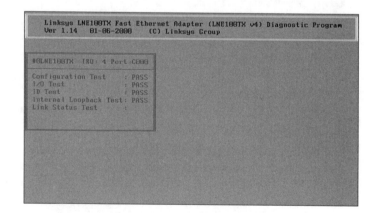

To get to an MS-DOS prompt with Windows 9x and run the diagnostic software, follow these steps:

1. Close all applications in Windows.

2. Select Start, Shutdown, Restart.

3. Press the F8 key (Windows 95) or Ctrl key (Windows 98) when the Starting Windows message appears.

4. Select Safe Mode Command Prompt Only from the startup menu.

5. Insert the disk containing the diagnostic program.

6. Change to the A drive by typing A: and pressing Enter.

7. Change to the folder on the A: drive that contains the diagnostics program by using the Change Directory command. For example, if the diagnostics program is stored in the DIAG folder, type CD DIAG and press Enter.

8. Run the diagnostics program and note the results; if the network card fails, replace it.

9. Remove the disk and press Ctrl+Alt+Del to restart the computer to the normal Windows desktop.

Get the Straight Dope from Your Diagnostic Software

Almost all network card diagnostic software is designed to be run from an MS-DOS prompt without Windows in the background; testing the card while Windows is running will create a false error message and may crash your computer.

When Fail Isn't a Failure

Some network card diagnostics feature a test that sets the card to listen for transmissions from other cards on the network. This test might give a false Fail message on a card that is connected to a DSL or other broadband device because these devices don't send data to your computer unless your computer requests it. If you see a Fail message onscreen, call the network card vendor if you don't understand it. Failures that happen on internal tests (tests that don't send or receive data) indicate the card is bad.

If you are using Windows Me, you must start your system with the emergency disk you created during the Windows Me installation process. If you didn't install Windows Me yourself, you can make this disk with this procedure:

1. Click Start, Settings, Control Panel, Add/Remove Programs.
2. Click the Startup Disk tab.
3. Click Create Disk.
4. Insert a blank disk when prompted; remove it after the files have been copied and label it as prompted.
5. Replace this disk in your floppy drive and restart your computer.
6. You eventually see an MS-DOS prompt displayed.
7. Remove the startup disk and insert your network card diagnostic disk.
8. Run the diagnostic program; note the results.
9. Replace the network card if it fails.
10. Remove the disk and press Ctrl+Alt+Del to restart your computer.

Using ping

The Ping command included with Windows is an excellent diagnostics tool for your network connection.

Tech Note

THAT WAY ▷

Pinging Your Way Across the Internet

Whenever you run the Ping command, you specify the IP address or the Web site URL (site name) of the computer you are trying to contact. The message you get back from Ping indicates how long it takes your computer to reach the remote computer and get a reply. If you don't get a normal response back from Ping, it might indicate you can't reach the remote computer, and as you'll see in this section, that can be used to figure out where the problem is.

If your DSL connection stops working, you can use ping to determine where the problem is taking place.

Start by pinging your own computer:

1. Click Start, Programs, (Accessories), MS-DOS Prompt.

2. Type ping localhost and press Enter.

3. You should see a reply similar to Figure 19.4.

Figure 19.4

When you ping yourself, a response similar to this one indicates that your computer's TCP/IP protocol is installed correctly.

4. You should then ping the IP address listed for your gateway in your network card's TCP/IP configuration; if you get no response or you get an Unknown host error message, check the following:

   ➤ Correct TCP/IP configuration—Use the notes you made when your technician installed your DSL service, or call the DSL provider for help (see Chapter 17 for details).

   ➤ Cable between the network card and the DSL modem—Make sure it's plugged in tightly to both units.

   ➤ Cable between the DSL modem and the wall socket—Make sure it's plugged in tightly to both the modem and the wall socket.

   If signal lights appear on the DSL modem in response to the ping, you know that the data packets you are sending with Ping are reaching the DSL modem.

5. Next, ping a Web site or IP address on the Internet. For example, you could ping your favorite news magazine or entertainment Web site. If you get a Request timed out message, the site is too busy to respond; try another site.

6. If you get no response or get an Unknown host error message, contact your DSL provider's help desk; the problem is between your home or office and the Internet.

Finding Line Problems

A completely dead line prevents ping tests from getting beyond your computer and your DSL modem. A more subtle problem is drastic speed drops in your DSL service. Unlike cable modems, where you share the same bandwidth with other users in your neighborhood, DSL service is not a shared medium. You have a one-to-one exclusive connection between your computer and the telco's central office, where the Internet connection is made. Because you don't share your connection with anyone, you are largely isolated from the high and low tides of cyber-traffic jams that can happen with shared-media services. So, if your 512Kbps DSL service suddenly starts doing an impression of a 56Kbps analog modem, you should suspect line problems.

Because DSL uses digital signals at a frequency different from those used for POTS (plain old telephone service) calls, weather problems like rain and moisture can degrade DSL service. This kind of thing has always occurred with phone lines, but it was never a big enough problem to have much of an effect on your ability to yak with Aunt Millie. DSL isn't that tolerant.

You should note when a drastic drop in speed takes place and then call your DSL provider. Look for patterns. Are you having a heavy rainstorm? Does the speed drop significantly at certain times of the day? Are speed changes seemingly random? The answers to these questions can help your DSL provider determine whether the problem is occurring on the DSL line connecting your location with the telco's central office.

Because many factors can change the performance of any Internet connection, including overall Internet traffic, you need to take a series of tests to show a significant drop in performance. You can use Ping to see what has happened to your line performance because it measures the time in milliseconds (ms) it takes to get a reply from the Web site you ping.

Tech Note

Ping Pong to Find Slowdowns

When you use Ping to test your line performance, be sure to ping a nearby Web site or IP address. Ask your ISP if there's a site they recommend for speed testing with Ping. You should ping the site when your Internet connection is running normally, and record the results for morning, after work, and late-night ping tests (which will vary according to Internet traffic). Then, if your downloads slow down drastically, ping the same site at about the same times of day. You should see a major difference. Report the problem with your line to your ISP.

DSL can also be affected by interference in your home. If you performed a DSL self-install, substandard components in the kit such as line splitters or microfilters could allow your phone to interfere with DSL. To see if this is the case, disconnect the phone from the DSL line. If your performance improves, call your ISP for replacement microfilters or splitters.

Common household appliances also produce a lot of electromagnetic interference that can poison a DSL connection. Dimmer switches, for example, are great for producing a romantic atmosphere for dinner, but if your DSL connection is nearby, you could also be creating enough electrical noise to degrade the connection.

You can fight back by making sure you use the cables that come in the DSL kit to connect your DSL modem to your computer and to the wall socket. Another simple solution is to attach metal donuts called *torroid chokes* to your network and telephone cables. These help block interference that can cause DSL line problems. You can get these torroid chokes at electronics stores such as Radio Shack.

Whether the problem is inside your home or outside, look for patterns. Does the performance drop and then recover? Do problems happen at a specific time every day? Are problems apparent only during the week or only on the weekend? Provide as much information as you can to help your DSL provider figure out where the problem is coming from.

Using Your DSL Modem to Troubleshoot Problems

DSL modems provide both another possible point of failure and a way to diagnose the source of the problem with your DSL connection. You must familiarize yourself with the signal lights on your DSL modem so you can use them for troubleshooting. Depending on your DSL modem model, your modem might use different signal lights for each function or use different light colors to indicate function, status, and errors.

The Alcatel STHome external DSL modem, a typical DSL modem used for residential service, has five signal lights (LEDs). Table 19.1 lists their use.

Table 19.1   Alcatel STHome Signal Lights

Light Name	Light Color	Light State	Meaning
PWR/Alarm	Green	On	Normal operation
	Red	Flashing	Power on and preparing for power on self test (POST)
		On	Power on but POST failed
LAN	Green	Flashing	Data traffic on Ethernet connection
		Off	No data

Table 19.1 CONTINUED

Light Name	Light Color	Light State	Meaning
Sync	Green	On	Modem synchronized to DSL line
		Flashing	Initializing DSL line
Line TX	Green	Flashing	DSL data being sent from modem
		Off	No data being sent
Line RX	Green	Flashing	DSL data being received by modem
		Off	No data being received

Here's how to use the signal lights to figure out where the problem is with your DSL connection:

1. If your DSL modem has no power light, it's either turned off or can't receive power from its AC adapter. Check the wall socket, power switch, and power line and turn on the modem.

2. If your modem indicates its power on tests have failed, turn off the modem for 30 seconds and turn it on again. If it continues to fail, contact your ISP for help.

3. Look at the LAN light while you try to go to a Web page. If this light isn't lit, check your 10BASE-T cable connection between your network card and DSL modem. If you have recently installed another card inside your computer, use the steps covered earlier in this chapter to check for a hardware conflict or failed network card.

4. If the Sync light indicates that your modem is attempting to synchronize to the DSL line, you must wait until it finishes this task before you can connect to the Internet. Check your manual or call the ISP to see how long this process should take. You might need to power down the modem and restart it. If your modem cannot synchronize with the DSL line, you might have a problem with the DSL line.

5. Look at the Line TX light while you attempt to go to a Web page; if this light isn't lit, your page request isn't being sent. Check the LAN light for activity; if it shows activity but the Line TX light shows no activity, you might have incorrectly configured your TCP/IP settings for your network card. Double-check them, and then call your ISP for help.

6. Look at the Line RX light while you attempt to receive a Web page; if this light isn't lit, your page isn't being received. If you saw activity on the Line TX light as you requested the page, you should see corresponding activity on the Line RX light. Call your ISP for help.

Tech Note

More Ways to See Your DSL Modem In Action

You can also use ping, as you saw earlier, to generate activity to help you use these diagnostic lights. Just ping a favorite Web site and repeat the ping as needed.

Some DSL modems place an icon on the Windows toolbar that can be used to report receive speed, transmit speed, and errors. Open this icon and check its information to help you find problems. You can see an example of this online at

    http://www.hiiwaay.net/support/dsl/troubleshooting.html

The Least You Need to Know

➤ You can improve the performance of your connection through Registry changes.

➤ Installing new network card drivers and switching from an ISA to a PCI network card can also boost DSL performance.

➤ Using a PCI network card also minimizes the odds of hardware conflicts.

➤ You can replace your normal browser with faster alternatives to improve performance.

➤ Creating a Hosts file helps your DSL connection find your favorite Web sites faster.

➤ The ping utility can be used to find the source of a DSL connection problem.

➤ Interference inside and outside your home can degrade the performance of your DSL connection.

➤ You can solve connection problems by checking cables and using the signal lights on the front of your DSL modem.

Chapter 20

Cable Modem Tips, Tricks, and Troubleshooting

In This Chapter

➤ Get the most out of your cable modem connection

➤ Solve problems with your cable modem connection, both by yourself and with the help of cable modem technicians

---

At least in the short term, I expect that cable modems will continue to be the favorite broadband solution for a lot of people (I installed the service at my home recently). The great thing about cable modem service is that at their best, cable modems give you terrific speed without tying up your phone line. However, cable modems can also be frustrating when overcrowded systems cause slowdowns or when you have a service outage.

In the first part of this chapter, I show you some tips and tricks to speed up your service, and in the second part I help you play Sherlock Holmes to discover where cable modem outages can come from and what you can do about them.

Cable Modem Tips and Tricks

Your cable modem's speed will blow you away, especially if you've been busy causing yourself repetitive stress injuries by drumming your fingers while waiting for Web pages to load up with your old analog-modem Internet service. Nevertheless, there's always room for improvement. The first part of this chapter shows you how to get even more speed out of your cable modem connection.

Many of the tweaks listed here also apply to other types of broadband connections, so the appropriate chapters are cross-referenced as needed for complete information.

You can increase your speed by

➤ Tweaking the Registry

➤ Replacing your network card drivers

➤ Switching to a PCI network card

➤ Tweaking your IE browser or replacing it with a faster Web browser

➤ Adding your favorite Web sites to a HOSTS file

➤ Using offline browsing, synchronization, and download managers to avoid network traffic jams

Increasing Speed Through Registry Tweaking

You can improve the speed of a cable modem, like other broadband connections, by changing settings in the Windows Registry. The changes needed for cable modems can be made by

➤ Installing and using Registry-tweaking software

➤ Making manual changes to the Windows Registry

The software and manual changes that can be used to tweak the Windows Registry are discussed in Chapter 3, "Speed Up and Fix Up Your Dial-Up." The Registry changes recommended for ISDN connections in Chapter 18, "ISDN Tips, Tricks, and Troubleshooting," are also recommended for use with cable modem connections. See those chapters for details.

Careful—That's Your Computer You're Playing With!

Just a friendly reminder that fiddling with the Registry isn't for the faint of heart. If you're satisfied with the speed of your cable modem, don't make any changes. However, if you've worked with Regedit before you can handle these changes, go ahead and go for more speed. If you already fiddled with your Registry to improve the speed of your analog modem, you'd better be prepared to wade back into the Registry and make the changes needed for broadband. If you don't, the optimizations that make an analog modem faster will make your cable modem slower.

New Network Card Drivers

The connection between your external cable modem and your computer is most likely made by a 10BASE-T Ethernet network card. Software drivers make your network card work (or not work) as well as possible. Out-of-date drivers can make your connection with your cable modem slower and less reliable. If you haven't upgraded to the latest drivers for your network card, take a few moments next time you're online and download them.

Tech Note

Built-In Ethernet or USB Changes Everything

If your computer has an Ethernet port on the motherboard, you'll typically contact your system or motherboard maker for new network drivers. Does your cable modem attach through a USB port? If so, you can skip this section.

You can determine the model number of your network card by using the Windows Device Manager. Apple iMac users should go straight to Apple's Web site for updates because your Ethernet connection is built in to your computer and is not a separate card.

You'll find complete instructions for upgrading your network card drivers in Chapter 19, "DSL Tips, Tricks, and Troubleshooting."

Replacing Your ISA Network Card with a PCI Network Card

If you installed an ISA network card to connect to your cable modem, consider replacing it with a PCI version. PCI cards are faster, are easier to configure, and will fit into most future computer models. You can pick up a decent PCI-based NIC for under $20, a small price to pay for better performance now and better compatibility with new computers later. In fact, if you are in the habit of stripping parts from old computers for reuse, you'll be disappointed the next time you try to reuse an ISA card. Over the last two or three years, the number of ISA slots in new computers has dropped from 2 to 1 to none on most new systems. Take a few moments of silence in memory of ISA (1984–2000, R.I.P.), and think PCI from now on.

Fast Ethernet Is Okay If It Can Go Slowly

You'll have a very hard time finding a "pure" 10BASE-T network card at stores these days. What happened? Network card manufacturers rolled out a faster Ethernet standard called, appropriately enough, Fast Ethernet a few years ago. Initially, Fast Ethernet cards could work only on a Fast Ethernet network, but network card makers now make dual-speed cards that run on both 10BASE-T and Fast Ethernet networks. These cards are usually referred to as 10/100 cards and can be used as a replacement for either a 10BASE-T or a Fast Ethernet card.

Browser Tweaks for Internet Explorer

Did you know that your browser can slow down your downloads? It can, but fortunately you have a couple of options. If you're an Internet Explorer fan, you can adjust how fast IE downloads pages by tweaking the Registry.

If you read Chapter 3's discussion of Registry tweaks, you have a pretty good idea of how the Windows 95/98 and Windows 2000 Registry tweaks speed up downloads. What about Internet Explorer? The more connections that Internet Explorer makes to a Web page's elements (the text and graphics included on the page), the faster you'll see it appear onscreen. The IE Registry tweak doubles the number of connections IE will make to a Web page you are downloading to speed up the page-fetch process.

A Night at the Opera

Opera has come a long way since it was introduced, and it's definitely worth trying and buying. To learn more about Opera or to download an evaluation copy, go to http://www.operasoftware.com

Alternatives to Internet Explorer

If you don't like Internet Explorer but aren't crazy about Netscape Communicator either, you're not stuck for options. If you're looking for faster Web browsing and downloading, try Opera 4.x, the browser from Opera Software. Opera has always been a lot faster than IE, and current versions also work well with multimedia-rich Web sites and high-encryption e-commerce sites. Opera costs $39, but you can try it free for 30 days. Get the Java-enabled version when you download it—the download is less than 10MB in size.

Get Those Pages Faster, Thanks to SpeedGuide

Do you want the benefits of Registry changes but don't want to fiddle with the Registry by hand or take time to experiment (and then recover from any faux pas)? The SpeedGuide Web site has the Registry fixes you need and best of all, you don't need to type in anything. The SpeedGuide site features Registry tweaks for

➤ Windows 95 and 98 to speed up cable modem connections

➤ Windows 2000 to speed up cable modem connections

➤ Internet Explorer Registry

You can even download patches to reset Windows 95/98 or 2000 back to the default (normal) condition.

Download these prefab Registry fixes from the Cable Modem patches section of

`http://www.speedguide.com`

If you prefer to stick with a browser based on Internet Explorer, take a look at the Voyager 5000 browser from Smartalec Corporation. It's faster than IE, maximizes screen area, and has a total download size that's under 2MB.

Beaming Up... er, Downloading Voyager

To download Voyager 5000, go to

`http://www.tweakfiles.com/misc/voyager5000.html`

For more information about other system-optimization products from Smartalec Corporation, visit its Web site at

`http://www.smartalec2000.com/`

Teaching Your PC to Memorize Your Favorite Sites

No matter how fast your cable modem service is, you'll notice that it still takes a few seconds to locate your favorite Web site after you click on a bookmark or Favorite, select a hyperlink, or enter its URL into your browser. What's going on? As you learned in Chapter 1, the Internet has a series of Domain Name Servers that contain databases that match Web site names to IP addresses. No matter how many times you've been to your favorite site, your computer still needs to ask your DNS Name Server "What's the IP address for that site again?" The DNS Name Server never gets tired of repeating the answer to the same question, but if you're trying to get every Kbps of performance, even a short wait might be too long to wait.

For the Most from Hosts and Much More

You can learn how to create a Hosts file and find many more speedup tips in Dustin "TimmyC" Jones's article on tweaking your connection. Read the entire article at `http://www.tweak3d.net/tweak/cable/print.shtml`

There are several ways to bypass this potential slowdown. One method advocated by some is to create a text file called Hosts that stores the IP addresses and URLs of the sites you go to most often on your hard disk. Does it work? Yes! Your computer can check the Hosts file and go straight to the sites listed there without asking the DNS Name Server for help.

Unlike IE's own browser caching (covered in the next section), Webcelerator can work with non-Microsoft browsers, and also offers many additional features, including

Webcelerator—For More Than IE

Webcelerator was recently selected by CNN as one of its top 11 Web tools. It's free (supported by ads) and available for download from `http://webcelerator.com/webcelerator/`

➤ Retrieval of pages linked to your current page— When you click on a link, you'll see it instantly

➤ Automatic checking for updated content— Minimizes the need to hit the refresh button

➤ Compressed storage of cached pages—Allows you to store lots of Web pages and sites on your system without running out of disk space

Webcelerator is easy to install and gives you faster access to your favorite sites.

Using Browser Synchronization to Preload Your Favorite Web Sites

At the best of times, cable modems offer blinding speeds, but because you share your connection with your neighbors, you might find traffic jams on the Web are as close as your next door neighbors' checking their email or news after work.

If you use Microsoft Internet Explorer version 5.0 or above, you can use the View Offline and Synchronize features to beat the after-work rush to the Web. These features can bring your favorite "hot off the Web" sites to your computer while you're on your way home from work. You need to follow two procedures to make this possible:

Tech Note

Using Netscape Navigator? Try Webcelerator Instead!

If you like the idea of offline browsing but prefer Netscape Navigator, Opera, or another non-IE browser, be sure to try Webcelerator as mentioned earlier in this chapter.

➤ Select sites for offline viewing—The contents of the site will be copied to your computer's hard disk for instant viewing.

➤ Select how and when to synchronize the sites you select—Synchronizing loads updated content to your system.

For the complete story on setting up offline favorites and browser synchronization, see Chapter 18, "ISDN Tips, Tricks, and Troubleshooting."

Using a Download Manager

A download manager enables you to download files much more quickly than your browser can by itself. In addition, it can be used to schedule downloads at night or other off-peak times to avoid peak-period congestion on cable modem networks. Download managers integrate with your Web browser to make it easy to download files more quickly and at your convenience.

To learn more about how download managers work, see Chapter 18, "ISDN Tips, Tricks, and Troubleshooting."

Cable Modem Troubleshooting

If you have problems with your cable modem service, you'll want to find help as quickly as possible. The solutions in this section are designed to help get you up and running as quickly as possible.

Problems with your cable modem service fall into these categories:

➤ Cable network problems beyond your control

➤ Cable modem problems

➤ Physical cable and connection problems

➤ Network card problems

➤ USB port problems

➤ TCP/IP configuration problems

Give Your Downloads a Speed Boost

Some of the most popular download managers include Go!Zilla, available from

```
http://www.gozilla.com
```

Download Accelerator Pro, available from

```
http://www.downloadaccelerator.com/
```

Most download managers, including these titles, are free (advertising-sponsored) programs.

Later versions of Netscape Communicator feature Netscape Smart Download, which provides faster downloading without the need for third-party software. If you like Netscape but are not using version 4.7 or above, download the latest version of Communicator from

```
http://home.netscape.com/computing/download/
```

No Cable TV Means No Cable Internet, Either

It's easy to forget that your cable TV and cable modem are sharing the same network cable until the splitter sends the Discovery Channel in one direction and www.discovery.com in another direction. However, because both cable TV and cable modem signals have a common source, a problem at your cable provider will whack both forms of news and entertainment.

So, if you can't get online with your cable modem, flip on the TV connected to your cable service. If you're getting nothing but snow on your cable channel but you can play DVDs and VHS tapes, you might think it's time to call the cable operator for help.

However, before you conclude the problem is beyond your control, take a look at the coaxial cable going to the splitter. The splitter prevents TV traffic from interfering with cable modem traffic. If the coaxial cable from your cable modem to your splitter is loose, you won't be able to get connected. If you've lost both cable TV and cable modem service, check the coaxial cable going back to the fiber-optic connection serving your neighborhood.

Cable Modem Problems

If your TV picks up cable channels okay but you can't get connected to the Internet through your cable modem, start by looking at your cable modem; its signal lights see all and know all—after you know the code.

Using the Signal Lights on Your Cable Modem

Signal lights on cable modems are similar to those used on DSL modems, providing indications of Ethernet traffic to and from the cable modem, traffic to and from the Internet, and modem status. The lights have different names, depending on which cable modem your provider uses. In this discussion, I use the most common terms for these signal lights and explain how your cable modem uses them to inform you of what's going on inside:

➤ Power—Your cable modem should be left on all the time to avoid problems with the modem and the cable network falling out of sync with each other. If this light is off, check the power switch and AC power source to the modem.

➤ Block sync/Cable Status—This light blinks for as long as 30 minutes if the cable modem has been turned off; if this light never stops blinking, your cable modem can't connect to the cable network. Check the cable running from out-side to your cable modem. This is called Cable Status or Link Status on some models.

Tech Note

Interference—Financial and Otherwise

One reason the block sync/cable status light won't stay on is if you forgot to pay your cable bill and your service has been suspended. If your cable modem provider does an automatic withdrawal from a credit or debit card, make sure you notify them before you change accounts or you could lose your service when they can't charge your closed account.

If your cable account is in good shape, check for interference. If you've just installed new speakers or an electric heater close to the cable modem line, turn them off or move them away from the line. If you can connect after you move or turn off these items, you've found the source of the problem.

➤ Cable activity/Data Rate—This light indicates that you are sending or receiving data from the cable modem network.

If the block sync light indicates you have a good connection to the cable network, but the cable activity light doesn't show activity when you try retrieve a Web page or ping a Web site, check the PC activity light.

➤ Modem status—This light (located on the rear of some models) can be used to indicate the result of power-on self tests, whether your modem is working correctly, and whether the modem is seeking a connection to the head end. It might use two colors of lights and different blink patterns to indicate different status messages.

➤ PC link status—This light indicates that your cable modem is connected to your computer. It's also called Ethernet on some models.

➤ PC activity—This light usually blinks when data is being transferred to and from your computer. It might be combined with the PC link status light on some models.

If neither the PC link status nor PC activity light comes on when you click a hyperlink or use ping to reach a Web site, check the Ethernet cable running between the cable modem and your computer.

Figure 20.1 shows a typical external cable modem, the 3Com HomeConnect Cable Modem external.

Resetting Your Cable Modem

Many external cable modems have a reset switch that can be used to reset the modem. If you are unable to make a connection and have ruled out cabling or other problems, you should reset your cable modem. Keep in mind that your modem will need to resynchronize itself with the cable network, and this can take as long as 30 minutes.

If you can't find a reset switch, unplug the modem for a minute or two and plug it back in again to reset it.

External One-Way Cable Modems

One-way cable modems can actually be more complex in configuration than two-way cable modems. External models connect to an external analog modem for uploading page requests and email. If you can't connect with your external one-way cable modem, be sure you check the serial cable that runs between the cable modem and analog modem, and make sure that the analog modem is powered on and is ready to run.

External one-way cable modems require special configuration. If you need to reset the modem, you might have to reset its configuration by using your Web browser. Keep the configuration instructions handy if this applies to your cable modem connection. External one-way cable modems have diagnostic and status lights similar to those used by two-way cable modems.

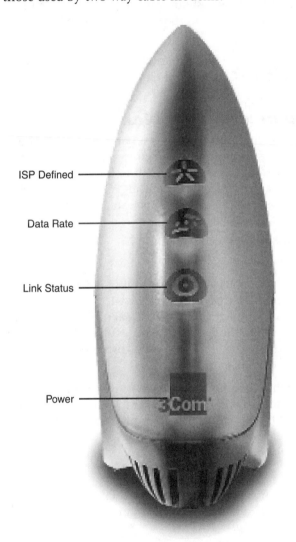

Figure 20.1

3Com's HomeConnect Cable Modem external is a typical two-way service cable modem (photo courtesy 3Com Corporation).

ISP Defined

Data Rate

Link Status

Power

Internal One-Way Cable Modems

Internal one-way cable modems can work with either external or internal analog modems. These models might have a few diagnostic lights on the card bracket or might provide diagnostic messages onscreen when you start your computer. See your modem's instruction manual for details. You must configure the modem's software to use your analog modem to dial up your ISP to make your connection.

Internal one-way cable modems can have hardware conflicts with other interface cards or with the built-in PS/2 mouse port found on many recent computers. You should disable power management on your system or make sure you hang up your Internet connection before your system goes into power-saving mode because this can cause some computers to lock up.

If you suspect a hardware conflict between your internal cable modem and another device, see "Solving Hardware Resource Conflicts" in Chapter 19 for full coverage.

Physical Cable and Connection Problems

As with any wired device, the weak link in the chain is usually the cables. Use the signal lights discussed in the previous section to find the most likely source of the problem with your cable modem connection. Start by examining the condition of the coaxial cable that runs into your cable modem from outside. Cracks in the cable's protective jacket or shielding visible on the surface of the cable can indicate problems with the cable construction.

Make sure the cable is tightly connected to the cable modem; if your block sync light is flashing, it can indicate a loose cable.

Do you have problems with Internet access after a heavy rain? A damaged cable will allow water to leak into the cable, interfering with your signal. A complete loss of service could indicate that your splitter (which splits the coaxial cable for computer and TV use) has failed. If you've had an electrical storm, take a good look at your cables and splitter. If you see burn marks, your cable might have absorbed a lightning strike, with ill effects possible for anything connected to it.

Other signal spoilers include adding or removing splitters after the initial installation. Splitters can change the signal strength and disrupt your cable modem reception. See Figure 20.2 for an overview of all the different places in your cable modem connection where loose cables can cause problems.

Tracking Down Interference

If you have intermittent problems with connections, chart them and note the times of day, days of the week, and other similarities. Contact your ISP and ask the help desk to check your cable for interference.

Network Card Problems

Unless you use a USB connection to your cable modem, your path to the Internet most likely starts with a 10BASE-T Ethernet network card. Your network card is the connection between your computer and your DSL modem. Network card problems can include the following:

➤ Loose cables

➤ IRQ and other hardware resource conflicts

➤ Damaged installation

➤ Hardware problems

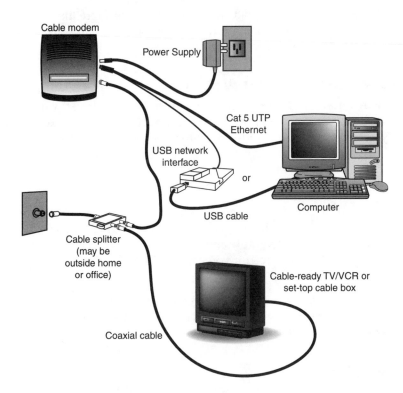

Figure 20.2

Loose coaxial, Ethernet (Cat 5) network, USB, or power cables can cause your cable modem connection to stop working.

Finding Loose Ethernet Cables with Status Lights

Most, but not all, network cards have one or two status lights near the 10BASE-T (Category 5) cable connector. These status lights can provide valuable clues about your cable modem connection.

10BASE-T–only network cards use a single light to indicate connection and activity, whereas dual-speed 10/100 cards use two lights—with the second light indicating the connection speed. If the network cable is disconnected, either at the network card or the cable modem, the lights will not be lit.

Solving Hardware Resource Conflicts

Network cards typically use two hardware resources:

➤ An interrupt request line (IRQ)

➤ A range of I/O port addresses

A conflict involving either setting is possible, but IRQ conflicts are far more likely, especially if your network card uses an ISA expansion slot. See "Solving Hardware Resource Conflicts" in Chapter 19 for full coverage of this issue.

Solving a Damaged Network Card Installation

If your network card is Plug-and-Play (it automatically installed its own drivers when you inserted it in the computer, or it came as part of a late model computer running Windows 95 or later), you can use the Plug-and-Play feature to "heal" the network card by removing and reinstalling the card. See "Solving a Damaged Network Card Installation" in Chapter 19 for full coverage of this process.

Does My Network Card Work?

The Windows Device Manager is notoriously unreliable at detecting whether hardware actually works; as long as the card doesn't become a black hole for electrons, the Device Manager will say it's working fine, even if you can't even surf across the room, let alone across the world on the Internet.

The best way to determine whether your network card is working is to use the diagnostic software that was shipped with it. See "Does My Network Card Work?" in Chapter 19 for full coverage of network card testing.

USB Port Problems

If the thought of taking a screwdriver to your PC gives you the willies, universal serial bus (USB) ports are a godsend. Imagine, just plug in a single cable and you can connect to practically anything, including many of the newest external cable modems. But, just because you have a USB port on the back of your computer doesn't mean you have a *working* USB port on a Windows PC (iMac users always have USB—and FireWire—ports as well).

Tech Note

The Shape of Things to Come?

The latest versions of the DOCSIS standard for cable modems, discussed in Chapter 12, now has provision for the FireWire (IEEE-1394 or i.Link) port. FireWire ports have become popular for directly connecting digital camcorders to high-performance PowerMac and Windows-based computers for digital editing. In the future, you may also connect your cable modem to a FireWire port that, like USB, also supports instant connection and removal from your system (hot-swapping).

Some cable modems use separate USB and Ethernet ports, while others, such as the 3Com Home Connect Cable Modem external illustrated later in this chapter, require you to attach an Ethernet adapter to your computer's USB port and connect to the Ethernet port on the cable modem.

If you can't connect with your USB cable modem, check the following:

➤ USB cables

➤ USB device detection

➤ USB hubs

➤ Disabled USB ports

USB Cable Problems

USB devices connect to USB ports. A USB port—unlike other types of ports such as serial, parallel, or SCSI—is designed for hot-swapping, meaning you can connect and disconnect USB devices on demand. Your computer redetects the USB device when you connect it and makes it available for use instantly.

A loose USB cable prevents your computer from detecting your USB cable modem, preventing you from using it. If you suspect a loose USB cable, check both ends of the cable, and see whether your USB modem shows up in the Windows Device Manager if your computer runs Windows.

If the cable looks tight but your USB modem appears to be missing in action, unplug it and reattach it to the USB port. This should cause your computer to redetect the modem and prepare to use it.

USB Device Detection

If your USB modem isn't being detected when you plug it into your USB port, check the following:

➤ Power—USB ports can't detect devices that are turned off; make sure your modem is turned on if you want it to be detected.

➤ USB ports—If the USB port is disabled, no devices can be detected.

➤ USB hubs—Most USB devices can be connected through a USB hub, an external box that enables multiple USB devices to attach to a single USB connector (also called a root hub) on your computer.

USB Hubs

For best results, USB hubs should use an external power source; self-powered hubs can have problems with some devices. If your USB modem is plugged into a USB hub but is not being detected by your computer, try bypassing the hub and plug the modem directly into a USB port on your computer. If the modem works, the USB hub might be defective or at least be incompatible with the USB modem.

Disabled USB Ports

If you have just upgraded to Windows 98, Windows Me, or Windows 2000 from Windows 95, your computer's USB ports might be disabled because most versions of Windows 95 don't support USB ports. Check the Windows Device Manager (Start, Settings, Control Panel, System, Device Manager tab) to see whether Universal Serial Bus Controller is listed as a device category (see Figure 20.3).

Figure 20.3

A computer with working USB ports has two entries: the USB Root Hub and the USB chipset, as seen here.

If you don't see Universal Serial Bus listed, look at the back of your computer to see whether you have one or more USB ports. They are rectangular ports about the width of a dime and are normally marked with a special fork-shaped USB logo (see Figure 20.4).

When Did We Get USB, and When Did Windows Know About It?

USB ports began to be introduced in 1997, but most PCs didn't feature them until 1998 or afterward. If you bought a new computer from mid–1998 on, you should have USB ports and the right operating system software (Windows 98 or above) to make them work.

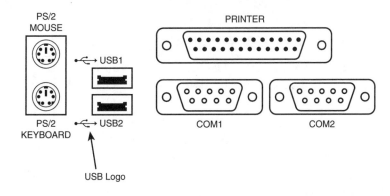

Figure 20.4

Typical location of USB ports and the USB logo in relation to other ports on a desktop computer.

If you see one or more USB ports, you must enable USB ports in your computer's BIOS. Save your data, restart your computer, and press the keys that activate your BIOS setup program. USB ports might be listed under a screen called Peripheral setup, Port setup, or something similar. After you turn on the USB port, save your changes and exit the configuration screen.

When your computer reboots, Windows detects the newly enabled USB port and loads the software drivers necessary to allow you to use it. You might need to insert your Windows CD-ROM to finish the installation.

If you have Windows 98 or above and don't have USB ports, don't panic (or start looking for a new computer, either). You can buy a card for about $30 from most computer stores that will retrofit your computer with a couple of USB ports

USB Support(?) in Windows 95

Late versions of Windows 95 also have USB support, but many USB devices don't work with any version of Windows 95. Windows 95's USB support was provided by a clumsy add-on patch, and I recommend that you upgrade to Windows 98 or Windows Me if you want USB done right!

What Else Is USB Good For?

Even though your cable modem can use either USB or Ethernet, you should still think about getting USB support if your computer doesn't have it. USB makes connecting things like Web cameras (great with high-speed Internet), printers, scanners, and lots of other devices very simple. Some of the newest low-cost computers have nothing but USB ports on-board.

TCP/IP Configuration Problems

If your cable modem hardware appears to be working correctly but you still cannot connect, the problem might be with your TCP/IP configuration. Check your configuration against the information supplied by your cable modem provider. For more information about TCP/IP configuration, see Chapter 17, "A Survivor's Guide to TCP/IP."

Releasing and Renewing Your IP Address

Most cable modem connections use a dynamic IP address. Occasionally, your connection will become corrupted because of IP address problems. Windows 9x/Me users can use WINIPCFG, and Windows NT 4.0 and Windows 2000 users can use Ipconfig to release the old IP address and renew (request) a new dynamic IP address.

For more information about using WINIPCFG and Ipconfig for releasing and renewing IP addresses, see Chapter 19, "DSL Tips, Tricks, and Troubleshooting."

Tech Note

Ping's a Thing That Can Help Your Cable Modem Sing!

The Ping utility, discussed in Chapter 19, can also help you locate problems with your cable modem connection. Ping works by sending a few data packets to a Web site or IP address you specify.

Check your cable modem documentation to see what IP address your cable modem is assigned to. For example, the 3Com Home Connect Cable Modem external I use at home has an IP address of 149.112.50.65. If you can't get a response when you ping the IP address of your cable modem, you should suspect problems with your Ethernet or USB cable to your modem or your computer's TCP/IP configuration.

If you get a response from your cable modem but not from a Web site, check the coaxial cable going from the modem out to the cable network.

Tech Note

Static Versus Dynamic IP Addresses

Most residential and small-business high-speed connections, including typical cable modem connections, use a dynamic IP address to identify your computer to the Internet. A dynamic IP address is different every time you turn on your computer and connect to the Internet.

Static IP addresses are used for servers and for other types of business computers that need to be located by other computers by their IP address. A static IP address doesn't change.

Remember, if your IP address isn't working, you can't connect to the Internet.

The Least You Need to Know

➤ You can improve the performance of your cable modem connection by making Registry changes.

➤ Installing new network card drivers and switching from an ISA to a PCI network card can also boost cable modem performance.

➤ Using a PCI network card also minimizes the odds of hardware conflicts.

➤ You can replace your normal browser with faster alternatives to improve performance.

➤ Using browser-caching features or a third-party page caching program can bring you your favorite sites faster.

➤ A one-way cable modem or a network card can conflict with other hardware in your computer; using PCI cards (which support Plug and Play with Windows) minimizes the odds of problems.

➤ If you want to use a USB port instead of an Ethernet card to connect to your cable modem, you need both working USB ports and Windows 98, Windows Me, or Windows 2000 (or a Macintosh computer with USB).

➤ The ping utility can be used to find the source of a cable modem connection problem.

➤ Interference inside your home can degrade the performance of your cable modem connection.

➤ You can solve connection problems by checking cables and using the signal lights on the front of your cable modem.

➤ Releasing your current IP addressing and renewing a new one and checking your TCP/IP configuration can help you fix connection problems.

Chapter 21

DirecPC Tips, Tricks, and Troubleshooting

In This Chapter

➤ Get the most out of your DirecPC connection

➤ Solve problems with your DirecPC connection, both by yourself and with the help of DirecPC technicians

---

This chapter is designed to help you get the most out of your DirecPC system. First, you'll learn some tips and tricks to help you get more out of your connection, then I'll dig into some more advanced troubleshooting that might help you avoid having to call tech support, pull out your hair in frustration, or both, of course.

DirecPC Tips and Tricks

DirecPC can blow the doors off your analog modem for downloading files; the first time you download a Web page with it, you won't want to go back. Unfortunately, many users have found that DirecPC loses some of its luster after the "honeymoon" period of initial ownership is over.

I cover the following tips and tricks in this section:

➤ How to configure DirecPC to work your way

➤ How to tweak Windows 95 and 98 for better performance

➤ How to use Windows Media Player 7 and nonsupported operating systems with DirecPC

➤ How to improve online game play with DirecPC

➤ Where to find DirecPC-approved tips and information

➤ How to troubleshoot connection problems

Many of these tips and tricks have been condensed from postings at the major DirecPC newsgroup:

```
alt.satellite.direcpc
```

Free Samples

If you want to sample this newsgroup before setting up your newsreader to sub-scribe to it, go to Deja's Web site:

```
http://www.deja.com/usenet
```

Search for DirecPC to see a sampling of recent postings. Although many posters are disappointed with DirecPC's overall performance, you'll learn a lot of additional ways around its limitations.

Configuring DirecPC Software

When you finish installing the DirecPC software, you can get online immediately, as you learned in Chapter 13. However, a bit of deeper digging into the DirecPC configuration enables you to customize the operation of DirecPC and bring content to your system automatically.

Like most software these days, DirecPC has many configuration screens and tons of features, many of which you probably won't care about. In this section I show you my picks for the most important features and help you get the most out of your DirecPC system.

Whenever you want to change a DirecPC setting, right-click the DirecPC Navigator icon in the Windows system tray, and you'll see the menu listed in Figure 21.1.

Figure 21.1

The DirecPC Navigation menu lets you configure all DirecPC programs.

Of the programs listed on the menu, you'll use Turbo Internet the most often because it is used to make, maintain, and disconnect your Internet sessions. To learn how to make Turbo Internet work harder for you, select Turbo Internet Properties from this menu.

Tips and Tricks for Turbo Internet

Select the General tab if you want to try the following tips and tricks (see Figure 21.2):

➤ DirecPC wants to send you a message, and you can choose how to get it or avoid being bothered. The User Notification section gives you three different ways for DirecPC to bug you when there's trouble in Internet land:

    ➤ Message box (default)

    ➤ Blinking Navigator icon

    ➤ Don't bother me

Choose your favorite way to be informed when DirecPC needs your help.

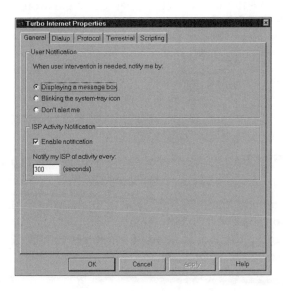

Figure 21.2

Use the General properties tab to adjust how DirecPC informs you of problems and how DirecPC notifies your ISP you're connected.

➤ Are you tired of having your ISP hang up on you? Because DirecPC uses your modem only for uploads, detouring downloads to your satellite dish, the lack of download activity coming through your modem might baffle some ISP's computers. The servers at your ISP might think you've fallen asleep at the keyboard and disconnect your system when you're really downloading like crazy from a DirecPC satellite. The solution is to adjust the Notify My ISP of Activity value to a shorter value than the default. This feature acts as a "keep-alive" feature, periodically letting your ISP know your computer is still alive, kicking, and online.

If you're still running into problems with your ISP pulling the plug on your connection, click the Dialup tab:

➤ If you want to try a backup dial-up number provided by your ISP, enter it in the Phone Number area and try your connection again.

➤ If you change modems, make sure DirecPC knows what to dial out with by selecting the new modem from the Modems section. Use the Properties button if you need to adjust any modem settings.

➤ If you're tired of dialing manually, make sure Auto-Dial is enabled, and whenever you open your browser, DirecPC will dial your connection. You also can adjust how long DirecPC will wait before pulling the plug on you when you're not surfing, and how long it will wait before redialing.

Go directly to the Protocol tab if you decide to change ISPs, if you get a message from your ISP that you must change some settings if you want to get online, or if you changed your password (see Figure 21.3).

➤ Whether you've changed to a new ISP or have just changed your password, use the PPP section of the tab to enter the correct username and password. Enter the password twice or DirecPC won't believe you know it!

Tech Note

Did You Change Your ISP? Change Everything or You'll Go Nowhere Fast!

If you switch to a new ISP after you install DirecPC, you must change the dial-up phone number on the Dialup tab as well as the username and password, and (sometimes) the protocol used on the Protocol tab. If you forget to change one of these, you can't connect to your new provider.

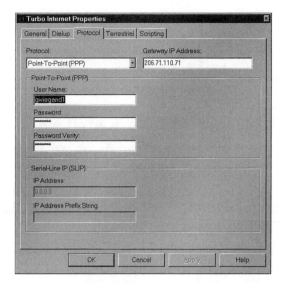

Figure 21.3

Use the Protocol tab when it's time to let another user try DirecPC with their own dial-up account, or if you change to a different ISP.

If you're an online gamer, go to the Terrestrial tab if you want a chance to live online for more than a few seconds. Why? The Terrestrial tab enables you to set up programs to use your ordinary dial-up modem in both directions (upload and download) instead of DirecPC.

➤ Because the latency (ping rate) for analog modems is better than for the normal modem plus DirecPC combination, you should use the Add button and use the dialog box that appears to include your online games one the Terrestrial listing.

Th-Th-That's Not All, Folks!

If you have more questions about using Turbo Internet configuration, go to the DirecPC online help files at `http://www2.direcpc.com/helpfiles/index.html`

All News, All the Time with Turbo Newscast

There seem to be two types of Internet users:

➤ Those who love newsgroups

➤ Those who have no idea what a newsgroup is

You don't need to use the DirecPC Turbo Newscast feature, but if you don't, you'll be missing out on a great source of user-to-user help and opinion about all types of topics.

I Pity the Fool Who Messes with Mr. T(errestrial)

When you click the Terrestrial tab, you'll see a couple of cryptic entries already listed by DirecPC. What are they?

> ➤ DNS (UDP) means that your contact with your ISP's DNS server is performed through Terrestrial mode. The matchups that say This URL Equals This IP Address come back through your modem.

> ➤ SMTP (TCP) means that your communication with your email server also runs in Terrestrial mode (SMTP stands for Simple Mail Transfer Protocol)

Don't change either of these settings unless you don't like getting online or getting your email...

What is it? Turbo Newscast is DirecPC's way of providing access to the thousands of newsgroups that exist in cyberspace. Despite the name, newsgroups aren't a repackaging of news from the AP or CNN. Instead, newsgroups feature lively, no-holds-barred discussions of whatever the newsgroup topic happens to be.

There are a lot of very opinionated and sometimes very useful information about DirecPC in the `alt.satellite.direcpc` newsgroup, and as you can imagine, there are multiple newsgroups for almost any technical (and non-technical) topic.

Turbo Newscast enables you to subscribe to any newsgroup you want and read the latest messages automatically delivered to your system. And, even if you're on the limited-hours Executive Surfer plan, Turbo Newscast won't cost you a minute of extra connection time.

You can use your Netscape browser or Microsoft Outlook Express to read newsgroups. See Figure 21.4 for an example of a typical newsgroup as seen in Microsoft Outlook Express.

If you want to try some newsgroups, use the newsgroup feature of Netscape Navigator or Outlook Express to select the `news.direcpc.com` news server and newsgroups you like. Here's how you set up your newsreader:

> ➤ Use the IP address 127.0.0.1 (also called localhost) for the news server address.

> ➤ Use 119 as the port number (if required by your news reader).

> ➤ Configure the newsreader to log on to the Newscast server if you have used a password to limit access to your newsgroups.

Tech Note

The DirecPC Newsgroup Difference

If you take a careful look at Figure 21.4, you can see that the DirecPC news server (news.direcpc.com) provides access to the newsgroup this user is relying on for help. This user's ISP's news server (news.iquest.net) is also listed, but news.direcpc.com has a big advantage—automatic delivery to your computer!

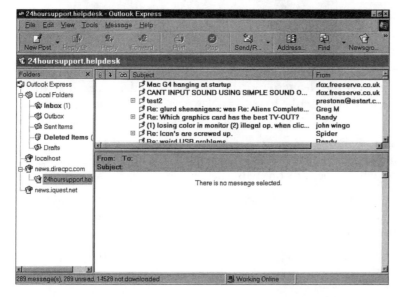

Figure 21.4

These are a few of the messages posted in the 24hoursupport.help *newsgroup as displayed by Microsoft Outlook Express.*

After you've set your newsreader to subscribe to a newsgroup, you can control how newsgroups work with the Turbo Newscasts properties sheet. You also can start your favorite newsreader and select your favorite newsgroups from the Electronic Program Guide.

To configure Turbo Newscasts, select Newscast Properties from the Navigator menu. On the General tab (see Figure 21.5), you can specify

➤ Where you want to store Newsgroup stories (the database)

➤ How much disk space to use for stories

➤ How long to keep stories

➤ Which news server you want to use for posting stories (and putting in your two-cents worth!)

Figure 21.5

Turbo Newscast's General properties tab.

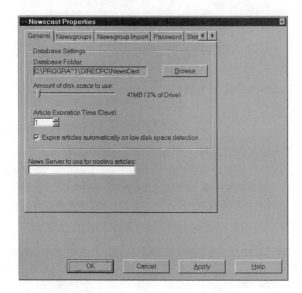

If you're using Netscape Navigator or Microsoft Outlook Express as your newsreader, you don't need to linger over the Newsgroups tab. These newsreaders can automatically send the newsgroups you subscribe to over to Newscast by using the options on the Newsgroup Import tab.

Some of the topics covered on newsgroups are, shall we say, for "mature" audiences only. You can keep snoopers out of the newsgroups you've selected (or from subscribing to any newsgroups without permission) with the Password tab.

If you're really, really bored you can use the Statistics properties sheet to see how much newsgroup activity your system has. Use the Advanced tab to adjust the performance and network use settings of your connection.

The latest newsgroup content will be delivered automatically to your computer through the DirecPC dish.

Automatic Updates with Turbo Webcast

If you like no-wait viewing of popular Web sites, you might also want to enable the Turbo Webcast feature. Select the Web sites (called Channels by DirecPC) you want downloaded to your system from the choices listed by the Electronic Program Guide, and adjust the properties through the Navigator menu's Webcast Properties sheet.

Use the General tab to specify what to do if you open a Turbo Webcast Web site that has been stored (cached) on your system and a page reference can't be found on your hard disk (see Figure 21.6).

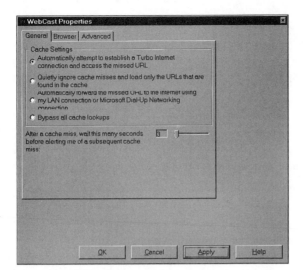

Figure 21.6

If you click a Turbo Webcast link that goes nowhere, use the General tab to tell DirecPC whether to chase it down or fuggetaboutit!

Because Turbo Webcast displays Web pages downloaded automatically to your system, it uses your Web browser. If you don't like offending anybody, you might have more than one browser installed. If you do, select the one you prefer with the Browser tab (see Figure 21.7).

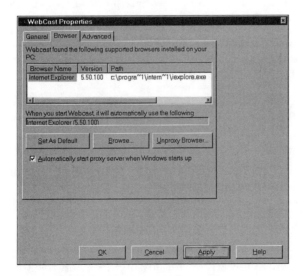

Figure 21.7

Pick any browser on your system with Turbo Webcast's browser tab.

You can use the Advanced tab to specify how often to tell the sites you download with Turbo Webcast that you've been there (hit-tracking).

Electronic Program Guide

If you need a very simple front end to the many features of DirecPC, you can start the major DirecPC programs from the Electronic Program Guide (EPG). Some users like it because it provides a home base for major features, but others find it slow and non-intuitive.

You don't need to use EPG for either Turbo Internet or Turbo Newsgroups, but if you want to subscribe to Turbo Webcasts, you must run the Electronic Program Guide to choose the sites you want downloaded to your system. You can start EPG by double-clicking the DirecPC desktop shortcut or from the DirecPC shortcut in the Program menu.

Email Alert

One of the biggest concerns that users of one-way systems such as DirecPC have is "Did I just get email?" Normally, the only way you can find out if an important email message has arrived is to keep a connection open to your email server. On a one-way system (which uses an analog modem), you normally either keep the phone line tied up while you wait for mail to arrive or hang up to free your line and call back in periodically. Of course, Murphy's law suggests that you might wind up getting your email late and missing important phone calls!

If you have DirecPC, there's a better way to find out when you have received new mail in your DirecPC mail account: Email Alert.

Email Alert uses your DirecPC dish connection to let you know when new email has arrived. You still won't know if it's your long-lost love saying "Yes, yes, yes!" or an invitation to multilevel market minor-league baseball cards, but at least you'll know you have new email.

Right-click the Navigator icon in the system tray and select Email Alert Properties to get started.

The Notification tab is displayed first. If you don't want to know that you have new email in your DirecPC account, select Disable Email Notification. Otherwise, choose your favorite notification method (see Figure 21.8).

Enter the name of your email server (`mail.direcpc.com`), and enter the account names you want notification to work with on the Mail Configuration tab (see Figure 21.9).

When you're notified that new email has arrived for any user listed on the Mail Configuration tab, go to the Status tab and click OK to indicate you've been notified.

If you want to read your email, dial up and go online, but remember Email Alert can take place whenever the computer running DirecPC is turned on.

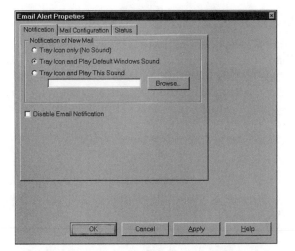

Figure 21.8

How obnoxious do you want Email Alert to be to get your attention? It's your choice; silent, standard sound, or choose your own sound.

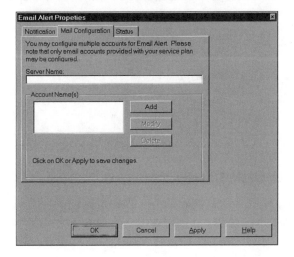

Figure 21.9

If you want email notification, take time to enter your DirecPC email server name and the users who want to be notified here.

Danger Danger

DirecPC Email Only, Please

Remember, Email Alert works only with your DirecPC.com email account. You'll still need to check manually for email on your other accounts.

Tweaking Windows 9x to Avoid Slowdowns

Because of how DirecPC's nuts and bolts operate, it often takes longer for Web pages to first appear with DirecPC than with other broadband systems. When the page starts to arrive, though, it finishes loading much more quickly. This is similar to the latency problem I discussed earlier with Internet gaming and DirecPC, but it can be a bigger problem for Web surfers because most computers running DirecPC are using Windows 95 or Windows 98, and these versions of Windows have a problem when they calculate how long to wait for TCP/IP (Internet) data before they say, "I guess it didn't work—please resend."

Windows 95 and Windows 98 make Web page downloads slower than they need to be, ironically, because they don't wait long enough for the Web page to appear. It's similar to a nervous guy who keeps calling his date to see if she's ready. She's spending so much time answering his frantic phone calls that she can't get ready in time.

Can you give Windows 95 and 98 a dose of digital Prozac so they won't keep calling for retransmits? Yes, you can.

You can download and install the appropriate patches from Microsoft's Web site.

A Little Patchwork

You'll find the MS Knowledge Base article #Q236926, "Windows 95 and Windows 98 TCP/IP May Retransmit Packets Prematurely," which contains links to the patches you need, at

`http://support.microsoft.com/support/kb/articles/Q236/9/26.ASP`

Click the correct link for your version of Windows to download the patch. Be sure to note the name of the file and where you saved it. To install the patch, run Windows Explorer, locate the folder you downloaded the file to, and double-click the file to install it. Follow the prompts, and restart your computer when requested.

The file the patch updates is called VTCP.386.

Optimizing Your Browser for Use with DirecPC

As with other broadband services covered in this book, a bit of Registry trickery can be useful in improving the performance of DirecPC. However, keep in mind that the performance of DirecPC's network operations center, which delivers files you request via satellite, has a bigger impact on performance than any tweak.

DirecPC offers a Registry tweaking program called Maxconn.exe made especially for DirecPC users running Windows 95. Maxconn.exe enables you to adjust how many connections your browser makes to a Web page from the default of four to eight or more. By making more connections to a Web page, your browser downloads it faster—and you see it faster!

Maximize Your Windows 95 Browsing

Learn more about how Maxconn works and find links to download the program from

        http://www.direcpc.com/consumer/owners/notes/app_config.html

This page also offers other browser–speed tips.

You also can visit the DirecPC FTP site at

        ftp://ftp.direcpc.com

Troubleshooting DirecPC with Terrestrial Mode

In addition to being useful for online gaming, terrestrial mode is also useful for troubleshooting problems with your DirecPC configuration. If you can connect to a Web site using only your modem, but not with the DirecPC dish, there's a problem with your dish, your satellite modem, or the DirecPC service itself. Terrestrial mode serves as a built-in backup to the normal DirecPC service.

To switch to terrestrial mode for troubleshooting, follow these steps:

1. Right-click the DirecPC Navigator icon in the system tray.
2. Click the Turbo Internet Properties option in the DirecPC Navigator menu.
3. Click the Terrestrial tab.
4. Click the check box to Use Terrestrial Mode for All Applications.

5. Click OK.

6. All Web traffic will use your modem for both inbound and outbound traffic until you clear the check box. If you don't reset this option, you won't be using your DirecPC dish for any traffic.

When Use Terrestrial Mode for All Applications is not checked, only applications that have been selected for terrestrial mode, such as Domain Name System (DNS) lookups, use your modem for incoming traffic.

You also can configure terrestrial mode for only certain applications, and you can add or remove applications from the list. You should configure games to work in terrestrial mode.

Extra Terrestrial Information

For more information on using terrestrial mode, see the following DirecPC document:

```
http://www2.direcpc.com/helpfiles/ti/ti_terrsettings.htm
```

If you want to assign some programs to use terrestrial mode on a full-time basis, you must provide a TCP or UDP port number to allow them to work properly. A list of common numbers is available from the main DirecPC help files page

```
http://www2.direcpc.com/helpfiles/index.html
```

or by contacting the software vendor of the game or other program you want to use in terrestrial mode.

Networking DirecPC to Solve Compatibility Problems

Because of the design of DirecPC, Internet-dependent services that require a two-way path between your computer and the Web site can't work with DirecPC. Windows Media Player 7 is one of the biggest offenders because it has several Web-dependent components, such as the Media Guide and Radio Tuner.

The following are other difficulties reported by DirecPC users:

➤ Slower computers (under 300MHz CPU speed) bog down when DirecPC is being used.

➤ Software conflicts might occur between the DirecPC USB satellite modem used for Windows 98 and other USB devices.

➤ An inability to use DirecPC with Windows 2000 occurs.

For these reasons, one of the leading suggestions for getting DirecPC to work better is to put it on a computer acting as a small network server. That computer will provide Internet connectivity to the network, allowing the client computers sharing the DirecPC connection to run Windows Media Player 7, ICQ, and other troublesome applications and devices.

You can use a wide variety of networking solutions for this task, including the following:

➤ Windows 98SE's Internet Connection Sharing (ICS)

➤ Sygate (www.sygate.com)

➤ Satserv (www.getsatserv.com)

Using DirecPC on a network server is the only way to connect nonsupported operating systems, such as Linux and Windows 2000 or Macs, with the Internet via DirecPC.

Don't Be a Hog—Share Your DirecPC!

For more information on setting up these networking solutions from an independent source, see Lloyd Parsons's technical notes at

http://www.lloydparsons.com/dpc_networking.htm

You'll also find information on setting up Windows 98SE's Internet Connection Sharing at the DirecPC Help Files site listed earlier.

Sharing an Internet connection isn't for everyone. In addition to having two or more computers you can connect, you'll need to have a network card for each one, some understanding of how networking works, and the willingness to experiment.

Don't Share If You Don't Understand How

Although networking has gotten simpler, you can still make a computer that was working fine all by itself a piece of digital hash when you try to network it. Read Chapter 15 carefully before you decide whether sharing your DirecPC connection is what you want to try.

The Official DirecPC Glossary

Some of the terminology that applies to DirecPC isn't used with any other broadband system. If you're confused by a DirecPC term, the official DirecPC glossary is available online. Here are a few of the more unusual terms you'll find there:

➤ AutoCommissioning—Also referred to as auto-setup, this describes the process of registering your satellite modem and account with DirecPC.

➤ DAK—The DirecPC Access Kit; the satellite modem and dish you use to receive the DirecPC signal.

In Plain English, Please...

If you're still finding DirecPC terms that puzzle you, the official DirecPC glossary is available at `http://www2.direcpc.com/helpfiles/troubleshoot/dpcglossary.html`

➤ NOC—Network Operations Center. DirecPC has several of these scattered across the world, sending page requests to the Internet, receiving the data. and beaming it to your system through satellite.

Troubleshooting DirecPC

Some of the major categories for DirecPC problems include

➤ Dish alignment
➤ Reassignment to a new satellite
➤ Installing the satellite modem
➤ Locating replacement software
➤ Fair Access Policy (FAP)
➤ Connection problems

This section of the chapter provides you with field-tested solutions and recommendations to help you overcome these problems.

Autosetup and Dish Realignment

DirecPC can use any one of several satellites in the sky over the equator for downloads to your DirecPC or DirecDuo dish. Each satellite requires different settings, and each satellite supports certain gateways used by DirecPC's NOC.

If you get a message from DirecPC asking you to rerun autosetup, what's happening behind the scenes is that the NOC is trying to perform load balancing. *Load balancing* switches some users from one gateway to another. Because different gateways use different satellites, load balancing can cause you to lose your satellite connection. If you run autosetup and your signal strength drops to 0, you've been switched to another satellite. Because your dish is no longer pointing in the correct direction, you'll get no service until something changes.

If this happens, you have two choices:

➤ Repoint the antenna—You might need to readjust everything, including the LNB, so be prepared for the possibility of several hours of grief as you readjust the antenna to the new satellite.

➤ Pick up the phone and ask the DirecPC tech support staff to assign you to a gateway that uses the same satellite—This might take some arguing, but it beats playing with the satellite dish.

Aiming for the Sky

If you must readjust the antenna, ask the DirecPC techs which satellite your gateway is using. Then, go to the Helios Web site's satellite aiming page:

```
http://www.helius.com/cgi-bin/dpcaim.pl
```

Look up your country, state, and city and specify the satellite you will be using to receive dish positioning information. This is often more accurate than the information produced by the DirecPC autosetup program.

Discovering Which Satellite You're Pointing To

You'll find it easier to deal with DirecPC on new gateway issues if you know which satellite and which frequency your system is currently using. Regedit, the Windows Registry Editor, can be used to display both sets of information. Perform these steps before you rerun autosetup.

1. Click Start, Run; type Regedit into the Open field, and press Enter.
2. Navigate through the following folders to see which satellite you are currently using:

    HKEY_Local_Machine/Software/Hughes Network Systems/Direcpc/Pointing

3. Record the values for SatLongitude and SatFrequency in the right-hand window.

When you call DirecPC, the techs can tell you which satellite you are using from this information. Ask them to assign you to another gateway using the same satellite. If they can, you won't need to fiddle with your dish.

Danger Danger

You Haven't Backed Up Your Registry Yet????

Don't, repeat, **don't** take the Windows Registry lightly. There's no Undo option if you make an accidental change while you're looking around. Follow the tips in Chapter 3 to make a backup copy before you change or look inside the Windows Registry.

Remember, a hosed Registry makes your computer a useless hunk of plastic and metal.

Troubleshooting DirecPC Satellite Modems

If you use Windows 95 or Windows NT4, you must use the internal PCI version of the DirecPC satellite modem. Windows 98 users can run the USB version.

Official Windows Support Is Limited

Other current versions of Windows are not officially supported by DirecPC. Many users have been able to use the Windows 95/98 software with Windows Me. What about Windows 2000? A version of DirecPC for Windows 2000 might be available by the time you read this. Otherwise, your best bet is to connect your Windows 2000 computer over a network to a Windows 9x or NT server running DirecPC as suggested earlier.

When Your Modem Is Making You Feel More Dumb

Your DirecPC satellite modem is critical to the success of your high-speed connection. If it goes on the blink, your satellite dish might as well be a big Frisbee. If you get an error during auto setup telling you that the setup program couldn't test your modem, check the following:

➤ Uninstall and reinstall your satellite modem as covered in Chapter 13.

➤ Use the Windows Device Manager to make sure the PCI satellite modem is listed as a Network adapter or that the USB version is listed under USB devices.

➤ After you reboot the computer at the end of the DirecPC setup program, check Device Manager again for the serial number of the PCI adapter or to verify that the USB satellite modem is listed as another network device. If you don't see your modem listed, your satellite modem installation failed.

Deep in the Heart of Your PC Might Lie the Answer

For other steps in the troubleshooting process, including how to check the Windows Registry for signs of a blown satellite modem install, see `http://www.direcpc.com/consumer/owners/notes/failuretoinitialize.htm`

419

Troubleshooting the USB Satellite Modem

If the lights on your USB satellite modem start blinking after a few minutes of use, the modem might be overheating. Until you can receive a replacement, try laying the modem on its right side; this workaround has helped a lot of USB DirecPC users. You should contact DirecPC for a replacement if the problem persists.

Troubleshooting the PCI Internal Satellite Modem

If you're not running Windows 98, you must use the PCI version of the DirecPC satellite modem. Although this is a Plug and Play card, many of today's resource-starved systems can still have problems locating a free IRQ (interrupt request line) for this card.

Before you try (and fail) to install the PCI satellite modem, check your Windows Device Manager to see whether your computer has IRQ routing (also called ACPI IRQ routing or IRQ steering) enabled; *IRQ routing* enables Windows to do a better job of avoiding IRQ conflicts between PCI Plug and Play cards, such as the DirecPC PCI satellite modem and older ISA cards and motherboard devices. You must have Windows 95B/95C, Windows 98, or Windows Me to use this feature; the original version of Windows 95 (including the upgrade version sold in stores) doesn't have this feature, and Windows NT 4 doesn't use the Plug and Play feature.

New systems have IRQ routing/steering enabled from the factory, as shown in Figure 21.10.

Figure 21.10

The ACPI IRQ Holder for PCI IRQ Steering message next to IRQ 11 indicates this computer has IRQ routing enabled.

To enable or check your settings for PCI bus IRQ steering, follow this procedure:

1. Open the Windows System Properties sheet (Start, Settings, Control Panel, System).

2. If the Windows version says Windows 95 or Windows 95a, stop; your version of Windows doesn't support IRQ steering.

3. If the Windows version says Windows 95B, Windows 95C, Windows 98, or Windows ME, your version of Windows does support IRQ steering. It is disabled by default with Windows 95B/95C but enabled with newer versions of Windows.

4. Click the Device Manager tab to continue.

5. Click the plus sign (+) next to System Devices.

6. Scroll down to PCI bus and click it.

7. Click Properties.

8. Click the IRQ Steering tab; click boxes to configure it, as shown in Figure 21.11. You will need to restart your computer after making changes.

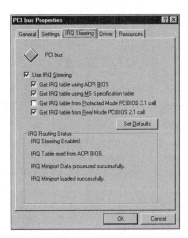

Figure 21.11

Defaults for enabling IRQ Steering.

Recent and older Pentium-class systems might need a patch file to enable IRQ routing; this should be installed if you have problems installing your PCI DirecPC satellite modem. To obtain the patch, check with your system or motherboard supplier. If your motherboard uses the VIA chipset, go to http://www.via.com.tw/drivers/index.htm to download the correct driver.

For information about other motherboards, you can go to Wim's BIOS page: http://www.ping.be/bios/index.html.

Don't Steer Me Wrong

For a good visual tutorial on PCI IRQ routing, see this page on Tim Higgins's Web site: http://www. practicallynetworked.com/ support/irqsteer.htm. Microsoft's Knowledge Base article #Q182604 on IRQ steering is found at http:// support.microsoft.com/support/ kb/articles/q182/6/04.asp.

Getting Software Upgrades from DirecPC's FTP Site

DirecPC software can be found at two FTP (file transfer protocol) sites, accessible with your Web browser:

➤ ftp://ftp.direcpc.com/direcpc/—The official DirecPC FTP site

➤ ftp://ftp.hns.com/pub/direcpc/—The DirecPC section of the Hughes Network Systems FTP site

What can you find there? The DirecPC FTP site has previous, as well as the latest, versions of the DirecPC software and miscellaneous driver files. Only the latest versions of DirecPC software are available at the Hughes Network Systems FTP site.

DirecPC software is supplied in self-extracting files; copy the version you need to its own temporary folder and open it to extract the files and start the installation process.

Can You Avoid Getting FAPed?

One of the most controversial features of DirecPC since its adoption has been the secrecy surrounding the so-called *Fair Access Plan (FAP)*, which is supposed to prevent a few users from hogging the bandwidth with heavy downloading. FAP substantially reduces the download speed of users who attempt to use up a great deal of bandwidth (a threshold that was not publicly revealed for a long time) to speeds at or below those found with analog modems. Ouch!

A 1998 class action lawsuit concerning this issue resulted in DirecPC's publishing guidelines for when FAP (also referred to as *download throttling*) is supposed to kick in.

The Letter of the Law

As a result of the 1998 class–action lawsuit, DirecPC's FAP guidelines are available online at `http://www.direcpc.com/consumer/cost/describe_fap.html`

These guidelines appear simple on the surface but in reality are confusing to many users; for example, the amount of data listed for peak and off-peak usage is not a download-per-hour limit. Many comments on the `alt.satellite.direcpc` newsgroup suggest that the published guidelines for FAPing are seriously misleading. Here's a digest of some suggestions that might help you avoid being FAPed:

➤ Don't download continuously—This seems to be the number one way to get FAPed. If you download a large file (more than 10MB–15MB), such as a new version of a Web browser, a movie trailer, or a software service pack, wait a little while before you download another large file.

➤ Watch out for streaming audio—A continuous audio stream, such as those generated by Internet radio, could trigger FAPing because it's on constantly. You might be able to set up streaming audio to run through your modem in both directions by using terrestrial mode, which bypasses the satellite download.

Tech Note

Maxconn Might Help You Get FAPed

The DirecPC Maxconn utility discussed earlier could make it even easier for you to get FAPed, because you can use it to increase the number of connections each browser window makes at one time. If you adjust the Maxconn value for your browser, open fewer windows accordingly to keep below the trigger value of 22 connections.

➤ Don't have more than four browser windows open at a time—FAP is triggered if you have 22 connections to the Web, and each browser window creates about 5 connections. Look at the taskbar to determine how many browser windows you have open; if you already have four open, close one before you open another one. Beware of the right-click Open in a New Window option because this can easily push you into FAP territory.

➤ If you get FAPed, try to determine how much you downloaded (in MB) in the current session—Some DirecPC users indicate that FAPing seems to take place each time they reach the same usage threshold that triggered FAPing in the first place.

➤ DirecPC has different published thresholds for peak and off-peak usage.

Using Netstat to Check Usage Yourself

You can run the Windows program Netstat on your computer to see how much Internet data you've sent and received since the last time you rebooted your system. If you restart your system each day, you can use Netstat to see your current day's Internet traffic.

You run Netstat from the MS-DOS (command) prompt. To open a DOS window with Windows 95 or 98, for example, click Start, Programs, MS-DOS Prompt, and then type Netstat -e.

This shows your uploaded and downloaded usage since the last reboot (see Figure 21.12).

Checking Your Record

You can see your current and two previous month's usage statistics at this site:

http://utilities.direcpc.com/db2/

You will need to provide your site ID to use this service. To learn how to locate your site ID, go to

http://www.direcpc.com/consumer/owners/faqs/billfaq.html

Follow the link to Where Do I Find my Site ID and the Serial # of the DirecPC Card? The method varies by the version of DirecPC software you are using.

Follow the link to Usage Questions for information about peak and off-peak usage.

Figure 21.12

This computer has received a bit over 2.5 million bytes since its last reboot.

Troubleshooting Connection Problems with DirecPC

Connection problems with DirecPC can result from

➤ DNS problems—DNS translates IP addresses into Web site names.

➤ Proxy server problems—By default, Webcast (the DirecPC software for Web browsing) uses a proxy server to provide Web pages rather than retrieving all page requests directly from the site. Web sites, such as eBay, that generate pages with scripts don't work properly when a proxy server intercepts the page before it arrives at your computer.

424

Solving DNS Problems

If you click on links and nothing's happening in your browser, you might have a problem with DNS, the Domain Name System you learned about in earlier chapters. If you do not use a valid DNS name server (a computer that can translate Web site names into IP addresses), you cannot surf the Web properly. The ping command can be used to determine whether you have a problem with DNS configuration. For more information about ping, see Chapter 19, "DSL Tips, Tricks, and Troubleshooting."

To use ping to determine a problem with DNS settings, start by opening an MS-DOS window. Click Start, Programs, (Accessories), MS-DOS prompt. Then, follow these steps:

1. Type the command ping www.direcpc.com and press Enter; you should see the IP address appear along with four replies indicating the speed of the ping.

2. Type the command ping 198.77.116.8 (the DirecPC DNS name server) and press Enter; you should see four replies indicating the speed of the ping.

3. If you can ping the IP address, but not the Web site, your DNS configuration is incorrect.

Type Exit and press Enter to close the MS-DOS window. See Figure 21.13.

Figure 21.13

This computer can ping the DirecPC Web site by name, indicating its DNS configuration is okay.

Adjust the properties for your Dial-Up Networking connection to your DirecPC ISP to include the DirecPC DNS name server (198.77.116.8) as your primary name server. See Chapter 17, "A Survivor's Guide to TCP/IP," for details.

Disabling Webcast's Proxy Server Option

If you cannot open certain Web pages with DirecPC, you might need to disable the use of a proxy server in the Turbo Webcast configuration. To access this option, perform these steps:

1. Right-click the DirecPC Navigator icon in the system tray.

2. Click the Webcast Properties option, and select the Browser tab.

3. Clear the check mark from Automatically Start Proxy Server when Windows Starts Up; this will turn off proxy server use for your Web browsers and DirecPC.

4. Click Yes and OK to confirm the change, and then restart your computer.

5. If you can now view the Web site in both satellite mode and terrestrial mode, keep this change; if the Web site still can't be viewed, the site is probably down.

Don't Develop a Thing About Ping

Ping is okay to use for diagnostics tests like the one covered here, but many sites on the Internet reject any attempt to ping them for security reasons, including the White House Web site and many others. Why? As you see from Figure 21.13, ping reveals a site's IP address, which makes it easier for a hacker to attack the site.

The Least You Need to Know

➤ DirecPC's Turbo Webcasting and Turbo Newscasting services deliver content to your computer automatically, but you must select Web sites and subscribe to newsgroups if you want to use these features.

➤ Email Alert enables you to get notification of mail coming to your DirecPC account without having to go online.

➤ Windows 95 and 98 should be patched for best performance with DirecPC.

➤ Consider networking computers to a server running DirecPC to work around compatibility problems.

➤ Reinstalling DirecPC software and satellite modems can be used to fix some connection problems, but you also might need to examine the Registry.

➤ To avoid being FAPed (which drastically slows down your download speed), take breaks between downloading large files and avoid continuous data streams from sources such as Internet radio.

➤ You can use Ping and DirecPC properties sheets to solve problems with your TCP/IP configuration.

Broadband Wireless Tips, Tricks, and Troubleshooting

In This Chapter

➤ Get the most out of your broadband wireless connection

➤ Solve problems with your broadband wireless connection, both by yourself and with the help of broadband wireless technicians

---

Broadband Wireless Tips and Tricks

You'll be in love the first time you connect to the Internet with your broadband wireless connection, especially if you've been condemned in the past to 56Kbps or slower analog phone lines.

However, after the first thrill is gone, you'll still be asking yourself, "Can it be even better?" Yes, it can! The first part of this chapter shows you how to get the most out of your broadband wireless Internet connection. Many of the tweaks listed here also apply to other types of broadband connections, so the appropriate chapters are cross-referenced as needed for complete information.

You can increase your broadband wireless speed through

➤ Upgrading to a faster service

➤ Registry tweaks

➤ Replacing your network card drivers

➤ Switching to a PCI network card

➤ Tweaking your Internet Explorer (IE) browser or replacing it with a faster Web browser

➤ Using offline browsing, synchronization, and download managers to avoid network traffic jams

Upgrading to a Faster Service

If your broadband wireless provider offers multiple speed options, the most straightforward and easiest way to pick up speed is to call and upgrade your service. A broadband wireless provider in my area (Ohio Valley Wireless) sells 512Kbps service for just $10 a month more than its 128Kbps service.

Keep in mind that if your provider offers committed information rate (CIR) service, a lower-cost way to get most of the benefits of faster speed without a big upward jump in pricing is to add the bursting option to your service. For example, one Midwest provider offers bursting as an option for just $5 a month more than fixed-speed services.

Tech Note

Speed Is Bursting Out All Over

As you learned in Chapter 14, "Getting Wireless," bursting enables you to use all available excess bandwidth as your own, bringing you big speed benefits when the network doesn't have a lot of active users. A burstable wireless connection will be very fast at times and much slower at other times, but the overall speed will be a good bit higher than for a service whose maximum speeds are fixed.

Combine upgrading to a faster service (preferably with bursting if available) with tricks such as accelerating your downloads and getting Web content downloaded to your system during the off hours and you'll get the most out of whatever speed your broadband wireless service provides.

Increasing Speed Through Registry Tweaking

If you're the type of computer user who isn't afraid of trying a trick or two, tweaking the Windows Registry might be just what you're looking for to get extra speed without upgrading your existing connection. As you learned in Chapter 3, "Speed Up and

Fix Up Your Dial-Up," there are two ways you can tweak your Registry for additional speed. You can

➤ Install and use Registry-tweaking software

➤ Make manual changes to the Windows Registry

Back Up Before You Plunge Ahead

The Windows Registry is the database of all hardware and software settings used by Windows 95 and later versions. Whether you decide to make changes by hand or use a Registry tweaking program, be sure you back it up first as discussed in Chapter 3!

You can use the same software discussed in Chapter 3 to make your changes, but the keys and settings you should use are different for broadband connections than for analog modems. The settings shown in Table 22.1 are designed to make downloads and online gaming faster.

Table 22.1   Registry Settings to Optimize Your Wireless Broadband Connection

Key	Value	Registry
MaxMTU	1500	System\CurrentControlSet\Services\Class\NetTrans\000x
MaxMSS	1460	System\CurrentControlSet\Services\Class\NetTrans\000x
RWIN	32120	HKEY_Local_Machine\System\CurrentControlSet\Services\VxD\MSTCP
TTL	32	HKEY_Local_Machine\System\CurrentControlSet\Services\VxD\MSTCP

See Chapter 18, "ISDN Tips, Tricks and Troubleshooting," for details on making these changes on your system.

If You Tweaked It Once, You'd Better Tweak It Again!

If you've previously changed some or all of these settings for your analog modem, you must make the preceding changes listed if you want the performance you paid for with your wireless broadband service. Why? Analog modems and broadband connections are so much different that analog modem speedups will slow down broadband connections.

New Network Card Drivers

In most cases, the connection between your external broadband wireless modem and your computer is made by a 10BASE-T or 10/100 Ethernet network card. Whether your card is fresh from the shrink wrap or a tattered orphan you rescued from the office junk room, it's useless without driver software and frustrating if you're not using the latest drivers. How important is that?

Move Over Ethernet, Here Comes USB!

More and more broadband devices are designed to connect to USB ports instead of to an Ethernet card. If your wireless broadband modem connects to the USB port, you'll have far fewer concerns than Ethernet card users about conflicts and driver issues.

If you install your network card using the drivers supplied with Windows 95, you're using drivers that are at least 4 years old! Using Windows 98 instead? Those drivers are as much as 2 1/2 years old! New drivers can make your network connection more stable and faster.

If you haven't upgraded to the latest drivers for your network card, take a few moments next time you're online and download them. You can determine the model number of your network card by using the Windows Device Manager; iMac users should go straight to Apple's Web site for updates because your Ethernet connection is built in.

You'll find complete instructions for upgrading your network card drivers in Chapter 19, "DSL Tips, Tricks, and Troubleshooting."

Replacing Your ISA Network Card with a PCI Network Card

If you installed an ISA network card to connect to your broadband wireless modem, consider replacing it with a PCI version. PCI cards are faster, are easier to configure, and will fit into most future computer models. You can pick up a decent PCI-based NIC for under $20, a small price to pay for better performance now and better compatibility with new computers later.

Browser Tweaks for IE

You can also adjust the Microsoft Internet Explorer Web browser for faster page downloads by means of a Registry tweak. You'll find complete instructions for tweaking your Internet Explorer Registry settings in Chapter 19, "DSL Tips, Tricks, and Troubleshooting."

Alternatives to IE

Although most providers support IE 5.x as their "official" browser, you don't need to be a Microsoft lemming. Many users have found that the Opera 4.x browser from Opera Software is worth examining—and worth paying for (it costs $39 after your 30-day free trial has expired). Like previous versions, Opera 4.x displays pages faster and downloads files much faster than IE, and Opera now features full Java support, support for major plug-ins, 128-bit encryption, and other enhancements to help it fit nicely into an IE world.

A little-known fact about IE is that it can be customized. The Voyager 5000 browser from Smartalec Corporation is based on IE, but it's faster than IE, maximizes screen area, and has a total download size that's less than 2MB.

Fast Tracks to Your Favorites Sites

As you work with your broadband wireless service, you'll notice that, regardless of its speed, it still takes a few seconds to locate your favorite Web site after you enter its URL or click a bookmark/favorite in your browser. Why? The reason for the slowdown is that the Internet's Domain Name System (DNS) name servers must translate the URL into the IP address for your site before retrieving the site. No matter how many times a day you go to the same site, your computer can't remember which URLs and which IP addresses go together.

Get Opera for Only 9.4MB!

To learn more about Opera or to download an evaluation copy (the Java-enabled version is only 9.4MB), go to http://www.operasoftware.com

Voyage to a Different Kind of Browser

To download Voyager 5000, go to

```
http://www.tweakfiles.com/misc/voyager5000.html
```

For more information about other system-optimization products from Smartalec Corporation, visit its Web site at

```
http://www.smartalec2000.com/
```

Tech Note

What's in a (Domain) Name?

As you learned in Chapter 1, "How the Internet Works," the Domain Name System was created to make finding Web sites easier; rather than entering the IP address for each site, you can type in the Web site's URL to go to the site you want. The price for this convenience is the need to look up every URL and match it to its IP address because the IP address is used to request information from the Internet.

There are several ways to speed up the access to your favorite pages:

➤ Create a Hosts file to store the URLs and IP addresses you access most often
➤ Use third-party site-caching software
➤ Use IE's built-in browser synchronization tools

Which way is best? If you want to create a Hosts file, you must determine the IP address that matches a Web site. The Ping utility supplied with Windows can be used to find this information. If you want to give Ping a try, here's how it works:

➤ Open a DOS window (Start, Programs, Accessories), MS-DOS Prompt

➤ Type the following command and press Enter: Ping *yourfavoritewebsite.com* (specify an actual Web site)

➤ You'll see the IP address of the Web site you entered, as seen in Figure 22.1.

Figure 22.1

Using Ping to learn the IP address of a specified Web site.

If you add the sites you use most often to a Hosts file on your system, the performance difference is amazing; sites literally pop onto your screen because you're bypassing the normal DNS to IP address translation step. Want to learn more? Get the full details from the Tweak3D.net Web site.

For the Most from Hosts and Much More

You can learn how to create a Hosts file and many terrific speedup tips from Dustin "TimmyC" Jones's article on tweaking your broadband connection. Read the entire article at

    http://www.tweak3d.net/tweak/cable/print.shtml

Keep in mind that creating a Hosts file by pinging sites is not the only method you should try to speed up your favorite sites. Here's why:

➤ Some very popular e-commerce and many government sites don't respond to pings—ignoring pings is a protection taken by some sites against so-called *Denial of Service (DoS)* attacks, which use rapid pinging to tie up a Web server. Although Ping sends out only four data packets, sites that won't reply to Ping won't reveal their IP addresses.

➤ Some popular search engines and indexes (such as Yahoo!) feature Dynamic DNS, changing the DNS numbers of servers to perform load balancing, which distributes Web traffic over multiple servers. Thus, the DNS number of such a site today might be different tomorrow.

I recommend experimenting with Hosts if you plan to use it for favorite sites that aren't on everybody's hot list. If you're looking for alternatives to creating a Hosts file, take a look at Webcelerator. Unlike IE's own browser caching (covered in the next section), Webcelerator can work with non-Microsoft browsers from AOL, Opera, and Netscape. What else can Webcelerator do?

➤ It automatically retrieves pages linked to your current page—When you click on a link, you'll see it instantly.

➤ It provides automatic checking for updated content—Minimizes the need to click the refresh button.

➤ It uses special techniques to store preloaded pages in a compressed format—Allows you to store lots of Web pages and sites on your system without running out of disk space.

Webcelerator is easy to install and gives you faster access to your favorite sites.

Webcelerator—For More Than IE

Webcelerator was recently selected by CNN as one of its top 11 Web tools. It's free (advertisers support it) and available for download from `http://webcelerator.com/webcelerator/`

Your Favorite Web Sites Are Already Loaded with Browser Synchronization

As you've already learned, your broadband wireless service can vary in speed because, like its cousin the cable modem, you are sharing the wireless spectrum with a varying number of users. The result? Speeds can drop like a rock during peak Web access hours (before and after work) while blazing along at non-peak periods.

If you must use a one-way (telco return) broadband wireless service, you put your callers through the endless "buzz-buzz-buzz" of busy signals because you're tying up your telephone line while you suffer through slower page downloads at these peak periods.

Don't Tell Your Callers to Buzz Off

Until your broadband wireless service is upgraded to two-way, you'll need to use your analog modem (and your phone line) to stay connected. In Chapter 3 you learned that you can set up voice mail on your computer so that callers can leave you a message while you're online.

Of the products available, BuzMe has the most features, including the capability to receive voice mail messages through your phone, even when you're away from home.

To try BuzMe, check out the BuzMe Web site:

```
http://www.buzme.com
```

What's the answer? If you use Microsoft Internet Explorer version 5.0 or above, you can use the View Offline and Synchronize features to beat the after-work rush to the Web. These features can bring your favorite "hot off the Web" sites to your computer while you're on your way home from work. You need to follow two procedures to make this possible:

➤ Select sites for offline viewing—The contents of the site are copied to your computer's hard disk for instant viewing.

➤ Select how and when to synchronize the sites you select—Synchronizing loads updated content to your system.

For the complete story on setting up offline favorites and browser synchronization, see Chapter 18, "ISDN Tips, Tricks, and Troubleshooting."

Using a Download Manager

A second way to avoid peak usage periods is to schedule large file downloads for off-peak periods. You can do this by using a download manager. Download managers integrate with your Web browser to make it easy to download files more quickly and at your convenience. To learn more about download managers, see Chapter 18.

Download Accelerator Plus—A Real Plus for Your System

If you've already decided that a download manager is for you, give Speedbit's Download Accelerator Plus a try. It's fast, free, and available from

www.downloadaccelerator.com

Broadband Wireless Modem and Antenna Troubleshooting

If you have problems with your broadband wireless service, you should find help as quickly as possible. The solutions in this section are designed to help get you up and running as quickly as possible.

Problems with your broadband wireless service fall into these categories:

➤ Network problems beyond your control
➤ Antenna problems
➤ Modem problems
➤ Physical cable and connection problems
➤ Network card problems
➤ TCP/IP configuration problems

No Wireless TV Might Mean No Internet

It's easy to forget that your wireless TV and broadband wireless Internet service share a common origin when you're staring into your computer screen on the prowl for MP3 music while the rest of your family is enjoying a movie on TV. However, because both wireless cable TV and broadband wireless Internet service have a common source, a problem at your wireless provider could whack both your Internet and TV plans for the evening.

So, if you can't get online with your broadband wireless modem and you also use the wireless cable TV service, see what's on TV. If the answer is "snow," you might be out of luck with your Internet connection as well.

It Might Not Be a Total Loss...

Problems at your wireless provider can affect just one of your services. Unlike cable modems, which use the same coaxial cable to deliver both TV and Internet content, broadband wireless/TV providers use different transmitters to send out TV and Internet data. A power failure would shut down both services, but other types of problems might affect only the TV or only the Internet side of the operation.

Antenna Problems

If you can't connect to the Internet after a windstorm, push yourself away from your computer and go outside. Take a careful look at your antenna. If it has been bent out of shape or has debris blocking the receiver, you won't be able to pick up information from your ISP.

Make a Kodak Moment—While It's Working!

You'll have a better idea of which way the antenna should be pointing if you'll take detailed pictures of the installation as soon as the technician finishes it. Even a minor misalignment caused by wind damage could put you off the air.

Don't try to realign the antenna yourself; call your provider for help. A visit from the site survey truck is probably in the offing, especially if your provider uses a single transmission antenna.

If your antenna looks okay, look at the cable; if it is damaged or has come loose from the antenna, this could also take you off the air.

Tech Note

THAT WAY ▷

Rainy Day Blues

Rain and snow can affect your signal reception as well, depending on the technology used to deliver the signal. MMDS–based systems, such as those supplied by Hybrid, are quite resistant to rain fade, but systems using different frequencies, as well as satellite-based systems, could have problems getting a good signal in bad weather.

Troubleshooting Overview

If your antenna alignment is okay, the problem with your connection could be relatively minor. In many cases, you can restore your broadband wireless service quickly and easily. After trying the following steps, check the rest of the chapter for more detailed information.

1. Turn off your modem(s) and your computer. Give your broadband wireless modem, your analog modem (if you have one-way service), and your computer a 30-second or longer break before continuing.

2. Turn on the modem(s) first to allow the computer to properly initialize them when it's turned on.

3. Turn on the computer after the modem(s) are turned on.

4. Check the coaxial, network, and RS-232 analog modem cables.

5. Check the power supplies to the digital receiver/transceiver, modem(s), and computer. Also check the power supply on the network hub or switch if you connect through a hub or switch to the wireless broadband modem.

6. Check the LINK light to make sure it's on.

7. Check the LOCK light to make sure it's on.

Are some lights not coming on? Still no connection? Try the detailed troubleshooting steps that follow.

Broadband Wireless Modem Problems

If your TV picks up wireless cable channels okay but you can't get connected to the Internet through your modem, start by looking at your modem. Its signal lights can help you figure out where the problem is with your connection.

Using the Signal Lights on Your Broadband Wireless Modem

Signal lights on broadband wireless modems are similar to those on cable modems, providing indications of Ethernet traffic to and from the cable modem, traffic to and from the Internet, and modem status.

The lights have different names, depending on which modem your provider uses. In this discussion, I use the terminology used by Hybrid—one of the leaders in wireless broadband Internet access—for these signal lights, and explain how your modem uses them to inform you of what's going on inside (see Figure 22.2).

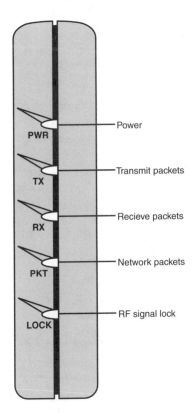

Figure 22.2

A typical wireless broadband modem's front panel.

➤ PWR (power)—Green light indicates power is reaching your modem.

➤ TX (transmit packets)—Green light blinks to indicate you are sending data; faster blinks indicate faster data transmission.

➤ RX (receive packets)—Green light blinks to indicate you are receiving data; blink rate speeds up when more data is received.

➤ PKT (network packets)—Orange light indicates power on; changes to green when network activity is high.

➤ Lock (RF signal lock)—Indicates that the modem is tuned to an active channel.

➤ Link—Yellow light indicates the Ethernet card is properly connected to your modem. Might be located on rear of modem.

Table 22.2 will help you use these signal lights to diagnose connection problems.

Table 22.2   Troubleshooting Your Connection with Modem Signal Lights

Signal Light	Problem	Solution
Power LED Off	No power reaching unit	Check power cord
		Plug modem into another power outlet
		Check power switch on surge protector
Lock LED Off	Coaxial cable might be loose	Check coaxial cable connection to modem and to transceiver/receiver
		Reset modem and wait for about 60 seconds for light to come on
LINK LED Off	Loose, damaged, or incorrect Ethernet cable/connection	Check cable connection at modem and computer/hub
		Check cable type (crossover to computer; straight-through to hub or switch)

Resetting Your Modem

Many external broadband wireless modems have a reset switch that can be used to reset the modem. If you are unable to make a connection and have ruled out cabling or other problems, you should reset your modem.

If your modem lacks a reset switch, turn off the modem for 30 seconds or more, and then turn it back on. If the modem doesn't have an on/off switch, just unplug the power supply and plug it back in again after 30 seconds or so.

External One-Way (Telco Return) Broadband Wireless Modems

One-way broadband wireless modems (which use a dial-up connection over telephone lines for page requests, email, and uploads) can have additional wiring considerations: The 9-pin jack on the rear of the modem connects to an external analog modem on some models. Others have a built-in analog modem.

Tech Note

THAT WAY ➤

You Don't Need a High-Tech Tool

If your reset switch is recessed into the side or rear of the modem, try my favorite tool for pushing the button: a bent paperclip. It works great!

If your connection uses a separate analog modem, check the following:

➤ Is the analog modem correctly cabled to both your telephone line and your broadband wireless modem?

➤ Is the analog modem turned on?

See Figures 22.3 and 22.4 (in the next section) to see how your analog and wireless broadband modems work together.

Physical Cable and Connection Problems

As with any wired device, the weak link in the chain is usually the cables. Use the signal lights discussed previously to find the most likely source of the problem with your connection. Start by examining the condition of the coaxial cable that runs into your modem from outside. Cracks in the cable's protective jacket or shielding that are visible on the surface of the cable can indicate problems with the cable construction. Figure 22.3 shows how and where cables connect to your wireless modem.

Make sure the coaxial cable to the antenna is tightly connected to the wireless modem; if your RF signal lock light is not lit, it can indicate a loose cable.

If you are unable to send information with a telco return model, the connection between the wireless modem and your analog modem might be loose, or the analog modem might be turned off (see Figure 22.4).

Figure 22.3

Rear view of a typical wireless broadband modem and cables.

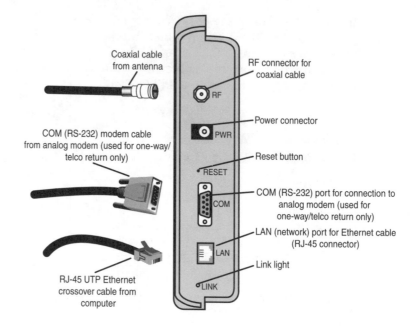

Figure 22.4

A one-way (telco return) broadband wireless system uses an ordinary analog modem to send data from your computer to the Internet. The COM port on the wireless modem connects to the analog modem, using the same cable you use to connect the analog modem to your computer.

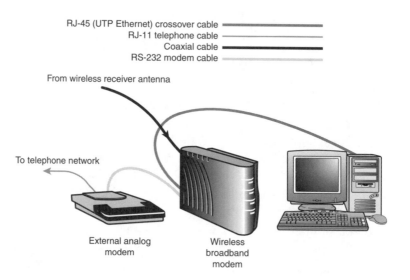

Do you have problems with Internet access after a heavy rain? A damaged cable will allow water to leak into the coaxial cable, interfering with your signal. Other signal spoilers include adding or removing splitters after the initial installation. Splitters can change the signal strength and disrupt your reception.

On one-way systems, rain can cause problems for your analog modem connection. If you hear crackling over your telephone line, your modem will have a difficult time making a connection. Although download speeds won't be affected because they are routed over the wireless connection, upload speeds and page requests will be very slow. Extremely noisy lines could cause you to lose your connection altogether.

Tracking Down Interference

If you have intermittent problems with connections, chart them and note the time of day, day of the week, and other similarities. Contact your ISP and ask the help desk to check your cable or site for interference.

If you are using a one-way (telco return) system, you are at the mercy of the telco's line quality. If your telephone line quality is very low, you could have connection problems even in good weather. Have your telco check the junction box where your household lines connect to the telephone company for damaged or corroded wires.

Tech Note

What if I Still Can't Get a Good Connection?

You might even need to have a new site survey performed if the problem persists. If you live in an area with a lot of new construction, a new building can disrupt your line of sight to the transmitter. If your broadband wireless service was installed in the fall or winter, you might have foliage blocking your line of sight in the spring or summer.

In either case, a higher antenna mount or tower might be required to clear the obstacle.

Network Card Problems

Your path to the Internet most likely starts with a 10BASE-T or 10/100 Ethernet network card, which connects your computer to the broadband wireless modem. Network card problems can include the following:

➤ Loose or incorrectly wired Ethernet cables

➤ IRQ and other hardware resource conflicts

➤ Damaged installation

➤ Hardware problems

Finding Ethernet Cable Problems with Status Lights

Most, but not all, network cards have one or two status lights near the 10BASE-T (Category 5) cable connector. These status lights can provide valuable clues about your cable modem connection.

10BASE-T–only network cards use a single light to indicate connection and activity, whereas dual-speed 10/100 cards use two lights, with the second light indicating the connection speed. If the network cable is disconnected, either at the network card or the cable modem, the lights will not be lit.

If the Ethernet cable is connected securely to both the modem and your network card but the link light is still out, make sure you are using a crossover cable (which reverses some of the wires). If you have replaced the cable that came with your modem with an off-the-shelf Ethernet cable, you are using the wrong type of cable. Go back to the store and buy a crossover cable, or use the cable that was used for your original installation (see Figure 22.5).

Tech Note

Getting the Right Cable

If you are using your wireless broadband connection with a network and connect your modem to a hub or switch, you need to use a standard straight-through Ethernet cable instead of a crossover cable.

If you're not sure which kind you have, hold both ends of the Ethernet cable next to each other and pointing in the same direction and look at the ends of the cables. The ends of the cable are clear, allowing you to see the twisted–pair wires inside the cable. If you see the same wire color pattern on both ends, the cable is straight–through. If some of the wire colors are different, it's a crossover cable.

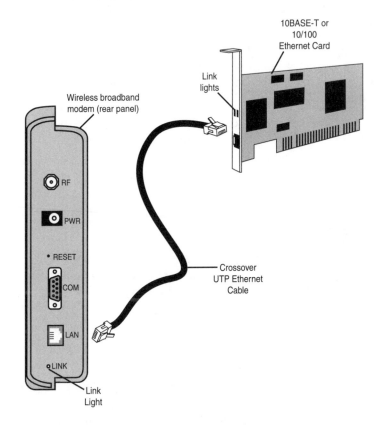

Figure 22.5

Look for the link light on the rear of your wireless broadband modem and network card. While your system is running and your modem is turned on, both devices' LINK lights should be on. If not, check for loose or incorrect cables.

Solving Hardware Resource Conflicts

Network cards typically use two hardware resources:

➤ An IRQ

➤ A range of I/O port addresses

A conflict involving either setting is possible, but IRQ conflicts are far more likely, especially if your network card uses an ISA expansion slot. If your wireless connection was working correctly until you installed another card inside your computer, you probably have a hardware resource conflict. Are you ready to solve the problem? See "Solving Hardware Resource Conflicts" in Chapter 19, "DSL Tips, Tricks, and Troubleshooting."

Solving a Damaged Network Card Installation

If your network card is Plug-and-Play (it automatically installed its own drivers when you inserted it in the computer, or it came as part of a late-model computer running Windows 95 or later), you can use the Plug-and-Play feature to "heal" the network card by removing and reinstalling the card. See "Solving a Damaged Network Card Installation" in Chapter 19 for full coverage of this process.

Does My Network Card Work?

The Windows Device Manager is notoriously unreliable at detecting whether hardware actually works; as long as the card doesn't become a black hole for electrons, the Device Manager will say it's working fine, even if you can't even surf across the room, let alone across the world on the Internet.

The best way to determine whether your network card is working is to use the diagnostic software that was shipped with it, or that you can download from the network card's maker.

See "Does My Network Card Work?" in Chapter 19 for full coverage of network card testing.

TCP/IP Configuration Problems

If your modem hardware appears to be working correctly, but you still cannot connect, the problem might be with your TCP/IP configuration. Check your configuration against the information supplied by your cable modem provider.

For more information about TCP/IP configuration, see Chapter 17, "A Survivor's Guide to TCP/IP".

Releasing and Renewing Your IP Address

Most broadband wireless connections use a dynamic IP address. Occasionally, your IP address can become invalid, which will cause your Internet connection to fail. Windows 9x/Me users can use WINIPCFG, and Windows NT 4.0 and Windows 2000 users can use Ipconfig to release and renew a dynamic IP address. For more information about using WINIPCFG and Ipconfig for releasing and renewing IP addresses, see Chapter 19.

Got a Brand-New Computer? Don't Forget To Reinstall Your Software!

If you've just changed computers, or if you've reformatted your hard disk and reinstalled your software, you'll need to rerun the installation program provided by your broadband wireless provider. The installation program will correctly configure your system to go online with your broadband wireless modem.

Danger Danger

Have CD—Can Fix!

Keep your operating system CD-ROM, network card drivers, and your provider's setup software in a safe place in case you need to reinstall your Internet software.

Are you thinking about trashing your computer's contents and starting over? Remember that if you run the recovery CD-ROM included with most new systems today you will reset your computer to its original factory-shipped condition. All software and information you added or created since you received the computer, including your Internet configuration, will be gone. Better back up your information and record your TCP/IP configuration before you say, "Go ahead."

The Least You Need to Know

➤ Wireless broadband modems offer many options for speedups, including service upgrades, switching to burstable services, Registry tweaks, and upgrades to network card hardware and software.

➤ You can use advanced browser features such as browser caching, as well as third-party programs such as download managers and page-caching utilities, to deliver content faster and during off hours.

➤ If you have a one-way service, you can prevent your callers from getting busy signals while you're online by setting up a voice-mail system.

➤ Wireless broadband modems offer built-in diagnostics through their signal lights.

➤ Correct cabling types and installation are essential to getting a good connection.

➤ One-way service has additional potential for problems because some providers use a separate analog modem.

➤ TCP/IP and setup software problems can also prevent a good connection.

➤ You must reinstall the connection software supplied by your provider when you reinstall software to your computer or switch to a new computer.

Speak Like a Geek: The Complete Reference

.EXE file   A Windows program file. Some archive files are stored as .EXE files, allowing them to self extract without requiring an unzipping program.

.INF file   A Windows driver installation file. This file contains instructions for installing and configuring an add-on card or other hardware device.

.ZIP file   An archive file (can contain one or more program and/or data files) created with a program such as WinZip or PKZip. Must be opened with WinZip, PKZip, or similar programs.

@Home   One of the leading U.S. cable modem ISPs.

10BASE-T   An Ethernet card that uses Category 3 or Category 5 unshielded twisted-pair cabling (UTP). Fast Ethernet 10/100 cards can be used in place of 10BASE-T cards.

16550   UART (serial port) chip that supports speeds up to 115200bps (115.2Kbps).

16650   UART (serial port) chip that supports speeds up to 230400bps (230.4Kbps); good choice for external ISDN TAs.

16750   UART (serial port) chip that supports speeds up to 460800bps (460.8Kbps); also good choice for external ISDN TAs.

2B+D   Refers to typical Basic Rate Interface (BRI) configuration of ISDN; two B(earer) channels of 64Kbps each, plus one D(elta) channel of 16Kbps.

activity   A light on some broadband modems used to display data transfer taking place.

ADSL   The most common type of DSL. A is short for asymmetrical, indicating the service is faster for downloads than uploads.

always-on   Most two-way broadband services don't require you to log on. The Internet is ready to access when you turn on the computer.

analog   The opposite of digital. Telephone data is analog because telephones carry high and low tones.

analog modem   Converts digital computer signals to analog telephone signals and back. It's the common type of modem supplied with most computers; also called a dial-up modem.

antivirus   Software used to detect viruses and stop them from infecting your computer.

AOL   America OnLine; the largest ISP and online service in the U.S.

ARPAnet   The ancestor of the Internet, it was developed by the U.S. Department of Defense to allow communication in case of a nuclear war.

asymmetrical   Refers to upload speeds for Internet services running slower than download speeds.

autosetup   DirecPC's setup program. It must be run to configure the system initially. If you run it later, it might indicate you are being switched to a new gateway (and maybe a new satellite).

azimuth   The angle in degrees, measured along the horizon from true (not magnetic) north and the point on the horizon directly below the satellite. It's always measured clockwise and always is a positive number (0–360). It's one of the settings required to point to a DirecPC satellite dish.

B-channel   Bearer channel; one of two 64Kbps channels used for data on an ISDN connection.

backbone   The high-speed fiber-optic connections that carry massive amounts of data across the Internet. ISPs connect to backbones to send and receive Internet data.

bandwidth   The speed of a connection in bits per second (bps). It also can be expressed in Kbps or Mbps. Broadband connections (over 100Mbps) have a larger bandwidth than analog modems (56Kbps maximum).

battery backup   Also referred to as a UPS (uninterruptable power supply), this is a useful accessory for computers and for ISDN connections used for voice phone calls.

bender   A reflector used by some fixed-base wireless broadband providers to reflect microwave data to subscribers who don't have a direct line of sight to the transmitter. Benders cannot return traffic, and can thus only be used for one-way connections.

bindings   The connection between a network adapter and a network protocol. When you install a network card on a computer running Windows, Windows will bind the installed network protocols to the card so the card can be used on a network.

block sync   A cable modem term used for the signal light indicating that the cable modem is connected properly to the cable network. If this light is blinking, you have lost your connection and must wait until it comes on again.

bonding   Using two or more analog modems (and/or ISDN TAs) to make a single Internet connection. The total speed of the connection is the sum of the modem's speeds, but each modem requires its own telephone line. Most ISPs do not support bonding.

bps   Bits per second; the common measurement of telecommunications bandwidth. Faster is better. 1000bps equals 1Kbps; 1000000bps equals 1Mbps.

BRI   Basic Rate Interface; the lower-cost form of ISDN. BRI uses two 64Kbps B(earer) channels and one D(elta) channel to provide 128Kbps upload/download connection when used with an ISP that supports both B-channels.

bridge tap   The common method for connecting additional telephones to an existing telephone circuit. The line runs from the phone to an existing line rather than all the way back to the telephone CO. The presence of a bridge tap and the length of the tap cable can cause problems with ISDN and DSL connections.

broadband   The general term for faster-than-analog modem Internet connections.

browser   Basic software for navigating the World Wide Web portion of the Internet. It can connect with both `http://` (Hypertext Transfer Protocol) Web sites and `ftp://` (File Transfer Protocol) file storage sites. Popular browsers include Netscape Communicator, Microsoft Internet Explorer, and Opera.

browser cache   The folder on your hard drive used as temporary storage for pages, pictures, and other files downloaded from the Internet. Windows Internet Explorer uses C:\Windows\Temporary Internet Files as its browser cache location. Netscape Navigator and Communicator use a folder called Cache that can be found in various locations.

browser synchronization   The process of downloading new content for sites you have selected to view offline with Internet Explorer 5.x or with DirecPC Turbo Webcast.

burstable   Speeds that can exceed the CIR speed guaranteed with some broadband wireless services. It allows your computer to download as fast as the connection permits rather than being capped at a fixed maximum speed.

bursty   Refers to the nature of Internet traffic. Because much Internet activity is the transfer of small amounts of data, a service that doesn't cap (limit) your speed can go faster when there is little traffic.

cable modem   Connects your computer to the Internet through the cable TV network. Because it modulates computer data into a signal that can be carried by a particular channel (frequency) on the cable, this term is accurate.

caching server   A device used by most cable modem providers to store frequently requested pages at the local cable provider's head end, allowing users to get the page faster than if the Internet had to be accessed separately for each user's request for the same information.

call forwarding   Originally designed to allow a call to follow you to another number, this telephone company service can also be used to send callers to an Internet mailbox to leave messages for a user whose phone is busy because they're online. You must install software such as CallWave to use this feature with an Internet connection.

CD-RW   A drive that can write CD-rewriteable and CD-recordable media. It's great for making low-cost backups of your computer.

central switch   Also called the central office, CO, and telephone exchange. The location where telephone calls are switched to the rest of the telephone network. It's also where DSL and ISDN equipment must be installed to permit these services.

central office   *See* central switch.

CIR   The Committed Information Rate; the minimum speed guaranteed for a connection with some broadband wireless Internet services.

CLEC   Competitive Local Exchange Carrier; a telephone company that competes with the original phone company in a locality (Incumbent Local Exchange Carrier or ILEC).

CO   *See* central switch.

coaxial cable   A round cable with a solid central core, insulation, metal mesh, and an outer rubberized layer. Commonly used to connect cable modem, satellite, and fixed wireless services to their respective modems. The usual type in common use is RG-6.

COM port   *See* RS-232 serial port.

commissioning   DirecPC's term for setting up your DirecPC satellite modem and account.

Control Panel   The Windows 9x/Me/2000 tool for setting up hardware and configurations.

D-channel   ISDN's Delta channel, which is used for signaling and making connections.

DCE   Data Communications Equipment; the technical term for the modem-to-modem connection.

DCLEC   Digital or Data Competitive Local Exchange Carrier; a type of CLEC that competes with other telephone companies for digital services. *See also* CLEC

device driver   Software installed by an operating system such as Windows to activate a device (such as an ISDN TA, network card, or analog modem).

DHCP   Dynamic Host Configuration Protocol. It allows computers using the TCP/IP protocol to be assigned an IP address automatically (dynamic IP) rather than requiring that a fixed IP address be assigned to the computer. Most residential broadband solutions use some form of DHCP and dynamic IP Addressing.

dial-up modem   *See* analog modem.

Dial-Up Networking   Windows software used to set up Internet and computer-to-computer connections with analog modems, ISDN TAs, and DSL lines that use PPPoE connections.

digital   The opposite of analog. Data is represented by 0 (off or low) and 1 (on or high). Computers must use an analog modem to convert digital data into analog form for transmission over ordinary phone lines.

digital loop carrier   A technique for extending voice-grade telephone lines a longer distance from a telco's central office without expensive signal boosters. It also is used to reduce the need to recable to add capacity. A digital loop carrier connection isn't suitable for high-speed connections such as ISDN or DSL.

451

Digital Subscriber Line   *See* DSL.

DirecDuo   A satellite dish used with DirecPC and/or DirecTV. The same dish can support either or both services at once.

DirecPC   A broadband solution that uses geo-synchronous satellite technology. It was developed by Hughes Network Systems.

DirecTV   A satellite TV system developed by Hughes Network Systems that can coexist with DirecPC when a DirecDuo dish is used.

DLC   *See* digital loop carrier.

DNS   Domain Name System. The system by which the Internet matches Web site names (URLs) with IP addresses. DNS information is distributed to DNS Name Servers set up at each ISP.

DOCSIS   Data Over Cable Systems Interface Standard, also known as CableLabs Certified Cable Modems. A standard for cable modems that allows the same cable modem to be used on any system that supports the DOCSIS standard.

Domain Name System   *See* DNS.

download   To receive data from a remote computer.

download manager   A type of program that speeds up downloads and can schedule downloads for off-peak periods.

downstream   The direction data flows from a remote computer to your computer; compare to download.

downtime   The opposite of uptime; when your Internet service or computer isn't working.

driver   *See* device driver.

DS1   Digital signal 1, the signaling portion of the T-1 carrier. It includes 24 64Kbps (DS0) signals.

DS3   Digital signal 3, the signaling portion of the T-3 carrier. It includes 28 DS1 signals (equivalent to 672 64Kbps DS0 signals).

DSL   Digital Subscriber Line; a technology that brings high-speed, high-frequency digital data to your home or office over ordinary phone lines. It's conceptually similar to ISDN but much faster and designed specifically for Internet and computer data usage. *See also* xDSL.

DTE   Data Terminal Equipment; refers to the RS-232 serial port used to connect external analog modems or external ISDN TAs to a computer.

DUN   *See* Dial-Up Networking.

dynamic IP address   An IP address that is assigned by a device acting as a DHCP server. A dynamic IP can be different each time you turn on your computer.

elevation   The angle between the horizon and a satellite, always measured in degrees. One of three factors needed to aim a DirecPC/DirecDuo satellite dish.

email   Short for electronic mail. Messages and files sent to and received from an electronic mailbox residing on an email server.

Ethernet   A popular network standard. The 10BASE-T card your computer needs to attach to cable, wireless cable, and DSL modems is a type of Ethernet device.

Exchange   *See* central office.

Fair Access Plan   *See* FAP.

FAP   DirecPC's policy of severely slowing down the download speed of subscribers deemed to be hogging bandwidth by downloading too much per hour. DirecPC has published FAP guidelines but these are regarded as misleading by many subscribers.

FCC ID#   An identification number assigned to all computer equipment by the FCC. It can be used to determine the make and model of so-called Brand X modems and other products.

File Transfer Protocol   A part of the TCP/IP protocol used for the transfer of files between computers. Your Web browser can act as a simple FTP client.

firewall   Software or hardware that can be used to block unauthorized access to computers from outside the network.

firmware   Software on a chip that controls how a device operates. Most modems have firmware that can be upgraded with software.

fixed broadband wireless   A technology that uses microwaves to deliver Internet content. The setup strongly resembles a cable modem inside your home.

FTP   *See* File Transfer Protocol.

G. lite   A form of DSL that you can install. It uses microfilters instead of a technician-installed splitter.

gateway   When one computer provides access to another network for other computers on a network. Windows's ICS is a simple gateway.

geosynchronous   A satellite orbit over the equator at a distance (a bit over 22,000 miles) that keeps the satellite in the same apparent position in the sky. The type of orbit used by DirecPC and similar satellite-based Internet services.

grounding block   A device that attaches between a satellite dish or microwave antenna and your computer. The ground wire is attached to it and runs to ground to protect your equipment.

hosts   A text file you can use in Windows for instant lookup of popular Web sites' IP addresses.

HTML   Hypertext Markup Language; the special type of text used on most Web sites. It can contain text attributes, tables, hyperlinks, and so on.

hub   A device that is used to connect two or more 10BASE-T or Fast Ethernet computers.

hybrid   A leading supplier of the fixed broadband wireless technology. It is used for many of the fixed broadband wireless installations in the U.S. and elsewhere.

hybrid fiber-optic/coax   The type of cable TV network needed to support two-way cable. Fiber-optic is used from the cable company's head end into the neighborhood, where individual homes connect using coaxial cable.

hyperlink   Text (often underlined) or a graphic on a Web page that links to a different part of the page, a different page on the Web site, or a different Web site.

hypertext   An ancestor of hyperlinking; many help systems use hypertext.

I/O port address   A hardware resource used by network cards and internal modems. No two devices can use the same range. Use the Windows Device Manager to see the I/O port address use for any device or overall.

ICS   *See* Internet Connection Sharing.

initialization string   A series of commands sent to an analog modem or ISDN TA before a number is dialed. The initialization string can change many of the modem's default behaviors.

Integrated Services Digital Network   *See* ISDN.

Internet   The network of networks; the interconnected worldwide network encompassing commercial, educational, governmental, nonprofit, and personal computers. Requires installation of the TCP/IP protocol and either dial-up, network, or broadband connection to access it.

Internet Connection Sharing   Microsoft's term for its simple Internet gateway software, which allows users on a small network to share a single Internet connection. Found in Windows 98SE, Windows Me, and Windows 2000. Also known as ICS.

Internet radio   Web sites that provide streaming media playback of all types of music.

Internet service provider   A company that connects you to the Internet. All types of Internet connections, both broadband and dialup, must be made through an ISP.

IP address   The numeric value by which all computers on the Internet are identified, such as 111.22.243.18.

IRQ routing   *See* IRQ steering.

IRQ steering   The method supported by Windows 95B (OSR2.x) and later versions of Windows and on recent motherboards to allow a single IRQ to be used by more than one PCI card. It might need to be adjusted to allow installation of the DirecPC PCI satellite modem.

IRQ   Short for Interrupt ReQuest. Different devices (whether on the motherboard or in an expansion slot) on a Windows PC must use an IRQ from 0–15 to talk to the CPU. If two devices use the same IRQ (unless IRQ steering can be used), a device conflict results and the devices can't be used.

ISA   Industry Standard Architecture. A slot design developed in 1981 with a single (8-bit data) connector, enhanced in 1984 with a second connector for 16-bit data, and finally disappearing from new computers.

ISDN   Integrated Services Digital Network. A telephone-based method for performing all-digital transmissions over phone lines. Originally developed for improved voice, fax, and teleconferencing, ISDN is also used as a broadband Internet solution by some people.

ISP   *See* Internet service provider.

K56flex   A proprietary modem design for reaching maximum 56Kbps download speeds. It has been replaced by V.90.

Kbps   Kilobits per second; 1000bps equals 1Kbps.

Kermit   A file transfer protocol used for direct computer-to-computer data transfer, not for Internet file transfers.

kludge   An inelegant workaround to a computer problem.

latency   The delay between sending a signal to a remote computer and getting a reply; also called the ping rate.

line RX   A signal light used on some broadband devices to indicate you are receiving a signal.

line TX   A signal light used on some broadband devices to indicate you are sending a signal.

link   A signal light used on some broadband devices to indicate your network card is properly connected to the device.

LNB   Low Noise Block. A part of the DirecPC or DirecDuo satellite dish where the coaxial cable is attached.

load balancing   Attempts to equalize the demand on DirecPC by moving users to different gateways. It often results in moving users to different satellites, which requires re-aiming the dish.

load coil   A device used on some phone lines to eliminate high-frequency noise to make voice calls sound better. It also prevents a line from being used for DSL.

low-noise block   *See* LNB.

M-PPP   Multilink Point-to-Point Protocol. A popular method for binding two or more phone lines together to make a single faster Internet connection.

MaxMSS   A Windows Registry setting that should be adjusted for faster downloading.

MaxMTU   A Windows Registry setting that should be adjusted for faster downloading.

Mbps   Megabits per second; one million bps equals 1Mbps.

megahertz   Measures a CPU's clock speed. Your CPU should run at 133MHz or faster if you want to use a broadband solution. Many services recommend a 200MHz or faster CPU.

MHz   *See* Megahertz.

microfilter   A device you attach to your telephone lines when you install DSL service yourself. It prevents your phone from interfering with DSL signals.

microwave   Signals received and sent by broadband wireless Internet services.

MMDS   Multichannel Multipoint Distribution Service. The most popular form of fixed broadband wireless Internet service.

modem   A device that changes one type of signal to another. The term is also used for any device that attaches your computer to the Internet, even if it doesn't convert signals (DSL "modem," for example).

Multichannel Multipoint Distribution Service   *See* MMDS.

multilink   Refers to bonding two or more phone lines together to create a single high-speed Internet connection.

name server   Also called DNS server. It matches Web site names to IP addresses.

NetBIOS A simple network protocol that is suitable for use in a small or home network. It cannot access the Internet.

network Two or more computers that can share information or resources with each other. Must be connected by cables or wireless devices.

network packets Data transmitted over a network is subdivided into packets.

newsgroups Internet discussion groups that must be accessed through a newsreader. The Internet Explorer Web browser can be used to read newsgroups, and newsgroup access is provided as part of most Internet access.

OC-48 Optical Carrier Level 48. A signal rate of 2.488Gbps (48 times the base signal rate of 51.84Mbps) used on some high-capacity fiber-optic backbone connections.

offline viewing Viewing Web pages that have been stored on your hard disk for viewing when you are not connected to the Internet.

one-way Broadband connections that use a modem for uploading, and the broadband connection for downloads only. It's less desirable than two-way connections.

patch A software fix for an existing program. Some patches (also called service packs) can be many megabytes in size.

PC Card Also called PCMCIA card. A credit-card sized add-on for notebook computers that can contain a modem, network card, or other accessories.

PCI Short for Peripheral Component Interconnect. A 32-bit fast expansion slot created by Intel in 1992 and standard on all computers since about 1995.

ping rate Also called latency. The delay between sending a signal to a remote computer and receiving it back. From the ping used by sonar to detect ships at sea. A low ping rate (under 100ms) is best for Internet gaming.

plumb Vertically straight; not leaning. The mounting arm for the DirecPC or DirecDuo dish must be plumb to make dish aiming accurate.

polarization The angle of clockwise or counterclockwise rotation of the DirecPC or DirecDuo dish. One of the three adjustments needed to set the dish to pick up your satellite.

POP Point-of-Presence (where you connect to the Internet) or Post Office Protocol (a popular email server type).

POP3 Post Office Protocol 3. The current version of the email server protocol.

POST Power On Self-Test; performed by computers and other devices when you turn them on. Failures are indicated by beeps or signal lights.

POTS Plain Old Telephone System.

PPPoE Point-to-Point Protocol over Ethernet. A connection method used by some DSL providers that requires you to use Dial-Up Networking to connect to the Internet.

PRI Primary Rate Interface. The corporate-oriented form of ISDN, which provides a 1.5Mbps connection to the telephone system for voice and data to share.

protocol A common communications standard for devices and software; TCP/IP is an example.

proxy server A computer that receives network data and relays it to other computers. It's used on many cable modem networks to reduce congestion, and can also be used to share an Internet connection in your office.

PSTN Public Switched Telephone Network; same as POTS.

quality of service Refers to any guarantees about uptime, equipment replacement, or other measures that will (or will not) be taken to keep your Internet connection working.

receive packets A signal light on some broadband devices that tells you the device is receiving Internet data.

refresh button An onscreen button in your Web browser you can click to retrieve a new copy of the current Web page.

Registry   The Windows files (User.dat and System.dat) used in Windows 95 and newer versions to store virtually all settings for hardware and software.

release   An option in software that displays IP address information to give up the current IP address. Useful for fixing connection problems with dynamic IP connections.

renew   An option in software that displays IP address information to receive a new IP address. Useful for fixing connection problems with dynamic IP connections.

Restore Point   Feature in Windows Me that allows you to reset the computer to that point if you have problems after installing new hardware or software.

RF signal lock   A signal light used on wireless broadband modems to indicate you are getting signals from the remote transmitter.

RG-59   An obsolete type of coaxial cable once used for cable TV and networking.

RG-6   Current coaxial cable type used for cable TV, cable modems, DirecTV, DirecPC, and fixed wireless broadband connections.

RJ-11   A standard two-wire telephone jack also used for DSL and sometimes for ISDN.

RJ-45   An eight-wire jack (resembling RJ-11 but larger) used for Category 5 UTP network cable between 10BASE-T Ethernet cards and cable, DSL, and fixed broadband wireless devices.

RoadRunner   One of the leading cable modem providers in the U.S.

routable   A network protocol that can connect to other networks. TCP/IP is routable, but NetBEUI and NetBIOS are not.

router   A network device that allows multiple PCs to connect to another network. Sometimes a part of a broadband device, or it can be connected to a broadband device.

RS-232 serial port   Also called a COM(munication) port, this is used for most external analog modems and for most external ISDN TAs. USB is preferred when available.

RWIN   A Windows Registry setting (Receive Window) you can adjust for faster download speed.

satellite modem   DirecPC's term for its broadband devices that connect to your computer.

SDSL   Symmetrical DSL; a form of DSL in which downloads and uploads run at the same speed

self-install   A popular option for some forms of DSL, this allows the user to install DSL hardware without a technician's service call.

serial port   *See* RS-232 serial port.

share-level   A type of network security in which each shared folder has its own password (if passwords are used). Presents a potential security risk on the Internet.

shared folder   A folder that can be shared with other network users.

shotgun technology   Diamond Multimedia's term for its version of modem bonding.

site survey   Service performed by fixed wireless broadband providers to make sure your home or office can receive the signal.

SPID   Service Profile Identifier. A number assigned by the telco to a device on an ISDN B-channel. The SPID often includes the area code and phone number that will be used for the device as well as additional information used to configure the ISDN service for that device.

splitter   A device used to split a single line for both data and other uses. Cable modem and DSL installations often use splitters.

static IP address   An IP address that never changes. It's more common in business Internet service than in residential.

subnet   A method of IP addressing that allows several computers on a network to share a single main IP address but still be identified individually.

switch   A device used to connect computers on a network. It resembles a hub but is much faster.

symmetrical   A type of broadband connection in which uploads and downloads are the same speed. Most residential and small business connections (except ISDN) are asymmetrical instead.

sync   A signal light used on cable modems to indicate the modem is properly connected to network.

T-1   The telephone company's term for a combination of 23 64Kbps B-channels and 1 64Kbps D-channel. It's a 1.5Mbps connection used by some ISPs to connect to the Internet.

T-3   The telephone company's term for a 45Mbps connection to an Internet backbone (it's like 30 T-1s put together).

TA   ISDN terminal adapter. It connects your computer to an ISDN line.

TCP/IP   Transmission Control Protocol/Internet Protocol. The protocol your computer must use to access the Internet.

TCP port   A logical connection that is part of the TCP/IP protocol. Some TCP ports are designated for particular jobs, but other ports can be exploited by intruders. Use a firewall to stop unauthorized use of TCP ports.

telco   Short for telephone company.

telco return   The term used by cable modem and fixed wireless broadband providers for one-way service. You use an analog modem with a TR system.

telephone exchange   *See* central switch.

telephony   Refers to devices like fax machines and analog modems that use telephone lines.

terminal adapter   *See* TA.

terminal emulation   Using software to make your computer look like a terminal. It was common before the advent of the Internet and still is used today to make a non-Internet connection with another computer.

Torroid chokes   A hollow, iron, donut-shaped device (usually split in two) that can be attached to coaxial cable to help reduce interference.

Traceroute   A command to trace Internet routing to an IP address or Web site you specify. Windows uses Tracert.

Tracert   A utility included in Windows. *See also* Traceroute.

two-way   Broadband connections that don't use an analog modem, such as ISDN, DSL, most cable modem, and some fixed wireless broadband services.

UART   Universal Asynchronous Receive Transmit. The part of the serial port that determines the maximum DTE speed of the port.

upload   Sending data from your computer to another.

UPS   Uninterruptible Power Supply. Refers to battery backup units.

upstream   The direction data takes when going from your computer to another. It's normally slower than downstream.

uptime   The amount of time your system is working; the ideal is 100% of the time.

URL   Uniform Resource Locator. The technical name for the name of a Web page or Web site.

USB   Universal Serial Bus. The port used by Windows 98, Windows Me, and Windows 2000 as an eventual replacement for serial and parallel ports. Some broadband devices can connect through USB ports, and more are coming.

V.90   International standard for 56Kbps analog modems. Replaced K56flex and X2.

Visual Basic   A Microsoft programming language that is used to create many useful programs, but can also be used to create email viruses.

wallfish   Term for pulling a network cable or wire through a wall.

Web browser   *See* browser.

Webcast   DirecPC's name for its Internet software.

WINIPCFG   Windows 95/98/Me program that can be used to view your computer's IP address and other IP settings.

WINS   Windows Internet Naming Service. A way that office networks sometimes use to assign IP addresses.

wire distance   The distance a telephone wire must travel from the central switch to your home. It's important in qualifying your location for ISDN or DSL.

wire feet   *See* wire distance.

World Wide Web   The part of the Internet you can visit with a Web browser. It allows hyperlinking.

X2   Proprietary 56Kbps standard for analog modems; replaced by V.90.

xDSL   The term sometimes used to refer to all forms of DSL. The x is a variable that can stand for ADSL, SDSL, and so on.

Xmodem   An early file-transfer protocol used before the Internet.

Ymodem   An improved version of Xmodem.

Zmodem   An improved version of Ymodem. Xmodem, Ymodem, and Zmodem are still used if you make a direct (non-Internet) connection with a computer and need to send or receive files.

Index

J - K

469

T

473

U